THE
BRITISH
POLITY
SECOND EDITION

PHILIP NORTON

Longman
New York & London

The British Polity, Second Edition

Longman, 95 Church Street, White Plains, N.Y. 10601

Associated companies:
Longman Group Ltd., London
Longman Cheshire Pty., Melbourne
Longman Paul Pty., Auckland
Copp Clark Pitman, Toronto

Senior editor: David J. Estrin
Production editor: Camilla T. K. Palmer
Cover design: Kevin Kall
Text art: Art Directions

Library of Congress Cataloging-in-Publication Data

Norton, Philip.
    The British polity / Philip Norton.—2nd ed.
      p.   cm.
    Includes bibliographical references.
    ISBN 0-8013-0123-8
    1. Great Britain—Politics and government. I. Title.
JN231.N669 1991
320.941—dc20

                                      90-31031
                                        CIP

2 3 4 5 6 7 8 9 10-AL-9594939291

3/94

UNIVERSITY OF WOLVERHAMPTON

LIB/LEND/001

Wolverhampton Learning Centre

St. Peter's Square
Wolverhampton   WV1 1RH

Wolverhampton (01902) 322305

This item may be recalled at any time. Keeping it after it has been recalled or beyond the date stamped may result in a fine.
See tariff of fines displayed at the counter.

Other Books by Philip Norton:

Dissension in the House of Commons 1945–1974 (*1975*)
Conservative Dissidents (*1978*)
Dissension in the House of Commons 1974–1979 (*1980*)
The Commons in Perspective (*1981*)
Conservatives and Conservatism (*with A. Aughey, 1981*)
The Constitution in Flux (*1982*)
Law and Order and British Politics (*editor*) (*1984*)
Parliament in the 1980s (*editor*) (*1985*)
The Political Science of British Politics (*editor, with J. Hayward*) (*1986*)
Legislatures (*editor*) (*1990*)
Parliaments in Western Europe (*editor*) (*1990*)
Politics U.K (*with B. Jones et al.*) (*1991*)

To Mr. and Mrs. R. A. Bradel

Contents

Part VI: Conclusion

Illustrations and Tables

Preface

In this edition I have taken the opportunity principally to update facts and narrative. The latter half of the 1980s was a fascinating period in British politics and the various changes that it witnessed have been incorporated in this volume. Where appropriate, either because of the extent of new material available or in response to reviews and readers' comments on the first edition, I have rewritten chapters and, more often, sections within chapters. However, the basic theme of the book remains the same. The events of recent years have served to reinforce rather than to dent the analysis offered originally in 1984.

For the preparation of this edition, my thanks are due especially to Paul Willis, who has been prodigious in researching contemporary data; without him, completion of this work would have been much delayed. My gratitude is owing also to David Estrin of Longman Inc. for his unfailing encouragement and professionalism. I am also very grateful to all those readers from around the world who kindly wrote to comment on the first edition. A number of helpful comments arose from correspondence and, wherever possible, these have been taken into account in this edition. The positive response to the first edition has also served to confirm my belief that the basic approach of the book should be retained.

Since the first edition was published, exchange rates have fluctuated considerably. In this volume, dollar equivalents are based on the August 1989 exchange rate of £1 = $1.65.

Responsibility for any errors, omissions, or misjudgments remains mine. I would, as ever, be delighted to hear from readers with corrections and comments.

Preface to First Edition

When in the United States, I have always been struck by the interest, sometimes the fascination, shown in Britain and its history, politics, and culture. However, for the serious student of British politics, satisfying the desire to understand and know more about the subject is difficult because of limited sources. Coverage of British events by television and newspapers in the United States is extremely limited and often superficial. There are a number of introductory texts on British politics, but the most popular and recent are written primarily for British students by British scholars. When I was invited to write the volume on British politics in Longman's *Polity* series, I grasped the opportunity to produce a book that appeared to be much needed: an introductory text on British politics written primarily for American students. Although I hope that the book may prove of interest to British readers as well, not least because of the comparisons it introduces, it has been written principally for the American reader.

The plan of the work is simply stated. The first three chapters (Part I) provide an introduction to Britain and its political culture and history. Parts II through V identify and analyze the main features of the contemporary British polity. Governments do not operate in a political vaccum. Part II considers the political environment created by the constitution, the electoral system, political parties, and interest groups. Part III dissects and studies the different levels of government: central government, local government, and the institutions of the European Communities. Government in Britain is politically accountable to Parliament and legally accountable to the monarch. Both institutions constitute the focus of Part IV. The assent of both is necessary for the enactment of legislation. Once passed, legislation is interpreted by the courts and enforced by the different agencies of the state, most notably by the police in the case of criminal law. The effects of law and of government activities are communicated to the lawmakers through various channels. The most important media of communication are television and newspapers, and by their reporting they can have a significant impact on political behavior. The courts, the police, and the mass media constitute the concern of Part V. The final chapter draws out the themes of the book and comprises my own analysis of the strengths and weaknesses of the contemporary British polity.

In each of the chapters in Parts II through V I have tried to provide a common structure. As far as possible, each embodies an illustrative comparison with the equivalent United States institution, a brief historical sketch, an analysis of the current position, and a discussion of the debate that surrounds the institution. Because the book is designed as a student text for class use, I have sought to construct chapters that are sufficiently self-contained to be read independent of one another. Where necessary, important points are repeated or a cross-reference is provided. I have avoided terms that are probably unfamiliar to American readers or, where such is unavoidable, I have provided an explanation. Also, important terms are defined in the glossary located at the end of the text. Where financial figures are mentioned, the sterling amount is followed by the approximate dollar equivalent, based on the July 1983 exchange rate of £1 = $1.50, unless otherwise stated.

In writing the book, I have incurred a number of debts. My intellectual debts will be apparent from the footnotes. For reading and commenting on all or part of the manuscript, my thanks are due to John Vanderoef, Jorgen Rasmussen, Ed Page, and Ken Batty. Irving Rockwood of Longman not only read and commented on the text but also provided valuable and considerate editorial guidance. Catherine Davies, Enid Tracy, and Melanie Bucknell provided much-appreciated help in typing the manuscript. It would not have been possible for me to write a work of this nature, designed for American students, without my own experiences of the United States. For these experiences my gratitude goes to the Thouron family and Scholarship Committee for the award of a Thouron Scholarship, allowing me to study at the University of Pennsylvania in 1974–1975, To Fairleigh Dickinson University for the opportunity in 1977 to teach American students, and to Mr. and Mrs. Robert Bradel for their unstinting hospitality on my regular visits to the United States. On this side of the Atlantic, my thanks go to colleagues and friends for continued support. Many of my ideas on British politics have been developed and refined as a result of teaching the subject at the University of Hull. The comments of students have proved an invaluable stimulus to my thoughts and have served to reinforce my long-held view that teaching and research are complementary rather than conflicting pursuits. I have learned a great deal myself through writing this book. Doubtless I shall learn more from student reaction to it.

My thanks are also owing to Professor Samuel H. Beer for his recent work *Britain Against Itself*. As will be clear from my conclusion, I profoundly disagree with his analysis. However, the appearance of his work has provided me with the opportunity to develop and think through my own analysis, and for that I am grateful.

Although I have drawn on the help and work of others, no one else can be held responsible for any faults, misguided interpretations, or omissions that follow. That responsibility is mine alone. I would be pleased to hear from any reader who spots errors or wishes to express comment on the work.

THE
BRITISH
POLITY

PART I
Introduction

CHAPTER 1

The Contemporary Landscape
British Society and
Political Socialization

Continuity and change are features of every political system. What makes each significant is the nature and the extent of that change. Some systems are characterized by rapid and sometimes revolutionary change. Others are noted for continuity with past experience and structures. The task of the student of politics is to discern the distinctive features of that continuity and change, to generate concepts, and, if possible, to construct models and theories that will aid understanding of and serve to explain those distinctive features and the relationship among them.

The distinctive features of a political system can be recognized by comparing that system with another or, better still, with many others. In discussing the merits of comparative politics, a student in a class of mine once objected to the whole exercise. "There's no point in comparing one country with another," he argued. "Every country is unique." As others in the class were quick to respond, the only way by which one knows that a country is unique is by comparing it with others. Just as one can know whether one is short or tall only by comparing oneself with others, so one can know whether one's own political system is "short" or "tall" only by putting it alongside other systems and noting the differences.

Space and resources preclude an exhaustive or even an extensive comparative study in this work. Instead, I will illustrate the distinctive nature of the British polity by comparing it, where appropriate, with the American. They are similar in many respects, with a shared language; advanced industrial economies; similar but not always identical political,

3

social, and economic values; and some mutual needs. Each has a sense of affinity with the other. As we shall see, however, there are significant dissimilarities, which make a comparative exercise useful. Such an exercise will serve not only to sensitize the American reader to the distinctive features of the British polity but also to make readers more aware of the features of their own polity. That, at least, is the hope.

In order to understand continuity and change within the British polity, I will stress the significance of the political culture. This emphasis will form the basis of the next chapter as well as the book's conclusion. Before we proceed to an analysis of that culture, a brief sketch of the salient features of contemporary Britain is necessary. This outline is especially pertinent for comparative purposes. There are important dissimilarities between the United States and Britain in terms of geography, demography, and social history. Britain is a small, crowded island, largely oriented in terms of industry and population to England (and especially the southeast of England), with a class-based society that has superseded but by no means discarded the characteristics of a status-based feudal society. The purpose of this chapter is to highlight those features and, for convenience, to consider also the media of political socialization in Britain. Such a study is a prerequisite for a consideration of the political culture and the institutions and processes that culture nurtures.

CONTEMPORARY BRITAIN

Land and Population

From the perspective of land distribution and usage, Great Britain could be described as a predominantly agricultural kingdom based on the three countries of England, Scotland, and Wales. (The United Kingdom comprises these three countries plus Northern Ireland: see Map. 1.1.) In terms of the distribution and activities of the population, it is predominantly English, nonagricultural, and town- or suburban-based.

Great Britain occupies a total area of 88,798 square miles. This compares with an area of 3,615,123 square miles for the United States. (The USSR occupies more than 8 million square miles. The small principality of Monaco, by contrast, comprises a modest 368 acres.) Within the United States, ten states each have a greater land area than Britain: Alaska (586,412 square miles), Texas (267,339), and California (158,693) being the most notable. England has approximately the same land area as New York State, Scotland the same as South Carolina, and Wales the same as Massachusetts.

The disparity in population size is not quite so extreme. In 1987 the

Map 1.1. The United Kingdom.

United Kingdom population was just under 57 million, up from 38.2 million at the turn of the century. The United States population in 1987 was almost 244 million, up from 76 million in 1900 (see Table 1.1). There is a more significant difference, though, in population growth. Between 1970 and 1987 the United Kingdom population increased by only 2.2%. (A continuation of the slow growth rate is anticipated, with the population projected to be no more than 57.5 million in 1991 and 59 million in 2001.) Between 1970 and 1987 the United States population increased by 19%. Much higher increases have been recorded in Third World countries. In South Asia over the same period, for example, the population increase was more than 40%.

When the population is put in the context of land size, Britain emerges as a crowded island. The number of people per square kilometer in 1986 was 233. By European standards, this is high but not exceptional: the Netherlands, Belgium, and West Germany are even more densely populated. The number of people per square kilometer in the United States in 1987 was less than 28. By worldwide standards, this is a low but not exceptional figure. The USSR, Brazil, New Zealand, Australia, and Canada were among the nations with lower population density. In Australia and Canada there were fewer than 3 people per square kilometer.

Within the United Kingdom, the population is heavily concentrated in one country. In 1987 more than 47 million people lived in England, compared with a little over 5 million in Scotland, 2.8 million in Wales, and 1.6 million in Northern Ireland. The number of people per square kilometer in England in 1987 was 363—the highest population density of

TABLE 1.1. UNITED STATES AND UNITED KINGDOM POPULATIONS, 1900–1987

Year	United Kingdom Population (millions)	United States Population (millions)
1900	38.2	76.1
1910	42.1	92.4
1920	44.0	106.4
1930	46.1	123.1
1940	48.3	132.4
1950	50.6	152.3
1960	53.0	180.7
1970	55.7	205.0
1980	56.0	227.7
1987	56.9	243.8

Sources: Adapted from Central Statistical Office, Social Trends 19 (Her Majesty's Stationery Office, 1989) and Statistical Abstracts of the United States 1988, 108th ed. (U.S. Department of Commerce, Bureau of the Census, 1988).

European countries and greater even than that of Japan. Within England, the greatest concentration of inhabitants is in the southeast of the country (that is, Greater London and the surrounding counties), with a population in excess of 17 million; the second largest concentration is in the northwest, with more than 6 million inhabitants.

The population resides predominantly in areas classified, for local government purposes, as urban. About 80% of the population in England, and more than 70% in Scotland and Wales, live in urban areas. One-fifth of the population lives in the ten largest cities (see Table 1.2). The shift from rural to urban areas has been marked in England, the proportion of the population living in nonurban areas declining from a little over 35% in 1951 to not much more than 20% twenty years later.

Although approximately three-quarters of the land surface is used for agriculture, very few people are employed in the agricultural industry. There has been a persistent drift from land work since industrialization in the eighteenth and nineteenth centuries, a trend that continues. More than 700,000 people were employed in agriculture, forestry, and fishing in 1961. By 1988, the figure was down to 313,000. Increased efficiency and greater mechanization have in part facilitated this development. (Britain has one of the heaviest tractor densities in the world.) There are more than 250,000 farm holdings in Britain, with three-fifths of the full-time farms being devoted mainly to dairying or beef cattle and sheep. Farms devoted to arable crops are predominant in the eastern part of England. Sheep and cattle rearing is a feature of the hills and moorland areas of Scotland, Wales, and northern and southwest England.

TABLE 1.2. THE TEN LARGEST CITIES IN THE UNITED KINGDOM, 1987

City[1]	Population (thousands)
Greater London	6,770.4
Birmingham	998.2
Glasgow	715.6
Leeds	709.0
Sheffield	532.3
Liverpool	476.0
Bradford	462.5
Manchester	450.1
Edinburgh	438.7
Bristol	384.4

[1]For locations, see Map 1.1. *Source:* Britain 1989: An Official Handbook *(Her Majesty's Stationery Office, 1989).*

Although Britain exports agrochemicals, agricultural equipment, and some agricultural produce and food products, it nonetheless has to import a substantial portion of its food supply. (In 1987, food accounted for 10% of the nation's imports by value.)[1] Indeed, Britain is heavily dependent on imports of its raw materials. Compared with other large industrialized (and some developing) nations, Britain is notably lacking in natural resources. The exception is energy resources—it is a major world producer of oil, natural gas, and coal—and since 1980 the country has been self-sufficient in energy in net terms. However, it is dependent on other nations either wholly or in part for products such as cotton, rubber, sulphur, bauxite, copper, lead, tungsten, tin, nickel, phosphates, potash, rice, corn, silk, coffee, tobacco and wool. The United States, by contrast, is self-sufficient in most of these products, with surplus supply in several cases; for example, it is the world's largest producer (and consumer) of lead. The USSR is even better served in its natural supply of raw materials. France, Germany, Canada, Japan, and India are also more self-sufficient than Britain. This lack of raw materials not only is important for an understanding of British industry in the 1990s but also provides a partial explanation for some of Britain's internationalist and imperial history.

Employment

Britain was the first major nation to experience industrialization. Most of the population moved from the land to find jobs in manufacturing industries in the towns and cities; the north of England in particular witnessed the growth of major industrial conurbations. Most of the economically active population came to be employed in primary industries and manufacturing. In the twentieth century, especially in the period since 1945, more and more workers have moved into service industries. The growth of service industries has been particularly marked in London and the southeast, where almost 75% of employees are now in the service sector. There has been a corresponding decline in employment in manufacturing, especially in the north. Today Britain can be described as having a predominantly service economy. In 1987, services accounted for approximately 60% of the gross domestic product (GDP) and for 68% of those in employment. Table 1.3 charts the growth in employment in the service sector between 1971 and 1988 and the decline in employment in all other sectors. As the figures demonstrate, there has been a significant increase in the number employed in the financial sector. Within the service sector, the 1980s witnessed also a significant growth in small businesses and self-employment.

In all categories other than the service industries, male employees outnumber females. In the service industries, more than half the workers

TABLE 1.3. EMPLOYMENT BY INDUSTRY, 1971–1988

Industry	Number in Employment (thousands)		
	1971	*1979*	*1988*
Agriculture, forestry, and fishing	450	380	313
Energy and water supply	798	722	459
Construction	1,198	1,239	1,022
Manufacturing			
Extraction of minerals and ores other than fuels, manufacture of metals, mineral products and chemicals	1,282	1,147	771
Metal goods, engineering, and vehicle industries	3,709	3,374	2,219
Other	3,074	2,732	2,108
Total Manufacturing	8,065	7,253	5,097
Services			
Distribution, hotels, catering, and repairs	3,686	4,257	4,551
Transport and communication	1,556	1,479	1,372
Banking, finance, insurance, business services, and leasing	1,336	1,647	2,468
Other	5,049	6,197	6,820
	11,627	13,580	15,211
All Industries and Services	**22,138**	**23,174**	**22,102**

Source: Social Trends 19 *(Her Majesty's Stationery Office, 1989), p. 73.*

are women and much of the increase in service jobs in the 1980s was accounted for by part-time, predominantly female, jobs. By mid-1987, female part-time employees accounted for 20% of all employees, compared with 13% in 1971. Approximately 25% of women held full-time jobs and 20% held part-time jobs. Of the total workforce in employment in 1987, 6.4 million worked in the public sector (a slight majority of them female—3.3 million to 3.1 million males) and 18.5 million in the private sector. Private sector growth since the late 1970s has been marked in the service industries, reversing the trend of the 1960s and early 1970s and reflecting government policy to reduce employment in public sector services.

In terms of employment, the service industries clearly represent the principal area of growth. In the 1970s and especially the first half of the 1980s the other main growth area was unemployment. In the 1950s and 1960s very few workers were unemployed. In 1961 only 1.5% of the workforce was registered as unemployed, but by 1971 the proportion had risen to 3.5%—a total of 792,000 people. The figure increased throughout the decade, reaching 7.4% in 1980. It continued to rise, reaching a peak in 1986 of 11.6%—3.2 million people. Unemployment levels were particularly high in areas dependent on manufacturing industry and in the inner cities. In the north of England, for example, the unemployment rate exceeded 15.0%. (In Northern Ireland it reached 18% at the beginning of 1987.) In southeast England, in contrast, the rate just topped 8%. After 1986 the level of unemployment fell, both nationally and in every region, and by the beginning of 1989 it was down to 7.0%; East Anglia enjoyed an unemployment rate of less than 4% and the southeast one not much higher.[2]

Within the workforce, the regional disparity in terms of unemployment remains—Scotland and the north of England have more than double the unemployment rate of the southeast, and Northern Ireland more than triple—and the proportion of long-term unemployed (those unemployed for more than one year) has risen sharply, reaching a peak of 41% of claimants for unemployment benefit in 1988. Within the workforce, unemployment is greater among immigrants (and their descendants) from the New Commonwealth and Pakistan than it is among native-born white citizens and those from other European Community countries. Males of West Indian or Guyanese origin, as well as those of Pakistani or Bangladeshi origin, are more than twice as likely to be unemployed than white males. Unemployment is also greater among teenagers and those in their early twenties than it is among those aged 35 to 59.

The level of unemployment remains high both in absolute terms and by comparison with many other major industrial nations. In the first half of the 1980s the United Kingdom had the highest level of unemployment among the seven major countries in the Organization for Economic Cooperation and Development (OECD). The decrease in unemployment since then has been at a faster rate than in many other countries, and the United Kingdom no longer tops this particular league table. The 8% unemployment rate in the United Kingdom in 1988 compared with 10.6% in France. (Belgium, Spain, the Netherlands, and possibly Italy also had higher rates than the United Kingdom.) Those with lower rates included West Germany (6.6%), the United States (5.5%), and Japan (2.5%). The governing Conservative party in Britain has been keen to note that unemployment in other countries would be higher were it not in some cases for conscription and a retirement age of 60 for men. Britain does not have conscription (compulsory national service in the armed forces was ended in 1960, the last call-up papers being issued on December 31), and the retirement age for men is 65.

Linguistic and Racial Differences

The population is predominantly English in birth as well as residence. It is concomitantly white and English-speaking. It is not, however, totally homogeneous. Not only is there a division between the English, the Scottish, and the Welsh; there is also a division in Scotland between those who do and do not speak Gaelic, and in Wales between those who do and do not speak the Welsh language. In both cases, those who speak the old traditional language are in a small minority. According to the 1981 census, only 19% of the inhabitants of Wales could speak the Welsh language. Only 80,000 Scots are believed to speak the indigenous Scots Gaelic, most of them concentrated in the Scottish highlands and islands. There is a further division in Northern Ireland, where the community is divided along mutually exclusive lines (see Chapter 9); a few families in the province still speak the Irish form of Gaelic. The influx of immigrants into Britain, especially in the 1950s and early 1960s (numbers have been limited since 1962), has also added to the diversity of the population and to linguistic differences.

The number of nonwhite people in Britain is now slightly over 2.5 million—up from just over a million in 1968—with the largest single nonwhite community being the Indian (Table 1.4). In 1987 some 45,500 people were accepted for settlement in Britain, a quarter of these from the South Asian subcontinent. A large proportion of the ethnic minority population—just over 40%—is United Kingdom–born. As a proportion of the total population, the nonwhite community is small: 4.5% of the total. It is not evenly spread throughout the country, however. It is heavily concentrated—a factor exacerbating racial tension—in a number of urban

TABLE 1.4. POPULATION BY ETHNIC GROUP, 1981–1987

Ethnic Group	Estimated Population (Thousands)		Percentage (1985–1997 average)
	1981	*1987*	
White	51,000	51,573	94.4
Ethnic minority groups			
West Indian[a]	528	489	1.0
African	80	116	0.2
Indian	727	761	1.4
Pakistani	284	392	0.7
Bangladeshi	51	116	0.2
Chinese	92	126	0.2
Arab	53	79	0.1
Mixed	217	263	0.5
Other	60	141	0.3
All ethnic minority groups	2,092	2,484	4.5
Not stated	608	467	1.0

[a] Includes Guyanese. *Source:* Population Trends 54, Winter 1988 *(Office of Population Censuses and Surveys, 1988), p. 29.*

areas, notably London, Leicester, Birmingham, Bradford, and various towns in the West Midlands and Yorkshire.

The United States has experienced analogous problems of concentration but has a much larger black population. In 1987, blacks accounted for more than 12% of the American population (29.8 million out of 243.8 million); there were also approximately 7 million other nonwhites, the largest single proportion being those of Spanish/Hispanic origin. Unlike the case in Britain, the black population in the United States is as indigenous as the white. (The principal indigenous population—the American Indian—totaled 1.4 million at the beginning of the 1980s.) The United States also has a far greater ethnic mix than Britain. The hyphen in American society (German-Americans, Polish-Americans) has no significant equivalent in Britain.

Religion

Britain is a predominantly Protestant but not particularly religious nation. Though religion has played a central role in the history of the British Isles, its significance in the twentieth century has, with certain exceptions, declined rapidly. Outside of Northern Ireland, church membership is a minority activity.

The largest church is the Anglican Church of England. It occupies a position that would be impossible for a church to occupy in the United States. It is "by law established" the official church in England. (The Presbyterian Church of Scotland is the established church there.) As such, it is variously involved in affairs of state. The monarch is the Supreme Governor (temporal head) of the church, and archbishops, bishops, and deans are appointed by the Queen on the advice of the prime minister. The coronation of a new monarch is conducted by the Archbishop of Canterbury, the senior churchman in the Anglican faith, and services of national celebration (or grief) are conducted in one of the principal Anglican churches, usually St. Paul's Cathedral or Westminster Abbey in London. The monarch must always be a member of the Church and promise to uphold it. Until the beginning of the 1970s there was also a statutory requirement that the Lord Chancellor, head of the judiciary, must be a Protestant.

A broad Protestant church, the Church of England was founded by King Henry VIII in the sixteenth century following his break with the Roman Catholic Church.[3] It comprises two provinces: Canterbury, headed by the Archbishop of Canterbury (titled Primate of All England), with 30 dioceses, and York, headed by the Archbishop of York (Primate of England), with 14 dioceses. Within the dioceses, there are more than 13,000 parishes. By virtue of its being the established church, the senior bishops—the two archbishops; the bishops of London, Durham, and Winchester; and 21 other bishops according to their seniority—sit in the House of Lords, forming the Lords Spiritual (see Chapter 11). Though a largely self-regulating (and self-financing) church, various measures concerning the governing principles of church organization require the approval of Parliament.[4]

Though about half the population is baptized into the Church (and somewhat more regard themselves as members of the Church), less than 10% are confirmed. Just over one million people are estimated to attend Church services on a normal Sunday. In recent years the Church has faced a schism on the issue of women priests. Only men are admitted to the priesthood. Pressure for women to be admitted led to the General Synod of the Church (the central governing body, comprising bishops, clergy, and lay members) voting in 1987 to proceed with legislation to permit the ordination of women, a process likely to take several years; a significant fraction of the existing clergy are expected to leave the Church when the process is completed.

There are a number of other Protestant churches in Britain, generally known as Free (or Nonconformist) churches, by virtue of their not being established. Like the Church of England, the Methodist Church is indigenous to England, having originated in the eighteenth century under the evangelical revival led by John Wesley. Today it has a membership of just under 500,000. Other Nonconformist churches include the Baptist (about 170,000 members), the United Reform Church (about 130,000 members), and the smaller but most visibly active Salvation Army (60,000), its uniform-clad members being seen regularly on missions of social welfare. Most churches have witnessed a declining membership, but one growth area has been in the house church movement: services and prayer meetings are held in private houses, members taking turns as host. Attendance, drawing largely on people from Protestant denominations, is probably now in excess of 100,000; membership stands at about 90,000.

The Roman Catholic Church, the "out" (and often legally discriminated against) church for most of the period since the Reformation in the sixteenth century, now enjoys the same freedoms as other religions. It is divided into seven provinces in Britain, each headed by an archbishop; the premier archbishop is the Archbishop of Westminster. There are thirty episcopal dioceses, and six more in Northern Ireland. Approximately 10% of the population claim to be Roman Catholics. Whereas adherence to the Church of England may be described as broad but not particularly deep, the reverse generally obtains in the case of the Roman Catholic Church. The Church places particular emphasis on religious education as well as devotion.

The Jewish community in Britain—numbering about 400,000—is the second largest in Europe. Most Jews are Orthodox Jews, headed by the Chief Rabbi, and about 20% are members of the Reform or Liberal and Progressive movements. There are about 300 Jewish congregations in the country. The Muslim community is believed to number at least 1.5 million people. There are 1,000 mosques and prayer centers throughout the country, the Islamic Cultural Center (and London Central Mosque) on the edge of London's Regent Park constituting the most important Muslim institution in the western world. There are also Sikh, Hindu, and Buddhist communities and a host of Christian movements of foreign origin. Religious movements originating in the United States with bases now in Britain include the Jehovah's Witnesses, Christian Scientists, and the Church of Jesus Christ of Latter-Day Saints (the Mormons). Though small in number, Jehovah's Witnesses and Mormons constitute the most active doorstep proselytizers in the country.

Though religion remains politically and socially central to the life of Northern Ireland—and important in certain British cities, such as Glasgow, as well as among various non-Christian denominations—its importance in Britain generally has declined throughout the twentieth century. In significance, it has been displaced by class.

Class

The United States does not have a feudal history. The significance of this fact was well described by Louis Hartz in his incisive work on the Lockean basis of American society.[5] Britain, by contrast, most certainly does have a feudal past. Furthermore, unlike some of its European neighbors with feudal histories, it has witnessed no revolutionary break with past experience. As a result, the class patterns of a capitalist society have been superimposed on the hierarchical social structure of a departing feudal society.

Status derives from the tendency of people to accord positive and negative values to human attributes and to distribute respect accordingly. In feudal society, a superior status was accorded to the land-owning aristocracy and gentry. They were deemed to have breeding and to be the best people to govern the land. They were accorded deference as a socially superior body. It was a status that was passed on by inheritance, not one that could be acquired by merit or work.

Whereas status is essentially the product of social structure, class is the product of the economic.[6] Defining the concept of class is not an easy task. Marx distinguished two classes, bourgeois and proletarian, based on the ownership of the means of production. This is not a particularly useful definition given the significant distinction between ownership and control.

TABLE 1.5. SOCIAL CLASSES IN BRITAIN

Class	Market Research Designation	Encompassing
Middle class		
Upper-middle	A	Higher managerial and professional
Middle	B	Lower managerial and administrative
Lower-middle	C1	Skilled or supervisory nonmanual, lower nonmanual
Working class		
Upper-working	C2	Skilled manual
Working	D	Unskilled manual
	E	Residual, pensioners

The problem is compounded by the fact that there is a difference between attempts at objective measurement and subjective self-assessment. In other words, how social scientists measure class—and there are an increasing number of measures used—and how others perceive it (particularly in terms of self-ascription) are often far from congruent. Though there are now several definitions of class, the most used is that of groups formed on the basis of occupational difference. In Britain there are essentially two classes, the middle and the working; as A. H. Halsey has observed, it is a characteristically British distinction.[7] Within each of the two classes, there are further divisions. Table 1.5 provides a simple delineation of them.

Class grew out of industrialization and the development of a capitalist economy. It did not displace status; it usurped it. In the nineteenth century, the upper class comprised the traditional landed aristocracy, but it was an aristocracy that had absorbed largely, if not wholly, the new men of wealth who had made their money from trade and industry. These new men were drawn into the new class until, eventually, they overwhelmed it.[8]

This combination of class and status was carried into the twentieth century. In recent decades, however, it has been weakened. Some of the features of a status society, such as peerages, can be passed from father to son: the inheritance is founded in law. Class can be inherited but it is an inheritance based on the market, which is less predictable than the law. Recent years have witnessed a growing social mobility. The children of many working-class parents have been upwardly mobile socially. The children of some middle-class parents have taken up working-class occupations. Indeed, a few members of that institutional survivor of a feudal era, the House of Lords, pursue manual occupations. Writes Halsey, "Men and women, moving and marrying between different occupational levels, both over the generations and also within their own working lives or careers, have become an increasingly common feature of British social life in the past half century."[9] The general pattern of change has been one of upward mobility. Greater mobility and affluence have eroded the claims to status. Mobility deprives one of claims to breeding. Acceptance of the principle of meritocracy is discordant with claims of inherited worth. Status remains important but it is no longer the central feature of British society that it was in preceding centuries.

The importance of class in contemporary society has been confirmed by a number of studies. In their 1970 survey, Butler and Stokes asked respondents to name the main social classes and the class to which they would ascribe themselves. They found that "virtually everyone accepted the conventional class dichotomy between middle and working class"[10] with 77% spontaneously ascribing themselves to one or the other. According to Butler and Stokes, "It is difficult not to see this as evidence of the acceptance of the view that British society is divided into two primary classes. This is much more than a sociologist's simplification: it seems to be deeply rooted in the mind of the ordinary British citizen."[11] Though increased social mobility and changes in the occupational profile of the nation appeared to reduce the significance (or, perhaps more accurately, the measurability) of class in the 1970s and 1980s, most citizens continue to consider themselves members of a particular class. A 1987 survey found less than 2% of respondents giving a "Don't know" response when asked which social class they believed they belonged to, and, as in Butler and Stokes' survey, most identified themselves with the class of their parents (Table 1.6). Insofar as there is a difference between the class of self and parents, the figures in Table 1.6 reinforce the thesis of upward mobility.

The importance of class is political as well as social. For most of the twentieth century, there has been a significant relationship between class

TABLE 1.6. SOCIAL CLASS BY SELF-ASCRIPTION, 1987

Q: Which social class would you say *you* belong to:

	Self %	Parents %
Upper-middle	1.5	2.3
Middle	26.0	17.7
Upper-working	21.3	12.1
Working	46.0	59.1
Poor	2.9	6.8
Don't know	1.4	1.2

Source: R. Jowell, S. Witherspoon, and L. Brook, British Social Attitudes, the Fifth Report, *1988–1989 edition (Gower, 1988), Q76, p. 227.*

and politics. The Labour party has attracted largely but not wholly the support of the working class, and the Conservative party that of the middle class. The significance of the class–party nexus will be explored in more detail shortly. There is recent evidence of decline in class identifications and in the correlation between class and party. Such decline, though, has been relative. Class remains a feature of British society. Most Britons continue to ascribe themselves to a particular class. Politicians analyze their support in class terms, and sociologists would be lost without it.

Education

Education in Britain is best seen in pyramidal terms. All children receive a primary and secondary school education. Thereafter, only a minority proceed to institutions of further education and a small percentage enter university. For children receiving education at private schools, the structure is less pyramidal: A greater proportion of those educated at private schools proceed to university than those attending state schools.

After entering primary school at the age of 5, children in England receive a common education until the age of 11, when they enter secondary schools. Most pupils now attend what are termed comprehensive schools, schools whose enrollment criteria are geographic rather than academic.

In the two decades following the Second World War, secondary schools were divided into grammar and secondary modern schools. The former stressed scholastic skills, and a large proportion of students stayed beyond the minimum school-leaving age (then 15) and proceeded to university. The latter emphasized practical skills such as technical drawing and woodwork; some pupils went on to some form of technical college but most left at the age of 15 and few if any achieved university entrance. Selection for grammar schools was based on an intelligence test known as the "Eleven-plus" examination, taken, as the name suggests, when primary schoolchildren reached the age of 11, at the end of their primary education. Labour party politicians came to view this examination and the consequent dichotomy between grammar and secondary modern schools as educationally questionable and socially divisive: those attending secondary modern schools were seen as "failures" and their subsequent job opportunities limited by virtue of their education. Grammar school pupils were drawn disproportionately from middle-class families.

In 1965 the Labour government introduced a scheme of reform requiring local authorities to take steps to dispense with the Eleven-plus and introduce a scheme of comprehensive education. Many authorities responded reluctantly, some resisting the government's wishes, and only in the 1970s did the number of pupils in comprehensive schools exceed the number attending selective schools. In 1971 only 38% of secondary schoolchildren in England attended comprehensive schools; by 1980 the proportion was 83%, and by 1987 it had reached 92%. In Scotland and Wales the proportion was even higher: 96% and 99% respectively.

The Conservative government of the 1980s introduced further reforms of the system. Foremost among these was the introduction, in England and Wales, of a national curriculum. Implemented in September 1989, it comprises three core subjects (English, science, and mathematics) and seven foundation subjects (history, geography, technology, art, physical education, art, and, at secondary level, a modern foreign language), each with nationally agreed-upon attainment targets and assessment arrangements. (Pupils' performance is to be assessed and reported on at four "key stages": at ages, 7, 11, 14, and 16.) Under an earlier change, taking effect in 1988, the public examinations taken by secondary school pupils were also reformed. The examinations previously taken at 16+ were the Ordinary Level ("O"-Level) General Certificates of Education, and the CSEs, or Certificates of Secondary Education; the former were for more academic students and the latter were more practically oriented. These were replaced by a single examination, the General Certificate of Secondary Education (GCSE), which placed a greater emphasis on coursework. The principal examination taken at 18+—Advanced Level ("A"-Level) General Certificates of Education, the primary qualifications for higher education—was left intact.

Although secondary education is compulsory, parents are not required to send their children to state schools but can opt to send them to private schools. Here the enrollment criterion is more financial than geographic. Private schools tend to stress scholastic skills and concentrate on developing the capacity to pass examinations and on building self-confidence. Believing their children will receive a better and more disciplined education, with a greater prospect of university entry than from a state school, many parents who can afford it send their children to such private institutions, known (confusingly) as "public schools." Fees at such schools will vary, depending on the status of the school. The more prestigious such as Eton, Harrow, and Winchester can afford to charge annual fees in excess of £7,000 (more than $11,500 in 1989 terms), whereas some less prestigious day schools may charge less than £2,000 per year. In 1988, fewer than 7% of the total school population were attending assisted and independent schools—yet more than a quarter of university entrants continued to be drawn from private schools.

From secondary school, a small proportion proceed to institutions of further and higher education. Only a small fraction of pupils take and pass the two "A"-Level GCE examinations that are the minimum requirement for university entrance. (In practice, passing three "A"-Level examinations with high grades is generally required for admission to study non-science subjects.) In 1986–1987, fewer than 30% of girls aged 18–24 and fewer than 25% of boys in the same age range were studying in institutions of further and higher education; of those in this age range, only 4% were attending universities (Figure 1.1). Only one out of every ten who leaves school goes on to study full-time for a degree.

There are different forms of higher and further education. There are various technical colleges and colleges of further education, as well as the institutions at the top of the pyramid—polytechnics and universities.

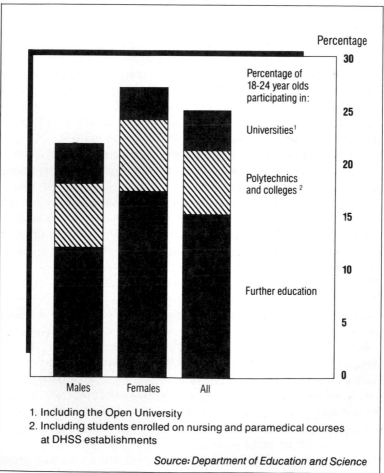

Figure 1.1. Proportion of 18–24 Year Olds in Further and Higher Education, 1986–1987 (Reproduced from *Social Trends 19* (Her Majesty's Stationery Office, 1989), p. 58.)

Polytechnics stress more vocational, practical subjects, often providing sandwich courses (part teaching, part practical job experience), and are a relatively new innovation; the first were established in 1967 and there are now 30. Universities tend to stress more academic subjects. Relative to the United States, there are few universities in the United Kingdom: a total of 47. Of these, 37 were founded after 1945. The most prestigious tend to be the oldest: Oxford, Cambridge, and, in Scotland, St. Andrew's. The Open University is notable for being a nonresidential university, providing tuition by correspondence and through special television and radio programs: it is the only university that requires no formal academic qualifications in order to enroll. One of the newest universities, Buckingham, receives no support from public funds—it is the only wholly private university.

A university education continues to provide occupational advantage. More than 80% of graduates have ended up in the professional and managerial classes. They constitute fewer than one-third of those in these classes, but it is these classes that will provide more children than any other for university entry. The likelihood that a person will go to university remains strongly linked to his or her social class. A majority of university applicants are drawn from the top two social classes (see Table 1.5), though the proportion of 18-year-olds in these two classes is less than 30%. "Roughly speaking, the lower the socioeconomic group of someone's father, the more likely it is that his or her full-time education ended in school, rather than college or university."[12] In recent years there has been little significant change in the number of university students drawn from working-class families.

Personal Wealth and Taxation

The distribution of marketable wealth among the population is skewed in favor of a minority. Marketable wealth comprises stocks and shares, cash, bank deposits, consumer durables, buildings, trade assets, land, and dwellings net of mortgage debt. In 1971 approximately one-third of the total marketable wealth in Britain was owned by 1% of the population; two-thirds was owned by the wealthiest 10% (see Table 1.7). Since then the proportions have declined: by 1985, 20% of marketable wealth was owned by the top 1% and just over half by the top 10%. More than 90% of marketable wealth remains in the hands of half the population.

When occupational and state pension rights are added to marketable wealth, there is a change in the pattern of distribution (Table 1.7). In 1971, 21% of this aggregate wealth was owned by 1% of the population and 49% by 10% of the population. Over the 1970s and less so in the early 1980s, there was a shift in the distribution of wealth in favor of slightly more equality; by 1985, the percentage owned by 1% of the population was about half what it was in 1971. As Table 1.7 clearly demonstrates, however, most wealth remains in the hands of the minority.

In income, approximately two-thirds of the total household income before tax comes from wages and salaries. In 1987 the average gross weekly earnings of a male manual employee was just over £185 ($306) and of a nonmanual employee £266 ($439). The equivalent figures for female workers were £115 ($190) and £157 ($259). The average wage for all employees was £224 ($369) (male) and £148 ($244) (female). Between 1982 and 1989, average earnings increased each year by between 5% and 10%.

Taxation is essentially progressive, though the various rates have been reduced to two: a basic income tax of 25% and a higher rate of 40%. (At one stage there was a maximum rate of 83%.) The proportion of tax paid by the highest 10% of earners has increased, however, since the period of the 1970s. In the latter half of the 1970s, the highest 10% of taxpayers paid 35% of the total. By 1987–1988 the proportion had increased to 41%, falling back slightly to 39% the following year after the reduction in the top rate of taxation to 40%. The bottom 50% of taxpayers pay only 17% of the total, a figure that has remained constant for most of the past decade.

Expressed as a proportion of GDP, total taxes in Britain account for between 30% and 40%, reaching a peak of just over 39% in the early and mid-1980s. The proportion of GDP taken in income tax has fallen from just over 11% in 1978–1979 to a little over 9% in 1988–1989. In part, this drop reflects a shift in the balance between direct and indirect taxes. Of total taxes and social security contributions paid, 39% were paid by households in direct taxation in 1975; by 1985 the proportion was down to 28%. Indirect taxes rose in the same period from 36% to 41% of the total.

TABLE 1.7. DISTRIBUTION OF WEALTH, 1971–1985

Percentage of Population	Percentage Owned of Marketable Wealth			Percentage Owned of Marketable Wealth Plus Occupational and State Pension Rights		
	1971	*1979*	*1985*	*1971*	*1979*	*1985*
1	31	24	20	21	13	11
5	52	45	40	37	27	25
10	65	59	54	49	37	36
25	86	82	76	69–72	58–61	57–60
50	97	95	93	85–89	79–83	81–85

Source: Derived from Social Trends 12 *(Her Majesty's Stationery Office, 1981), p. 99, and* Social Trends 19 *(Her Majesty's Stationery Office, 1989), p. 100.*

(There was also a rise in the direct taxes paid by corporations, rising from 6% to 13% of the total.) This contrasts with a shift in the opposite direction in the United States, where direct taxes paid by households rose from 34% of the total in 1975 to 39% in 1981 and then 37% in 1985. The U.S. proportion is now higher than in West Germany, Japan, and France as well as the United Kingdom. The proportion of indirect taxes paid in the United Kingdom for most of the past decade has been higher than that in most other major industrialized nations, rivaled only by France for part of the period but now surpassing it.

POLITICAL SOCIALIZATION

The various values and beliefs that coalesce to maintain, reinforce, or sometimes modify the political culture are not generated in a vacuum; they are acquired through a process of socialization. In that process, the most important influences are usually family, education, occupation, geographic location, and to a lesser extent, the mass media. Such influences serve to instill an awareness of one's place in or relationship to society and the political system.

Family

Although much emphasis is placed on the individual, the family remains the most important social unit in Britain. Most households in Britain comprise married couples, in most cases with dependent children. The average size of a household in 1985 was 2.6 persons. The number of people living on their own has increased—there were 5.3 million one-person households in 1987 (double the number in 1961)—and the number is expected to increase.[13] This increase does not necessarily signify social detachment from a family, however. For many people living on their own—the largest number comprising people over state retirement age —their social world may revolve around visits to and from relatives. Family units are also provided by couples living together but not married. In 1985, for example, 16% of nonmarried women aged 18 to 49 were cohabiting, compared with 14% the previous year.[14] Although marriages are becoming less stable in that divorce rates continue to rise (Britain has both the highest marriage rate and highest divorce rate in the European Community), many divorcees remarry or cohabit with another partner. One-third of marriages in 1987 involved at least one divorced partner. Marriage remains the ultimate goal for most men and women: the proportion who have ultimately married has shown little variation in this century. One change has been an increase in the proportion of women getting married.[15] According to the authors of *British Social Attitudes: The 1987 Report*, "In their attitudes towards marriage and other family matters, the British emerge as highly and consistently conventional."[16]

It is from parents that children inherit social values. Indeed, children often acquire their class orientation from parents not only in thought but also in practical terms. As we have seen (Table 1.6), most people ascribe themselves to the same class as that of their parents. Though the proportion has declined since the 1960s, most children obtain jobs in the class bracket of their fathers. (Where social mobility does occur, upward mobility is twice as likely to take place as downward mobility.)[17] That this should be so is not surprising. Children raised in a middle-class family in which the parents and grandparents were university educated are likely to be brought up in an environment in which reading and learning are stressed and going to university is encouraged. A university education is more likely to result in a better-paying job than is a nonuniversity education. Hence, graduates are more likely to obtain middle-class occupations than are nongraduates. Working-class families, by contrast, are less likely to provide an environment that encourages scholastic skills. This may not be out of unwillingness but rather ignorance on the part of parents: they do not know how to go about encouraging such skills. In some cases they may not wish to. The need to supplement the family income motivates some parents to encourage children to go out and earn a wage as soon as possible. Years spent at university are financially unrewarding from the parents' perspective. An attachment to class may also limit the ambitions of both parents and children. Existing in a working-class milieu reinforced by the still-existing perception of status can create a cocooning effect: it provides a sense of the familiar and the comfortable (in psychological if not financial terms). To leave a working-class environment is to head for the unknown. From parents, children can acquire habits and tastes that are peculiar if not exclusive to a particular class. Certain sports are working-class sports (for example, darts), others middle-class (squash, for instance). Such tastes are passed from one generation to the next, reinforced by the environment in which a family exists.

Political habits and values also are passed from parent to child. Children are more likely to be politically interested and active if their parents have been similarly interested or active.[18] More important, children tend to inherit their parents' partisan preferences. The influence is strongest when both parents share the same preference and that preference is known to the children.[19] There is evidence of some decline in this parent–party nexus,[20] and in recent elections a significant fraction of the electorate voted for parties for which earlier generations could not have voted (the Liberal/Social Democratic Party Alliance in the 1983 and 1987 general elections, for example, and the Green party in the European

Parliament elections of 1989). Despite this decline, parents' preferences remain a significant predictor of partisan preference.[21] This partisanship is reinforced when parents' preferences are congruent with the influences to be identified below.

Family remains the most important primary influence in the process of political socialization. Divergent influences may modify or dispel values imbued as a result of parental influence, but in seeking to make sense of the social and political environment in which he or she lives, an individual's first and foremost point of reference is provided by father and mother (the father more likely in terms of partisan preference).

Education

Formal education is important in political socialization, less for its effect on partisan support (family remains the predominant influence) than for helping shape awareness of the political system and explicitly or, more often, implicitly, the values that underpin it.

In their classic but now dated study of the civic culture, Almond and Verba found that there were differences in attitude toward government between those with different levels of education, and between those who had received some formal education and those who had received none. The more extensive the education, up to university level, the greater the perceived significance of government action.[22] Nonetheless, the overwhelming majority of those with some formal education, primary or above, considered that national government had some effect. In the countries studied in which a proportion of the population had received no formal education (Italy and Mexico), only a small proportion of those without an education felt that national government had some effect. (The proportion of those with a formal education ascribing influence to the government was lower than in the United States and in Britain, albeit still a majority among the university educated.) From this, one may infer the importance of education for the purposes of political socialization.

The correlation between education and political socialization in Britain is not greatly dissimilar to that in the United States. Almond and Verba discovered that those with higher levels of education were more likely to attach significance to government, to pay attention to politics and elections, and to believe that they had some influence on government.[23] More recent survey data have reinforced these findings. A 1986 survey "shows that those with educational qualifications, and graduates in particular, are more liberal in their moral values, more confident in their ability to understand politics and generally more inclined to participate in politics than are the unqualified."[24] Table 1.8 reveals the greater level of political participation among graduates than among nongraduates.

TABLE 1.8. POLITICAL PARTICIPATION BY LEVELS OF EDUCATION, 1986

Political Acitivity	Graduates	Those with Intermediate Qualifications	Those with No Qualifications
	%	%	%
Have contacted Member of Parliament	29	11	8
Have signed a petition	52	37	29
Have gone on a demonstration	17	7	2

Source: R. Jowell, S. Witherspoon, and L. Brook, British Social Attitudes: The 1987 Report *(Gower, 1987), p. 65.*

Where Britain and the United States differ is in the way that the subject of politics is taught. In Britain, manifest teaching of the subject, insofar as it is manifest, can best be described as subtle. There is little emphasis on symbolic acts (there is no obvious British equivalent to saluting the flag) and little formal teaching of politics as such. The media of other subjects have usually been employed. As Stradling noted, "Until comparatively recently the prevailing view on political education in England was either that it was already adequately taken care of through History, Geography, Social or General Studies or that it was a wholly unsuitable subject for the school curriculum."[25] Only recently has the opportunity to study politics as a distinct and legitimate subject been expanded within secondary schools. Relative to other subjects, it remains a little-taught subject. Despite an increase in the 1980s, only 8,000 students were studying "A"-Level politics by 1987 and the subject was not included among the foundation subjects for the national curriculum. Earlier studies, both in Britain and in the United States, suggested that the study of politics had little impact on political knowledge and attitudes.[26] A more recent study, by Denver and Hands, has found that "the teaching of Politics, at least to senior students at 'A' Level, has a substantial effect on levels of political knowledge, issue awareness and ideological sophistication."[27] Students of politics may thus constitute the tip of a pyramid, with those with advanced levels of education but without a training in politics being immediately below them.

Attendance at school, and particularly at certain schools, can be important also in providing an environment that can serve to reinforce certain norms and traditions. At leading public schools, most notably Eton, there is a tradition of providing MPs, government ministers, and prime ministers. At such schools, a pupil is more likely to consider pursuing a political career than are pupils attending an inner-city comprehensive school with no such tradition. A majority of Conservative members of Parliament, for example, went to public schools (followed by study at Oxford or Cambridge University). In most cases, the school environment tends to reinforce the influence of the home background.

Occupation and Class

Occupation and class, as we have seen, are closely related. The former is usually employed as the primary criterion for assessing the latter. Both are important in the context of political socialization.

Occupation, by virtue of its nature, status, or the interaction with others that it offers, can significantly affect the process of social and political integration. Holding jobs that are well paying or rewarding in terms of personal satisfaction are likely to increase one's level of contentment with existing society. Conversely, pursuing a mundane, poorly paid job or no job at all may provoke a sense of alienation from society. Certain jobs by their nature may lead to greater social awareness or to a greater degree of social intercourse than others.

Class is an abstraction and the concept acquires meaning only as a result of the socialization process just outlined. From one's parents, education, occupation, and associated lifestyle one acquires an awareness of social class. Such awareness becomes important in helping clarify one's place in society and, thus, one's relationship to others in that society. It serves to give some meaning and shape to one's social existence.

There is an important but not complete relationship between class and political efficacy. Those in the working class, for example, are more likely than those in the middle class to consider governments as not particularly able to change things.[28] There is also a significant—and much charted—relationship between class and partisan support. Such a relationship is not surprising. Those in middle-class occupations are more likely to be better paid and to pursue a preferred lifestyle than those in working-class occupations (though the emphasis should be on the likelihood, not the certainty). Hence, one might expect the middle class to opt for the political party most likely to conserve the existing state of affairs. Those in working-class jobs and those with no jobs at all might be expected to opt for a party that offers some degree of social change and appears more disposed toward the "have nots" than toward the "haves." This hypothesis has been generally but not wholly borne out by the empirical evidence.[29] Middle-class voters have tended to support the Conservative party in Britain, and working-class voters the Labour party. The relationship has never been a complete one, however. Some middle-class voters have supported the Labour party and about one-third of working-class voters have traditionally cast their ballots for Conservative candidates. In recent years, the significance of the class–party tie has markedly declined; nonetheless, as we shall see, class provides the most important indicator of partisan support. No other indicator—despite recent changes—has proved so reliable.

Location

Location can be important in the process of political socialization in a number of senses. The location of one's residence is important. Living in an area of expensive detached houses can serve to reinforce one's sense of being middle class. The area provides a social milieu that reinforces that awareness. Conversely, living in an area of less expensive terraced accommodation or of council houses (estates composed of houses rented from local authorities are common, though declining in number) reinforces one's identification with the working class. Within such areas, there is often a particular lifestyle.

The independent influence of location is borne out when correlated with partisan support. As Miller found, "At a minimum, the class characteristics of the social environment have more effect on constituency partisanship than class differences themselves, perhaps much more. The partisanship of individuals is influenced more by where they live than what they do."[30] In other words, voters who live in class-specific communities are more likely to vote for the relevant class-specific party than are those not living in such communities. There is also a correlation between partisan support and urban versus rural location. There is a further correlation between partisan support and regions. These correlations have become more pronounced since the 1960s, the regional concentration becoming particularly marked. The north and northwest of the country have shifted markedly toward the Labour party, the south and the east toward the Conservatives.[31] This shift has been apparent in succeeding general elections. In the 1987 general election the Conservative share of the poll increased in London and the southeast but fell markedly in Scotland— reinforcing a trend apparent since 1959—as well as in the north and the northwest. This correlation is not surprising, given changes in employment and demographic patterns. As Curtice and Steed have noted, "the peripheral areas of Britain, with their higher unemployment, and the declining inner parts of conurbations, have become steadily more Labour; while the expanding, more prosperous areas have become more Conservative."[32]

The Mass Media

The mass media of communication—principally television, radio, and newspapers—are also important. They constitute the most used sources for knowledge of what is going on in society. As in the United States, television in Britain now constitutes the most used source (see Table 1.9). Perceptions of the reliability of the different media are also similar in the two countries. Given conflicting reports from the different media, 53% of U.S. respondents in a 1982 survey said they would consider television the most believable of the three sources; in a similar survey in the United Kingdom in 1984, 57% gave the same response.[33]

The mass media are important not only as means of transmission (hence their collective name) but also for what they choose to transmit. By choosing to transmit some stories rather than others, those in control of television and newspapers can have some impact on political perceptions and values. Various studies suggest that stories chosen serve to reinforce existing, particularly elite, values (see Chapter 14). In Britain it is likely that the media serve also to reinforce a national, as opposed to regional, attachment. The size of the country and the dual position of London as the nation's capital and its largest city have facilitated a national—primarily a London—orientation not possible in the United States.

The partisan influence of the media in Britain is unclear. The broadcasting media are statutorily required to be impartial. Newspapers can and do express partisan preferences: most support or are sympathetic to the Conservative party. Though by international standards Britain has a high level of newspaper readership, a significant proportion of the population (about one-quarter) do not read a newspaper regularly;[34] of those who do, few read newspapers with significant political coverage. Television news programs, in contrast, are regularly among the most watched programs. Readers of the popular (tabloid) press in particular are likely to use television as their main source of news.[35] There is evidence, however, that newspapers can have what Butler and Stokes characterized as a "magnetizing" effect, a finding reinforced by Dunleavy and Husbands' analysis of the 1983 general election: they found that the greater the exposure to Conservative newspapers, the greater the propensity to vote Conservative.[36] Manual workers exposed to Conservative newspapers

TABLE 1.9. MAIN SOURCE OF NEWS, UNITED STATES AND UNITED KINGDOM

Main Source(s) of news	USA 1982[a] %	UK 1984 %
Television	65	61
Newspapers	44	20
Radio	18	15

[a] U.S. respondents were permitted multiple responses. *(Source: R. Jowell and S. Witherspoon,* British Social Atittudes: The 1985 Report *(Gower, 1985), p. 46.)*

were four or five times more likely to vote Conservative than manual workers not exposed to such newspapers.

A Complex Mix

The process by which an individual becomes politically socialized is a complex one. The influences just outlined are in most cases the more important but by no means the only ones—nor are they exclusive. They clearly interact with one another, as has been obvious from the foregoing. It has been virtually impossible to discuss one influence without drawing out the impact of another. Also, these influences are far from static. Changes in family structures, the educational system, the nature of employment, and demographic and housing patterns may affect the socialization process. As we have noted, children staying longer in formal education appear to acquire a greater interest in politics than those leaving school earlier. More children than before are acquiring a formal education beyond the minimum school-leaving age. Unemployment may generate a sense of political alienation. As we have seen, unemployment for the past two decades has been at historically high levels.

The importance of some of these changes will be touched on later in this work, particularly in the context of partisan support. However, such changes are relative. In terms of the basic values being transmitted in the process of political socialization, the most significant feature is not change but rather continuity. The media for political socialization in Britain are not dissimilar to those in the United States and many other polities. To know this is useful, but to identify those media is to identify the *means* for transmitting the values and beliefs that coalesce to form the political culture, and not to identify the political culture itself. That is a separate exercise, undertaken in the next chapter. Having identified some of the salient features of contemporary Britain and, as a prerequisite, the process of political socialization, we can now progress to the more analytically useful study of British political culture.

NOTES

1. Central Office of Information, *Britain 1989: An Official Handbook* (Her Majesty's Stationery Office, 1989), p. 305.
2. Central Statistical Office, *Economic Trends*, No. 426, April 1989 (Her Majesty's Stationery Office, 1989), p. 40.
3. Henry VIII was excommunicated by the Pope in 1533, following the crowning of Ann Boleyn as Queen, the Pope having refused to annul Henry's previous marriage to Catherine of Aragon. Parliament responded with various Acts

establishing Henry's position as head of the church. By the Act of Supremacy of 1534, the king was recognized as "the only supreme head of the Church of England, called *Anglicana Ecclesia*."

4. The power is more than formal: in July 1989 the House of Commons rejected a Church measure that would have permitted divorced men to be ordained.
5. L. Hartz, *The Liberal Tradition in America* (Harcourt, Brace & World, 1955).
6. See A. H. Halsey, *Change in British Society*, 2nd ed. (Oxford University Press, 1981). This section draws heavily on this work.
7. Ibid.
8. Ibid., p. 47.
9. Ibid., pp. 53–54.
10. D. Butler and D. Stokes, *Political Change in Britain*, 2nd ed. (Macmillan, 1974), p. 69.
11. Ibid.
12. J. Statham and D. Mackinnon, with H. Cathcart, *The Education Fact File* (Hodder & Stoughton in association with the Open Unviersity, 1989), p. 160.
13. *Social Trends*, 19 (Her Majesty's Stationery Office, 1989), p. 35.
14. *Population Trends*, 51, Spring 1988 (Office of Population Censuses and Surveys, 1988), p. 3.
15. J. Haskey, "Trends in Marriage and Divorce, and Cohort Analyses of the Proportions of Marriages Ending in Divorce," *Population Trends*, 54, Winter 1988 (Office of Population Censuses and Surveys, 1988), p. 21.
16. R. Jowell, S. Witherspoon, and L. Brook, *British Social Attitudes: The 1987 Report* (Gower, 1987), p. 140.
17. R. Jowell and S. Witherspoon, *British Social Attitudes: The 1985 Report* (Gower, 1985), p. 3.
18. Butler and Stokes, p. 50.
19. See especially M. N. Franklin, *The Decline of Class Voting in Britain* (Oxford University Press, 1985), pp. 69–71 and 78–79.
20. R. Rose and I. McAllister, *Voters Begin to Choose* (Sage, 1986), p. 104–6.
21. Franklin, pp. 69–71, 78–79.
22. G. Almond and S. Verba, *The Civic Culture* (Princeton University Press, 1963), pp. 86–87.
23. Ibid., pp. 380–81.
24. Jowell, Witherspoon, and Brook, p. 65.
25. R. Stradling, *The Political Awareness of School Leavers* (Hansard Society, 1977), p. 1.
26. Stradling, p. 37; K. P. Langton and M. Kent Jennings, "Political Socialisation and the High School Curriculum in the United States," *American Political Science Review*, 62, 1968, pp. 852–67.
27. D. Denver and G. Hands, "The Effects of 'A' Level Politics: Literacy, not Indoctrination," *Social Studies Review*, 4 (1), 1988, p. 40.
28. Jowell and Witherspoon, *1985 Report*, p. 18.
29. R. J. Johnston, C. J. Pattie, and J. G. Allsopp, *A Nation Dividing?* (Longman, 1988), p. 49.
30. W. L. Miller, *Electoral Dynamics* (Macmillan, 1977), p. 65. See also Johnston, Pattie, and Allsopp, pp. 61–63.

31. J. Curtice and M. Steed, "Electoral Choice and the Production of Government," *British Journal of Political Science*, 12, 1982, pp. 249–98.
32. J. Curtice and M. Steed, "An Analysis of the Voting," in D. Butler and D. Kavanagh, *The British General Election of 1979* (Macmillan, 1980), p. 402.
33. Jowell and Witherspoon, p. 47.
34. Ibid., p. 46.
35. Ibid.
36. P. Dunleavy and C. T. Husbands, *British Democracy at the Crossroads* (Unwin & Hyman, 1985); see especially the extract, P. Dunleavy and C. T. Husbands, "Media Influences on Voting in 1983," in J. Anderson and A. Cochrane (eds.), *A State of Crisis: The Changing Face of British Politics* (Hodder and Stoughton, 1989), pp. 287–95.

CHAPTER 2

Continuity and Change
The British Political Culture

Continuity and change, as we have observed, are features of every political system. In order to understand the extent and nature of that change, one has to generate some analytically useful framework. The opening chapter provided largely descriptive material of the society with which we are concerned. It did not generate a framework that would help us understand the nature of continuity and change in Britain. The purpose of this chapter is to provide such a framework.

The emphasis of the chapter will be on the political culture. As I shall seek to show, however, that culture cannot be divorced from the constraints of history and of physical and spatial resources. Each has had a significant impact on the other. The impact has not been in one direction only: the political culture has served to shape political perceptions and actions, and hence to influence the nation's political history. Conversely, those actions have been constrained by the experiences of history. They have also been constrained by Britain's geographic location and limited resources.

A number of problems have to be borne in mind. As we shall see, there are problems inherent in trying to give shape to such an abstract concept as political culture. There is the danger of tautology and of failing to distinguish between how a system operates and the way in which people believe it should operate. There is the problem also of attempting to discern the cause-and-effect relationships among culture, history, and resources. The problem here is analogous to that embodied in the familiar conundrum, "Which came first, the chicken or the egg?" The existence of a stable political culture in Britain has been ascribed by some to the effectiveness of government. But what has enabled government to be effective? Has it been a distinctive political culture, citizens being prepared to acquiesce in and, when called on, to support the demands made of them by government? If so, what explains the existence of such a political culture? Is not a partial explanation the effectiveness of government? The problem is an acute one in the case of Britain, given the absence of any clear point of departure. Where does English, Scottish, or Welsh history begin? At what point is a political culture discernible? The question is largely an unanswerable one, and all we can do at this stage is to bear it in mind. Fortunately, it does not present an insurmountable obstacle; as I shall seek to show, the importance of the relationship is one of mutual reinforcement.

What, then, is the British political culture? How important have been the constraints of history and of resources? How does it compare with other polities? And is it, as some writers have suggested, in a state of collapse?

THE POLITICAL CULTURE

Political culture is a vague, abstract concept that has been subject to various definitions.[1] In its simplest form, it may be described as denoting the emotional and attitudinal environment within which a political system operates.[2] Various political scientists have sought to define and identify different types of political culture. Almond and Verba, for example, identified three ideal types: participant, subject, and parochial.[3] Others have sought to generate criteria by which to assess the distinctive features of a political culture.

In his work on political oppositions in western democracies, Robert Dahl observed that patterns of opposition may have something to do with widely shared cultural premises. He noted that four kinds of culturally derived orientations toward politics seem to have a bearing on the pattern of opposition.[4] Those four orientations can usefully be employed to help one understand and explain attitudes not just toward political opposition in Britain but to the political culture as a whole. They enable one to draw out the distinctive features of that culture, in a more useful manner than does the framework provided by others, and to consider the impact of both history and resources. Those four orientations, listed not in the order provided by Dahl but in the order I believe to be most significant to an understanding of British political culture, are toward (1) problem solving, (2) the political system, (3) cooperation and individuality, and (4) other people.

Orientation toward Problem Solving

Giovanni Sartori has distinguished two approaches to problem solving: the empirical and the rational.[5] The empirical approach is concerned with what is and what can be seen and touched, proceeding on the basis of testing and retesting and largely rejecting dogma and abstract or coherent grand designs for change. The rationalist approach, by contrast, is concerned with abstraction rather than facts, stressing the need for deductive consistency and tending to be dogmatic and definitive. According to Dahl, "While the empirical approach takes the attitude that if a program does not work in practice there must be something wrong about the theory, the rationalist will retort that what is true in theory must also be true in practice—that it is the practice, not the theory, that is wrong."[6]

France has been identified as employing a rationalist approach. Germany and Italy, to some extent, tend also to find such an approach useful. Britain and the United States, by contrast, are seen as the exemplars of an empirical approach. Indeed, it is my contention that this approach is *most* marked in the British case and that it constitutes the most significant aspect of British political culture.

Although oriented more toward an empirical approach, the United States has exhibited some elements of the rationalist. While tempered by experience and (according to Beard) self-interest, the framers of the United States Constitution were informed by Lockean values and sought to impose a political framework in line with a Lockean conception of society.[7] Those values and that conception of society have permeated the American consciousness, so much so that they have largely gone unstated. They have been so pervasive and so self-evident that there has been little point in articulating them. Hence, the United States might be described as being oriented toward a mix of the empirical and the rationalist, albeit with the former being clearly the more dominant of the two.

Britain, by contrast, has a distinct orientation toward the empirical approach. Even the political system, however strong the attachment to it, tends to be justified in pragmatic terms. Democracy, having been implemented in largely pragmatic fashion, has been lauded on the grounds that "it works." The point has been well put by Vivien Hart in comparing American and British approaches: "In America the emphasis has been on what democracy is and *should* be, while Britain has been characterised by a more pragmatic and less urgent emphasis on what democracy is and *can* be."[8] Empiricism seems appropriate to the English consciousness. Instinct, trial and error, and incremental change are the essence of the English approach to problem solving. "I believe in the instinctive wisdom of our well-tried democracy," declared Churchill in 1945—shortly before going down to election defeat.[9]

Such an orientation to problem solving has been a distinctive feature of English political culture for many centuries, discernible, I would suggest, since at least the thirteenth century. It is an approach that has informed political actions and hence the political history of the country. An empirical orientation has in turn been reinforced by the experience of history—it is the approach that has always been employed and no external constraints have managed to force themselves on the nation to generate conditions in which a rationalist approach would be possible. In the wake of the War of Independence, Americans were able to sit down and generate a political system from first principles. Invasions by foreign powers and subsequent liberation (or absence of liberation) have put other states in similar positions. England, by contrast, has never been faced with or sought such an opportunity. The closest it came was during the Protectorate of Oliver Cromwell in the seventeenth century. When that failed, the country resorted as far as possible to the conditions prevailing prior to its creation. English history is scattered with philosophers generating theories that have failed to find congenial soil in the nation's consciousness. Ideologies have been either discarded or else molded to fit with the experience of history. Prevailing theories, once they no longer seem appropriate, have been dispensed with. The act of dispensing with them has not always met with common assent nor has it always been smooth— the English historical landscape is scattered with periods of violence and upheaval—but once the dispensing process is achieved, it has largely been accepted. Hankering after the old order is congenial to some minds, but seeking to revert by force or civil unrest to the *status quo ante* is not. In the English perception, empiricism is both a descriptive and a prescriptive term. To the Englishman, it is both what is and what he believes always has been.

Orientation toward the Political System

Orientation toward the political system may be classified as allegiant when attitudes, feelings, and evaluations are favorable to the political system; apathetic or detached when feelings and evaluations are neutral; and alienated when such feelings and evaluations are unfavorable.[10] Italy and France have been cited as examples of political cultures that generate alienation and a large measure of apathy. West Germany has been put forward as having a culture that generates detachment. In contrast, Britain and the United States are among those countries cited as exhibiting a strong allegiant orientation.[11]

Almond and Verba found that evaluation of the political system in Britain was the product of a mix of participant and deferential orientations.

A participant orientation was developed in Britain (citizens being oriented to the input as well as the output side of the political system, believing that they enjoyed access to it), but it was one adapted to an existing deference to the independent authority of government. The participant orientation in Britain, unlike in the United States, did not displace the deferential;[12] it remained important.

The participant orientation finds expression in citizens' beliefs that they can influence government at both the national and local level. Although Almond and Verba found few people in their survey who actually sought to exert such influence, the proportion who believed that they *could* do so was significant. Of British respondents, approximately three out of five believed they could influence national and local government. (Only the United States managed to produce a higher proportion.) The proportion believing that they had no influence was only one in five. The 1974 survey of Kaase and Barnes demonstrated the extent to which these levels of political efficacy had been maintained.[13] Almond and Verba found significantly lower levels in Germany, Italy, and Mexico; Kaase and Barnes found lower levels in the Netherlands and Austria.[14] More recent evidence of high levels of political efficacy in Britain have been found in the *British Social Attitudes* surveys of the 1980s.[15]

Deference to the authority of government has found expression in a number of ways. It has been shown in a voluntary compliance with basic political laws. Criminal acts tend to be antisocial rather than conscious acts against "the state." (Indeed, the concept of "the state" is one that is not well entrenched in English consciousness.) There has been little overt opposition to the parliamentary form of government in Britain. Some may want to modify its form but do not challenge the principle of it, nor do they seek to change its form through unlawful and certainly not violent means. When government authority has been challenged, citizens have expressed themselves in favor of maintaining that authority. When called on by government to act in time of war, citizens have been prepared to respond.

Such deference has often been seen as allied with a social deference, citizens according certain skills of government to those drawn from a particular group. Walter Bagehot, in his classic work *The English Constitution*, identified England as a "deferential nation," one that had a structure of its own. "Certain persons," he wrote, "are by common consent agreed to be wiser than others, and their opinion is, by consent, to rank for much more than its numerical value."[16] Such deference, though possibly weakened, survived into the era of mass suffrage and the democratic ideal. It has been seen as a significant feature of contemporary Britain and has been variously offered as a partial explanation of the continuing success of the Conservative party and its socially atypical leadership.[17]

Such deference, though, has been contingent rather than certain. It has been based on a reciprocity between governors and governed. The populace has deferred to the independent authority of government and to those who occupy government in return for the satisfaction of expectations. Those expectations have covered the substance of policies (improving material well-being, for example) as well as the form of government. Almond and Verba, for example, found that an overwhelming majority of Britons expected equal treatment from politicians and from bureaucrats.[18] Conversely, those to whom citizens accord deference have been characterized by having an inbred sense of duty. A stress on responsibilities as well as rights has been a significant and long-standing feature of the British culture and has been well imbued by a large part of the nation's political elite. A paternalistic concern for the well-being of the nation has been a feature of most if not all monarchs and has been associated with a particular and often predominant tradition within the Conservative party.

As long as the political system has been able to maintain the capacity to meet the demands and expectations of citizens, they have demonstrated an allegiant orientation. The longer the system has been able to do this and the longer people have been socialized into accepting the efficacy of the system, the stronger and more enduring the allegiance has been. In Almond and Verba's survey, more Britons expressed pride in their governmental and political institutions than in any other feature of the nation that was mentioned. (The same pride was found in Americans, on a larger scale.)[19] More recently, a 1983 *Euro-Barometre* survey found a majority of Britons (56%) believing Parliament to be "very important" to the life of the country, more than double the number giving a similar response in France, Italy, the Netherlands, and Belgium, and 21% more than in West Germany (Table 2.1); nine out of ten Britons believed Parliament to be "very important" or "important."[20]

TABLE 2.1. IMPORTANCE OF PARLIAMENTS IN WESTERN EUROPE, 1983

Q: How important, would you say, is our own national parliament in the life of our country nowadays?

Response	Britain %	West Germany %	Netherlands %	Belgium %	France %	Italy %
Very important	56	35	28	27	25	25
Important	33	56	53	49	53	47
Not very/Not at all important	11	9	19	24	22	28

Source: Euro-Barometre survey, April 1983.

Orientation toward Cooperation and Individuality

Some cultures emphasize the values of cooperating with others, conciliating opposing views, and being prepared to compromise and submerge one's own ideas in a broader and more popularly acceptable solution. Others, by contrast, stress the virtues of maintaining the distinctiveness, ideas, and integrity of the individual, such virtues being considered superior to those of compromise and cooperation.[21]

France and Italy have been cited as examples of countries in which the maintenance of group and individual integrity is stressed in both the general culture and in political life.[22] Britain and the United States are included among those countries in which the political culture emphasizes the virtues of compromise and conciliation, without threatening personal integrity.

The Anglo-American perception was well expressed by Edmund Burke in 1775. "All government, indeed every human benefit and enjoyment, every virtue, and every prudent act," he declared, "is founded on compromise and barter."[23]

In Britain there is an almost instinctive distaste for conflict, both in personal relationships and in political life. The formal political framework facilitates an adversary relationship among political parties, but the underlying reality is a quest for compromise. Parties play according to the rules of the constitutional game. Similar observations can be made about groups in industry and in society generally. There is a penchant, almost, for resolving disputes by discussion, by sitting around a table and ironing out differences. It is an orientation compatible with the others already identified and it is eminently congenial to a society that stresses the responsibilities as well as the rights of the individual. It remains an orientation that Britons not only find congenial but also take as the source of a certain pride.

Orientation toward Other People

A belief that one can have faith and confidence in others has been put forward as a culturally rooted phenomenon, with potentially important implications for political life. Research by Morris Rosenberg has shown that "faith in people" is related to democratic and internationalist values and attitudes.[24] In their study, Almond and Verba found that the Americans and the British "tend to be consistently most positive about the safety and responsiveness of the human environment."[25] The Germans and the Italians, by contrast, were found to be more negative, and the Mexicans inconsistent.

A 1985 Gallup Poll found that Britons regarded themselves to be friendly, polite, hard-working, fun-loving, and with a sense of humor.[26] Eighty percent declared themselves to be very or quite proud of being British; the proportion was fairly well spread throughout different groups in society (see Table 2.2). Only 4% were not at all proud to be British. (A 1983 survey found levels of pride to be notably higher in Britain than in other West European countries.)[27] Trust also remains a significant feature of British society. A 1980 Gallup Poll found that 85% of respondents considered other Britons to be very or fairly trustworthy.[28] The experience of history may have helped to consolidate such a sense of trust. Britons have stood successfully shoulder-to-shoulder in order to win battles abroad and to repel foreign invaders from their shores. During the Second World War the nation did not have to contend with a significant fifth column or with the equivalent of Vichy collaborators. There is little or nothing in recent history that would give Britons cause to distrust their compatriots.

Similarly, the experience of history, island isolation, and shared values may serve to explain differing levels of trust that Britons have in other people. Britons tend to retain trust in the inhabitants of countries in which Britain has had or retains colonial interests; countries that share a common language, values, and (in some cases) ancestry; and countries that have stood together in times of crisis. There are strong emotional ties to old Commonwealth countries such as New Zealand, Canada, and Australia. There is also a high level of trust in one or two other European countries, most notably Holland, and usually—but not consistently—the United States.[29]

Survey data have revealed lower levels of trust in those countries and peoples that historically have been Britain's enemies. To the island inhabitants of Britain, such peoples remain distant (the English Channel constituting as much a psychological as a physical barrier), with alien cultures, different interests, and different thought processes. Englishmen and Scots-

TABLE 2.2. PRIDE IN BEING BRITISH, 1985

Q: How proud are you to be British?

Response	General Public %	Aged 16–19 %	Aged 65+ %	Cons. %	Labour %	Lib./ SDP %	Northern England %
Very proud	47	31	61	56	41	45	51
Quite proud	33	44	19	35	31	35	30
Not very proud	12	18	14	5	15	15	13
Not at all proud	4	5	3	2	7	4	3
Don't know	3	1	3	2	6	1	3

Source: G. Heald and R. J. Wybrow, The Gallup Survey of Britain *(Croom Helm, 1986), p. 276.*

men, as Anthony King observed, have tended not to think like Europeans nor to think of themselves as Europeans.[30] In the 1980 Gallup Poll only 32% of the Britons who were questioned regarded the French as very or fairly trustworthy (a perception confirmed by the findings of the 1985 Gallup Poll); only 6% of those questioned would trust the French a great deal as allies in time of war, 4% would trust the Spanish, 4% the Italians, and only 3% the Turks. Germans, perhaps surprisingly, fared much better: 60% of respondents considered them very or fairly trustworthy, and 22% would trust them a great deal as wartime allies.

What is apparent from the data is that, despite the travails of recent times, trust in one's fellow countrymen and a discriminating, possibly confident, perception of other people remain central features of the British political culture.

A DECLINING CULTURE?

The political culture of Britain may then be characterized, in broad terms, as having the four orientations identified: empirical in terms of problem solving and change, allegiant in terms of the political system, cooperative in making decisions, and trusting with relation to fellow countrymen and allies. These, it is important to stress, are generalizations—there are always individuals or subcultures that may not have such orientations. What is important is that they are and remain the orientations of most Britons, both at the mass and the elite level.

The strength of the culture may be said to lie in the convergence of these orientations—that is, they are compatible with and reinforce one another, and similarly are compatible with and are reinforced by the experience of history. The stress on cooperation and compromise, an emphasis compatible with an empirical approach to change, has facilitated the integration of groups and individuals into the political system. Such integration may be seen as reinforcing an allegiant rather than a neutral or alienated orientation to the political system. History, as we have mentioned, has been kind: the country has staved off invasion by its enemies, and the resources have been available for government to make and meet commitments in response to changing demands and expectations. As a result, it has been possible to interpret the experience of history as justifying or reinforcing an attachment to empirical problem solving and to the virtues of cooperation and trust. The interplay of these variables generated what Almond and Verba characterized as "the civic culture," "a pluralistic culture based on communication and persuasion, a culture of consensus and diversity, a culture that permitted change but moderated it."[31]

What of the civic culture today? My argument is simply stated: Although subject to modification, the civic culture remains. What has been the subject of radical, almost revolutionary, change over the past decade or so has not been the civic culture but the perceptions of that culture. In short, it has not changed as much as observers think it has.

I do not argue that the political culture of Britain remains unchanged. The culture not only allows for change, usually incremental but occasionally radical, but itself can and does change. In good British fashion, however, that change has tended to be piecemeal rather than comprehensive. Some values, attitudes, and emotions have been subject to modification over time, but the essential orientations outlined above have not been discarded. They remain the orientations that converge to form the predominant element of the British political culture.

What has changed, and changed radically over the period since the 1960s, has been the perception of that culture. Analyses of the British political culture have swung, pendulum fashion, from one extreme to the other. At times of apparent stability, contentment, and political success, there has been a tendency to see the political culture in idealized terms, to hold it aloft and laud it as a culture to be admired and possibly even envied. Although Almond and Verba drew attention to some of the inconsistencies and problems inherent in the civic culture, it was nonetheless difficult not to ascribe positive connotations to that culture.

There are a number of problems inherent in the political culture. A disposition to incremental change can deflect one from considering or even comprehending wider and more fundamental problems. The combination of an empirical orientation and historical continuity has produced a political system that is complex and disparate. While the American federal system has been likened to a marble cake, the British political system can be likened to a patchwork quilt. It may look to some extent like the original, it may even retain traces of the original, but the many pieces that make the whole were added at different times and have been the subject of change and much repair work. It includes structures that (according to some observers) have facilitated policy discontinuity—a discontinuity not incompatible with an empirical orientation to change—yet it comprises such an interdependent complex of political bodies that it has become increasingly difficult for government to govern and to initiate radical and comprehensive change. Such difficulty has been exacerbated by the desire to resolve problems by compromise. Problems that cannot be resolved by reasoned debate have tended to be ignored in the hope that they will go away.

Such inherent problems tend to be discounted, ignored, or even interpreted in a favorable light at times when the political system appears to be successfully meeting the demands and expectations of the populace.

When the system appears to be malfunctional, usually at times of economic difficulty for the country, some commentators identify such inherent problems as providing at least a partial explanation for the system's poor showing. Since the latter half of the 1970s, for example, policy discontinuity arising from an electoral and political system that encouraged an "adversary style" of politics has been offered as a partial explanation for Britain's poor economic performance.[32]

Other commentators have sought to identify the nation's problems not in terms of the effect of some aspects of the political culture but as agents generating and reflecting a decline in the culture itself. In the 1970s and early 1980s a number of observers began to chart a decline in the civic culture.[33] In 1982, on the basis of some survey evidence, Samuel Beer concluded that "it is no exaggeration to speak of the decline in the civic culture as a 'collapse.'"[34] He argued that as old institutions failed to meet new expectations, so legitimacy in government would falter and trust in its equity and effectiveness would decline. He hypothesized and sought to show that the consequences of this included a greater self-assertion by participants, a decline of leadership, a weakening of party government, and a loosening of the nexus of class and party. "In an ironic sense," Beer declared, "Britain is maintaining its leadership. As it once showed the way toward democratic success, today it blazes the trail toward democratic failure."[35]

While Beer's hypothesis is plausible as to the effect of institutions that fail to meet new expectations on legitimacy in government, it is arguable as to the extent to which such a failure to meet expectations has taken place. This is a point to which I shall return in the concluding chapter. Although government capacity to meet expectations is variously limited, its capacity to meet expectations in the past built up a body of diffuse support, support that now exists independently of particular failures to meet demands.[36] Furthermore, there is evidence that the expectations themselves may be changing, converging more with the capacity of the system to meet them.

Certainly, it will be my case that the political culture has neither declined nor been threatened to the extent suggested by Beer and other Jeremiahs.[37] Certain institutions may be under threat (as subsequent chapters will show) but not in a manner inconsistent with the existing political culture. The civic culture may be weakened but it has not collapsed. Its position is similar to that of Mark Twain: reports of its death would be greatly exaggerated. As I shall seek to show, the political culture remains predominantly an allegiant one, and the important question to be addressed is not "Why has there been a decline in the civic culture?" but rather "Why has that decline not been greater?"

NOTES

1. See D. Kavanagh, *Political Culture* (Macmillan, 1972), pp. 10–11.
2. Ibid., p. 10.
3. G. Almond and S. Verba, *The Civic Culture* (Princeton University Press, 1963), Ch. 1.
4. R. A. Dahl (ed.), *Political Oppositions in Western Democracies* (Yale University Press, 1966), p. 353.
5. G. Sartori, *Democratic Theory* (Wayne State University Press, 1962), p. 233, cited in Dahl, p. 354.
6. Dahl, p. 355.
7. L. Hartz, *The Liberal Tradition in America* (Harcourt, Brace & World, 1955). For the Beard analysis, see C. Beard, *An Economic Interpretation of the Constitution* (Macmillan, 1913).
8. V. Hart, *Distrust and Democracy* (Cambridge University Press, 1978), pp. 202–3.
9. Eve of election broadcast, July 4, 1945.
10. Dahl, p. 353.
11. Almond and Verba, Ch. 14.
12. Ibid., pp. 455–56.
13. Reproduced in D. P. Conradt, "Changing German Political Culture," in G. Almond and S. Verba (eds.), *The Civic Culture Revisited* (Little, Brown, 1980), p. 232.
14. Ibid., and Almond and Verba, p. 186.
15. See R. Jowell and S. Witherspoon, *British Social Attitudes: The 1985 Report* (Gower, 1985), pp. 11–17; and R. Jowell, S. Witherspoon, and L. Brook, *British Social Attitudes: The 1987 Report* (Gower, 1987), pp. 55–59.
16. W. Bagehot, *The English Constitution* (first published 1867; Fontana, 1963 ed.).
17. See, e.g., R. McKenzie and A. Silver, *Angels in Marble* (Heinemann, 1968).
18. Almond and Verba, p. 108.
19. Of Americans, 85% expressed pride in their institutions, compared with 46% of Britons. Almond and Verba, p. 102.
20. Reproduced from D. P. Conradt, *The German Polity*, 3rd ed. (Longman, 1986), p. 152.
21. Dahl, p. 354.
22. Ibid.
23. Speech on conciliation with America, March 22, 1775.
24. M. Rosenberg, "Misanthropy and Political Ideology," *American Sociological Review*, 21, pp. 690–95; and "Misanthropy and Attitudes towards International Affairs," *Journal of Conflict Resolution*, 1, 1957, pp. 340–45, cited in Almond and Verba, p. 266.
25. Almond and Verba, p. 268.
26. G. Heald and R. J. Wybrow, *The Gallup Survey of Britain* (Croom Helm, 1986), p. 277.

27. Ninety-three percent of Britons were "very" or "quite proud" to be British, 75% of French respondents were proud to be French, and 56% of Germans were proud to be German. The average of strong pride in European Community countries was 77%. *Euro-Barometre* survey, June 1983.

28. N. Webb and R. Wybrow, *The Gallup Report* (Sphere Books, 1981), pp. 103–4.

29. Levels of trust in Americans have fluctuated considerably. In the 1980 Gallup Poll, 70% of respondents considered Americans to be very or fairly trustworthy; in the 1986 Gallup Poll, more respondents felt Americans could not be trusted than believed could be trusted.

30. A. King, *Britain Says Yes* (American Enterprise Institute, 1977), p. 6. See also L. Barzini, *The Impossible Europeans* (Weidenfeld & Nicolson, 1983).

31. Almond and Verba, p. 8.

32. See, e.g., S. E. Finer, *Adversary Politics and Electoral Reform* (Wigram, 1975), A. M. Gamble and S. A. Walkland, *The British Party System and Economic Policy 1945–1983* (Oxford University Press, 1984), and below, Ch. 5.

33. See, e.g., D. Kavanagh, "Political Culture in Great Britain: The Decline of the Civic Culture," in G. Almond and S. Verba (eds.), *The Civic Culture Revisited* (Little, Brown, 1980).

34. S. H. Beer, *Britain Against Itself* (Faber and Faber, 1982), p. 119.

35. Ibid., pp. xiv–xv.

36. For the concept of "diffuse support," see D. Easton, *A Systems Analysis of Political Life* (Wiley, 1965), p. 273.

37. The term "Jeremiahs" is taken from William Gwyn's chapter, "Jeremiahs and Pragmatists: Perceptions of British Decline," in W. B. Gwyn and R. Rose (eds.), *Britain: Progress and Decline* (Tulane University Press, 1980).

CHAPTER 3

Past and Present
Historical Perspective and Contemporary Problems

A number of introductory texts on British politics do not have chapters devoted specifically to political history. The omission is a surprising one. When the proposal for this book was under consideration by the publishers, a number of American professors were asked for their comments. One responded with this advice: "Make sure you incorporate as much historical detail as possible. American students don't know much about British history." It was a shrewd response. The need for such detail, however, is not confined to Americans interested in the subject; it encompasses all those who seek to make some sense of the institutions and complex relationships that form the British polity.

There has been no point in British history at which the prevailing method of government has been completely swept away, allowing those in power to sit down and create from first principles a new and clearly delineated form of government. The country has witnessed continuous and sometimes dramatic change. In the past 300 years alone, the nation has experienced industrialization, the advent of democracy, and the introduction and growth of the welfare state—yet the changes have never been such as to be described as revolutionary. They have been built upon and have adapted that which already existed. The body politic may have undergone radical surgery and it may have aged considerably, but it has continued to endure.

What, then, are the significant features of British history that help us understand the contemporary political system and the political culture?

Limitations of space preclude a lengthy dissertation on what is a vast subject. That vastness is apparent when put in comparative perspective. The *Magna Carta*, for instance, was signed more than two centuries before Christopher Columbus set sail. A Parliament was summoned more than 500 years before the United States Congress first assembled. And an American president, unlike a British monarch, cannot trace his forebears in office back more than 1,000 years. Nonetheless, it is possible to provide a brief but structured sketch that furthers our understanding of contemporary British politics. This can be done under two headings: the emergence of parliamentary government, and the development of the welfare state and the managed economy.

The structure and relationships of the contemporary organs of government can be understood only in historical context. A study of the emergence of the welfare state highlights the increased demands and responsibilities borne by government. Both studies provide a necessary background for an understanding of some of the problems now faced by government. They serve also to highlight certain features of the political culture.

HISTORICAL PERSPECTIVE

The Emergence of Parliamentary Government

One of the essential features of the British Constitution is a parliamentary government under a limited, or symbolic, monarchy. The formal elements of this type of government will be more fully outlined in the next chapter. For the moment, what concerns us is that this government is the product of change extending over several centuries, coming to fruition only in the past century. Its development has sometimes been characterized as being evolutionary, but in practice it is the outgrowth of piecemeal change.

Let us begin in the thirteenth century. Traditionally, the sovereign power in England resided in the monarch. Nonetheless, the king was expected to consult with his tenants-in-chief (the earls, barons, and leading churchmen of the kingdom) in order to discover and declare the law and to have their counsel before any levies of extraordinary taxation were made. This expectation was to find documented expression in the Great Charter (*Magna Carta*) of 1215, by which the king recognized it as a right of his subjects "to have the Common Council of the Kingdom" for the assessment of extraordinary aids—that is, taxation. Such consultation was undertaken through a Great Council, from which evolved what was to be recognized as a *parlement* or Parliament. The Great Council itself was essentially the precursor of the House of Lords. The House of Commons evolved from the summoning to council, in the latter half of the thirteenth century on a somewhat sporadic basis, of knights and burgesses as representatives of the counties and towns. At various times in the fourteenth century the Commons deliberated separately from the Lords, and there developed a formal separation of the two bodies.

During the period of the Tudor monarchs in the sixteenth century, Parliament acquired enhanced status. It was generally supportive of the monarch but became more powerful because the monarchs depended upon it for that support, especially during the reign of Elizabeth I. The relationship between Crown and Parliament under the subsequent Stuart dynasty was one of conflict. The early Stuart kings James I and Charles I sought to assert the doctrine of the divine right of kings and to deny many of the privileges acquired or asserted by Parliament. This conflict was to lead to the civil war and the beheading of Charles I in 1642. With the abolition of the monarchy came a brief period of rule by a Council of State elected by what was termed the Rump Parliament. (Some attempts were actually made to formulate a form of written constitution, but they came to nothing.)[1] Rule by the Council of State was succeeded by Oliver Cromwell's unsuccessful military dictatorship, and in 1660 Charles' son returned to assume the throne as Charles II. The period between 1642 and 1660 proved an aberration in British history. The Restoration witnessed an attempt to return, unconditionally, to the country's position as it was at the beginning of 1642.[2] Through this attempt, the Restoration lent itself to a repetition of the earlier struggle between King and Commons. Relations between the two gradually deteriorated during the reign of Charles II and became severe in the reign of his successor, James II. James sought to reassert the divine right of kings, and Parliament combined against him. In 1688 James fled the country. At the invitation of Parliament, the throne was taken by William and Mary of Orange, James' son-in-law and daughter. The new occupants of the throne owed their position to Parliament, and the new relationship between them was asserted by statute in the Bill of Rights. Although the Bill of Rights was important for enumerating various "Liberties of this Kingdom" (some of which were to be similarly expressed during the following century in the Bill of Rights of the United States Constitution),[3] its essential purpose was to assert the position of Parliament in relation to the Crown. The raising of taxes or the dispensing of laws without the assent of Parliament was declared to be illegal. The monarch was expected to govern, but to do so only with the consent of Parliament. The Act of Settlement of 1701, which determined the succession to the throne, affirmed that the laws of England "are the Birthright of the People thereof and all the Kings and Queens who shall ascend the Throne of this Realm ought to administer the Government of the same according to the said Laws and all their Officers and Ministers ought to serve them respectively according to the same."

The monarch thus became formally dependent on Parliament for consent to the raising of taxes and for the passage of legislation. In practice, he or she became increasingly dependent also on ministers for advice. The importance of ministers grew especially in the eighteenth century. The Hanoverian kings were not uninterested in political life but they had difficulty comprehending the complexities of domestic and foreign affairs. According to the historian J. H. Plumb, both George I and George II were "crassly stupid" and "incapable, totally incapable, of forming a policy."[4] During the period of their reigns, the leading body of the king's ministers, generally known as the cabinet, began to meet without the king being present.[5] The period also witnessed the emergence of a minister who was to become popularly known as the prime minister. (Not until the twentieth century was the office of prime minister to be mentioned in a statute.) The relationship among Crown, ministers, and Parliament in the century was one in which the king relied on his ministers to help formulate policy. Those ministers were chosen by the king on the basis of his personal confidence in them, and they remained responsible to him. They also were responsible to Parliament in order to achieve their ends, a fact recognized by both the king and his ministers. Nonetheless, parliamentary support was not difficult to obtain; the king and his ministers had sufficient patronage and position usually to ensure such support. A ministry that enjoyed royal confidence could generally take the House of Lords for granted, and provided it did not prove incompetent or seek to impose excessive taxation, "its position was unassailable in the Commons."[6] The position was to change significantly in the nineteenth century.

Britain underwent what has been popularly referred to as an industrial revolution from the middle of the eighteenth century to the middle of the nineteenth. Seymour Martin Lipset has characterized the United States as the "first new nation," but Britain has been described as "the first industrial nation."[7] Industry became more mechanized, improvements took place in agricultural production techniques, and there were improvements in transport and in the organization of trade and banking. There was a notable growth in the size of cities, particularly in the early part of the nineteenth century. Men of industry and commerce began to emerge as men of some wealth. In 1813 Robert Owen referred to the "working class," a term brought into common speech by Lord Brougham.[8] By the 1830s, a nonlanded middle class, artisans, and an industrial workforce were important constituents of the country's population.

Parliament remained dominated by the aristocracy and by the landed gentry. Representation in the House of Commons was heavily weighted in favor of the rural counties. Some parliamentary constituencies had only a handful of electors: known as "rotten boroughs," they were often in the pocket of an aristocrat or local landowner.[9] Pressure for some parliamentary reform, with a redistribution of seats and a widening of the franchise, began to develop. It was argued that a Parliament full of men of wealth and property was unlikely to view industry, trade, and agriculture from the point of view of the laboring classes. Rotten boroughs were criticized as being used by the ministry to help maintain a majority. Unrest in a number of areas, both agricultural and industrial, and the French Revolution of 1830 (a spur to radical action) increased the pressure for change. One political group in particular, the Whigs, who had been the "outs" in politics for the 25 years prior to 1830, began to see the need for some response to this pressure. The concession of some parliamentary reform was seen as necessary in order to prevent worse happenings. The result was to be the Reform Act of 1832.

The Reform Act, introduced, ironically, by the most aristocratic Whig government of the century, reorganized parliamentary constituencies and extended the franchise. The electorate increased in size from a little under 500,000 to 813,000 electors.[10] Although much remained the same as before—the new electorate constituted but one-thirtieth of the population, 31 boroughs still had fewer than 300 electors in each, voting remained by open ballot (secret ballots were considered rather un-English), and the aristocracy still held great sway politically—the act precipitated important changes both within and outside the House of Commons.

The redistribution of seats and the extension of the franchise helped loosen the grip of the aristocracy and of ministers on the House of Commons. The size of the new electorate encouraged the embryonic development of political organizations. Members of Parliament (MPs) became less dependent on aristocratic patrons without acquiring too great a dependence on the growing party organizations. The result was to be a House of Commons with a greater legitimacy in the eyes of MPs and electors and with an ability to assert itself in its relationship with government. The House proved willing to amend or reject legislation put before it as well as to remove individual ministers, and on occasion the government itself. In his classic work on the constitution, Walter Bagehot attached much importance to this "elective function"; the House of Commons, he declared, was "a real choosing body: it elects the people it likes. And it dismisses whom it likes too."[11] Debates in the House really counted for something and, with the exception of the period from 1841 to 1846, party cohesion was almost unknown. The House of Commons did not itself govern, but government was carried on within the confines of its guidance and approval.

The period after 1832 witnessed also important changes in the relationships within and among the different elements of Crown, government, and Parliament. The monarch retained the formal prerogative power to appoint the prime minister, but the changed political circumstances essentially dictated that the person chosen should be able to command a majority in the House of Commons. Royal favor ceased to be an essential condition for forming the government. Within Parliament, the relationship between the two Houses also changed. Members of the House of Lords sat by virtue of birth, holding hereditary peerages. The acceptance of the Commons as the "representative" chamber underminded the authority of the peers to challenge or negate the wishes of the other House. After the 1830s, the Lords tended to be somewhat restrained in their attacks on government measures. "This," as Mackintosh noted, "followed from the view that while a ministry retained the confidence of the elected representatives it was entitled to remain in office. The peers on the whole accepted these assumptions, though many found the explicit recognition of the situation hard to bear."[12] The Lords' remaining authority was in practice to be removed in consequence of the 1867 Reform Act, though not until the twentieth century was the House forced formally to accept its diminished status.

Whereas the 1832 Act helped ensure the dominance of the House of Commons within the formal political process, the passage of the Reform Act of 1867 began a process of the transfer of power from Parliament to Ministers. The act itself was the product of demands for change because of the limited impact of the 1832 Act and because of more immediate political considerations.[13] Its effect was to increase the size of the electorate from 1,358,000 to 2,477,000. (The number had grown since 1832 because of increased wealth and population.) Other significant measures followed in its wake. Secret voting was introduced by the Ballot Act of 1870. Other acts sought to prohibit as far as possible corrupt practices and limited the amount of money a candidate could spend on election expenses. Single-member districts (known in Britain as constituencies) of roughly equal electoral size were prescribed as the norm.[14] The 1884 Representation of the People Act extended the franchise to householders and tenants and to all those who occupied land or tenements with an annual value of not less than 10 pounds. The effect of the act was to bring into being an electorate in which working men were in a majority. The consequence of these developments was to be party government.

The size of the new electorate meant that the voters could be reached only through some well-developed organization, and the result was to be the growth of organized and mass-membership political parties. The Conservative National Union and the National Liberal Federation were formed in order to facilitate and encourage the support of the new electors. However, contact with the voters was insufficient in itself to entice their support. Not only had a large section of the population been enfranchised, it was a notably different electorate from that which had existed previously. The new class of electors had different and greater demands than those of the existing middle-class electors. If the votes of working men were to be obtained, the parties had to offer them something. And the parties could fulfill their promises only if they presented a uniform program to the electorate and achieved a cohesive majority in the House of Commons to carry through that program. What this was to produce was a shift of power away from the House of Commons to the cabinet and the electorate, with political parties serving as the conduit for this transfer.

The electorate proved too large and too politically unsophisticated to evaluate the merits of an individual MP's behavior. Political parties provided the labels with which electors could identify, and elections became gladiatorial contests between parties rather than between individual candidates. The all-or-nothing spoils of an election victory and the method of election encouraged (if it not always produced) a contest between two major parties.[15] And having voted for party candidates, the electors expected the members returned to Parliament to support the program offered by their leaders at the election. Party cohesion soon became a feature of parliamentary life.[16] The House of Commons in effect lost two of the most important functions ascribed to it by Bagehot, those of legislation and of choosing the government: the former passed to the cabinet and the latter to the electorate. The cabinet constituted the leaders of the party enjoying a parliamentary majority. It assumed the initiative for the formulation and introduction of measures of national policy and became increasingly reluctant to be overruled by the House. The growth in the number and complexity of bills further limited the influence of the individual MP. Increasingly, his role became one of supporting his leaders. The cabinet had previously rested its authority on the support of the House; now it derived its authority from the electors. As Mackintosh states, "The task of the House of Commons became one of supporting the Cabinet chosen at the polls and passing its legislation. . . . By the 1900s, the Cabinet dominated British government."[17]

Further modifications and addenda took place in the first half of the twentieth century. The House of Lords was forced by statute in 1911 to accept its diminished status. The franchise was variously extended, most notably to half the population previously excluded because of their sex. (The first female MP to take her seat in the House of Commons did so in 1919.) The monarch's political influence further receded. The growth and increasing economic weight of groups generated more extensive and complex demands of government. And the size of government grew as its responsibilities expanded.

Basically, though, the essential features of the political system were those established in the preceding century. The responsibility for making public policy rested with the government, a government derived from and resting its support upon a political party. That same party's majority in the House of Commons ensured that the government's measures were approved. Formal and political constraints limited the effect of any opposition from the House of Lords. The monarch gave formal assent to any legislative measure approved by the two houses. Thus, within the formal framework of deciding public policy, the government was dominant. The role of Parliament became largely but not wholly one of legitimating the measures put before it. For the monarch, that became the exclusive role (that is, in respect of legislation). Government, as we shall see, operated within a political environment that imposed important constraints, but the limitations imposed formerly by Parliament and the monarch were largely eroded. Britain retained a parliamentary form of government, but what that meant was not government by Parliament but government through Parliament.

The Welfare State and the Managed Economy

To comprehend some of the problems faced by contemporary British government, it is necessary to know not only the structure and relationships of the political system but also the popular expectations and the burden of responsibilities borne by government. Those expectations and responsibilities have not been static. Just as the governmental structure has been modified in response to political demands, so the responsibilities of government have grown as greater social and economic demands have been made of it.

Toward the end of the nineteenth century and more so in the twentieth, the responsibilities of government expanded. In part this expansion was attributable to the growth of the Empire. (As prime minister in the 1870s, Benjamin Disraeli had played the "imperial card," the British Empire expanding rapidly: by 1900 it covered virtually a quarter of the globe.) It was also attributable to the increasing demands and expectations of the newly enfranchised working population. Government began to conceive its duties as extending beyond those of maintaining law and order and of defending the realm. The statute book began to expand, with the addition of measures of social reform. Various such measures were enacted prior to 1867, though the most notable were to be enacted in the remaining decades of the century. They included measures to limit working hours for women and children, to improve housing and public health, to make education for children compulsory, to provide for the safety of workers (including the payment of compensation by employers in the event of accidents at work), and even to extend the right to strike.[18] Such measures, exploited for electoral advantage, were within the capabilities of the government to provide. The did not create too great an economic burden; they were not themselves economic measures.

The growth of expectations and the greater willingness of government to intervene in areas previously considered inviolate was to be continued and become more marked in the twentieth century. The general election of 1906 was something of a watershed in British politics. It was the first election to be fought essentially on national issues and it witnessed the return not only of a reforming Liberal government but also, and in some respects more significantly, of 27 Labour MPs. The Labour party had been created for the purpose of ensuring working-class representation in Parliament, and from 1906 onward class became a significant influence in voting behavior. The nature of electoral conflict changed as the Labour party succeeded the Liberal as the main opposition party to the Conservatives. The franchise was further extended, notably in 1918 and 1928, and new expectations were generated by the experience of the two world wars.

During the First World War (1914–1918), socialists within the Labour party argued the case for the conscription of wealth (public ownership) to accompany the conscription of labor (the drafting of men into the armed forces). Politicians fueled rather than played down the belief that Britain should become, in the words of one politician, "a land fit for heroes" once "the war to end all wars" was won—in other words, that provision should be made for those who had fought for King and Country. The period of the Second World War (1939–1945) witnessed a significant shift of attitudes by a sizable fraction of the electorate. One informed estimate was that by December 1942 about two out of five people had changed their political outlook since the beginning of the war.[19] Opinion was moving toward the left of the political spectrum. There was a reaction against (Conservative) government unpreparedness for war in the 1930s and against those who had not done more to solve the nation's problems during the Depression. There was support for calls for equality of sacrifice. There was some degree of goodwill toward the Soviet Union as a wartime ally. There was also, very importantly, the enhanced position of the Labour party. It had entered into Coalition in 1940 (its leader, Clement Attlee, became deputy prime minister to Churchill) and had demonstrated its claim to be a capable partner in government. As the 1940s progressed, there developed a notable movement, including within the Conservative party, for a greater degree of social and economic intervention by government. This was to find some authoritative expression during the war years themselves and especially in the years after 1945, when a general election resulted in the return of the first Labour government with a clear working majority in the House of Commons. The 1940s and the 1950s were to produce what Samuel Beer has referred to as the welfare state and the managed economy, or what some commentators have referred to as the period of the social democratic consensus.

The welfare state and the managed economy did not suddenly emerge full-blown in this period. The preceding decades had not witnessed governments unresponsive to electoral expectations and the nation's problems. The Liberal government before the First World War had made the first tentative steps in the introduction of old-age pensions (1908) and national health and unemployment insurance (1911). The interwar years had seen the introduction of a number of significant measures of social reform, especially those associated with a Conservative, Neville Chamberlain, as minister of health. He proposed to the cabinet 25 measures and secured the enactment of 21 of them. These included unemployment insurance, public health and housing, and the extension of old-age pensions. Much of this legislation, as one biographer noted, "has an important place in the development of the Welfare State."[20] The Conservative government also began to engage in certain measures of economic management. It embarked on a protectionist policy and, in return for the grant of a tariff to an industry, demanded that its major producers reorganize themselves. Such producers were encouraged to reduce capacity and maintain prices. The gold standard was abandoned, the pound was devalued, and interest rates were lowered. The government even proved willing to take certain industries into public ownership: broadcasting, overseas airways and the electricity-generating industry. By indulging in such policies, Beer has contended, government was beginning to move in the direction of a managed economy.[21] The movement, though, was modest. Government adhered to the prevailing orthodoxy that balanced budgets were necessary and desirable and that deficit financing was neither. Ministers showed little desire to emulate the innovative approach adopted in the United States by Franklin Roosevelt during the period of the first New Deal. (Indeed, Conservative leader Stanley Baldwin commented at one point that the United States Constitution had broken down and was giving way to dictatorship.)[22] Britain and the United States were similar, though, in that both were to be brought out of the Depression of the 1930s not by government economic policies but by rearmament and the Second World War.

Two major documents published in the war years provided the planks for the final emergence of the welfare state and managed economy. These were the Report on Social Insurance and Allied Services by Sir William Beveridge (the so-called Beveridge Report), published in November 1942, and the White Paper on Full Employment, published in 1944. The former proposed a comprehensive scheme of social security, one to provide "social insurance against interruption and destruction of earning power and for special expenditure arising at birth, marriage or death."[23] The latter was significant because of its opening pledge: "The Government accepts as one of their primary aims and responsibilities the maintenance of a high and stable level of employment after the war." There was also one particularly significant measure of social reform enacted during wartime: the 1944 Education Act, pioneered by R. A. Butler. It provided for the division among primary, secondary, and higher education—and, within secondary education, between secondary modern and grammar schools—that was to form the basis of the educational system for almost a generation.

The welfare state was brought to fruition by the establishment of the National Health Service (NHS) in 1948, entailing the nationalization of hospitals and the provision of free medical treatment, and also by the passage of the 1945 Family Allowance Act, the 1946 National Insurance Act, and the 1948 National Assistance Act. The principle enunciated by the Beveridge Report was largely put into practice. National insurance ensured a certain level of benefit in the event of unemployment or sickness. For those who required special help there was "national assistance," the provision of noncontributory benefits dispensed on the basis of means-testing. There were family allowances for those with children. The state now provided something of a protective safety net from the cradle to the grave. It was still possible to pay for private treatment in the health service, but for most people it was a case of having treatment "on the national health." The NHS became a feature of some pride at home and of considerable interest abroad.

Acceptance and usage of techniques pioneered by the economist J. M. Keynes ushered in the managed economy. Government accepted responsibility for keeping aggregate monetary demand at a level sufficient to ensure full employment or what was considered as far as possible to constitute full employment (an unemployment rate of 1% or 2% was considered acceptable), and the annual Budget was to be used as the main instrument of economic policy. The Labour government proved unwilling to pursue a more overtly socialist approach; physical controls acquired during wartime were eventually discarded and those industries that were nationalized, such as steel and the railways, were basically essential and loss-making concerns. Government was prepared to pursue a managed rather than a controlled economy.

The Conservative party was returned to office in 1951 and was to remain there until 1964. It accepted, or appeared to accept, both the welfare state and Keynesian techniques of demand management. Indeed, it gave the impression of making a success of both. As heir to the Disraelian belief in elevating the condition of the people and as a party seeking to enhance its image among working-class voters, the Conservative party could claim both a principled and a practical motive for maintaining the innovations of its predecessor. At the same time, it was reluctant to pursue policies that would increase the tax burden or the public sector of the economy. Good fortune was with the government: world economic conditions improved and heralded a period of sustained growth in industrial output and trade. Government revenue was such that not only was it possible to sustain and indeed expand expenditure on the national health service, it was possible to do so without substantial increases in taxation. Indeed, reductions rather than increases in tax rates were a feature of the period. There was an extensive and successful house-building program. Economic prosperity allowed government to maintain peace with the labor unions by allowing high wage settlements. It was also possible finally to abandon many of the controls maintained since wartime. Government was able to claim to have maintained full employment, an expanding economy, stable prices, and a strong pound. Despite the agonies of withdrawing from Empire and various undulations in economic performance, the 1950s was seen more than anything as "an age of affluence."[24] In July 1957 Prime Minister Harold Macmillan was able to declare that, for most of the people, "You've never had it so good."

The 1960s witnessed a downturn in economic performance and a growing realization that, in comparative terms, Britain was faring less well than many of her continental neighbors. The Conservative government of Harold Macmillan responded with various novel proposals, including indicative economic planning and an application to join the European Economic Community. The succeeding Labour government of Harold Wilson, returned to office in 1964, sought a more comprehensive method of national economic planning as part of its grand design of modernization. Inflation and unemployment became move visible problems.

Despite the economic problems and some unrelated political problems of the 1960s, the country remained a relatively prosperous one. Living conditions continued to improve. The rise in wages exceeded the rise in inflation. Where economic conditions impinged on the ability to maintain the welfare state, it was essentially at the margin: government imposed nominal charges for medicines obtained on NHS prescriptions. Parties tended to argue more about means rather than ends. The consensus that developed in the 1950s remained intact.

POLITICAL CULTURE AND CONTEMPORARY PROBLEMS

This brief survey not only provides some historical depth to an understanding of contemporary British government—its structure, responsibilities, and political dominance—it also serves to reinforce our grasp of the political culture and to provide in part an explanation for some of the problems now associated with government.

History and Political Culture

From the foregoing sketch one can recognize not only the features of the political culture outlined in the preceding chapter but also the convergence of those features and their interplay with the experience of history. An empirical orientation to change and a conditional relationship between governors and governed are long-standing characteristics of political life. Clearly, government has been shaped by no grand design. Change has been piecemeal and largely incremental. Although the governed have been largely prepared to defer to those in power, their deference has been conditional. If presumed rights and privileges were ignored or dispensed with, the appropriate action was taken to restore them (e.g., the *Magna Carta*, the beheading of Charles I). The other orientations can be identified from the experience of reform in the nineteenth and early twentieth centuries.

The reforms of the nineteenth century were facilitated not only by an empirical orientation to change but also by the paternalism of political leaders. *Noblesse oblige* (privilege entails responsibility) is a foreign phrase but it embodies a very British concept. Many of the country's aristocratic leaders believed that they had a duty to help improve the condition of the working man. This point should not be overemphasized, since on occasion this sense of duty was not so much a cause of action as a *post hoc* justification of it. Nonetheless, it was important. It combined with need (to avoid social unrest) and political expediency (to steal the thunder of one's opponents) to produce franchise extension.

Increasingly, change was more easily accommodated as political relationships changed. By the twentieth century, the hegemony of government in the political process ensured that measures could be carried through Parliament without too much difficulty. Equally important, once Parliament approved these reforms, they were accepted by the populace and by those at whom they were directed. The widening of the franchise in the nineteenth century, House of Lords reform, and votes for women in the twentieth century are all issues that aroused great emotion and were fiercely opposed but on which reform was accepted once the government of the day had gotten the measure accepted by Parliament. This in part reflects the orientation toward cooperation. It also may be seen as the product of an allegiant orientation to the political system. The widening of the franchise extended the input of citizens into the political system. The passage of measures of social and economic reform appeared to be meeting their needs.

Equally important, Britons have been taught that the political system works. Although the media of political socialization have changed over time, the content has not. There has been an emphasis on, and lauding of, the continuity and stability. Historically, as we have seen, the country has been rent by various upheavals, sometimes of a quite violent nature. The English Civil War was far from bloodless. The opinion of foreigners, wrote an English scholar in 1704, is "that there have been more shakes and convulsions in the government of England than in that of any other nation."[25] There have been various shakes since—social, economic, and political. In the popular mind, though, such convulsions have not figured largely. "What makes the history of England so eminently valuable," wrote T. H. Buckle, "is that nowhere else has the national progress been so little interfered with, either for good or evil."[26] British government has been accepted as the product of the collected wisdom of many generations, indeed of many centuries. It flatters the British mind, and certainly the English mind, to look upon it as the envy of the world. The Constitution has been lauded as "a living organism in a condition of perpetual growth."[27] George III described it as "the most perfect of human formations."[28] In 1981 one member of Parliament declared that, distinguished from other constitutions, "our constitution is the envy of the world."[29] The virtues of the Westminster model of government have been widely extolled. They became embodies in what was taught in British schools. They became part of received wisdom, and to some extent they remain so.

The British have not been alone in such teaching. British parliamentary government has variously found its admirers abroad as well, and not least in the United States.[30] Especially in the 1950s and 1960s, the capacity of the party in government to enact a party program was compared with the brokered politics of the American system. It was a comparison that generated some calls for reform; most notable were those of James MacGregor Burns in the 1960s and Charles Hardin in the 1970s. In *The Deadlock of Democracy*, published in 1963, Burns argued the case for what amounted to the equivalent in the United States of a "responsible party system." Hardin cited British experience in contending that "party government—if it can be attained—provides the best hope that our government will be able to meet its problems."[31] In the wake of Watergate, it was an argument with a certain persuasive appeal. Although not all observers wished to emulate British experience, their analyses appeared edged with a touch of envy. Within a matter of a few years, envy turned to amazement. Attempts to emulate British processes were replaced with attempts to explain "the British disease."

Contemporary Ills and Analyses

In the 1950s and 1960s Britain, as we have noted, experienced relative economic decline. Because it was relative rather than absolute, the implications were hazily rather than fully grasped. After 1970, as economic conditions worsened, there was a more acute awareness of Britain's problems. Unemployment rose, as we have seen, to historically high levels, reaching a peak in 1986; by international standards, it remains high. Inflation reached double-digit figures: the annual average in the 1970s was 13% and at one point reached 27%. Industrial disputes in the 1970s became more frequent; more working days were lost as a result of industrial disputes in the 1970s than in the preceding quarter of a century. During that decade Britain had the lowest growth rate of the major industrialized nations. The 1980s witnessed a relative improvement (Britain's growth rate exceeding that of West Germany and France), but the country still lagged behind the United States and Japan, and the annual rate of growth still trailed behind the average for the big industrial seven (Table 3.1). The nation's manufacturing base declined (see Chapter 1), and in 1981 the country for the first time became a net importer of manufactured goods. Continuation of this trend produced major trading deficits in 1987 and 1988.

Since the 1970s there has been a major and extensive debate as to the causes of the nation's failure to catch up with—and match—the performance of its international competitors. The explanations have been numerous; the only agreement appears to be that the causes are deep-rooted. The diagnoses can be grouped under three, albeit not exclusive, heads: economic, sociological, and structural. The economic explanations have been the most prominent.

One economic explanation for poor economic performance is a failure

TABLE 3.1. GROWTH RATES: INTERNATIONAL COMPARISONS, 1968–1987

Country	Annual Average Rate of Growth GDP (1980 prices)		
	1968–73 %	*1973–79* %	*1979–87* %
United Kingdom	3.2	1.4	1.9
United States	3.0	2.6	2.3
Japan	8.4	3.6	3.9
West Germany	4.9	2.3	1.5
France	6.2	2.8	1.7
Italy	4.6	2.6	2.3
Canada	5.4	4.2	2.8
Average	4.3	2.7	2.4

Source: OECD.

to modernize. There has been a tendency to retain old plants and to rely on traditional but declining industries, such as textiles. There is a popular view that Britain won the Second World War militarily but lost it economically. (The United States won on both counts, a cause of some residual resentment among a small portion of the political elite.)[32] The country was left in serious debt—economically dependent on the United States—and with a large portion of its industrial plant still intact. There was neither the capacity nor the incentive to start afresh; a number of other countries had no option but to begin anew, both politically and economically.

Other economists have laid the blame for economic failure at least partially on the emphasis given by successive governments to maintaining a balance of payments surplus in order to fund overseas military commitments and foreign investment, a policy pursued at the expense of economic growth.[33] A consequence of Empire has been that Britain has tended to retain a number of overseas commitments beyond what many regard as its financial capacity to do so, and to continue to harbor international pretensions. (A major and continuing burden on Britain's defense budget since 1982 has been the commitment to defend the Falkland Islands following the military repossession of the islands after the Argentine invasion that year.) Related diagnoses have focused on the legacies of attitudes and institutions, derived from the days when Britain was at the center of the world economy, acting as a barrier to change.[34]

A more contemporary explanation has been that the nation's decline is attributable to the failure of successive governments in the postwar era to manipulate supply as well as demand. This explanation has found favor especially with the Conservative government returned in 1979 and has provided some of the underpinning of its economic policy (see Chapter 6). Committed to a free market economy, it has been keen to remove all obstacles that stand in the way of its realization. Trade unions and public sector institutions with restrictive practices have been particular targets. Believing that a free market economy is the solution to the nation's economic ills, the government has been prepared—indeed, has regarded it as a *sine qua non* of its policy—to reject the social democratic consensus of the postwar years. Tackling inflation and freeing the market have been its essential goals; the objectives of the managed economy have not. By the end of the 1980s it could claim some success: there was greater economic stability and the economy was growing faster than some of its principal competitors. Its opponents could point to rising inflation and interest rates, a substantial balance-of-payments deficit, and a reduction—on their analysis, a collapse—of the nation's manufacturing base. The Labour party argued that government policy was part of the problem rather than part of the solution.

Though predominant, economic explanations have not been the only ones offered. Some have been primarily sociological. As we have seen (Chapter 1), class did not displace status in British society. Preindustrial aristocratic attitudes were carried over into an industrial age. These attitudes included looking down on the pursuit of trade and commerce as somewhat inferior socially. Low priority was given to industry and science and, so the analysis goes, a tendency grew for those with wealth and some ability to avoid management in favor of the professions such as law.[35] Such attitudes are still apparent today, though on a less significant scale. The "old school tie" (that is, which school—usually a public school—one went to) still provides an important route of entry to many important posts in the business world. By international standards, British management remains poorly trained and, consequently, amateurish. This weakness is most apparent in the international marketplace, British exporters lacking the skills and persistence of their competitors. British boardrooms have remained highly conservative and unadventurous. They earned the enmity of Conservative Prime Minister Edward Heath in the early 1970s when they failed to respond to government incentives to invest in new plant and machinery. There is evidence that many firms are not well prepared—especially in terms of language skills—for the Single European Market of the 1990s. At various times the Conservative government under Margaret Thatcher has proven willing to bring in businessmen who are foreign born or trained to run public bodies.

Some blame for sluggish economic performance has also been imputed to the egalitarianism of the labor movement, harboring dislike of profits and risk taking as well as the values of thrift and self-reliance that underpin the operation of the free market. This view has been argued in particular by some who have been close to Margaret Thatcher.[36] Unlike the case in America, there is no culture that favors ambition among blue-collar workers to achieve a junior managerial post and then a post above that. In short, bringing the two sociological explanations together, the attitudes of both the social elite and the labor movement—generating an "us" and "them" mentality in industrial relations—has hindered economic growth.

The other diagnoses are essentially structural. They are important in the context of later chapters and hence deserve some attention. The historical background provided in this chapter helps us understand some of these diagnoses as well as some of the resulting prescriptions. The three main diagnoses are those of adversary politics, centralization, and—fashionable in the 1970s but less discussed today—pluralist stagnation.

Adversary Politics.   This thesis contends that attempts to generate solutions to long-term problems are thwarted by a political system that encourages an adversary relationship between the two main political parties, one that historically has enabled them to alternate in office so that each undoes the work of the other.[37] The consequence, it is argued, has been policy discontinuity, making it difficult if not impossible for industrialists and investors to plan ahead. The adversary relationship encourages an escalation in promises that outstrip the capacity of the parties to fulfill them when in office. When the resources are not there to fulfill promises, disenchantment with the political system grows. Furthermore, the parties themselves are unable to break out of a cycle that works to their mutual advantage. The result is a political system that is dysfunctional and not amenable to radical reform.

The adversary politics thesis was developed in the mid-1970s and—despite ten years of uninterrupted Conservative government—was still prominent by the end of the 1980s; indeed, it appears to have attracted even greater support since 1987. In part, this is attributable to the view that the maintenance of adversarial relations between the parties in the 1980s made it impossible for government—despite a large parliamentary majority—to mobilize support to tackle the nation's problems; and, since 1987, to the political revival of the Labour party and its declared intentions to reverse various policies of the Conservative government if it were returned to office. For those who advance this thesis, the structure of government does not offer the means of resolving the nation's problems; rather, the structure itself is seen as part of the problem.

Centralization.   The thesis of centralization dovetails to some extent with that of adversary politics. As government responsibilities in the twentieth century have expanded, so government has become increasingly centralized in Whitehall; the centralization has been both political (Whitehall as the center of the executive) and geographical (Whitehall being in the heart of the nation's capital). In recent decades, as the responsibilities of government increased, the capacity of government to fulfill them has decreased. The combination of these two features has produced what was characterized in the 1970s as "government overload."[38] The problem, according to various writers, has been exacerbated in recent years by a further centralization of power. In order to implement the goal of a free market economy, the Conservative government of Margaret Thatcher has variously found it necessary to strengthen its own powers, creating what Andrew Gamble has titled "the Strong State."[39]

This further centralization of power is seen as part of a vicious circle. The government, by virtue of a political system that allows it largely unfettered law-making power (through a parliamentary majority), is able to extend its formal powers. However, the adversarial nature of that same system militates against its mobilizing the support of disparate groups—and the population generally—in order to tackle economic problems.

Consequently, in order to tackle them, it takes more and more powers. The more powers it takes, the more distant it becomes from those groups it needs to mobilize; hence, a government with strong legal powers but increasingly limited political capacity to mobilize support. That, on this analysis, has been the dilemma, indeed the paradox, of the period of Conservative government under Mrs. Thatcher.

Pluralist Stagnation. This thesis suggests that the problem lies with the growth of groups in Britain, each group pursuing its own interests and bringing pressure to bear on governments to provide resources or pursue policies to the benefit of its members. Such has been the economic leverage of some groups that the role of government has become one of arbiter between competing group demands.[40] A tendency of governments to avoid conflict has encouraged inertia, governments being unwilling to pursue policies that would generate sustained opposition from well-entrenched groups.[41] The problem has been made worse, according to Samuel Beer, by the numerical growth of such groups. (Of the groups listed in a 1979 directory of pressure groups in Britain, approximately 40% had come into existence since 1960.)[42] Because there are so many, self-restraint in making demands of government would bring no discernible benefit to any one group. As a result, even though recognizing the need for restraint, a group is tempted to raise its own claims. Other groups then compete to raise their own claims. "The source of the problem," argues Beer, "is not a lack of knowledge, but the structure of the situation, which continues to have compelling force even when participants recognize its tendencies."[43] Government consequently is overwhelmed by the multiplicity of self-serving demands.

This thesis declined in prominence in the latter half of the 1980s. That this should be so is not surprising. The Conservative government demonstrated a clear willingness to lead rather than arbitrate, and it distanced itself from group bargaining at the level especially of economic policy. Groups, and certain ones in particular (such as the trade unions), were viewed as increasingly marginalized. The thesis nonetheless retains a degree of plausibility, calling attention to certain features of group activity in recent years. Though groups have been marginalized at the level of high policy making, they remain as active as before at the level of intermediate and what may be termed low or day-to-day policy making; small policy communities of civil servants and group representatives flourish. Groups have increasingly resorted to professional lobbying of government (and Parliament) in order to achieve their demands; the growth of political lobbyists in Britain has been a particular feature of the past decade. Government departments continue to be faced with competing group demands. Even at the level of high policy, government has been constrained by the demands (and in the case of various proposed reforms, by the opposition) of various entrenched groups. Group pressure has contributed, in part, to government not fulfilling a neo-liberal economic policy to the extent that the Prime Minister and her suporters would have wished.

These, then, constitute the main analyses that conclude that the problem is a structural one. There are other analyses that go beyond the structural and economic analyses, providing more complex explanations. One of the most sophisticated was that offered in 1982 by Samuel Beer in his book *Britain Against Itself*, in which he argued that there was no single causal explanation for Britain's decline; rather, he contended, it resulted from a convergence of disparate causes, encouraged by and contributing to a decline—indeed, a collapse—of the "civic culture" in Britain, producing distrust in government. Coupled with pluralist stagnation, this generated fragmentation and an incapacity to mobilize popular support. "The defeating logic of short-run self-interest has won out."[44]

Beer's thesis also became less prominent in the latter half of the 1980s, predominantly for the same reasons that the pluralist stagnation thesis (part of Beer's overall analysis) receded in prominence. Nonetheless, adherents of Beer's argument could point to increased social unrest in the years following publication of *Britain Against Itself*, to some degree of alienation on the part of particular groups and regions, and consequently— in common with those advancing the structuralist diagnoses—they contend that government was proving unable to mobilize the support necessary to tackle the nation's economic—and social—problems.

I shall return to these analyses in appropriate chapters. For the moment, two points need to be made. The first, rather obviously, is that no one approach is without its critics. Each approach has its limitations and these I shall seek to draw out at appropriate points in the text. The second and possibly equally obvious point is that, given the disparate diagnoses, a number of different prescriptions have been offered for dealing with the presumed causes of the country's ills. Exponents of the adversary politics thesis favor a new electoral system, for reasons to be explained in Chapter 5. Those who stress the effect of the centralization of power argue for devolution of power of elected assemblies in Scotland, Wales, and the English regions and for a decentralization of power below that to local bodies. Pluralist stagnation, according to Beer's analysis, can be overcome only by mobilizing popular consent through restoring trust in government.[45] So wide are the analyses and the resulting prescriptions that one might be tempted to wonder whether the concept of pluralist stagnation might more appropriately be applied to the analyses of Britain's problems.

My own argument I will draw together in the conclusion. For the moment, suffice it to say that I take a skeptical view of the structural analyses offered. They are largely unproven and exaggerated and they miss the essential point. The problem is not primarily a structural one; structures are dependent variables. The independent variable on which one has to focus is the political culture. That culture has not suffered the "collapse" suggested by Beer: instead, as I have already intimated (Chapter 2), it remains in strong shape. And that culture provides government with the breathing space necessary to attempt to tackle the nation's essential problems, which are economic and social. The political system facilitates rather than militates against government's tackling essential problems— the obverse of the situation that exists in the United States. If government fails, the failure may be the product of poor policies, of a deteriorating global economy, or of poor management and unions. Changing structures will not help solve the nation's problems; it could, though, add to them.

NOTES

1. See A. H. Dodd, *The Growth of Responsible Government* (Routledge & Kegan Paul, 1956), pp. 43–44.
2. B. Kemp, *King and Commons 1660–1832* (Macmillan, 1957), p. 3.
3. Its provisions included, for example, "That excessive Baile ought not to be required nor excessive Fines imposed nor cruell and unusuall Punishments inflicted." Compare this with the Eighth Amendment to the United States Constitution, which prescribes that "Excessive bail shall not be required, nor excessive fines imposed, nor cruel and unusual punishments inflicted."
4. J. H. Plumb, *England in the Eighteenth Century* (Penguin, 1950), p. 50.
5. J. Mackintosh, *The British Cabinet*, 2nd ed. (Methuen, 1968), pp. 50–51.
6. Ibidl., p. 64.
7. S. M. Lipset, *The First New Nation* (Heinemann, 1964); P. Mathias, *The First Industrial Nation* (Methuen, 1969).
8. Sir L. Woodward, *The Age of Reform 1815--1870*, 2nd ed. (Oxford University Press, 1962), p. 3.
9. A table compiled in 1815 revealed that 144 peers, along with 123 commoners, controlled 471 seats (more than two-thirds of the total number) in the House of Commons. M. Ostrogorski, *Democracy and the Organisation of Political Parties*, Vol. 1: England (Macmillan, 1902), p. 20.
10. J. B. Conacher (ed.), *The Emergence of British Parliamentary Democracy in the Nineteenth Century* (Wiley, 1971), p. 10. Different authors cite different figures.
11. W. Bagehot, *The English Constitution* (first published 1867; Fontana ed., 1963), p. 150.
12. Mackintosh, p. 113.
13. See Conacher, pp. 68–69, for a summary.
14. See H. J. Hanham, *Elections and Party Management*, 3rd ed. (Harvester Press, 1978), p. xii.

15. Similarly, in the United States the all-or-nothing spoils of presidential victory have encouraged two rather than many parties. See M. Vile, *Politics in the USA* (Hutchinson, 1976 ed.), pp. 62–63.
16. A. L. Lowell, *The Government of England*, Vol. II (Macmillan, 1924), pp. 76–78.
17. Mackintosh, p. 174.
18. Many of the reforms were introduced by Conservative governments. See C. E. Bellairs, *Conservative Social and Industrial Reform* (Conservative Central Office, 1977).
19. P. Addison, *The Road to 1945* (Quartet, 1977), p. 127.
20. I. Macleod, *Neville Chamberlain* (Muller, 1961), p. 123.
21. S. H. Beer, *Modern British Politics* (Faber, 1969 ed.), pp. 278–87.
22. Addison, p. 29.
23. *Social Insurance and Allied Services—Report by Sir William Beveridge*, Cmnd. 6404 (Her Majesty's Stationery Office, 1942), para. 17, p. 9.
24. Based on the title of Vernon Bogdanor and Robert Skidelsky (eds.), *The Age of Affluence 1951–1964* (Macmillan, 1970).
25. G. Botero, *The Reason of State*, quoted in K. Thomas, "The United Kingdom," in R. Crew (ed.), *Crises of Political Development in Europe and the United States* (Princeton University Press, 1978), pp. 45–46.
26. H. T. Buckle, *History of Civilization in England*, quoted in Thomas, p. 44.
27. S. Low, *Governance of England* (1904), quoted in G. Marshall and G. Moodie, *Some Problems of the Constitution,* 4th rev. ed. (Hutchinson, 1967), p. 18.
28. Quoted in P. Norton, *The Constitution in Flux* (Basil Blackwell, 1982), p. 23.
29. *House of Commons Debates*, Sixth Series, Vol. 2, col. 1213.
30. See L. D. Epstein, "What Happened to the British Party Model?" *American Political Science Review*, 74 (1), March 1980, pp. 9–22.
31. C. M. Hardin, *Presidential Power and Accountability: Towards a New Constitution* (University of Chicago Press, 1974), p. 139.
32. This was apparent in the parliamentary debate in November 1945 on the loan that Britain had negotiated with the United States. Its terms were viewed by a number of Conservative Members of Parliament as part of an attempt to open up world markets to the benefit of the United States; there were also fears that it would, in the words of one Labour Member, hitch the nation "to the American bandwagon, and may eventually land us in the position of being America's Heligoland off the coast of Europe." See P. Norton, *Dissension in the House of Commons 1945–74* (Macmillan, 1975), p. 3. Further resentment was caused by the active opposition of the U.S. government to Britain's attempt to occupy the Suez Canal Zone by force in 1956.
33. See, e.g., W. A. P. Manser, *Britain in Balance* (Penguin, 1973).
34. See A. Gamble, *Britain in Decline* (Macmillan, 1981).
35. See, e.g., M. Postan, *An Economic History of Western Europe 1945–64* (Methuen, 1967); and A. Gamble, "Explanations of Economic Decline," Paper presented to the Annual Conference of the Political Studies Association of the United Kingdom, Newcastle-Upon-Tyne, 1983. This section has benefited substantially from this latter paper.

36. See especially Sir K. Joseph, *Stranded on the Middle Ground* (Centre for Policy Studies, 1976).
37. See especially S. E. Finer (ed.), *Adversary Politics and Electoral Reform* (Wigram, 1975), which had a seminal influence. See also D. Coombes, *Representative Government and Economic Power* (Heinemann, 1982); and A. M. Gamble and S. A. Walkland, *The British Party System and Economic Policy 1945–1983* (Oxford University Press, 1984).
38. See A. King, "The Problem of Overload," in A. King (ed.), *Why Is Britain Becoming Harder to Govern?* (BBC, 1976), pp. 8–30.
39. A. Gamble, *The Free Economy and the Strong State* (Macmillan, 1988).
40. See S. H. Beer, *Modern British Politics* (Faber & Faber, 1969 ed.).
41. See I. Gilmour, *The Body Politic*, rev. ed. (Hutchinson, 1971); and J. E. S. Hayward, *Political Inertia* (University of Hull Press, 1975).
42. P. Shipley, *Directory of Pressure Groups and Representative Organisations*, 2nd ed. (Bowker, 1979).
43. S. H. Beer, *Britain Against Itself* (Faber & Faber, 1982).
44. Ibid., p. 2.
45. Ibid., Conclusion.

PART II
The Political Environment

CHAPTER 4

The Uncodified Constitution

A constitution may be defined as the body of laws, customs, and conventions that define the composition and powers of organs of the state and that regulate the relations of the various state organs to one another and to the private citizen.[1]

The United States has a constitution; so does the United Kingdom. Expressed in purely formal terms (Table 4.1) there is very little similarity between them. Indeed, the differences are such that to the student weaned on a study of the United States Constitution, the British Constitution is nearly incomprehensible. Even to the student of British politics it is not well understood. Nonetheless, the differences should not be emphasized to the exclusion of certain common features. Both Constitutions are strong in that they reflect and reinforce their respective political cultures.

The United States Constitution is considered by Americans to embody the principles of a higher law, to constitute "in fact imperfect man's most perfect rendering of what Blackstone saluted as 'the eternal immutable laws of good and evil, to which the creator himself in all his dispensations conforms: and which he has enabled human reason to discover, so far as they are necessary for the conduct of human actions.'"[2] As the embodiment of a higher law, it thus not only needs to be distinguished from ordinary law but also needs to be protected from the passing whims of

TABLE 4.1.   AMERICAN AND BRITISH CONSTITUTIONS

| Characteristics | Constitutions | |
	United States	United Kingdom
Form of expression	Written	Part written but uncodified
Date and manner of formulation	1787 by a constitutional convention	No one date of formulation; no precise manner of formulation
Means of formal amendment	By two-thirds majorities in both Houses of Congress and by ratification of three-quarters of the states, or by conventions	No extraordinary provisions for amendment
Location of its provisions	The written document (also judicial decisions, custom usage, works of authority)	Statute law, common law, conventions, works of authority
Bodies responsible for interpretation of its provisions	The judiciary primarily (can be overridden by constitutional amendment)	The judiciary (statute and common law), scholars and politicians (conventions)
Main provisions	Document as "supreme law," judicial review, separation and overlap of powers, federal system, bill of rights, republican form of government	Parliamentary sovereignty, "rule of law," unitary system, parliamentary government under a constitutional monarchy, membership in the European Community
Public promulgation of its provisions (in textbooks, etc.)	Extensive	Infrequent

politicians—hence the introduction of extraordinary procedures for its amendment.

By contrast, the British Constitution is admired by Britons for reflecting the wisdom of past generations, as the product of experience—in short, a constitution that stipulates what should be on the basis of what has proved to work rather than on abstract first principles. The empirical orientation to change that underpins such a constitution also favors flexibility in amendment: as conditions change, so some amendment may be necessary. Formal extraordinary procedures for its amendment have not been found necessary.

The differences in political culture have thus produced somewhat different constitutions, but the attachment to them is similar in the two countries. Also, as we we shall see, there are certain similarities in sources and in the means of interpretation.

FORMS OF EXPRESSION

New nations from the eighteenth century onward have found it both necessary and useful to codify their constitutions. At the time that the Founding Fathers promulgated the United States Constitution in Philadelphia, a written constitution was exceptional. Today it is the norm. Having lacked the opportunity to create a new constitutional framework afresh from first principles, Britain now stands out as one of the few nations lacking such a document.

The absence of a written constitution similar to that of the United States and other nations has led to the British Constitution being described as unwritten, but such a description is misleading. As we shall see, various elements of the Constitution find expression in formal, written enactments. What distinguishes the British Constitution from others is not that it is unwritten, but rather that it is part written and uncodified. The lack of codification is of special importance. It makes it difficult to identify clearly and authoritatively what constitute the provisions of the Constitution. There are certain principles that are clearly at the heart of the Constitution, parliamentary sovereignty being the prime example, but there are many provisions, be they expressed through statute law or the writings of constitutional experts, that are of constitutional significance but on which there is no clear agreement that they form part of the British Constitution. It is this lack of codified certainty that makes a study of it so fraught with difficulty.

SOURCES

Because one cannot have recourse to one simple authoritative document to discover the provisions of the British Constitution, one has instead to research four separate sources: statute law, common law, conventions, and works of authority. Such sources are also relevant in analyses of the United States Constitution. Congress may pass measures of constitutional significance, such as certain stipulations of electoral law or the War Powers Act. Provisions of the Constitution are developed and molded by judicial decisions. In seeking to interpret the Constitution, the courts may have recourse to works by constitutional experts. The difference between the two countries is that in Britain such sources are primary sources, and in the United States the primary source is the written document.

Of the four sources, statute law is perhaps the best understood and, nowadays, the most extensive. It provides the main source for the part-written element of the British Constitution. It comprises acts of Parliament and subordinate legislation made under the authority of the parent act.

Many acts of Parliament that have been passed clearly merit the title of constitutional law. Acts that define the powers of the various state organs (for example, the 1911 and 1949 Parliament Acts) and acts that define the relationship between Crown and Parliament (notably the Bill of Rights of 1689), between the component elements of the nation (the Act of Union with Scotland of 1706, for example), between the United Kingdom and the European Communities (principally the 1972 European Communities Act and 1986 European Communities [Amendment] Act), and between the state and the individual (as with the Habeas Corpus Act of 1679 or the Police and Criminal Evidence Act of 1984) clearly constitute important provisions of the Constitution. They are published in authoritative, written form and, as acts of Parliament, are interpreted by the courts. This is the most important of the four sources both in quantitative and qualitative terms. It has increasingly displaced common law as the most extensive form of law in Britain and it is the most definitive of the four. It takes precedence over any conflicting common law and is superior to the conventions of the Constitution and to works of authority. Its precedence derives from the concept of parliamentary sovereignty.

Common law constitutes rules and customs of ancient lineage that are so well established that they have been upheld as law by the courts in cases decided before them. Once a court has upheld a provision as being part of common law, it creates a precedent to be followed by other courts. In past centuries, when few statutes were enacted, common law constituted the main body of English law; today, it has been largely but not wholly displaced by statute law. Certain principles derived from common law remain fundamental to the Constitution, and these include the principle of parliamentary sovereignty.

Under the heading of common law comes also prerogative powers— the powers and privileges recognized by common law as belonging to the Crown. Although many prerogative powers have been displaced by statute, many matters at the heart of government are still determined under the authority of the prerogative. These include the appointment of ministers, the making of treaties, the power of pardon, the dispensing of honors, and the declaration of war. By convention, such powers are normally exercised formally by the monarch on the advice of ministers (the ministers, in practice, take the decisions). There is no formal requirement that Parliament assent to such decisions. This is in stark contrast to the position in the United States, where Congress alone has the formal power to declare war and the Senate's consent is necessary for the ratification of treaties and the appointment of federal public officers. (In practice, the differences are not that great: "presidential wars" have been waged without a congressional declaration of war, while in Britain a government taking military action abroad will seek the consent of Parliament.) In 1972 the Treaty of Accession to the European Community was signed under prerogative powers. In 1982 a naval task force was dispatched to the Falkland Islands under the same authority. Although diminishing in number, prerogative powers clearly remain of great importance.

Generally included under the generic heading of common law is the judicial interpretation of statute law. Unlike those in the United States, British courts have no power to hold a measure unconstitutional. They are limited to the interpretation of provisions of acts of Parliament. Even in exercising their power of interpretation, they are limited by rules of interpretation and by precedent. (The exception is the House of Lords, the highest domestic court of appeal, which is not now bound by its previous decisions.) Nonetheless, judges retain the power to distinguish cases, and by their interpretation they can develop a substantial body of case law. In interpreting acts of Parliament, they assume Parliament to have meant what, on the face of it, the words of an act appear to mean. Unlike the United States Supreme Court, which can delve deep into the deliberations of the Founding Fathers to try to elucidate what was meant by a particular provision of the Constitution, British courts are not permitted to look at the proceedings of Parliament in order to determine what Parliament really meant.

The third and least tangible source of the Constitution is that of convention. Conventions of the British Constitution are most aptly described as rules of behavior that are considered binding by and upon those who are responsible for making the Constitution work, but rules that are not enforced by the courts or by the presiding officers in either house of Parliament.[3] They derive their strength from the realization that not to abide by them would make for an unworkable Constitution. They are, so to speak, the oil in the formal machinery of the Constitution. They help fill the gap between the constitutional formality and the political reality. For example, ministers are responsible formally to the monarch. Because of the political changes wrought in the nineteenth century, they are by convention responsible now also to Parliament. By convention, the government of the day resigns or requests a dissolution of Parliament if a motion of no confidence is carried against it in the House of Commons. By convention, the monarch gives the Royal Assent to all legislative measures approved by Parliament. The last time a monarch refused assent was in 1707, when Queen Anne vetoed a Scottish Militia Bill. Queen Victoria in the nineteenth century contemplated refusing her assent to a measure but wiser counsels prevailed.

No formal, authoritative documents set forth these rules, and they find no embodiment in statute law. The courts may recognize them but have no power to enforce them. They are complied with because of the recognition of what would happen if they were not complied with. For the Queen to refuse her assent to a measure passed by the two Houses of Parliament would draw her into the realms of political controversy, hence jeopardizing the claim of the monarch to be "above politics." A government that sought to remain in office after losing a vote of confidence in the House of Commons would find its position politically untenable: it would lack the political authority to govern. For ministers to ignore Parliament completely would prove equally untenable.

Some conventions may be described as being stronger than others. Some on occasion are breached, while others are adhered to without exception. On three occasions in this century, the convention of collective ministerial responsibility has been suspended temporarily by the prime minister of the day. In contrast, no government has sought to remain in office after losing a parliamentary vote of confidence. The point at which a useful and necessary practice is accorded the status of a constitutional convention is not clear. Once a practice has become well established in terms of the relationship within or between different organs of the state, finding recognition in works of authority and by those involved in its operation, then it may be said to have reached the status of a convention. At any one time, though, there are a number of relationships that may be said to be in a constitutional haze. Is it a convention of the Constitution that the government of the day must consult with interested bodies before formulating a legislative measure for presentation to Parliament? A noted constitutional lawyer, Sir Ivor Jennings, once argued that it was.[4] Prime Minister Harold Wilson appeared to give some credence to this view in 1966 when he said in the House of Commons that it was the *duty* of the government to consult with the Trades Union Congress and the Confederation of British Industry.[5] Few other authorities have supported Jennings' assertion and it has not found acceptance by most practitioners of government. It is usual for governments to engage in such consultation, but it is not a convention of the Constitution that they do so.

The fourth and final source of the Constitution is that of works of authority. These have persuasive authority only. What constitutes a "work of authority" is rarely defined. Various early works are accorded particular standing by virtue of the absence of statutes or other written sources covering a particular area. The statements of their writers are presumed to be evidence of judicial decisions that have been lost and are therefore accepted if not contrary to reason.[6] Among the most important early sources are Fitzherbert's *Abridgment* (1516) and Coke's *Institutes of the Law of England* (1628–1644). More recent works have been called in to aid on those occasions when jurists and others have sought to delineate features of the contemporary Constitution; this has been the case especially in determining the existence or otherwise of conventions. Given that conventions are prescribed neither by statute nor by judicial interpretation, one must study instead scholarly interpretations of political behavior and practice. Especially important authoritative works in the nineteenth century were those by John Austin and A. V. Dicey. Important names in the twentieth century have included Sir Ivor Jennings, Sir Kenneth Wheare, O. Hood Phillips, and E. C. S. Wade.[7]

Given the disparate sources of the British Constitution and the fact that important relationships within and between organs of the state are not laid down in any one formal or binding document, it is not surprising that one must have recourse to books by constitutional scholars to discover the extent and nature of those relationships. Works of authority tend to be consulted more frequently in the field of constitutional law than in any other branch of English law.

MEANS OF AMENDMENT

Given the disparate primary sources of the British Constitution and the difficulty in determining where the Constitution begins and ends, it is perhaps not surprising that there are no extraordinary procedures for its amendment. Statute and common law of constitutional significance are subject to amendment by the same process as that employed for other legislative enactments. Conventions can be modified by changes in behavior or by reinterpretations of the significance of certain behavior. Works of authority can be rewritten or subjected to different interpretations in the same way as can other texts.

Much the same can be said about constitutionally significant statute law, judicial decisions, and works of authority in the United States. Even the provisions of the formal document, the United States Constitution, may be amended by judicial decisions and custom usage. The difference between the two countries is that the formal wording of the United States Constitution can be amended only by an extraordinary process, that is, one that goes beyond the provisions employed for amending the ordinary law. (Because of the extraordinary procedures necessary for amendment, the provisions of the Constitution are commonly referred to as "entrenched.") No such formal amending procedures exist in Britain, where there is no formal document.

INTERPRETATION

As may be surmised from the foregoing, there is no single body endowed with the responsibility for interpreting the provisions of the Constitution. As in the United States, statute and common law are subject to judicial interpretation, but there is no power of judicial review, at least not as the term is understood in the United States. The courts cannot declare a legislative measure or an executive action contrary to the provisions of the Constitution.

The courts can influence and to some extent mold certain provisions through their interpretation of statute and common law. Indeed, their use of common law has been of special importance in outlining and protecting certain rights of the individual. However, at the end of the day they are subject to the wishes of Parliament. Judicial interpretation of statute law can be overridden by a new act of Parliament. By virtue of the concept of parliamentary sovereignty, the act would be definitive. The judges serve to enforce and interpret such acts: they cannot strike down an act.

Identification and interpretation of conventions has little to do with the courts. Conventions arise as a result of changes in the relationships within and between different organs of the state. Their delineation rests with scholars, and their enforcement rests with those at whom they are aimed.

The Constitution, in short, is subject to interpretation by different bodies, the most prominent being politicians, judges, and scholars. The same can be said of the United States Constitution, but in Britain there is no body that stands in a position analogous to that of the United States Supreme Court. This is an important difference, reflecting the differences in political culture. The Lockean basis of constitutional interpretation in the United States—a higher law cognizable by independent, rational magistrates operating free of outside interests[8]—finds no parallel in Britain.

MAIN PROVISIONS

The central provisions of the British Constitution are listed in Table 4.1: parliamentary sovereignty, the rule of law, a unitary (as opposed to a federal) system, what I have termed parliamentary government under a constitutional monarchy, and membership in the European Community. Although there is some dispute as to whether it should remain so, the preeminent provision is that of parliamentary sovereignty. In the nineteenth century the great constitutional lawyer A. V. Dicey identified it as being one of the two main pillars of the Constitution, the other being the rule of law.[9] Dicey's work has had a major and lasting impact. Despite subsequent criticisms, the two pillars identified by Dicey still stand. While some critics have considered them weak and (in the case of parliamantary sovereignty) unnecessary pillars, supporting a crumbling edifice, they remain crucial to an understanding of the British Constitution.

Parliamentary Sovereignty

The most succinct definition of parliamentary sovereignty was offered by Dicey. Parliamentary sovereignty, he wrote, means that Parliament has "the right to make or unmake any law whatever; and, further, that no person or body is recognized by the law of England as having a right to override or set aside the legislation of Parliament."[10] An act passed by Parliament will be enforced by the courts, the courts recognizing no body other than Parliament as having authority to override such an act. Parliament itself can substitute an act for an earlier one. One of the precepts derived from the principle is that Parliament is not bound by its predecessors. Once Parliament has passed an act, it becomes the law of the land. It is not open to challenge before the courts on the grounds of being unconstitutional.

Although Dicey claimed more ancient lineage for it, the principle of parliamentary sovereignty became established as a judicial rule in consequence of the Glorious Revolution of 1688 and subsequent Bill of Rights, which established the relationship between the Crown and Parliament (see Chapter 3). It was the product of an alliance between Parliament and common lawyers and of the intimidation of judges by the House of Commons. Assertion of the principle served to do away with the monarch's previously claimed powers to suspend or dispense with acts of Parliament and it served to deny judges the power to strike down measures. It came to occupy a unique place in constitutional law. The principle finds no expression in statute or any other formal enactment. It exists in common law but enjoys a special status beyond that enjoyed by other principles of common law. Its underpinnings are not only legal but also political and historical. It is now too late to challenge the principle. Judicial obedience to it constitutes what H. W. R. Wade referred to as "the ultimate political fact upon which the whole system of legislation hangs."[11] No statute can confer the power of parliamentary sovereignty, for that would be to confer the very power being acted upon. It is therefore considered to be unique. As Hood Phillips states, "It may indeed be called the one fundamental law of the British Constitution."[12]

The Rule of Law

The second pillar identified by Dicey was that of "the rule of law." Identifying what is meant by the term is extremely difficult. Few students of the Constitution would deny the importance of the tenet. Dicey himself argued that it comprised "at least three distinct though kindred conceptions": "that no man is punishable or can be lawfully made to suffer in body or goods except for a distinct breach of law established in the ordinary legal manner before the ordinary courts of the land"; that "no man is above the law [and] every man, whatever be his rank or condition, is subject to the ordinary law of the realm and amenable to the jurisdiction of the ordinary tribunals"; and that "the general principles of the constitution [are] the result of judicial decisions determining the rights of private persons in particular cases brought before the courts." These three conceptions have been subject to various criticisms: that many of the discretionary powers are vested in officials and public bodies, that many officials and bodies have powers and immunities that the ordinary citizen does not have, and that certain rights have been modified by or enacted in statute. Furthermore, it is not clear why Dicey's third conception should be considered "kindred" to the other two. Some students of the Constitution find Dicey's analysis useful, and others tend to be dismissive; even Dicey later revised his own definition. The important point for our purposes is that there is no agreed-upon definition.

The rule of law, then, stands as a central element of the British Constitution, but no one is sure precisely what it means. It remains "one of the most elusive of all political concepts."[13] Some writers, especially in recent years, have tended to accord it a wide definition, encompassing substantive rights. On their argument, the rule of law cannot be said to exist unless basic human rights are protected. Others have adopted a narrow and more long-standing definition, contending that the concept entails certain procedural (or "due process") rights, that government must be subject to the law, and that the judiciary must be independent. The problem is one of determining what those rights are, how they are to be protected, and how the independence of the judiciary is to be maintained.

There is a further problem. The concept of the rule of law is not logically compatible with that of parliamentary sovereignty. Parliament could if it so wished confer arbitrary powers upon government. It could fetter the independence of the judiciary. It could limit or remove altogether certain rights presumed to exist at common law. The rule of law, in short, could be threatened or even dispensed with by parliamentary enactment. Dicey himself recognized this problem and sought to resolve it. He argued, in essence, that the rule of law prevented government from exercising arbitrary powers. If government wanted such powers, it could obtain them only through Parliament (Parliament itself has never sought to exercise executive powers) and the granting of them could take place only after deliberation and approval by the triumvirate of monarch, Lords, and Commons.[14]

Such an argument serves to explain potential impediments to a government intent on acquiring arbitrary powers. It does not deny the truth of the assertion that Parliament could, if it wished, confer such powers upon government. Indeed, many observers would argue that given the growth of cabinet government, the potential for government to seek and receive such powers is significantly greater now than was the case at the time when Dicey was writing. For many critics of the existing Constitution, parliamentary sovereignty no longer constitutes an encouragement to the rule of law but rather exists as an impediment to its attainment. So long as parliamentary sovereignty remains "the one fundamental law" of the Constitution, there is no way in which substantive rights can be entrenched and put beyond the reach of Parliament.

Unitary System

The third feature of the Constitution that I have listed—that the United Kingdom is a unitary state—is a less difficult one to comprehend. The United States is a federal nation. The power vested in the federal government is that delegated in the United States Constitution: all other powers not delegated rest with the states or the people. In the United Kingdom, no powers are reserved to national or regional bodies. If they were, Parliament would not be omnicompetent. Parliament exercises legal sovereignty. It can confer certain powers and responsibilities upon regional and local authorities, and it can also remove those powers.

The unitary nation is that of the United Kingdom of Great Britain and Northern Ireland. Wales was integrated with England in 1536 by act of Parliament (the Laws in Wales Act), and Scotland and England were incorporated in 1707 by the Treaty of Union and by the Act of Union with Scotland. Ireland entered into legislative union in 1801. Following an armed uprising, the emergence of the Irish Free State was recognized in 1922 and given the status of a self-governing dominion. (The Irish Constitution of 1937 declared the country to be a sovereign independent state, a position recognized by the Westminster Parliament in 1949.) Excluded from the Irish Free State were the northern six counties of Ireland, forming part of the traditional region of Ulster. The Protestant majority in Ulster wished to remain part of the United Kingdom, and the province of Northern Ireland has so remained.

Parliamentary Government under Constitutional Monarchy

The fourth element of the constitution is one that I have described as a parliamentary government under a constitutional monarchy. It is this element that is especially important in terms of the current relationships among the different organs of the state and the one in which conventions of the Constitution are predominant. It constitutes an assembly of different relationships and powers, the product of traditional institutions being adapted to meet changing circumstances. The developments producing this form of government were sketched in Chapter 3. The result as we have seen, was parliamentary government in the sense of government *through* Parliament rather than government *by* Parliament, with a largely ceremonial head of state. The essentials of this form of government may be adumbrated as follows.

In the relationship among government, Parliament, and the monarch, the government dominates. Although lacking formal powers, the cabinet is recognized by convention as being at the heart of government. It is responsible for the final determination of policy to be submitted to Parliament, for the supreme control of the national executive in accordance with the policy prescribed by Parliament, and for the continuous coordination and delimitation of the interests of the several departments of state.[15] It is presided over by the prime minister. The prime minister is appointed by the monarch. By convention, the monarch summons the leader of the party with a majority of seats in the House of Commons. (In the event of a party having no overall majority, the monarch summons whoever he or she believes may be able to form an administration.) The prime minister then selects the members of his or her cabinet and other government ministers and submits their names to the monarch who, by convention, does not deny the prime minister's choice. By convention, ministers are drawn from Parliament and, again by convention, predominantly from the elected house, the House of Commons. Although the government is no longer chosen by the Commons, it nonetheless is elected through the House of Commons: there is no separate election of the executive. There is a separation and overlap of powers between the government and the House of Commons in Britain but no equivalent separation of personnel. Government ministers are drawn from, and remain within, Parliament.

Legally, ministers are responsible to the monarch. Politically, they are responsible for their policies and actions to Parliament. Ministers are responsible to Parliament through the convention of individual ministerial responsibility, which assigns to them control of their departments, for which they are answerable to Parliament. The cabinet is similarly responsible to Parliament through the convention of collective ministerial responsibility. This convention, one scholar writes, "implies that all cabinet ministers assume responsibility for cabinet decisions and actions taken to implement those decisions."[16] It also has begotten two other conventions. It is a corollary of collective responsibility that any minister who disagrees publicly with a cabinet decision should resign and that a government defeat in the House of Commons on a vote of confidence necessitates either the resignation of the government or a request for a dissolution of Parliament (there is no convention as to which of these alternatives the government should select). Party cohesion ensures that the cabinet usually enjoys a parliamentary majority, but political parties remain unknown to the Constitution.

The cabinet approves government bills to be presented to Parliament. (In drawing up measures, it is aided primarily by its officials—that is, civil servants—and will consult normally with interested bodies: such consultation, though, enjoys no formal recognition in constitutional terms.) Within Parliament, the most important house is the Commons. It is expected to submit bills to sustained scrutiny and debate before giving its assent to them (or not giving its assent to them, but the influence of party usually precludes such an outcome). Formally, the Commons is free to pass or reject bills as it wishes. The House of Lords is more constrained (see Chapter 3); it was forced to accept a restricted role under the terms of the 1911 and 1949 Parliament Acts. Under the provisions of the 1911 Act (a measure to which the Lords acquiesced under threat of being swamped with a mass of new Liberal pro-reform peers), the Lords could delay passage of nonmoney bills for only two successive sessions, such bills being enacted if passed by the Commons again in the succeeding session. Money bills, those certified as such by the Speaker of the House of Commons, were to receive the Royal Assent one month after leaving the Commons, whether assented to by the House of Lords or not. The only significant power of veto retained was that over bills to prolong the life of a Parliament. (The delaying power over nonmoney bills was reduced by a further session under the terms of the 1949 Parliament Act, itself passed under the provisions of the 1911 Act.) In practice, it is rare for the Lords to reject government measures, and there is a gentleman's agreement among the parties in the House that a bill promised in a government's election manifesto should be given an unopposed Second Reading (see Chapter 11).

Once a bill has received the assent of both houses, it goes to the monarch for the Royal Assent. By convention, this assent is always forthcoming. As was already mentioned, not since Queen Anne's reign has a monarch refused assent. Queen Victoria contemplated such refusal but was persuaded otherwise. By convention, the Queen exercises her powers on the advice of her ministers. In certain extreme circumstances, Her Majesty may find herself in a position in which she is called on to use her discretion in making a political decision. Such cases are rare, though the Queen would probably prefer them to be nonexistent. The strength and the value of the contemporary monarchy derives from being above and avoiding political decisions.

The moment a bill receives the Royal Assent it becomes an act of Parliament. It is then enforced and upheld by the agencies of the state. It is binding and, by virtue of the doctrine of parliamentary sovereignty, cannot be challenged by the courts, nor can it be overridden by any other authority. The development of a form of representative democracy in the nineteenth century led Dicey to distinguish between legal sovereignty, which continued to reside with the triumvirate of the monarch, Lords, and Commons, and political sovereignty, which he deemed to rest with the electorate. This somewhat clumsy distinction has a certain utility. The electorate may have the power to choose the members of the House of Commons, but the will of the electorate is not something formally recognized by the courts. The courts recognize and will enforce only acts of Parliament.

Under the provisions of the 1911 Parliament Act, the maximum life of a Parliament is five years. (Previously, the period was seven years.) Within that period, the prime minister is free to recommend to the monarch a dissolution—in effect, to call a general election. Unlike the United States, Britain has no fixed-term elections at a national level. The ability of a prime minister effectively to call a general election has been regarded by some writers as the most important weapon in ensuring parliamentary support. The prime minister can threaten to recommend a dissolution if he or she does not receive the necessary support to get a measure through. Such a threat may constitute a bluff in that the prime minister would have more to lose if an election was called than would most MPs (the prime minister could lose office: most seats are safe seats and so most MPs could expect to be reelected), but nonetheless it has proved a potent influence in determining parliamentary behavior. It would be exceptional, albeit not unknown, for MPs of the government party to vote against their own side on a vote of confidence. No government in the twentieth century has lost a vote of confidence as a result of dissent by its own supporters[17]—hence the dominance of government.

In summary, then, the fourth element of the Constitution—parliamentary government under a constitutional monarchy—may be seen to comprise different relationships and powers, which are the product of traditional institutions being adapted to meet changing circumstances and are prescribed by a variety of measures of statute and commom law and by convention. The working of the various relationships within the framework established by law and convention is made possible by the operation of bodies not formally recognized by the Constitution, namely political parties. To understand contemporary British politics, one has to understand this framework.

European Community Membership

To understand British politics fully, one now has also to go beyond this framework. This brings us to the fifth and most recent constituent of the

Constitution, one for which there is no parallel in North America: membership in a supranational body, the European Community (EC). The United Kingdom became a member of the Community on January 1, 1973, and the effect of membership has been to add a new dimension to the formulation, approval, and enforcement of measures of public policy.

By virtue of Community membership, decision-making competence in a number of sectors has passed from the British government to the principal executive institutions of the Community: the Council of Ministers, comprising the relevant ministers drawn from the member states, and the Commission, the permanent bureaucracy headed by a College of Commissioners. (The commissioners are appointed by, but required to be independent of, the member states.) The Council is the ultimate decision-making body; the Commission alone has the power to propose legislation.

British ministers thus form part of a wider, collective decision-making body. Under the terms of the treaties forming the Community, the Council and Commission can issue different forms of Community legislation (see Chapter 10). Under the terms of the European Communities Act of 1972, which provides the legal basis necessary for membership, the force of law is given in the United Kingdom to EC legislation. Such legislation has immediate and general applicability. The assent of Parliament is not required: it has, in effect, been given in advance under the provisions of the 1972 Act. In the event of any conflict between domestic (known as municipal) law and EC law, EC law is to prevail. Disputes concerning Community law are to be treated by British courts as matters of law, and cases that reach the highest domestic court of appeal—the House of Lords—must, under the provisions of the Treaty of Rome, be referred to the Community's Court of Justice for a definitive ruling. Requests may also be made from lower courts to the Court of Justice for a ruling on the meaning and interpretation of Community treaties.

Membership in the Community has thus had profound constitutional implications for the United Kingdom. These implications are even more pronounced now as a result of the implementation of the Single European Act, which constitutes an amendment to the treaties of the EC and came into force on July 1, 1987. (As a treaty amendment, it required parliamentary approval and this was given under the provisions of the European Communities [Amendment] Act of 1986.) The effect of the act was to change the power relationship *between* the institutions of the Community and the member states, and *within* the Community between the different institutions. The act extended the provision for weighted majority votes in the Council of Ministers: what this means is that one or a small minority of ministers can be outvoted by the ministers from the other countries. (Each minister enjoys a stipulated number of votes, depending on the size of the country, with a total of 54 votes out of 76 being necessary for a measure to be adopted; the British minister has 10 votes.) A measure can thus be opposed by the British government and Parliament and yet, if it achieves the necessary number of votes in the Council, be enforced as law in the United Kingdom. Within the institutions of the Community, the act also accorded a stronger role to the European Parliament (a 518-member body, directly elected since 1979, in which the United Kingdom has 81 seats); it now is more directly involved in the discussion and amendment of Council proposals and, in certain circumstances, can fulfill a significant blocking role.

Membership in the Community has been added on, and as far as possible, integrated with the existing provisions of the British Constitution. The "fit" has not necessarily been complete. The doctrine of parliamentary sovereignty remains intact in that Parliament retains the power to repeal the EC Acts of 1972 and 1976. (To do so would be a breach of the nation's treaty obligations, under which membership is in perpetuity, but the courts would enforce the act of repeal.) The British government retains its autonomy in several significant sectors. Most significant measures of public policy arise from the domestic process of lawmaking. There is, though, a capacity for tension between the established national institutions and those that were grafted on at a supranational level in the 1970s and 1980s. The superior source of constitutional law in Britain is, as we have seen, statute law. Two provisions of statute law—the European Communities Act of 1972 and the Amendment Act of 1986—may be seen as constituting a Trojan Horse, allowing the introduction of a new layer to the British Constitution. Existing institutions and procedures have not yet become fully accommodated to this new dimension.

CONCLUSION

The shifting and complex web of relationships and powers that forms the British Constitution is not an easily discernible one. There are some powers and relationships that recognizably fall within the rubric of the Constitution. Others are less easy to classify. Sometimes a feature of the Constitution is discerned as such only at the time when it has just ceased to have much relevance. Walter Bagehot's *The English Constitution*, published in 1867, constituted a classic description of a Constitution that had not previously been so well sketched, yet a Constitution that was to undergo significant modifications as a result of the passage that very same year of the Second Reform Act. Bagehot's work continued to be regarded as an authoritative work long after the Constitution had undergone fundamental change.

Grasping the essentials of the Constitution at any given moment is clearly a demanding and confusing task. It is confusing even to those charged with its interpretation and to those who seek to make it work. To the student of the subject, the British Constitution appears complex, confusing, ill defined, and in many respects amorphous. Such a reaction is both natural and understandable: the Constitution does exhibit those very characteristics.

At the heart of the difficulty of delineating clearly the essential features of the Constitution is its ever-changing nature. Statute law, as we have seen in the case of membership in the European Community, can introduce new bodies of government. Constitutional norms serve to influence and mold political behavior. Conversely, political behavior helps influence the contours of the Constitution. As we have seen, such changes are made possible by the assimilating influence of conventions. "The conventions of the constitution," as Professor LeMay observed, "have meaning only when they are looked at against a background of continuous political change. It is very difficult to say with certainty what they were at any particular moment. Above all, they cannot be understood 'with the politics left out.'"[18]

The Constitution has proved adaptable to changing political conditions. In recent years, however, its relevance has been questioned. The patchwork quilt of powers and relationships has been criticized for no longer being either useful or relevant. There is, as we shall see, pressure from many influential sources for the Constitution not only to be further amended but also to be radically altered. In some cases there are calls for a new constitutional settlement. It is this pressure for change and its implications that subsequent chapters will explore.

NOTES

1. O. Hood Phillips, *Constitutional and Administrative Law*, 6th ed. (Sweet & Maxwell, 1978), p. 5.
2. C. Rossiter, prefatory note to E. S. Corwin, *The "Higher Law" Background of American Constitutional Law* (Cornell University Press, 1979 ed.), p. vi.
3. See G. Marshall and G. Moodie, *Some Problems of the Constitution*, 4th rev. ed. (Hutchinson, 1967), p. 26.
4. I. Jennings, *The Law and the Constitution*, 5th ed. (University of London Press, 1959), p. 102.
5. A. H. Hanson and M. Walles, *Governing Britain*, rev. ed. (Fontana, 1975), p. 156.
6. Phillips, p. 25.
7. P. Norton, *The Constitution in Flux* (Basil Blackwell, 1982), p. 9.
8. See L. Hartz, *The Liberal Tradition in America* (Harcourt, Brace and World, 1955), p. 9.

9. A. V. Dicey, *An Introduction to the Study of the Law of the Constitution*, 10th ed. (Macmillan, 1959, first published 1885).

10. Ibid., pp. 39–40.

11. H. W. R. Wade, "The Basis of Legal Sovereignty," *Common Law Journal*, 1955, cited by E. C. S. Wade in his introduction to the 10th ed. of Dicey, p. lvi.

12. Phillips, p. 46.

13. "The Rule of Law in Britain Today," *Constitutional Reform Centre: Politics Briefing No. 6* (Constitutional Reform Centre, 1989), p. 1.

14. See Norton, pp. 16–17.

15. As listed by *The Report of the Machinery of Government Committee* (His Majesty's Stationery Office, 1918).

16. S. A. de Smith, *Constitutional and Administrative Law* (Penguin, 1971), p. 176.

17. The government of Neville Chamberlain effectively fell in 1940 because of dissent by its own backbenchers, though it retained a majority in the parliamentary vote that took place. The government, in effect, got the message without having to be defeated formally. On three occasions in this century, government has actually lost a vote of confidence—in 1924 (twice) and 1979—but in each instance the government party did not enjoy an overall parliamentary majority.

18. G. LeMay, *The Victorian Constitution* (Duckworth, 1979), p. 21.

CHAPTER 5

The Electoral System
Fair and Workable?

In the United States, citizens are presented with the opportunity to go to the polls at frequent and fixed intervals to elect at national, state, and local levels a host of legislators, executive heads, councilpersons, officials, and even, in some states, judges. It has been estimated that there are approximately one million elective offices to be filled. In any given year there may be 120,000 or 130,000 elections held, most of them for local school boards.[1] Before polling day, the citizen is faced with a lengthy election campaign: there are primary campaigns, the primary elections, the general election campaign, and the general election itself. The presidential election campaign lasts for nearly a year; with all the preplanning, advance publicity, and fund raising, it lasts for much longer. Given the short interval between elections, campaigns for the United States House of Representatives are virtually continuous. Once in the polling booth, the voter is faced with a daunting array of candidates: given the number of offices to be filled and the number of people seeking to fill them, the number of names may be a three-figure one. Voting and its subsequent tabulation are much eased by the use of voting machines. Choosing between Republican and Democratic candidates is not always an easy task, and ticket splitting is a well-recognized phenomenon. Such characteristics of United States elections are well known. They have little in common with those of British elections.

In the United Kingdom, a citizen may have the opportunity to vote in the election of a national body only once every five years. That election is for the House of Commons and the House of Commons alone. The members of the House of Lords are not elected: they serve by virtue of birth or, for life peers, by appointment for life. There is no separate election of the executive: the leader of the party with a majority of seats in the House of Commons is invited to form a government. (The choice of party leaders is a matter for the parties themselves.) The date of an election is not known until approximately four weeks before the event, when the prime minister recommends to the Queen a dissolution of Parliament. Although there is much anticipatory planning, the election campaign proper extends over approximately three weeks. There are no primaries: candidate selection is an internal matter for the parties. As we shall see, there are also significant differences in registration procedures. The campaign is fought on a national, and party, basis. Funding and organization in the constituencies as well as nationally is undertaken by the established parties, not by individual candidates or campaign organizations created by the candidates. The amount of money spent on electioneering during this period is strictly limited by law. On polling day the elector is faced with a small ballot slip on which are printed the names usually of only three or four candidates. (Six or more candidates standing in any one constituency would be unusual.) The voter places his or her cross next to the name of one of them. With each elector having only one vote to cast for only one candidate, there is no such thing as ticket splitting. At the close of polling, the votes are collected in one central area in each constituency and counted by hand. The process of counting is an efficient one, and a sufficient number of results are usually announced within a few hours of the close of the polls to know which party has won the election. If the party in office has lost, the prime minister goes to Buckingham Palace to tender his or her resignation. The leader of the party newly returned with a majority of seats is then summoned. The new cabinet and other ministerial appointments are announced within a matter of days, sometimes within a matter of hours. Within a month of an election being called, Britain may find itself with a new government.

Since 1979, British electors have also had an opportunity to vote in a supranational election, electing the United Kingdom's 81 members in the European Parliament (see Chapter 10). Britain is exceptional in that, unlike every other country in the European Community, it employs (other than for the three seats in Northern Ireland) the plurality, first-past-the-post method of election. There are consequently similarities to elections to the House of Commons: candidates of the main parties compete in single-member constituencies, each elector having just one vote to cast. Though the elections are held on a fixed-term basis once every five years, election campaigns are short.

For elections to national and supranational bodies, the demands made on British electors are thus not onerous. Coupled with the shortness of

TABLE 5.1. UNITED STATES AND UNITED KINGDOM NATIONAL ELECTIONS

Characteristics	United States	United Kingdom
Bodies elected	President and Vice President United States Senate United States House of Representatives	House of Commons
Constituencies	President: national Senate: state House: districts	Single-member constituencies (650)

Terms of office	President: 4 years (two-term
	   maximum)
	Senator: 6 years (one-third
	   elected every 2 years)
	Representative: 2 years (no limits
	   to seeking reelection by
	   Senators or Representatives)
		Maximum of 5 years (no limit to
		   MPs seeking reelection)

Eligibility for
candidature
	President: citizen, aged 35 or
	   over, 14 years resident in U.S.
	Senator: aged 30 or over, 9 years
	   a citizen, inhabitant of state
	Representative: aged 25 or over,
	   7 years a citizen, inhabitant of
	   state
		Citizen aged 21 or over (certain
		   exceptions)

Fixed-term or irregular elections	Fixed-term	Irregular (but must not go beyond 5-year intervals)

Mode of
election
	Plurality vote for Senate and
	   House, popular vote and
	   electoral college for president
		Plurality vote

Date of
election
determined
by
	Provisions of United States
	   Constitution
		Recommendation of prime
		   minister to monarch (within
		   limits of 1911 Parliament
		   Act and subject to certain
		   qualifications)

Franchise	Citizens aged 18 and over
	   (certain exceptions)
		Citizens aged 18 and over
		   (certain exceptions)

Registration
procedures
	Generally required to register in
	   person at stipulated times and
	   places (certain state excep-
	   tions)
		Head of household required by law
		   to complete annual registration
		   form, submitted by mail

Turnout at elections	Less than 60% post-1968 (40% or less in midterm elections)	Regularly over 70%

election campaigns, they do not impinge upon electors' lives on any extensive basis. Greater opportunities to vote exist in local elections. An elector can vote for members of councils at district and country levels and sometimes at parish levels as well (see Chapter 9). However, only council members (councillors) are elected; no executive officers are subject to election. Councils choose their own chairmen, and the chief administrative officers are appointed professionals. There is no election of any local official, be it police chief, register of wills, city auditor, or judge. The one similarity between local elections in Britain and the United States is the turnout. Normally two-thirds of electors stay away from the polls.

The essential characteristics of national elections in the United States are contrasted in Table 5.1. Let us consider in a little more detail some of the main features of national elections in Britain—that is, to the House of Commons—and of electoral behavior before proceeding to a consideration of the current controversy surrounding the electoral system. Elections to the European Parliament and to local councils are considered in later chapters.

THE ELECTORAL STRUCTURE

Electors

As we have seen (Chapter 3), the franchise was variously extended in the nineteenth century. The basis on which the vote was given was that of property. Not until 1918 was universal manhood suffrage introduced on the basis of (six months') residence. In the same year, women aged 30 and over, if already local government electors or married to such electors, were given a vote in general elections. The vote was extended to all women aged 21 and over in 1928. It was extended to 18- to 20-year-olds in 1969. The various extensions of the franchise during the course of the century, much more radical in numerical terms than the various extensions of the previous century,[2] and the growth in population have resulted in the electorate growing from 6,730,935 in 1900 to 43,181,321 in 1987. The 1949 Representation of the People Act effectively brought to final fruition the principle of "one person, one vote." The only people excluded from the franchise are peers (they have their own House), imprisoned criminals, those of unsound mind, people convicted of certain election offenses, and aliens.

In order to exercise one's right to vote, it is necessary to be on the electoral register, which is compiled annually. Each year every household receives an electoral registration form. The head of the household is required by law to complete it and to list all those who are resident in the dwelling on October 10 of that year and are eligible for inclusion, including those who will attain the age of 18 years during the period that the new register comes into effect. These forms are returned by mail to the Registration Officer for the Constituency. Once the register is compiled, it is open for inspection; it takes effect the following February, and is in force for one year. Electors who move to another constituency during the course of the year are entitled to apply to vote by post in the constituency in which they are registered.

Compared with registration practice in most American states, the British method is both simple and effective. Given that people die, sometimes fail to complete the registration forms or fill them in incorrectly, or move without applying for a postal vote, the electoral register is never 100% accurate. According to a survey following the 1981 census, almost 7% of the names on the register should not have been included and almost 7% of qualified citizens had been left out.[3] In registration there is no procedure analogous to the American practice of registering as a Republican, Democrat, or Independent; given the absence of primary elections in Britain, there is no logical reason why one should.

Constituencies

The United Kingdom is divided into single-member constituencies. There are currently 650, though the number can and does vary. From 1974 until 1983 there were 635, and at one time earlier in this century there were over 700.

The drawing of boundaries is the responsibility of bodies known as boundary commissions: there is a commission each for England, Scotland, Wales, and Northern Ireland. Each commission is chaired by the Speaker of the House of Commons (a nonparty figure) and each has a judge as deputy chairman. Assistant commissioners, usually lawyers, are appointed to supervise local inquiries, and the staff of the commissions includes the country's main officials dealing with population and geographic surveys.

In redrawing boundaries the commissions are guided by rules laid down by act of Parliament. They are supposed to ensure that constituencies are as equal as possible in size of their electorates. However, they are permitted to deviate from this equality if special geographic considerations (for example, the size, shape, and accessibility of a constitutency) appear to render such a deviation desirable. Other rules further complicate the position. The commissioners are enjoined not to cross local authority boundaries in creating parliamentary constituencies. They also have to work within the context of regional disparities. To compensate for the absence of its own national assembly, Scotland has a greater number of constituencies allocated to it than its population strictly allows, and the same exception applies to Wales. Hence, the electoral quota (the national electorate divided by the number of seats) is greater in England than in Scotland or Wales.

Under existing legislation, the commissioners are required to review electoral boundaries every 10 to 15 years. (It used to be at more frequent intervals, but this was found to be too disruptive.) Before making their recommendations, the commissioners consider submissions from interested bodies, primarily the local political parties. If a proposed change has the support of the local parties, it is usual for the commissioners to accept it. Once they have completed their work, their recommendations are presented to a government minister, the home secretary, who is then required to lay them before the House of Commons for approval. They are rarely free of criticism. Boundary reviews in 1948 and 1955 were the subject of protests, and in 1969 the Labour home secretary advised his supporters in the House to vote against the commission's recommendations, which they did. As a result, the 1970 general election was fought on the basis of the old boundaries. The Commission's recommendations were implemented in the new Parliament. The next review by the commission was completed in 1982 and challenged unsuccessfully in the courts by the Labour party. The recommendations were subsequently approved by Parliament, and the 1983 general election was fought on the new boundaries. The next review should be completed in about 1995.

A combination of population shifts (about three-quarters of a million people move every year in Britain), the disparity among constituency electorates recommended by the commissioners in favor of other criteria (maintaining local government boundaries and the like), the lapse of time between reviews, and the disparity in the number of seats allocated to the different countries in the United Kingdom has meant that there are often marked differences among the sizes of electorates. Prior to the 1983 boundary revisions, 39% of seats deviated from the electoral quota by $\pm 20\%$. Even after the revisions, 5% of seats still deviated from the quota to the same extent; by the 1987 general election, the proportion was 15%. In the 1987 general election, the smallest and largest constituency electorates were, coincidentally, at opposite ends of the British Isles: the constituency of Orkney and Shetland (constituencies are given names, not numbers), covering the Orkney and Shetland islands off the north coast of Scotland, had an electorate of 31,047; the Isle of Wight, off the south coast of England, had an electorate of 98,694. In the 1970s some constituencies had electorates in excess of 100,000 and some had fewer than 25,000.

Campaigns

Election campaigns are short, sharp, and dominated by the political parties. In British elections, unlike those in America, the personalities of candidates (except for national leaders) and their personal wealth play but a marginal role. The campaign is fought in practice on a national level between the two main parties, the candidates and the local campaigns serving to reinforce the national campaigns of their leaders. Candidates are selected locally by the parties, and the parties provide the finance and the organization for the campaign. Election expenses are limited by statute and have been since 1883. Expenditure is permitted only where authorized by a candidate, a candidate's election agent, or a person authorized in writing by the agent. The maximum permitted expenditure is calculated on the basis of a fixed sum plus a limited amount based on the number of electors: in an average-sized English county constituency in 1987 the ceiling was £5,800 (just over $9,500). There are certain types of expenditure that are illegal (for example, paying an elector to exhibit an election poster or paying for voters to be taken to and from the polling booths), and separate committees to promote a candidate are not permitted. Even with the modest expenditure that is permitted, most candidates fail to spend the maximum allowed.[4] Some devices for keeping costs low are employed and these can, where required, provide up to an extra 20% of expenditure:[5] a popular ploy is to purchase stationery in advance and then resell it cheaply to the candidate as second-hand stock. Few candidates, though, are prepared to run too many risks for fear of having their elections challenged and declared void: expenses have to be declared and opponents keep a wary eye open for any infringements of election law. Two other constraints also operate: the parties have difficulty raising sufficient money to fight campaigns (national and local appeals are common when an election is in the offing) and there is little evidence that increased expenditure in local campaigns helps win elections.[6]

Each candidate is permitted one postage-free mailing of one piece of election literature. Other literature is distributed by the unpaid party activists. The main item of literature is the candidate's election address. This will usually incorporate a summary of the main points of the party's national election manifesto. The candidate will spend most of the campaign making speeches throughout the constituency, not infrequently at thinly attended meetings, and canvassing door to door where possible. He or she will be aided by volunteers who do doorstep canvassing to try to determine where supporters live: on election day they will keep a running tab on who has voted in order to ensure that support is maximized.

The main focus of the campaign is a national one. The party leaders will make regular and well-publicized appearances throughout the country, ensuring that the national press and television reporters follow in their wake, as well as holding daily press conferences. The national party organizations increasingly make use also of press advertising. As long as expenditure cannot be said to apply in support of specific candidates, national party campaigns do not fall foul of the election finance restrictions. In the 1987 election the Conservative, Labour, and Alliance parties spent a total of $15 million (almost $25,000,000) centrally, about twice the amount expended by their candidates in the local campaigns. The largest single item of expenditure was advertising.[7] The parties enjoyed also the benefit of free but limited television time. Paid political advertising on television is not allowed: each party is allocated a set number of 10-minute party political broadcasts that are transmitted on all television channels. The allocation of the number of broadcasts to the parties is a somewhat contentious one. The broadcasts themselves are often regarded by voters as the least appetizing part of election campaigns.[8]

    The basis of the parties' appeal to the country is the election manifestos that they issue. In recent elections these have become increasingly lengthy and specific documents, detailing the intended policies and measures to be pursued by a party if returned to office. They constitute a topic of some controversy. It has been argued that very few electors actually read them and that many of the commitments made do not enjoy widespread support among voters, even among those voting for the parties that issued them.[9] They are also viewed by some observers as hostages for the future, parties in office being perceived as often doing the reverse of what was promised in their manifestos.[10] In practice, they constitute something of a guide to interested bodies and provide a framework for the main items of legislation introduced by an incoming government in the first session or two of a new Parliament: most manifesto promises are usually implemented.[11] A more relevant criticism is that manifesto promises may not address themselves to the country's real problems. Some would argue that, by virtue of the manner of their compilation and their utilization as a means furthering the adversary relationship between the parties, manifestos add to those problems rather than offering solutions.[12]

Candidates

Any citizen aged 21 years or over is eligible to be a candidate for election to the House of Commons. There are certain limited exceptions. Precluded from serving in the House of Commons are those who are disqualified from voting, as well as policemen, civil servants, judges, members of the boards of nationalized industries, undischarged bankrupts, members of the armed services, and clergy of the Churches of England, Scotland, Ireland, and the Roman Catholic Church. The exclusion of public servants has an acceptable rationale to reinforce it; they are free to resign their positions should they wish to stand for election. The exclusion of certain clergy is less easy to justify (a relic of the time when religious disputes were at the heart of national affairs), as is the exclusion of 18- to 20-year-olds: when the voting age was lowered in 1969, the age of eligibility for candidature was not.[13] To

TABLE 5.2. GENERAL ELECTION RESULTS, 1945–1987

General Election (Winning party in capital letters)	Votes Cast[a]	Seats Won[a]
July 1945		
LABOUR	11,995,152 (47.8%)	393 (61.4%)
Conservative	9,988,306 (39.8%)	213 (33.3%)
Liberal	2,248,226 (9.0%)	12 (1.9%)
Others	854,294 (2.8%)	22 (3.4%)
Turnout: 72.7%	25,085,978 (99.4%)	640 (100.0%)
February 1950		
LABOUR	13,266,592 (46.1%)	315 (50.4%)
Conservative	12,502,567 (43.5%)	298 (47.7%)
Liberal	2,621,548 (9.1%)	9 (1.4%)
Others	381,964 (1.3%)	3 (0.5%)
Turnout: 84.0%	28,772,671 (100.0%)	625 (100.0%)
October 1951		
CONSERVATIVE	13,717,538 (48.0%)	321 (51.4%)
Labour	13,948,605 (48.8%)	295 (47.2%)
Liberal	730,556 (2.5%)	6 (1.0%)
Others	198,969 (0.7%)	3 (0.5%)
Turnout: 82.5%	28,595,668 (100.0%)	625 (100.1%)
May 1955		
CONSERVATIVE	13,286,569 (49.7%)	344 (54.6%)
Labour	12,404,970 (46.4%)	277 (44.0%)
Liberal	722,405 (2.7%)	6 (0.9%)
Others	346,554 (1.2%)	3 (0.5%)
Turnout: 76.7%	26,760,498 (100.0%)	630 (100.0%)
October 1959		
CONSERVATIVE	13,749,830 (49.4%)	365 (57.9%)
Labour	12,215,538 (43.8%)	258 (40.9%)
Liberal	1,638,571 (5.9%)	6 (0.9%)
Others	142,670 (0.8%)	1 (0.2%)
Turnout: 78.8%	27,746,609 (99.9%)	630 (99.9%)
October 1964		
LABOUR	12,205,814 (44.1%)	317 (50.3%)
Conservative	12,001,396 (43.4%)	304 (48.2%)
Liberal	3,092,878 (11.2%)	9 (1.4%)
Others	347,905 (1.3%)	0 (0.0%)
Turnout: 77.1%	27,647,993 (100.0%)	630 (99.9%)
March 1966		
LABOUR	13,064,951 (47.9%)	363 (57.6%)
Conservaive	11,418,433 (41.9%)	253 (40.2%)
Liberal	2,327,533 (8.5%)	12 (1.9%)
Others	422,226 (1.2%)	2 (0.3%)
Turnout: 75.8%	27,233,143 (99.5%)	630 (100.0%)

TABLE 5.2. (CONTINUED)

General Election (Winning party in capital letters)	Votes Cast[a]		Seats Won[b]	
June 1970				
CONSERVATIVE	13,145,123	(46.4%)	330	(52.4%)
Labour	12,179,341	(43.0%)	287	(45.6%)
Liberal	2,117,035	(7.5%)	6	(0.9%)
Others	903,299	(3.2%)	7	(1.1%)
Turnout: 72.0%	28,344,798	(100.1%)	630	(100.0%)
February 1974				
LABOUR				
Conservative	11,639,243	(37.1%)	301	(47.4%)
Liberal	11,868,906	(37.9%)	297	(46.8%)
Others (Great Britain)	6,063,470	(19.3%)	14	(2.2%)
Others (Northern Ireland)[b]	1,044,061	(3.4%)	11	(1.7%)
Turnout: 78.7%	717,986	(2.3%)	12	(1.9%)
	31,333,666	(100.0%)	635	(100.0%)
October 1974				
LABOUR	11,457,079	(39.2%)	319	(50.2%)
Conservative	10,464,817	(35.8%)	277	(43.6%)
Liberal	5,346,754	(18.3%)	13	(2.0%)
Scottish National Party	839,617	(2.9%)	11	(1.7%)
Plaid Cymru	166,321	(0.6%)	3	(0.5%)
Others (Great Britain)	212,496	(0.8%)	0	(0.0%)
Others (Northern Ireland)	702,094	(2.4%)	12	(1.9%)
Turnout: 72.8%	29,189,178	(100.0%)	635	(99.9%)
May 1979				
CONSERVATIVE	13,697,690	(43.9%)	339	(53.4%)
Labour	11,532,148	(36.9%)	269	(42.4%)
Liberal	4,313,811	(13.8%)	11	(1.7%)
Scottish National Party	504,259	(1.6%)	2	(0.3%)
Plaid Cymru	132,544	(0.4%)	2	(0.3%)
Others (Great Britain)	343,674	(1.2%)	0	(0.0%)
Others (Northern Ireland)	695,889	(2.2%)	12	(1.9%)
Turnout: 76.0%	31,184,015	(100.0%)	635	(100.0%)
June 1983				
CONSERVATIVE	13,012,602	(42.4%)	397	(61.1%)
Labour	8,457,124	(27.6%)	209	(32.1%)
SDP/Liberal Alliance	7,780,577	(25.4%)	23	(3.5%)
Scottish National Party	331,975	(1.1%)	2	(0.3%)
Plaid Cymru	125,309	(0.4%)	2	(0.3%)
Others (Great Britain)	198,834	(0.6%)	0	(0.0%)
Others (Northern Ireland)	764,474	(2.5%)	17	(2.6%)
Turnout: 72.7%	30,670,895	(100.0%)	650	(99.9%)

TABLE 5.2. (CONTINUED)

General Election (Winning party in capital letters)	Votes Cast[a]	Seats Won[b]
June 1987		
CONSERVATIVE	13,760,525 (42.3%)	376 (57.8%)
Labour	10,029,944 (30.8%)	292 (35.2%)
SDP/Liberal Alliance	7,341,152 (22.6%)	22 (3.4%)
Scottish National Party	416,873 (1.3%)	3 (0.5%)
Plaid Cymru	123,589 (0.4%)	3 (0.5%)
Others (Great Britain)	127,329 (0.4%)	0 (0.0%)
Others (Northern Ireland)	730,152 (2.2%)	17 (2.6%)
Turnout: 75.3%	32,529,564 (100.0%)	650 (100.0%)

Speaker seeking reelection included with original party.
[a] Figures do not always add up to 100% because of rounding.
[b] Prior to 1974, Ulster Unionists were affiliated with the Conservative party. They thereafter sat as a separate parliamentary party.

be a candidate one has to obtain the signature of ten electors in the constituency and submit a deposit of £500 ($825), returnable in the event of receiving 5% of the votes cast. (From 1918 to 1985 the deposit was £150, returnable in the event of receiving one-eighth of the votes cast.) Unlike in the United States, there are no residence requirements: hence, parties enjoy a wider range of choice in the selection of candidates.

In practice, candidates are party candidates. As a result of a change in the law in 1969, this fact is now more formally recognized: candidates are permitted to include their party designation on the ballot paper. It is generally assumed that an individual candidate has little influence on voting behavior. Party is the decisive factor, though the candidate can have some impact. In recent general elections there have been examples of locally popular candidates holding their marginal seats against the national swing (even in some instances increasing their majorities in the 1987 election), and recent research has suggested that the "personal vote" achieved by candidates may be higher than was previously assumed.[14] Such personal votes can make a difference in some marginal seats, but the instances are limited. Party remains the primary and almost exclusive influence. Since 1950, only four MPs have been elected in Britain (excluding Northern Ireland) without the support of a major party, and those four were all incumbent party members who had broken with their parties.

Virtually all constituencies, with the exception of the seats in Northern Ireland, are contested by Conservative and Labour candidates. In the 1970s there was an increase in the number of Liberal candidates, and in the general elections of 1983 and 1987 the Liberal/Social Democratic Alliance fielded candidates in all 633 seats in Britain. The Conservative, Labour, and (since merged) Liberal and Social Democratic parties are the only parties to each obtain several million votes in general elections (see Table 5.2). They are also the only ones to be successful in recent years in winning seats in England.

In Scotland there is the challenge of the Scottish National Party (the SNP), which grew especially in the first half of the 1970s. In February 1974 it won 7 seats, the number rising to 11 seats in the October election of the same year. Though it remained an electoral force in Scotland, its representation in the 1980s was much reduced, with the return of only 2 MPs in 1979 and 1983 and 3 in 1987; in 1988 it added another member when the party won another seat—Glasgow Govan—in a by-election. The activity and electoral support of the SNP make the electoral competition in Scotland a four-party one, each party enjoying parliamentary representation (see Map 5.1). In Wales there is Plaid Cymru (the Party of Wales), which since 1974 has held two (in 1979 and 1983) or three (in 1974 and 1987) of the 38 seats in the principality. In Northern Ireland the dominant force is that of the Ulster Unionists, though it is divided now into different parties: in 1987, Unionists of different hues, committed to the union with Britain, won 13 of the 17 seats in the province. Of the remaining 4 seats, 3 were won by candidates of the Social Democratic and Labour party (SDLP) and one by a Sinn Fein candidate (Gerry Adams in Belfast West), who refused to take his seat in the House of Commons. Though the House of Commons is dominated by the two major parties, who held 604 of the 650 seats in 1987, the presence of members representing various minority parties brings to eleven the total number of parties actually represented in the House.

Other parties, or fringe groups, also ostensibly are keen to be represented in the House of Commons. The 1970s and early 1980s witnessed a growth in the number of candidates contesting seats. The 1951 general election was fought by 1,376 candidates, that of 1983 by 2,579, an average of four per seat. It was in order to deter nonserious candidates that the deposit for candidature was raised to £500 in 1985, but the deterrent effect was modest. Though the right-wing National Front (which had fielded 303 candidates in 1979) gave the increased deposit as the reason why it did not contest any seats in 1987, the number of candidates in 1987 was not much less than in 1983: a total of 2,325. The Communists had 18 candidates; the Red Front, 12; the Workers Revolutionary party, 10; and the "Loony Official Monster Raving party," 5. (The Workers party and the Alliance party of Northern Ireland also contested most of the seats in Northern Ireland.) There were also a host of candidates with individually tailored labels, including Fancy Dress party, Lets Have Another Party party, Blancmange Thrower, Christian Socialist Opposing Secret Masonic Government, Bread Creek Road Fresh Bread party, and—the most esoteric combination of name and label—the Gremloids, represented by a candidate who had taken the name of "Lord Buckethead." With one exception, all lost their deposits: the exception was the candidate of the Orkney and Shetland Movement in Orkney and Shetland, who secured 14.5% of the vote.

Candidate Selection

The candidates of the main parties are selected locally, though the national party in each case retains some veto power. In Britain, unlike in the United States, there are no primary elections and the selection of a candidate is in practice usually in the hands of a small group of party activists. Given that most seats are (increasingly) safe seats for one party or another, this selection is usually tantamount to election. Within the Conservative party, aspiring candidates have to be on a candidates list maintained by the party's national headquarters. (A local party may choose someone not on the list, but it must obtain approval from the national party for its choice.) A local Conservative association seeking a candidate will invite applicants, and in a safe Conservative seat several hundred aspiring candidates can be expected to put their names forward. The association will then appoint a selection committee, usually comprising representatives from its different branches and associated groups such as the Young Conservatives. This committee will sift through the applications and then recommend three or more names to the executive council, the main decision-making body of the association. The council may then recommend one name for approval to a general meeting of the association, or it may put forward more than one name and leave it to the general meeting to decide.

The research of both Austin Ranney and Michael Rush found that, despite the political importance of choosing a candidate, the political views of applicants are not important considerations in the selection process.[15] Selection committees have tended to be influenced by an applicant's knowledge of the constituency, his or her stature and delivery of speech, and whether there are the makings of a good "constituency member" (one who will represent diligently the interests of constituents) or, in some cases, of a national figure. On occasions, more esoteric considerations may apply, as I can testify, having served on a selection committee. "Can't we interview him? He has a nice name" was one comment made during the selection deliberations. (The response: a polite "no.") Other influences can include, in some areas, religion and quite often age and sex: local parties are reluctant to adopt women candidates (the folklore being that women voters dislike voting for them) and anyone under 30 or over 50 years of age. There is also a tendency to prefer married men (single men over 30 are considered somewhat suspect), and wives are often asked to appear before selection committees. Because wives are looked on as surrogates for their husbands while the latter are at Westminster, their

attitudes to constituency work and their appearance are considered important. In the selection I was involved in, one prominent candidate—a
nationally known figure—suffered from the poor impression his wife gave
to some of the selectors. Arrogant or pretentious wives can sometimes kill
the political ambitions of their husbands.

Although the Labour candidates selected are increasingly similar in
background to Conservative candidates, the selection procedure in the
Labour party is not quite the same. A local Labour party will seek a
candidate by inviting nominations. Nominations may be made by local
ward committees, party groups such as the women's section, and affiliated
organizations, principally trade unions. (An aspiring candidate can
approach such groups to solicit a nomination.) Once nominations are
received, the executive committee, responsible for the day-to-day running
of the party, will draw up a short list of candidates for interview. The final
choice is made by the governing body, the General Management Committee, comprising representatives from the different ward committees and
affiliated organizations. The candidate then requires the endorsement of
the party's National Executive Committee.

In 1980 the Labour party conference approved the principle of mandatory reselection of sitting Labour MPs. What this meant was that sitting
MPs should no longer be reselected automatically by local parties just
before a general election was held. Instead, a full selection procedure was
to be gone through during the lifetime of a Parliament, thus allowing other
aspiring candidates to be considered. It was a contentious issue and was
generally seen as an attempt by the party's left wing to try to remove some
Labour members of whom they disapproved. In practice, the number of
members denied reselection has been small (only eight by the time the 1983
election was called and six by the time of the 1987 election), but the issue
serves to highlight the more overt emphasis placed by Labour activists on a
candidate's political stance than is the case on the Conservative side. In the
Conservative party, there is no procedure for mandatory reselection,
though on rare occasions MPs (for reasons of age, laziness, unpopularity,
or personal scandal) have been replaced—against their wishes—by new
candidates.

The principle of local selection is also a feature of the other national
parties in Britain with parliamentary representation—the Social and Liberal Democratic party (SLD) and the Social Democratic party (SDP).
During the two general elections of 1983 and 1987, when the then Liberal
and SDP parties had an alliance, national bargaining was necessary in
order to determine which party was to contest what seat, but generally the
practice has been to approve whoever has been selected by the local party.
For third parties, recruiting candidates to contest a large number of seats
has often proven a problem, hence a traditional willingness by the national

leadership to accept whomever the local party has managed to recruit.

The candidates selected by the major parties tend on the whole to be middle-class, middle-aged, male, and white. Female and nonwhite candidates are exceptional, but not as exceptional as in the past. (In the 1987 general election Labour had 92 female candidates, the Conservatives had 46; a total of 41 female MPs were elected—a record number. Four black MPs, including one woman, were also elected.) The successful candidates more than the unsuccessful ones tend to be middle-aged, university educated (and, in the case of most Conservative MPs, public school educated), and drawn from the ranks of business and the professions (see Chapter 11). In postwar years there has been a tendency for MPs to be even more middle-class than previously.[16] Past years, according to some observers, have witnessed the emergence of a more professional member of Parliament.

Elections

In each of the 650 single-member constituencies, the method of election employed is the plurality or "first-past-the-post" method. What this means is that the candidate receiving more votes than any other candidate is declared elected. An absolute majority is not required. It is the same method as that employed in the Senate and House elections in the United States. As the example of Brecon and Radnor in Table 5.3 shows, it is possible for a candidate to win election with fewer than 40% of the votes cast. In some instances, the proportion has been even smaller than in Brecon.

In practice, most seats are considered to be safe for one or the other of the two main parties—that is, the winning candidate has been returned with a majority that represents 10% or more of the votes cast. In the safest seats, the majority may constitute as much as 40% or 50% of the votes cast, and in exceptional cases even more; the result in the Rhondda constituency in 1987 (Table 5.3) is a good instance of one of the exceptional cases. Largely for demographic reasons and some change in economic activity, the number of safe seats has increased in recent years: Conservative and Labour support has become more concentrated. Urban areas, especially in the north, have become more strongly Labour, rural areas more strongly Conservative. In 1955 the number of seats held by Conservative or Labour candidates with majorities that were less than 10% of the total poll was 172; in 1987 the number was 80.[17] It is in these marginal seats that general elections are effectively fought. Their small number in the 1980s posed a particular problem for the Labour party. For the party to win an overall majority of seats it had—and, following the 1987 general election, has—to win not only the marginal seats (in some of which it came in third place)

TABLE 5.3. SELECTED CONSTITUENCY RESULTS, 1987

Rhondda

Electorate: 60,931
A. Rogers (Labour)	35,015 (73.4%)
G. R. Davies (Plaid Cymru)	4,261 (8.9%)
J. R. York Williams (SDP/Alliance)	3,930 (8.2%)
S. H. Reid (Conservative)	3,611 (7.6%)
A. True (Communist)	869 (1.8%)
Labour majority	30,686 (64.5%)

Total vote: 47,686
Turnout: 78.3%

In the heart of the Welsh mining community, an area of traditional Labour strength and Conservative weakness, Rhondda is the safest Labour seat in Britain.

Huntingdon

Electorate: 86,186
J. Major (Conservative)	40,530 (63.6%)
A. J. Nicholson (SDP/Alliance)	13,486 (21.1%)
D. M. Brown (Lab)	8,883 (13.9%)
B. Lavin (Green)	874 (1.4%)
Conservative majority	27,044 (42.4%)

Total vote: 63,773
Turnout: 74.0%

Huntingdon, in the east of England, produced the largest Conservative majority in the 1987 election. The seat is held by John Major, first elected in 1979 and Chancellor of the Exchequer since October 1989.

Brecon and Radnor

Electorate: 49,394
R. A. L. Livsey (Liberal/Alliance)	14,509 (34.8%)
J. P. Evans (Conservative)	14,453 (34.7%)
F. R. Willey (Labour)	12,180 (29.2%)
J. H. Davies (Plaid Cymru)	535 (1.3%)
Liberal–Alliance majority	56 (0.1%)

Total vote: 41,677
Turnout: 84.4%

A former Conservative seat, Brecon and Radnor was won by Liberal/Alliance candidate Richard Livsey in a 1985 by-election; he retained the seat in 1987 with the smallest majority in the election. (The Labour member in the seat of Mansfield had an identical majority.) The smallest majority in the 1983 general election was 7 in Leicester South.

but also a number of "safe" Conservative seats. The electoral arithmetic suggests that it may take more than one election in the 1990s for it to gain an overall majority of seats.

The results from the 650 constituencies, as was already mentioned, determine which party will form the government. In all but one of the general elections since (and including) 1945, one party has won an absolute majority of the seats and the leader of that party has formed a government. The Labour party has achieved an overall majority in five elections, on three occasions by slim margins (with one-figure majorities). The Labour party formed the government following the February 1974 election, in which it won more seats than any other party but did not obtain an overall majority (see Table 5.4). The Conservatives have won overall majorities by clear margins in seven elections since 1945, including the most recent election.

VOTING BEHAVIOR

Traditional Voting Patterns

Britain has often been portrayed as being the very model of a stable two-party system.[18] This perception derives in particular from characteristics of electoral behavior in the 1950s and 1960s. Three characteristics of elections in this period are of particular relevance:

1. There was a high turnout of electors.
2. Of those who voted, virtually all voted for either the Conservative or Labour party.
3. The most significant predictor of party voting was class.

TABLE 5.4. PARLIAMENTARY MAJORITIES, 1945–1987

Parliament	Party Returned to Office	Overall Majority[a]
1945–1950	Labour	146
1950–1951	Labour	5
1951–1955	Conservative	17
1955–1959	Conservative	60
1959–1964	Conservative	100
1964–1966	Labour	4
1966–1970	Labour	98
1970–1974	Conservative	30
1974	Labour	−33
1974–1979	Labour	3
1979–1983	Conservative	43
1983–1987	Conservative	144
1987–	Conservative	101

[a] Overall majority following general election. The Speaker is included in the party of which he was previously a member. A negative number indicates that a minority government was returned to office.

The first two generalizations are borne out by the data in Table 5.2. In every general election held from 1950 to 1966 inclusively, more than three-quarters of those on the electoral register turned out to vote and, of those who did so, 87% or more voted for either the Conservative or Labour candidates. In the 1950 election, turnout reached 84%. In the election of the following year, almost 97% of those who voted cast their ballots for one or other of the two main parties.

The third generalization is drawn from survey data, which demonstrate the close relationship of class and party in this period. In the general elections held in the 1950s, 70% or more of middle-class voters cast their votes for the Conservative party. In the 1960s, 60% or more of working-class voters cast their votes for the Labour party.[19] Party support was most marked at the two extremes of the social scale. In 1951, 90% of the upper middle class voted Conservative. In 1966, 72% of the "very poor" voted Labour.[20] Class was not an exclusive predictor of voting behavior, nor was the relationship between class and party symmetrical: the middle class was more Conservative than the working class was Labour. One-third of working-class voters regularly voted Conservative. Nonetheless, class remained the most important predictor of how an elector might vote—so much so that one writer, Peter Pulzer, was to declare in 1967 that "class is the basis of British party politics: all else is embellishment and detail."[21]

The 1970s and 1980s provided a somewhat different picture. Turnout was more variable: in three of the six general elections held between 1970 and 1987 inclusively it dropped below 73%. After 1970 the percentage of voters casting ballots for the Conservative or Labour parties reached 80% in only one election (1979); in the remaining four elections—February 1974, October 1974, 1983, and 1987—the average was 73.3% (Table 5.5). This is approximately 20% lower than the average achieved in the four elections in the 1950s. The year 1983 marked the low point in terms of turnout and two-party voting.

TABLE 5.5. TURNOUT AND TWO-PARTY VOTING, 1959–1987

General Election	Percentage Turnout	Of Those Voting, Percentage Voting Conservative or Labour
1959	78.8	93.2
1964	77.1	87.5
1966	75.8	89.8
1970	72.0	89.4
1974 (Feb.)	78.7	75.0
1974 (Oct.)	72.8	75.0
1979	76.0	80.8
1983	72.7	70.0
1987	75.3	73.0

The class–party nexus also began to wane. The Conservative and Labour parties' hold on their "natural" class support declined. The relative decline in this support is borne out by survey data from the general elections of 1983 and 1987 (Table 5.6). Support for the SDP/Liberal Alliance in both elections was drawn fairly evenly from different social classes. The Labour Party failed to achieve even half of the working-class votes. In 1983, the gap between its share of the manual and nonmanual votes was only 21%, compared with 40% in 1959.[22] The Conservatives made no significant inroads among their traditional class supporters, though attracting the support in both elections of almost one in three trade unionists. Although social class continues to structure party choice, it is no longer as reliable a predictor as it was in the 1950s and 1960s.

Also of declining significance have been the variables of gender, religion and age. Traditionally, women have been somewhat more likely than men to vote Conservative. In most postwar elections, more men have voted Labour than have voted Conservative whereas more women have voted Conservative than have voted Labour. However, the bias was a slight one. According to the Gallup Poll, it disappeared in 1983, the Conservatives drawing more support from men than women (46% to 43%).[23] According to Market and Opinion Research International (MORI) data, the bias disappeared in 1987, when precisely the same percentage of men voted Conservative—as well as Labour and Alliance— as did women (see Table 5.7). Gender has been of marginal utility in predicting voting behavior; today it would appear that even that marginality has dwindled to none at all.

Religion has also declined in importance. It was significant in the nineteenth century but declined rapidly in the twentieth, as class became more important. Butler and Stokes found the relationship between religion and party of declining relevance with each generation. However, in some areas where religious loyalties remain strong, such loyalties can still alter the pattern of class voting. An obvious example is Northern Ireland (see Chapter 9), though mainland examples can be found in certain cities,

TABLE 5.6. VOTE BY SOCIAL CLASS, 1987

Party	Professional and Managerial (AB) %	Office and Clerical (C1) %	Skilled Manual (C2) %	Semiskilled, Unskilled, Residual (DE) %
Conservative	57 (60)[a]	51 (51)	40 (40)	30 (33)
Labour	14 (10)	21 (20)	36 (32)	48 (41)
Lib/SDP Alliance	26 (28)	26 (27)	22 (26)	20 (24)

[a]1983 percentages in parentheses. *(Source: MORI.)*

TABLE 5.7. PARTY SUPPORT BY GENDER, 1974–1987

	General Elections							
	October 1974		1979		1983		1987	
	Men	*Women*	*Men*	*Women*	*Men*	*Women*	*Men*	*Women*
Conservative	32%	39%	43%	47%	42%	46%	43%	43%
Labour	43%	38%	40%	35%	31%	26%	32%	32%
Liberal	18%	20%	13%	15%	–	–	–	–
Liberal/SDP	–	–	–	–	25%	27%	23%	23%

Source: MORI.

notably Glasgow. In such cities there is a sizable Irish Catholic vote, and this swells the Labour vote in elections.[24] Elsewhere, the impact of religion is small, though those who are not members of the Church of England are less likely than others in their class to support the Conservatives.[25] The marginality of religion in terms of electoral behavior is reflected in the fact that it did not figure in analyses of the 1983 and 1987 general elections.

Age has a greater relevance, but it is still limited. The older the elector, the greater the likelihood of voting Conservative (Table 5.8). Among those aged 55 or over who voted in the 1987 election, the Conservatives enjoyed a 15-point lead over Labour; among those aged 18 to 24, Labour enjoyed a lead of 3 points. In 1983 the Conservatives achieved a far better result among first-time voters, achieving a 9-point lead over Labour among the 18- to 24-year-olds. Those voting for the first time in 1987 gave a plurality of their votes to Labour. It is possible that this shift reflects a generational cohort change; Butler and Stokes found in their survey that it is not age as such that influences voting behavior but rather the period at which one becomes politically aware. Those voting for the first time in 1983 are likely to have been able to recall the period of Labour government and the 'Winter of Discontent' of 1978–1979, the latter having a particularly negative impact on Labour support. In 1987 many first-time

TABLE 5.8. PARTY SUPPORT BY AGE, 1987

	Age				
Party	18–24 %	25–34 %	35–54 %	55+ %	Pensioners %
Conservative	37 (42)[a]	39 (40)	45 (44)	46 (47)	47 (51)
Labour	40 (33)	33 (29)	29 (27)	31 (27)	31 (25)
Lib/SDP Alliance	21 (32)	25 (29)	24 (27)	21 (24)	21 (23)

[a] 1983 percentages in parentheses. *(Source: MORI.)*

voters would have had no salient political perceptions other than those of Conservative government and might thus have been more willing to contemplate change. Even so, the differences are not great and as a predictor of voting behavior, the generational cohort thesis is of little value.[26]

Class, then, is of declining relevance as a predictor of voting behavior and it has not been displaced by the other variables we have identified. What then, if any, are the variables that explain and predict contemporary voting behavior?

Explanation of Current Voting Behavior

The analysis of electoral behavior has been a significant growth industry in British social science. Butler and Stokes' pioneering study dominated in the 1970s. Since then there have been several, often competing models of electoral behavior. The most significant have been those that seek to explain voting in terms of (1) class, (2) consumption, (3) location, (4) attitudes, and (5) performance evaluation.

Class.   The class–party nexus, as we have seen, declined in the 1970s and 1980s. Class became a less useful predictor of voting behavior, apparently because of changing social patterns, rendering class itself less relevant, and because of class dealignment, those within a class less likely to vote for the "natural" class party. Class, nonetheless, has not ceased to be relevant. As we have seen, middle-class voters are more likely to vote Conservative than Labour; the more one moves up the social scale the greater propensity to vote Conservative. Those at the bottom of the social scale remain more likely to vote Labour. In the 1987 election, in only one of the three social groupings shown in Table 5.6 is the difference between Conservative and Labour support less than 18%.

Some psephologists have also sought to demonstrate that there has not been a significant decline in class-based voting. They have done so through a redefinition of class. Instead of relying upon the occupation of the heads of households, they have utilized more sophisticated criteria. Heath, Jowell, and Curtice, for example, take into account authority at work and those who are self-employed.[27] The problem with these new variables is that those with the greatest predictive value cover but a small proportion of the population. In the analysis of Heath *et al.*, only about one in three voters are in categories where as many as half of the voters support one party. "No party secures as much as half the vote among the working class, foremen and technicians, or routine non-manual electors. Most of their strata are split three ways, rather than being predominantly for one party."[28] Class thus has its limitations.

Consumption.   One of the most controversial of recent studies has been that advanced by Patrick Dunleavy.[29] He contends that not only has there been a class dealignment but there has also been a realignment: the cleavage based on production has been replaced by one based on consumption. In other words, class voting—derived from one's stance in relation to the means of production—has been replaced by voting based on public and private consumption. Those who rely on services provided by the state (housing, education, health, transport) are most likely to vote Labour; those who rely on services provided by the private sector are most likely to vote Conservative. The greater the degree of private-sector consumption, the greater the likelihood of voting Conservative. Thus, home-owning households with two cars are 4.39 times more likely to vote Conservative than those with no car who rent their homes from the local authority. The problem with this analysis is the same as that with the redefinition of class: the ideal type (home owning, car owning, private education, private health care) is very small. One test of the consumption cleavage thesis found that it did not explain anything that could not be explained through existing approaches.[30]

Location.   Where one lives is an increasingly important influence on voting behavior. The north–south and urban–rural divide is increasingly observable, and various spatial studies have been undertaken to determine its significance. Research by Curtice and Steed found that the spatial divisions began to emerge after 1955. "A North–South cleavage began to emerge in the 1955–59 swing . . . while the urban–rural cleavage became clearly evident in the 1959–64 swing."[31] Conservative support has become more pronounced in the south of England, Labour support has increased in the north and Scotland. In 1979 and the two subsequent elections of 1983 and 1987, Mrs. Thatcher carried her party to victory largely on the votes of the electorate in the southern half of England, below a line drawn from the River Severn to the Wash (see Map 5.1). In the 1979 and 1983 elections, the swing to the Conservatives was highest in the southern half of the country and in the east. The Labour vote declined least in Scotland and in the north, and in the 1987 election there was a substantial swing to Labour in both areas (see Table 5.9). The Conservatives in 1987 saw their parliamentary representation in Scotland more than halved, while in London and the south they actually achieved an increase in their share of the vote, and of parliamentary representation. As Map 5.1 vividly demonstrates, there is now only one part of Britain which, in terms of the competition for seats, can be described clearly as a two-party area.

The urban–rural divide has been equally pronounced. Conservative support in the larger cities has been declining for thirty years. In the 1983 election the party won less than half the number of seats it had won in the

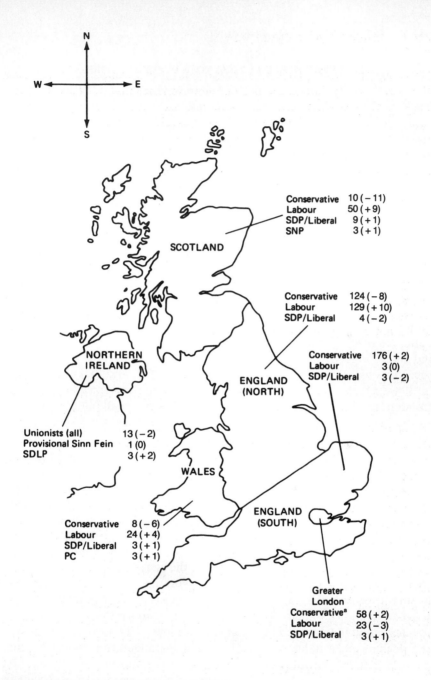

N

W ← → E

S

Conservative 10 (−11)
Labour 50 (+9)
SDP/Liberal 9 (+1)
SNP 3 (+1)

SCOTLAND

Conservative 124 (−8)
Labour 129 (+10)
SDP/Liberal 4 (−2)

Conservative 176 (+2)
Labour 3 (0)
SDP/Liberal 3 (−2)

NORTHERN
IRELAND

ENGLAND
(NORTH)

Unionists (all) 13 (−2)
Provisional Sinn Fein 1 (0)
SDLP 3 (+2)

WALES

Conservative 8 (−6)
Labour 24 (+4)
SDP/Liberal 3 (+1)
PC 3 (+1)

ENGLAND
(SOUTH)

Greater
London
Conservative[a] 58 (+2)
Labour 23 (−3)
SDP/Liberal 3 (+1)

Net gains and losses from 1983 shown in parentheses.
[a] Includes Speaker (Note: South of England comprises Avon, Bedfordshire, Berkshire, Buckinghamshire, Cambridgeshire, Cornwall, Devon, Dorset, Essex, Gloucestershire, Hampshire, Hertfordshire, Isle of Wight, Kent, Norfolk, Northamptonshire, Oxfordshire, Somerset, Suffolk, Surrey, Sussex and Wiltshire.

Map 5.1. General Election Results by Region, 1987

TABLE 5.9. CONSERVATIVE AND LABOUR VOTE BY REGION, 1987

Region	Conservative Vote %	Labour Vote %
London	46.4 (+2.5)[a]	31.4 (+1.6)
Rest of southeast	55.8 (+1.2)	16.8 (+0.8)
Southwest	50.5 (−0.8)	16.2 (+1.5)
East Anglia	52.0 (+1.1)	21.7 (+1.2)
East Midlands	48.6 (+1.4)	30.1 (+2.1)
West Midlands	45.6 (+0.6)	33.3 (+2.1)
Yorkshire and Humberside	37.5 (−1.2)	40.6 (+5.3)
Northwest	38.0 (−2.0)	41.2 (+5.2)
North	32.0 (−2.3)	47.0 (+7.1)
Scotland	24.0 (−4.3)	42.4 (+7.3)
Wales	29.5 (−1.5)	45.0 (+7.5)

[a] Change from 1983 in parentheses. (Source: ITN/Harris exit poll, published in The Independent, June 13, 1987.)

larger cities in 1959, the last election when it was returned with a three-figure majority. The position became more pronounced in 1987. In 1959, in the three large cities of Glasgow, Liverpool, and Manchester, the Conservatives won 15 seats. In 1983 they won only one, and that seat was lost in 1987. Of the ten British cities listed in Map 1.1, excluding Greater London, the Labour party holds a majority of seats in all but two of them. In the 1987 election it won 45 seats in these ten cities: the Conservatives won 14. Within London, Labour's remaining strength is in inner London, where it has the same number of seats as do the Conservatives; Conservative dominance is provided by outer, suburban London.

Various studies have demonstrated the independent influence of location on voting behavior. A middle-class voter in an urban area is more likely to vote Labour than is a middle-class voter in a rural area. A trade unionist in a rural area is more likely to vote Conservative than is a trade unionist in an urban area. Two reasons in particular would appear to explain this. One is essentially long term: the socialization process. Living for a long period of time in an urban, working-class environment, one begins to absorb the values of the local culture. This point we briefly touched upon in Chapter 1. The other reason is more short term and also touched upon in Chapter 1: economic conditions. The north has witnessed the decline of its industrial base, the old manufacturing industries that made it Britain's manufacturing heartland in the late nineteenth and first half of the twentieth century. The decline of the past decade, especially in the cities, with its attendant high levels of unemployment, has reduced support for the Conservative party, while the growth of the service economy in the south, with attendant low levels of unemployment, has increased support for the party. Economic optimism has been greater in the south, and such optimism has been found to strengthen identification with the party in power.[32] Location, clearly, is not an exclusive explanation of voting patterns—the Conservatives, as we have seen (Map 5.1), hold almost as many seats as Labour in the north—but it is increasingly important.

Attitudes. As class was perceived to have declined as a determinant of voting behavior, various analysts asserted the increasing significance of attitudes. The most sophisticated analysis has been that offered by Mark Franklin in *The Decline of Class Voting in Britain*. He charts the decline in class voting since 1964, a consequence, he argues, of changing social structures and a reduced appeal of the Labour party to its traditional class groups. "The decline in the class basis of voting amounts to a weakening of constraints on volatility and self-expression and the consequence was to open the way to choice between parties on the basis of issue preferences."[33] In other words, political attitudes have become more important. Voters develop attitudes through the process of socialization, but these are then reevaluated in the light of changing circumstances. As the constraint of class has declined, so those attitudes have played a greater role in shaping voting choice. The consequence, according to Franklin, is a rise in issue voting. It has also thereby produced electoral volatility. Class voting produced stable voting patterns for a large portion of the voting population, but being influenced by issues that change over time produces less certain behavior. The result, according to Franklin, has been "an era of uncertainty in electoral outcomes unparalleled in fifty years."[34] Though the Conservative party has won three successive general election victories, its success has been relative; it won in 1987 with a lower share of the poll than it had achieved in any previous postwar election victory; as we have seen, there has been a relative decline in support for the two main parties.

Such an analysis offers an explanation—albeit variously challenged and defended[35]—of electoral change and of voting behavior, but it is not one that has a predictive value. There is uncertainty about this analysis in the future. "For the indefinite future," writes Franklin, "we can expect to continue living in interesting political times."[36]

Performance Evaluation. Class, however important as a variable in shaping voting behavior, has never been an exclusive influence. If it were, elections would have demonstrated a more consistent outcome. Other variables have served to make the essential difference between success and failure in a general election. Various studies have served to reinforce the accepted wisdom that what has made the difference has been the evaluation of parties' performance in office. One of the most recent sophisticated analyses has been that of Paul Whiteley. According to his analysis, retrospective evaluation (of how parties have performed in office) and prospective evaluations (of how parties are likely to behave in office) are, along with social attributes, important influences on voting. Utilizing data drawn from the 1979 Election Study, he concluded that subjective judgments were better predictors of voting behavior than objective factors, and that of retrospective and prospective evaluations, the former were much more significant than the latter for explaining support—and the decline in that support—for the Labour party. "This is consistent with the performance hypothesis in which voters are passing judgement on Labour's record in office, rather than on its future policy proposals. The dealignment is explained by the failure of the party to represent adequately the objective and subjective interests of its supporters."[37] Labour had lost office because it had failed to fulfill particular expectations of its previously committed supporters.

The problem with this particular hypothesis is that it presupposes a reasonably high level of political awareness and an intellectual capacity to assess specific performance in office, whereas the largest switch away from the Labour party in an earlier election that it lost, in 1970, came from the least educated of its supporters.[38] Other studies suggest that evaluation is important rather at a general level. Voters are influenced by general economic performance. According to one study, "the electorate does not need to be sophisticated in order to be affected by the 'more good news' or 'more bad news' interpretations which are offered by the mass media when they report on fluctuations in . . . macro-economic indices."[39] Hence, voters are less concerned with the government's fulfillment of specific manifesto commitments than they are with its ability to deliver economic well-being. For much of 1980s the Conservative government has benefited from an upturn in the economy and greater levels of economic optimism. In 1983 the Conservatives won the biggest electoral victory since 1935; the "Falklands factor," following success in the Falklands conflict the previous year, was clearly important, but so too, according to one analysis, was an improvement in economic indicators.[40]

These various explanations of voting behavior serve to provide important insights into that behavior and the changes of the past twenty to thirty years. None by itself provides a sole explanation of voting behavior in Britian. Most serve to explain some degree of that behavior. Rose and McAllister, for example, found that about 80% of voting variance could be explained by five influences, those of pre-adult socialization, socioeconomic interests, political principles, current performance of parties, and party identification.[41] Others, as we have seen, have demonstrated the influence of other variables, including location. Elections in Britain, to use

Rose and McAllister's term, have become more open. As they have, the study of them has become more sophisticated.

THE CURRENT DEBATE

Electoral behavior, then, has been the subject of extensive academic analysis. That behavior occurs within the context of a particular electoral system, and in recent years that system itself has been the subject of public debate. The debate became prominent in the latter half of the 1970s and reemerged toward the end of the 1980s as part of a wider discussion about Britain's constitutional arrangements. The electoral system, according to its critics, is a dysfunctional one, in need of replacement. The view is not one that enjoys universal support.

A Dysfunctional Electoral System?

By the middle of the twentieth century, Britain had developed an electoral system whose basic characteristics were delineated above: single-member constituencies, first-past-the-post election to determine the winner in each, and each adult citizen having the right to cast a vote. That system was both perceived and expected to perform three related functions: through election to the House of Commons it was expected to produce a government;[42] through a purportedly democratic franchise and mode of election, it was expected to confer legitimacy upon the government to govern, subject to the approval of Parliament; and through facilitating a choice between parties propounding specific programs, it was expected to influence public policy, the party in government carrying through the promises embodied in its election manifesto. In the 1950s and 1960s such expectations were assumed to have been met. Governments were returned with overall majorities. There were few complaints about the mode of election. Governments appeared to carry out their promises. The electoral system appeared to form an intrinsic part of a stable polity.

In the 1970s, and especially in the wake of the two general elections of 1974, the extent to which the electoral system was capable of fulfilling such functions became a matter of controversy. In the February 1974 election no party was returned to office with an overall majority of seats. In the election of October of the same year the Labour party achieved an overall majority of only three seats: as a consequence of by-election losses and defections, it lost its majority in April 1976, and by the end of the Parliament it was in a minority by 17 seats. The Conservative party achieved a swing of 5.2% in its favor in the May 1979 election, being returned with a majority of 43 seats. In previous decades a similar swing would have produced a much higher majority. Shifts in the distribution of party support within the country were, according to one important study, likely to increase the likelihood of "hung" Parliaments, no one party being returned with an overall majority.[43] The ability of the electoral system to produce a government in the way previously expected of it was thus called into question. This analysis appeared to lose some of its persuasive appeal in the wake of the 1983 and 1987 elections. The results of those elections, though, gave greater force to another criticism. The system came under attack as being unfair—hence undermining consent by calling into doubt the legitimacy of both the mode of election and the government produced by it—and for facilitating the adversary relationship between the parties, a relationship that significantly influenced public policy but that did so in a manner harmful to the interests of the country. The effects of this adversary relationship on public policy in terms of both continuity and substance was considered to threaten rather than enhance the effectiveness of government.

The accusation that the electoral system is an unfair one is not new. It has been advanced for some time by both the Liberal—now the Social and Liberal Democratic—party and the Electoral Reform Society. It gained ground as a result of the election results of the 1970s and the development of the adversary politics thesis. The first-past-the-post plurality method of election in single-member constituencies, it is argued, does not allow realization of the principle of "one person, one vote, one value." Each adult citizen may have one vote but each vote is not of equal value. The disparity in the size of constituency electorates means that a vote cast in a constituency with a small electorate such as Orkney or Shetland is worth more than one cast in, say, the Isle of Wight. Furthermore, the extensive number of safe seats means that many electors cast "wasted" votes. What is the point of voting Conservative in a constituency such as Rhondda, for example, where the Labour candidate has a majority in excess of 30,000? An elector consistently voting Conservative in the constituency would never contribute toward the election of an MP.

The two most central criticisms, though, have been directed at the aggregate effects of such a method of election. Given the difference in the spread of support between the parties, it is possible for one party to get more votes than its opponent party but receive fewer seats. For example, party A could win two marginal seats by the barest of margins while party B won one seat with an overwhelming majority; the aggregate vote for party B in the three seats could well exceed that of party A, but party A has won twice as many seats. (A similar spread of support among states in the United States presidential elections may result in a president obtaining a majority in the electoral college without obtaining a majority of the popular vote.) On two occasions in postwar elections, such a situation actually occurred. In the 1951 general election, the Conservatives won a majority of seats but the Labour party won more votes (see Table 5.2). In the February 1974 election, the position was reversed, the Conservatives winning more votes nationally than Labour but Labour winning more seats. In terms of forming a government, it is the number of seats that count: the Conservatives formed the government in 1951, the Labour party in 1974.

The other major and related criticism, the one emphasized most often, is that the plurality system of voting works against national third parties. Those who benefit most from such a system are the two largest parties and those with regionally concentrated support. This is as true in the United States as it is in Britain. In presidential elections, a third-party candidate with concentrated support, such as George Wallace in 1968, can carry some states and hence win some electoral college votes. A candidate with support that is broad but not deep, such as John Anderson in 1980, can amass several million votes but carry no state at all. The system favors the Republican and Democratic parties. Similarly in Britain, a party can win several thousand votes in each constituency yet not come out top of the poll in any; in consequence, it amasses a large popular vote but no seats in Parliament. This is almost the position in which the Liberal party found itself in the 1970s (see Table 5.2). In 1979, for example, it won in excess of 4 million votes yet topped the poll in only 11 seats, less than 2% of the total. This phenomenon was even more marked in the case of the SDP/ Liberal Alliance in the 1980s: in both 1983 and 1987 it achieved more than 20% of the votes cast yet won less than 4% of the seats in Parliament. The largest party, by contrast, can top the poll in most constituencies with, say, 40% of the poll, the remaining votes split among the other party candidates, thus achieving a majority of seats without receiving an absolute majority of the votes cast. Indeed, at no election since 1935 has a party obtained more than 50% of the votes cast, yet at only one election since that time has a government been returned without a majority of seats. In the election of October 1974 the Labour party obtained a bare majority of seats for fewer than 40% of the votes cast. Not surprisingly, the Social and Liberal Democratic party, formed by a merger of the Liberal party and SDP in 1988, is in the vanguard in arguing for a reform of the electoral system to eliminate such anomalies. It has been joined by the recently formed Green party. The Conservative and Labour parties, by contrast, retain a preference for the existing system.

The other more recent criticisms of the electoral system have derived from the characterization of the existing political system as an adversary one. The "adversary politics" thesis was developed following the 1974 elections by a number of academics, led by S. E. Finer (see Chapter 3).

The essence of their argument was that the electoral system encouraged a polarized contest between two parties for the winner-take-all spoils of a general election. One party would be returned to office with an overall majority and implement its manifesto program, a program neither known nor supported by most electors and one drawn up on the basis more of party dogma than of a dispassionate and well-informed analysis of Britain's problems. The other party would then win at a subsequent election, enter office, and largely undo the work of its predecessor, implementing instead its own program. Given that the two parties were perceived as representing different poles of the political spectrum, government policy would lurch from being right of the political center under one administration to being left of center under another. The results, in short, were unrepresentative governments—pursuing policies more politically extreme than those favored by the more centrist electorate—and policy discontinuity. Policy discontinuity frustrated industrialists and investors who wished to engage in forward planning: they could not anticipate stability in government programs. Adversary politics and changes in government may make for "exciting politics," but they produced "low-credibility Government strategies, whichever party is in power."[44]

Indeed, the conditions created by the electoral system were seen as being the heart of Britain's current problems. In order to win an election, a party would make extravagant promises, doing so in order to outbid the other party. In office, it would find it could no longer raise the resources to meet those promises. It therefore had to change tack, further adding to confusion in governmental policy making. However, it also had to act in a way that would not jeopardize its chance of winning the next election. Hence it was reluctant to take the unpopular measures deemed by some to be necessary to tackle Britain's long-term problems. Even when, as in the 1980s, a government gained reelection, the adversary relationship militated against its being able to mobilize popular support in order to achieve its goals. The response of the Conservative government, according to critics, has been to strengthen its own power, thus further reducing its capacity to mobilize necessary, and voluntary, support. The result, in short, has been a vicious circle.[45]

The solution to the problem, or at least a partial one, was perceived by these critics as the introduction of a new electoral system, one that introduced a method of proportional representation (PR). Proportional representation, it was argued, would be fairer than the existing electoral system, ensuring that a party received the share of parliamentary seats equivalent to its national vote. Furthermore, given existing voting behavior, it would deprive any one party of an overall majority of seats. Forming a government with an overall parliamentary majority would thus necessitate a coalition. This would likely involve one of the main parties having "to co-operate with a party or parties taking a more central stance," hence leading to greater moderation in policy.[46] Given that such a coalition would enjoy the support of more than 50% of electors and that the turnover of seats under PR is small (Finer estimated that a swing of 1% would result in the loss of only six seats), it would most likely remain in office for the foreseeable future and hence be in a position to ensure a degree of policy continuity. The overall effect of PR would thus be to put an end to the worst features of adversary politics and its unfortunate consequences.

Of the systems of proportional representation, the one favored by Social and Liberal Democrats and the Electoral Reform Society is the single transferable vote (STV) system. This is the method of election currently employed in the Republic of Ireland, in Tasmania, and in Malta and for elections to the Australian Senate. Under STV there are multi-member constituencies, with each elector able to indicate a preference on the ballot paper, putting the number 1 beside the name of the candidate most preferred, 2 against the name of the elector's second choice, and so on. A quota is established by the formula of dividing the number of valid ballots cast by the number of seats, plus one: to the resulting figure, one is added. Thus in a five-member constituency in which 120,000 ballots are cast, the formula would be

$$\frac{120,000}{5 + 1} + 1.$$

Hence the quota (the number of ballots required to elect one member) would be 20.001. Any candidate receiving this number of votes is declared elected. The second preferences of any of the candidate's surplus votes, plus those of the candidate at the bottom of the poll, are then redistributed, and so on until the necessary number of candidates reach the quota.

The other main system that has been advocated is the additional member system, similar to that employed in West Germany. Under this system, single-member constituencies would be retained, with the first-past-the-post method of election retained in each—in other words, the same as at present. However, there would be additional seats allocated to parties on a regional basis, a minimum of 5% of the vote in any area of allocation being necessary to obtain additional seats. Additional seats would go to the parties on the basis of the proportion of votes received in the region. Under a scheme proposed by the Hansard Society for Parliamentary Government, there would be 480 single-member constituencies and 160 seats allocated on a regional basis.[47] Proponents of this system and of STV argue that the effect would be a representative House of Commons, the proportion of seats going to parties being the same as the proportion of the votes won in the election.

Support for a new electoral system has developed since the mid-1970s, encompassing academics and politicians. The Conservative and Labour parties have witnessed the creation of bodies within their own ranks favoring such reform.[48] Various attempts were made in the 1974–1979 Parliament to introduce PR throughout the United Kingdom for elections to the European Parliament and to the proposed assemblies in Scotland and Wales. The attempts failed, but they helped keep the issue of electoral reform on the agenda of political debate. The outcome of the 1983 and 1987 elections added a further spur to the reform movement. Social and Liberal Democratic MPs now regularly introduce bills in the House of Commons to utilize a system of PR in local elections.

Despite this pressure for reform, the existing system retains its supporters. A majority of both the Conservative and Labour parliamentary parties prefer the first-past-the-post method of election. One keen defender is the present prime minister, Mrs. Thatcher. The arguments deployed against the reformers' case are varied. The essential line of argument is that a reformed electoral system could constitute a greater threat to the maintenance of political authority than any defects of the existing system. The STV system, it is argued, could threaten the essential link between an elector and his MP, given that it would necessitate in rural areas constituencies of massive size. Given the reformers' argument that PR would enhance the likelihood of coalition government, consent could be undermined if government were to result from post-election bargaining between parties, or by a small center party holding the balance of power and hence wielding undue influence over government policy, or by the alienation of voters who support a party excluded on a long-term basis from becoming a partner in coalition.[49] Such rebuttals are based on accepting the assumption made by PR advocates about the likely consequences of electoral reform. Some observers have drawn attention to the fact that such assumptions themselves rest on flimsy foundations, however. The reformers argue their case on the assumption that voting behavior experienced under the current mode of election would most likely continue under a new mode: this is, as Geoffrey Alderman has pointed out, a most unlikely hypothesis.[50] Arguments that PR works well in countries such as West Germany are countered by pointing to the experience of Italy, where turnover in governments is rapid and a significant fraction of the population vote for a party that is consistently excluded from government. Given the different political cultures that exist, seeking to anticipate what would happen in Britain on the basis of experience abroad is an undertaking of limited usefulness.

The adversary politics thesis developed by the reformers has also been variously challenged. There are two mutually exclusive arguments deployed against it. One line of argument accepts the notion of an adversary relationship between the parties but considers this a beneficial rather than a harmful process: it offers a clear choice to the electorate and it results in one party with a mandate from the people getting on with the job of governing. If the electorate disapproves of the policies or their outcomes, it has the opportunity to replace the government at the next election. There may be some discontinuity in policy occasioned by governments of different political persuasions pursuing different paths, but that is the price—an acceptable price—one has to pay for the advantages offered by the existing system. Proportional representation, it is feared, would facilitate a blurring of the choice before the electorate and prevent a party from being returned with a mandate clearly approved by the people.

Such a line of argument is pursued especially by the two largest parties. It is in their own interests to do so: each wants to pursue its own policies, which it believes to be in the best interests of the country, without having those policies tempered or abandoned because of the need to enter into alliance with another party. For a brief period of one year, 1977–1978, the Labour government of James Callaghan entered into a pact with the Liberal parliamentary party: in return for voting support in the House of Commons (necessary to maintain its majority), the government modified certain policies of its own and introduced certain measures favored by the Liberals.[51] The experience was not one much enjoyed by the Labour party, certain sections of which were extremely hostile to the arrangement. Both the Conservative and Labour parties appeared to draw the conclusion that it was an experience to be avoided rather than encouraged.

The other argument deployed against the adversary politics thesis calls into doubt the relevance of the notion itself. The rhetoric of adversary politics, it is argued, hides a more consensual substance. In terms of government legislation, empirical research has indicated that a consensual model is indeed more applicable.[52] In this view, parties are seen as being not quite as central to formulation of public policy as both reformers and the politicians themselves believe. The external demands on government are such that it can often act only as arbiter between competing demands and respond, under guidance from civil servants, to international events and trends over which it has no direct influence. The Conservative government of Margaret Thatcher, for example, has been constrained by external events, and its capacity to achieve its goals has been determined largely by an upturn in the international economy after 1982. Whichever party is in power makes some but not a great deal of difference. Elections may help produce the personnel at the apex of government but they tell us little about likely public policy.

The electoral system, in summary, has again become a subject of political debate. In terms of the political system, it can be said to provide the means by which a government is chosen but, despite the results of the 1983 and 1987 general elections, the extent to which it will continue to be capable of providing a government (at least in the way it has previously done) remains under question. It operates on the principle of "one person, one vote," but there is now some dispute as to its legitimacy and that of the government it produces on the grounds that the principle of "one person, one vote, one value" has not been fully realized. And there is debate and notable disagreement about the consequences that elections not only do have but should have for public policy. The debate is very much a current one. It revolves around arguments for and against a reform of the electoral system. Whether Britain will witness electoral reform in the next decade or so rests on the outcome of that debate and, more significantly, the outcome of general elections in the 1990s.

NOTES

1. M. J. C. Vile, *Politics in the USA* (Hutchinson, 1976 ed.), p. 91.
2. See G. Alderman, *British Elections: Myth and Reality* (Batsford, 1978), pp. 9–22.
3. D. Butler, *British General Elections since 1945* (Blackwell, 1989), p. 56.
4. The average expenditure by a Conservative candidate in the 1987 campaign was £4,400 and that by a Labour candidate £3,900. D. Butler and D. Kavanagh, *The British General Election of 1987* (Macmillan, 1988), p. 236.
5. M. Pinto-Duschinsky, *British Political Finance 1830–1980* (American Enterprise Institute, 1981), p. 249.
6. See A. P. Hill, "The Effect of Party Organisation: Election Expenses and the 1970 Election," *Political Studies*, 22, 1974, pp. 215–17.
7. The Conservatives are believed to have spent £3.6 million on press advertising in 1987. Butler, *British General Elections since 1945*, p. 105.
8. See M. Pilsworth, "Balanced Broadcasting," in D. Butler and D. Kavanagh, *The British General Election of 1979* (Macmillan, 1980), p. 229.
9. See S. E. Finer, *The Changing British Party System, 1945–79* (American Enterprise Institute, 1980), pp. 125–26.
10. Alderman, pp. 25–27.
11. See D. Kavanagh, "The Politics of Manifestos," *Parliamentary Affairs*, 34 (1), 1981, pp. 13–14.
12. For a thorough discussion, see Kavanagh, "The Politics of Manifestos," pp. 7–27.
13. See P. Norton, "The Qualifying Age for Candidature in British Elections," *Public Law*, 1980, pp. 55–73.
14. B. Cain, J. Ferejohn, and M. Fiorina, *The Personal Vote* (Harvard University Press, 1987); P. Norton and D. M. Wood, "Constituency Service by Members

of Parliament: Does It Contribute to a Personal Vote?" *Parliamentary Affairs*, 43 (2), pp. 196–208, 1990.

15. M. Rush, *The Selection of Parliamentary Candidates* (Nelson, 1969); A. Ranney, *Pathways to Parliament* (Macmillan, 1965).
16. C. Mellors, *The British MP* (Saxon House, 1978).
17. Butler, *British General Elections since 1945*, p. 51.
18. See G. Sartori, *Parties and Party Systems: A Framework for Analysis* (Cambridge University Press, 1976), pp. 185–89.
19. B. Särlvik and I. Crewe, *Decade of Dealignment* (Cambridge University Press, 1983), p. 87.
20. The Gallup Poll, "Voting Behaviour in Britain, 1945–74," in R. Rose (ed.), *Studies in British Politics*, 3rd ed. (Macmillan, 1976), p. 206.
21. P. Pulzer, *Political Representation and Elections in Britain* (Macmillan, 1967), p. 98.
22. I. Crewe, "The Disturbing Truth Behind Labour's Rout," *The Guardian*, June 13, 1983.
23. Ibid.
24. R. Rose, *The Problem of Party Government* (Penguin, 1976), p. 43.
25. Ibid., p. 44.
26. See R. Rose and I. McAllister, *Voters Begin to Choose* (Sage, 1986), pp. 68–69.
27. A. Heath, R. Jowell, and J. Curtice, *How Britain Votes* (Pergamon Press, 1985), pp. 22ff.
28. Rose and McAllister, p. 46.
29. P. Dunleavy, "The Urban Basis of Political Alignment: Social Class, Domestic Property Ownership and State Intervention in Consumption Processes," *British Journal of Political Science*, 9, 1979, pp. 409–44.
30. M. Franklin and E. Page, "A Critique of the Consumption Cleavage Approach in British Voting Studies," *Political Studies*, 32, 1984, pp. 521–36.
31. J. Curtice and M. Steed, "Electoral Choice and the Production of Government," *British Journal of Political Science*, 12, 1982, p. 256.
32. See especially R. J. Johnston, C. J. Pattie, and J. G. Allsop, *A Nation Dividing?* (Longman, 1988), Ch. 6.
33. M. Franklin, *The Decline of Class Voting in Britain* (Oxford University Press, 1985), p. 176.
34. Ibid.
35. Cf. Rose and McAllister, p. 147, and Johnston, Pattie, and Allsop, p. 59.
36. Franklin, p. 176.
37. P. Whiteley, *The Labour Party in Crisis* (Methuen, 1983), p. 106.
38. Franklin, p. 161.
39. D. Sanders, H. Ward, and D. Marsh, "Government Popularity and the Falklands War: A Reassessment," *British Journal of Political Science*, 17, 1987, p. 298.
40. Ibid., pp. 281–313.
41. Rose and McAllister, pp. 128–33.
42. That is, the political apex of the executive formed by ministers. See the

comments of A. King, "What Do Elections Decide?" in H. Penniman (ed.), *Democracy at the Polls* (American Enterprise Institute, 1980), pp. 295–96.

43. J. Curtice and M. Steed, "Electoral Choice and the Production of Government," *British Journal of Political Science*, 12 (2), 1982, pp. 249–98.
44. M. Shanks, *Planning and Politics* (Political and Economic Planning, 1977), p. 92.
45. See the comments of P. Jay, "Englanditis," in R. E. Tyrell, Jr., *The Future that Doesn't Work* (Doubleday, 1977), p. 181. See also S. Brittan, *The Economic Consequences of Democracy* (Temple Smith, 1977).
46. S. E. Finer (ed.), *Adversary Politics and Electoral Reform* (Wigram, 1975), pp. 30–31.
47. *The Report of the Hansard Society Commission on Electoral Reform* (Hansard Society, 1976).
48. See P. Norton, *The Constitution in Flux* (Blackwell, 1982), p. 230.
49. See ibid., p. 240.
50. Alderman, p. 39.
51. See A. Michie and S. Hoggart, *The Pact* (Quartet, 1978).
52. I. Burton and G. Drewry, *Legislation and Public Policy* (Macmillan, 1981); R. Rose, *Do Parties Make a Difference?* 2nd ed. (Macmillan, 1984).

CHAPTER 6

Political Parties
A Two-party or a Multiparty System?

In the United States, political parties serve to provide some measure of choice among candidates at election time. They do little else. American politics remain characterized by faction rather than by party.[1] Consensus on basic values,[2] federalism, and the separation of powers has served to mold political parties that are basically nonprogrammatic and decentralized and that operate within a political system structured in such a way as to favor stalemate or compromise. Political parties are not geared to presenting a coherent program to the electorate. The parties are too decentralized, the elections too tiered, to be conducive to such an approach. Even if parties were so geared, the political structure would militate against carrying a coherent program into effect: a party would need to be cohesive and to capture the White House and would need to achieve the return of a majority of its supporters in both houses as well as overcoming internal procedural constraints within Congress. The occasions when these constraints have been overcome, as during the New Deal era, are notable for their rarity—and their brevity. It has proved impossible to sustain strong party government. In their writings, American political scientists often give little priority to a discussion of the importance of political parties. When parties are mentioned, it is not unusual for their minimalist role to be mentioned. When they are considered as programmatic bodies having an influence on the shaping and implementation of public policy, it is usually in order to lament their absence from that role.[3]

Britain lacks those features that have facilitated a weak party system within the United States. A unitary and parliamentary form of government has favored the development of centralized and cohesive parties geared to offering a programmatic choice to the electors and to carrying out that program once the all-or-nothing spoils of a general election have been gained. The executive dominance of the House of Commons ensures legislative approval of the party program: the doctrine of parliamentary sovereignty puts its implementation beyond the challenge of the courts. It is, in short, the very model of a strong party government. It is a model that for years was much admired. It was admired by many American scholars because of its apparent ability to ensure the realization of social reform.[4] It was contrasted with the brokered politics of the United States.

To stress the differences of the two systems is both important and necessary. However, it runs the risk of obscuring some important similarities. American parties may be weak and British parties strong by comparison, but both the United States and Britain are notable examples of two-party systems. In elections in the United States, electoral contests are dominated by Republicans and Democrats. Elections in Britain have usually been dominated by the Conservative and Labour parties. There are also *some* similarities between the parties themselves. The Republican party in the United States and the Conservative party in Britain are, in broad terms, right-of-center parties that tend to attract support from similar constituencies, notably the middle class. The Democratic party and the British Labour party are left-of-center parties that tend to appeal to working-class voters. (In the 1960s, Labour party leader Harold Wilson was reputed to have wanted to model himself on John Kennedy and his party on the Democratic party.) These are broad generalizations and should not be pursued too far. Nonetheless, they are relevant and it is instructive to note the apparent empathy in the 1980s between a Republican president, Ronald Reagan, and a Conservative prime minister, Mrs. Thatcher. Furthermore, parties in both countries have in recent years witnessed similar but not identical falls in support and partisan identification among electors. The analyses of this decline in support also display similarities. This decline in support and the debate surrounding it I shall explore later.

It is important first to consider the growth and the nature of the two main political parties in Britain. In their origins and growth, they are distinctly British and can be understood only within the context of British history and the political culture.

THE PARTIES IN BRITAIN

The first principle of party, according to Edmund Burke in the eighteenth century, was "to put men who hold their opinions into such a condition as may enable them to carry their common plans into execution." At the time that he was writing, that "condition" meant gaining the confidence of the king. With the widening of the franchise in the nineteenth century, it came instead to depend on the confidence of the electors. As bodies that seek electoral success in order to form the government, political parties may be said to have developed in Britain following the Reform Act of 1832; as bodies seeking that success in order to fulfill a particular program—a stage arguably never reached by American parties—they are more especially the product of the Reform Act of 1867.

The need for electoral support after 1832 and the difficulty of establishing direct personal contact with the enlarged electorate encouraged the development of embryonic political *organization*: political clubs were formed, election funds were established, registration societies—to ensure that supporters were registered to vote—were brought into being, and in some parts of the country (notably Lancashire) constituency associations were formed. Nonetheless, as we have seen (Chapter 3), the differences between pre- and post-1832 days were not as marked as some might have supposed: the aristocracy remained politically eminent, voting was still by open ballot, and corrupt practices were still common. All this was to change as a result of the Reform Act of 1867 and the reforming measures of the next eighteen years. The electorate was now of such a size (2.5 million: see Chapter 3) and of such a nature that highly organized parties became necessary both for facilitating contact and for aggregating the interests of voters through some form of party platform. Bribery and other corrupt practices, as well as the open ballot, were formally done away with by statute, though the size of the electorate alone did much to remove bribery as an effective weapon of influence. Organized corruption, as Richard Crossman observed, was gradually replaced by party organization,[5] and the two main parties of the day, to employ Maurice Duverger's terminology, were developed from cadres into mass-membership parties. The Liberal party created the National Liberal Federation to widen its appeal to the newly enfranchised voter. The Conservative party created the Conservative National Union in 1867 and Conservative Central Office in 1870, the latter to provide professional support to the voluntary wing of the party. Highly organized, mass-membership political parties became a feature of British political life.

In the latter half of the nineteenth century the two dominant parties were the Conservatives and the Liberals.[6] Both adhered to a hierarchical conception of party structure and both had parliamentary parties that predated the creation of the extraparliamentary parties. The voluntary organizations were created primarily to mobilize support for the parliamentary leaders: they were not expected to formulate policies or to give instructions. The conventions of the Constitution also facilitated this form of "top down" leadership within the parties. Although both parties began to appeal to the country on the basis of particular platforms, the notion of "the manifesto" was not well developed. The party leaders were expected to make an appeal to the country and, if elected, were expected to proceed with the task of governing.

Such approaches were to be modified in the twentieth century. One important influence was the development of the Labour party. It was created to achieve the return to Parliament of representatives of the working classes and it adhered to the concept of intraparty democracy. Implementation of the party's election manifesto became the touchstone by which party activists could determine if party leaders were adhering to the party's program. The party's internal norms were not altogether compatible with those of the Constitution. The party favored the election of party leaders, which in government would mean the members of the cabinet, whereas the Constitution conferred such power on the prime minister. Under the leadership of Ramsay MacDonald, the first Labour prime minister, this conflict was resolved largely in favor of the Constitution. Nonetheless, tension between a "top down" form of political leadership, in which the party defers to the guidance given by its leaders, and a "bottom up" form, in which leaders are bound by decisions taken by party members, has been a recurrent feature of Labour party politics. As we shall see, it remains a central feature of the contemporary Labour party.

The Labour party displaced the Liberal party as one of the two main parties in Britain in the 1920s. In 1922 it was recognized as the main Opposition party in Parliament. The interwar years, between 1918 and 1939, were years of Conservative dominance. The years from 1945 to 1970 constituted a period of balance between the Conservative and Labour parties: the Conservatives were in office for thirteen years, the Labour party for twelve years. The years since 1970 have seen a reemergence of Conservative dominance, the Labour party experiencing disarray within its ranks for much of the 1980s, a period of significant third-party challenge. The two parties are similar in that they have developed national organizations and cohesive parliamentary parties with complex infrastructures,[7] and at election time they issue detailed and specific manifestos. Both, not surprisingly, favor the existing party duopoly in British politics. In other respects, as well shall see, the two differ significantly.

The Conservative Party

Although British Conservatism can be traced back several centuries, indeed to Hooker in the sixteenth century, the emergence of a political party with the name *Conservative* took place in the fourth decade of the nineteenth century. The name Conservative was first used by an anonymous writer in 1830, and the term was in common usage by 1832.

The party set up an election fund in 1835.[8] It was the successor to the Tory party, the party of the land-owning gentry, which had largely disintegrated under the leadership of the Duke of Wellington in the 1820s. It inherited both the base of Tory support and the party's central tenets. Foremost among these was a belief in the organic nature of society. Society was seen as a historical product, a thing of slow and natural growth, an organic entity with unity and character. Concomitantly, the party inherited from the philosophy of Edmund Burke a belief in gradual change: society was evolutionary, not static. Change, though, had to be evolutionary, not revolutionary. It had to improve, not destroy. Change had to take place without doing violence to the existing fabric of society. The party was committed to the defense of existing and worthwhile institutions: it stood for the defense of Constitution, Crown, and Church. If there was to be reform it should be to save the Constitution, not to subvert it. It was a corollary of such beliefs that the party adhered to an ordered society, one in which law, order, and authority were upheld. It stood for the defense of property. Private property, as Burke contended, was a bulwark against tyranny: without private property, the over-powerful state could not be resisted. One could identify the party as adhering also to limited but not necessarily weak government. Government was perceived as having but a limited role to play in society, primarily that of defending the realm, but if strong government was on occasion necessary to maintain the King's government, then so be it. In short, then, the party stood basically for the existing order of things but was prepared to admit of the need for occasional change, change not for the sake of change but in order to preserve.

The party's base of support was initially a restricted one. It was essentially a party of the landed interest. It had no national appeal and for the middle years of the century was very much the "out" party in politics. It was transformed into a national party by Benjamin Disraeli. He had to devise an appeal that made the party relevant to the problems of the day. This he did: to the corpus of Conservative beliefs he added adherence to the notion of One Nation—that is, One Nation at Home and One Nation Abroad. Domestically, this meant that the party would not divide the nation in the interests of one class but would look after the interests of all classes. The party would balance social forces and establish common goals. Internationally, it meant the development and maintenance of Empire. This concept identified the party with the achievements of the nation; it provided an inspiring theme to unite in patriotic harmony all Englishmen, if not all Britons. As part of the theme of One Nation, Disraeli was to demonstrate concern for the welfare of the people—much of the social reform legislation of the latter half of the century was Conservative-inspired[9]—while stressing the imperative of maintaining institutions and social stability. Coupled with this national appeal was the development of the party as a mass-membership organization, one that ensured that the party's message reached the new electors. By the time of Disraeli's death in 1881, the Conservative party had laid claim to be a national party, one of responsibility and government. For the last quarter of the century and for much of the twentieth, the party was to dominate British politics.

As the party developed to acquire its national status, so it acquired new support. It obtained the support of a substantial fraction of working-class voters, in large part because industrialists and mill owners—the employers of the workers—were associated with the Liberal party. It acquired defectors from the ranks of the Liberals, notably the Liberal Unionists toward the end of the nineteenth century. The influx of Liberals tended to move it more in the direction of a capitalist party, supporting the making of money by individual enterprise rather than looking down on it as a slightly degrading pursuit. By the twentieth century the Conservative party was cohesive but constituted a coalescence of different strands of thought.

Within British Conservatism, there are two main strands: the "Tory" and the "Whig," each of which may be further subdivided.[10] The Tory strand of thought places emphasis on social discipline, on authority, on continuity, and on ensuring that change does not do violence to the essential fabric of society; it tends to adhere strongly to the Disraelian concept of One Nation. The Whig strain is more concerned with future goals and places emphasis on the creation of wealth and the most efficient form of economic organization. It is thus more concerned with economics, whereas the Tory strain is more concerned with morals. Within the party, there is the potential for tension between continuity and change, between those favoring change in more radical or rapid form and those favoring moderation, and also between the Tory emphasis on social unity and the Whig neoliberal element, which stresses creative tension and competitive struggle. On occasion, such tension has been realized: in the 1840s and again in the first decade of the twentieth century on the issue of tariff reform (the liberal strain within the party favoring free trade, the Tory element favoring the erection of tariff barriers to protect British industry), and in the 1970s and 1980s on the issue of economic policy, to which we shall return shortly. Such occasions, though, are the exceptions rather than the rule. Cohesiveness is a distinguishing feature of the party.

The cohesiveness of the Conservative party may be attributed largely to the fact that, unlike the Labour party, it is a party of tendencies rather than of factions[11]—that is, it lacks permanent factions organized in order to promote a specific set of beliefs. Rather, it comprises a set of differing but not mutually exclusive strands of thought that are not aligned in consistent opposition to one another. On some issues there may be dissent within the party, but the composition of the dissenting body changes from issue to issue, almost like a chemical reaction. One may be a Tory on one issue and something of a Whig on another. The distinction between Whig and Tory is not so clearly and starkly drawn as to permit a permanent divide. Within each Conservative there is a Tory element and a Whig element, though one element may tend to be more dominant at certain times and on certain issues. In consequence, a party member may disagree with the party on one issue but agree with it on other issues. This is in marked contrast to the Labour party, in which there is a factional divide: someone on a particular wing of the party on one issue is likely to be on that wing across the whole gamut of current political issues. There is in essence a mutually exclusive struggle between left and right.

The Conservative party traditionally has been led by leaders drawn more from the Tory than the Whig strain within the party. The postwar leaders up to 1965—Winston Churchill (1940–1955), Sir Anthony Eden (1955–1957), Harold Macmillan (1957–1963), and Sir Alec Douglas-Home (1963–1965)—were men essentially in the Tory paternalist mold, more concerned with social harmony and order than with the intricacies of economic management. In the 1960s the party's fortunes took a turn for the worse. The economy began to falter, and the party suffered a bitter, public battle for the party leadership in 1963 and seemed unable to offer a young and dynamic leadership to match that which the Labour party was providing. Macmillan had married into the family of the Duke of Devonshire and was often photographed on the Scottish moors shooting grouse. Sir Alec Douglas-Home was able to assume the office of prime minister only after renouncing his title as the 14th Earl of Home. (The prime minister, by convention, must sit in the Commons, not the House of Lords.) The party seemed to be out of touch with the tenor of the times, and in 1964 it lost the general election.

In July 1965 Douglas-Home resigned the party leadership. Previously the leader had not been elected but had been allowed to "emerge" following private consultations within the party hierarchy. Following the struggle for the leadership in 1963, rules for the election of the leader were adopted in 1964 and first employed in 1965. The electorate was the parliamentary party and the MPs chose as leader Edward Heath in preference to former Chancellor of the Exchequer Reginald Maudling. Maudling was in the traditional Tory mold, though lacking the aristocratic background of previous leaders. Heath was seen by his supporters as a neoliberal and as capable of challenging the Labour party under the leadership of Harold Wilson. Both Heath and Wilson came from relatively humble origins, they were of similar age, and both stressed the need for economic efficiency.

The first four years of Heath's leadership were inauspicious ones. The party badly lost the general election of 1966, and Heath proved no match for Wilson in parliamentary debates. However, as economic conditions worsened in the late 1960s, the unpopularity of the Labour government increased. In the 1970 general election, Heath dominated the Conservative campaign, pursuing a rigorous schedule and doggedly putting across his message. When the party won the election, the credit for victory was given to Heath, and he dominated the party for the next four years.

In the first two years of government, Heath pursued an essentially neoliberal policy, eschewing a prices-and-incomes policy and preferring the operation of the free market to intervention by government. The aim was to force British industry to be more efficient. This goal provided part of the motivation also for British membership in the European Community, which Heath achieved in 1972 (see Chapter 10). However, the government's economic policy failed to stem the rise in inflation. Unemployment also began to rise. Given these developments, the Heath government in 1972 embarked on a number of policy changes, dubbed "U-turns" by critics. Public money was made available to aid regional development and to assist ailing companies. An attempt was made to reach voluntary agreement with unions and employers on a prices-and-incomes policy. When that failed, a statutory policy was introduced, beginning with a 90-day freeze on pay and prices.[12]

The government's economic policy encountered opposition from the trade unions. The National Union of Mineworkers introduced an overtime ban in pursuit of a pay claim and then announced plans for a national strike. When negotiations with the government broke down, Heath in February 1974 called a general election, ostensibly to be fought on the issue of "Who Governs? The Government or the Miners?" In practice, other issues intervened during the campaign, and despite winning more votes than the Labour party, the Conservatives won fewer seats. Heath sought to arrange an alliance with the small parliamentary Liberal party in order to stay in office. He failed, and Harold Wilson was summoned to Buckingham Palace and asked to form a Labour government.

The loss of the election and his U-turns in office much reduced Heath's popularity within the party. He was heavily criticized by the growing neoliberal wing within the party. A number of Conservatives began to argue for a vigorous neoliberal policy, allowing the forces of a free-market economy to prevail, with government merely providing the conditions in which that economy could flourish. The means of achieving this was through control of the money supply, and the name of American monetarist economist Milton Friedman began to be much quoted. When the Conservatives lost the general election of October 1974, pressure for Heath to resign as party leader built up, and early in 1975 he was persuaded to offer himself for reelection, an event for which there was no precedent. His main challenger in the election was Mrs. Margaret Thatcher, who had served in his government as education minister. She espoused the rhetoric of the neoliberal wing of the party and offered the party a new style of leadership. In the first ballot, she won 130 votes to Mr. Heath's 119. (A third candidate received 16 votes.) Mr. Heath then withdrew from the contest. Under the election rules, a second ballot could be held in which new challengers could come forward. A number did but proved unsuccessful against Mrs. Thatcher's growing support: she received 146 votes and her nearest rival (William Whitelaw) 79 votes. For the first time in its history, the Conservative party had elected a female leader, one who was more clearly identified with the neoliberal wing of the party than any previous leader.

Mrs. Thatcher led the party in Opposition until 1979, when the minority Labour government was defeated on a vote of confidence in the House of Commons. A general election ensued. Labour unpopularity following a period of strikes by public employees helped the Conservatives to victory, and Mrs. Thatcher entered 10 Downing Street as Britain's first female prime minister. Under her leadership, the government pursued a policy of controlling the money supply, reducing direct taxation, and keeping public expenditure within stipulated limits. The government soon encountered difficulties. Techniques for controlling the money supply proved inadequate for the purpose. Attempts to reduce planned public spending generated political opposition from within the party (and, indeed, from some members of the cabinet) as well as from political opponents. Mrs. Thatcher failed to persuade her own government to accept more stringent measures. Subsidies to nationalized industries were continued. Despite maintaining neoliberal rhetoric, the government ceased to pursue a rigorous neoliberal economic policy.

Within two years of entering office, the government was trailing in the opinion polls, bitterly divided internally between those who supported the government's restrictionist economic policy and those who opposed it (known as the "Wets," a term of abuse used by the Prime Minister),[13] and had failed to produce the economic fruits that might produce a change in its fortunes. These conditions were to change in 1982. The government's response to the Argentinian invasion of the Falkland Islands—despatching a naval task force to expel the invaders—restored it to popular favor. Following the successful recapture of the islands, the Conservative lead in the opinion polls held until the 1983 general election, sustained by some change in economic indicators (inflation and interest rates both fell) and by disarray within the Labour party. The Falklands campaign also served to provide a boost to the Prime Minister's popularity: the campaign transposed her from a very poorly rated to a very highly rated prime minister in the perception of electors (the proportion of electors satisfied with her leadership prior to the campaign was less than 30%: after the campaign, it was nearly 60%).[14] In the 1983 general election the Conservative party was able to offer the image of a relatively united party that had pursued with determination harsh but necessary policies at home and had stood up for Britain's interests abroad. Facing a divided Labour party, with the non-Conservative vote split between Labour and the Liberal-SDP Alliance, it won its largest parliamentary majority in postwar history. During the new Parliament, the government was deflected by a national miners' strike: determined not to repeat the failure of the Heath government, it adopted a strong, nonconcessionary policy—the police ensuring that nonstriking miners were not prevented from working—and after eleven months the strike collapsed. Later, at the end of 1985 and beginning of 1986, government support slipped as a result of the Westland affair: a dispute between two Cabinet ministers as to the most appropriate rescue package for Britain's ailing helicopter manufacturer (Westland) led to the resignation of both, the appearance of a directionless Cabinet, and accusations of a cover-up over the leaking of certain documents to the press.[15] The political fallout from the affair proved relatively short-lived. Economic indicators proved favorable to government: unemployment peaked in 1986 and began to drop, inflation continued its downward trend. Economic stability generated greater optimism for the future. The government also embarked upon an extensive program of privatization, returning variously publicly owned bodies to the private sector. Some sales, such as of the government's holding in British Petroleum (BP), proved especially popular. The proportion of the population owning shares quoted on the Stock Exchange doubled. In 1987 the Prime Minister considered the time appropriate to seek a renewal of the government's mandate and a general election was held in June. Although the Labour party was credited with fighting a professional campaign—indeed, a better one than that of the Conservatives—the Conservatives were still considered by electors to have the better policies. (According to Gallup Polls, the Conservatives were also judged to have the better leaders.)[16] Though losing seats, especially in Scotland, the Conservative government was returned to office with an overall parliamentary majority of 101.

With the Parliament returned in 1987, the Prime Minister was determined not to give the impression of having run out of ideas, and the government embarked upon a radical program of reform. In the first session alone, major bills were introduced to reform the education, social security, and tax rating systems. None of the measures proved particularly popular: the one to reform the rating system, replacing the local rates (basically a property tax paid annually) with a community charge (known popularly as the poll tax, based on individuals), was notably unpopular. The government nonetheless retained its lead in the opinion polls. It appeared confident in office, and unemployment and inflation both continued to fall. Early in 1988 the inflation rate fell below 4%. In 1989, however, government popularity waned. Inflation began to increase, the Prime Minister was involved in a semipublic disagreement with the Chancellor of the Exchequer as to how to deal with the problem, and the party appeared increasingly divided over Britain's role as a member of the European Community. In the European Parliament elections held in June, the Conservatives lost 13 of their 45 seats, all to Labour candidates. In 1987 and 1988 Mrs. Thatcher had appeared as invincible. In the summer of 1989 she—and her party—looked vulnerable. Electoral arithmetic made it look unlikely that they would lose the next general election; but there was no longer any certainty that they would win it.

Conservative fortunes declined further as the year progressed. In the autumn, Chancellor of the Exchequer Nigel Lawson resigned. In December, one Conservative MP, Sir Anthony Meyer, challenged Mrs. Thatcher for the party leadership. He acknowledged he was not a serious challenger (he was 69-years-old with no ministerial experience) but was entering the race so that Conservative MPs could register this disquiet, especially on the issue of the European Community. Conservative MPs voted on December 5. The results of the ballot were:

Margaret Thatcher	314 (84%)
Sir Anthony Meyer	33 (9%)
Spoilt ballots	24 (6%)
Absent	3 (1%)

Spoilt ballots constituted a form of deliberate, but private, "abstention." Sixty Conservative members had withheld their support from the Prime Minister; a number of others were known to have voted for her but to have written to her campaign manager making known their disagreement with her style of leadership and her stance on European integration. The result was politically embarrassing for Mrs. Thatcher without being disastrous. In the weeks following the ballot, she was observed to have adopted a more conciliatory tone. However, economic indicators continued to worsen. Industrial disputes became more prominent. Introduction of the community charge in 1990 led to civil disorder in London and elsewhere.

Ironically, the change in the government's popularity in 1989 came at the very time that the Prime Minister was setting a record. On May 4, 1989, Margaret Thatcher celebrated ten years in office. She was already Britain's longest continuously serving Prime Minister since Lord Liverpool at the beginning of the nineteenth century. She was also the first since Lord Liverpool to lead her party to three successive election victories. Those victories had served to ensure that the record of the Conservative party in the twentieth century was one of dominance. The Conservative party remains the only party in Britain with a successful political history—either being the party in government or (less usually) the principal party challenging to be in government—over a period of more than a century.

Party Organization. In terms of its internal organization, the party is hierarchical. It brings to bear for its own organization the principles it seeks to apply in society. Weight is given to seniority and experience as well as to the wisdom of past generations. The fount of all policy is the party leader. The party's annual conference as well as other organs of the party (see Figure 6.1) serve in an advisory role only. At the end of the day, the leader determines the policy of the party and the contents of the election manifesto. Although the leader is now elected, other leading party officials, including the party chairman and the parliamentary spokesmen when in Opposition, are appointed by the leader. While some writers have sought to apply a monarchial or a Hobbesian model of leadership to the party, a traditional family model may be more appropriate, emphasizing as it does the mutual dependence and trust that exists between the leaders and the led within the party.[17] Each needs the other. As long as the leader appears likely to lead the party to electoral success, the party defers to that leader. If the party looks doomed to electoral defeat, the position of the leader becomes vulnerable. Mrs. Thatcher was in a vulnerable position in 1981, early 1986, and 1989.

Like other parties, the Conservative party recruits dues-paying members. (In Britain, one cannot register as Conservative or Labour: one has to make the conscious effort, independent of voter registration, to join a party.) Unlike the Labour party, the Conservative party has no indirect dues-paying membership through affiliated organizations. Instead it recruits individuals directly as members. Although there are no definitive figures available, it is believed to have a membership of about 1.0 to 1.5 million. Members are organized in constituency associations, based on the parliamentary constituencies. Each local association is responsible for holding various fund-raising activities, recruiting new members, and organizing election campaigns, both at the parliamentary and local government levels. About half of the associations employ full-time agents, paid executive officers responsible for the efficient running of the organization.

Of the political parties, the Conservative is the best financed (see Table 6.1). Its income derives from three sources: business donations, individual donations, and constituency associations. Each constituency association is given a quota that it is expected to contribute each year to national party funds. Some associations give more than the quota and a number give less (in some cases, nothing at all). Annual income from this source has generally been constant at a little over £1 million, forming a

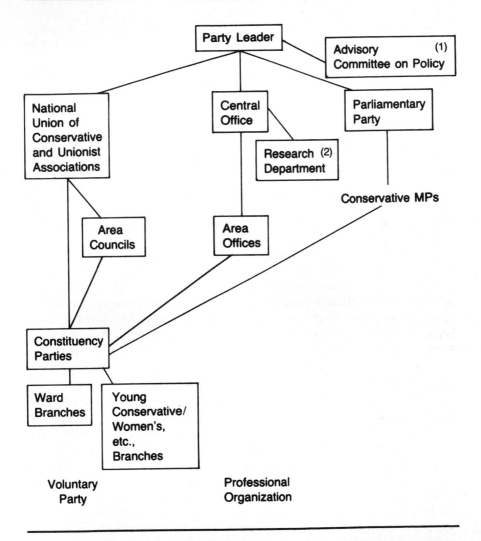

Figure 6.1. Conservative Party Organization

[1] Formally, the Advisory Committee on Policy provides advice on policy, working usually through policy groups composed on MPs and outside experts; in practice, it has been little used in recent years—ad hoc groups being utilized instead—and effectively is now in abeyance.

[2] The Research Department undertakes research for the party, publishes research briefs and pamphlets, assists in drawing up the manifesto, and services the Advisory Committee on Policy and parliamentary party committees. This department was previously independent of Central Office but is now under its roof both organizationally and physically.

TABLE 6.1. PARTY INCOME AND EXPENDITURE: 1982–1987

Year	Conservative Party		Labour Party	
	Income *(£m)*	*Expenditure* *(£m)*	*Income* *(£m)*	*Expenditure* *(£m)*
1982	4.8	4.7	3.9	4.0
1983 [a]	9.4	8.6	6.2	6.1
1984	4.3	5.6	4.2	4.2
1985	5.0	5.5	4.9	4.8
1986	8.9	7.5	6.1	6.2
1987[b]	15.0	15.6	10.0	11.3

[a] Calendar year for the Labour party, financial year (1982–1983 etc.) for the Conservative party.
[b] Election year. (*Source: Derived from M. Pinto-Duschinsky, "British Party Funding 1913–87," Parliamentary Affairs, 42 (2), April 1989, pp. 198 and 200.*)

decreasing proportion of the total income. The party is seen as the one most sympathetic to the interests of business, and a number of large companies give the party a proportion of their profits each year. In 1987–1988 about thirty large corporations each donated £50,000 or more. (These included British Airways, Hanson Trust, Rolls-Royce, and General Electric.) However, as a proportion of the party's income, such corporate giving is of decreasing significance; in 1979–1980 it comprised about 57% of central income and in 1987–1988 about 28%.[18] The party's financial strength derives increasingly from what are deemed individual donations; these now provide the bulk of the party's central funds. Such donations come from a variety of sources: small companies, partnerships, bequests, individuals, and quite possibly foreign corporations (which are not required to disclose such giving). The recent increase in such donations, according to the speculation of one authoritative source, may well come from individuals, a consequence of a lowering of the rate of taxation and the increasing opportunities for wealth creation.[19] Outside of election years, party income is spent on routine administration, salaries, and maintainence of the services that the central party provides to local associations. In election years, the party usually outspends its opponents: in the 1987 election campaign, for example, it is estimated to have spent about £9 million (almost $15 million), while the Labour party spent approximately half that amount.

A second tier of money-raising takes place at the local level. Constituency associations are essentially self-financing bodies (some poorer ones receive support from Central Office) and are active fund-raising organizations. Most money comes from events such as dinners and coffee mornings rather than individual subscriptions (there is no minimum subscription, and in some associations the recommended subscription is remarkably small); the money raised is spent on routine management, primarily the agent's salary and office expenses. Local appeals are normally made to raise money for election campaigns. Parties are constrained by the election finance limits (see Chapter 5), though in practice few local parties have funds that would allow them to exceed the limitations even if they wished to. In the 1987 general election, local associations spent £2.8 million.[20]

Like its main competitor, the party has had difficulty in recent years in raising funds sufficient to meet all its organizational commitments. The party maintains a sizable staff in expensive headquarters close to the Houses of Parliament. Even with various attempts at streamlining since the 1970s, costs have variously exceeded income (Table 6.1). The party's overall deficit in the period from 1984–1985 to 1987–1988 was estimated at £1.0 million; at one point in that period there was a deficit in the amount of £3 million or more.[21] Nonetheless, it continues to demonstrate a capacity to raise considerable funds, especially in election years.

The Labour Party

The Labour party is best described as a coalition of disparate interests. It was formed, in effect, on February 27, 1900, at a conference comprising representatives of the socialist Independent Labour party (the ILP), the marxist Social Democratic Federation (the SDF), the Fabian Society (which believed in socialism by gradual means), and 65 trade unions. It called for "establishing a distinct Labour Group in Parliament, who shall have their own whips and agree upon policy, which must embrace a readiness to cooperate with any party which for the time being may be engaged in promoting legislation in the direct interest of labour, and be equally ready to associate themselves with any party in opposing measures having an opposite tendency." The conference refused to accept an SDF motion linking it with socialism and the class war, and the SDF withdrew subsequently from the movement. An executive committee, the Labour Representation Committee, was set up, consisting of representatives from the different organizations, the trade union representatives being in the majority. There was thus witnessed, in Carl Brand's words, "an alliance between socialism and trade unionism"; he added, "It was done in characteristically British fashion: with scant regard for theory, the best tool possible under the circumstances was fashioned. In spite of the fact that for two decades the drive had come from the socialists, they did not insist upon their name or programme."[22] In the general election of 1906, 29 Labour MPs were elected and the Labour Representation Committee thereupon changed its name to the Labour party. The Labour party had established itself on the British political scene.

The next major event in the party's history was the adoption of a new constitution in 1918. There was a strong socialist element within the party, notably represented by the ILP, and the First World War had appeared to make socialist principles more relevant than they had been previously. It has also been argued that adopting a socialist program served a functional purpose in differentiating the party from the Liberals.[23] In any event, the party adopted what has been termed a Socialist Commitment and, in clause four of its new constitution, committed itself to the common ownership of the means of production. (The words "distribution and exchange" were added in 1928.) At its subsequent conference it adopted a program, *Labour and the New Social Order*, incorporating four principles: the enforcement of a national minimum (in effect, a commitment to full employment and a national minimum wage); the democratic control of industry, essentially through public ownership; a revolution in national finance (financing of social services through greater taxation of high incomes); and surplus wealth for the common good, using the balance of the nation's wealth to expand opportunities in education and culture. The program was to form the basis of party policy for over 30 years.[24] At the same time, however, the party amended its own procedures in a way that weakened the socialist element within its ranks: the trade unions, on whom the party depended for financial support, were given greater influence through the decision to elect members of the party's national executive committee at the party conference, where the unions dominated; and the ILP was weakened by the decision to allow individuals to join the Labour party directly. Previously, membership was indirect, through membership of affiliated organizations, and the ILP had been the main recruiting agent for political activists. Socialists within the party were to become increasingly wary of the attitude adopted toward the party's program by those who dominated the party leadership.

At the 1918 general election 63 Labour MPs were returned. In 1922 the number rose to 142, making the party the second largest in the House of Commons. In the 1923 general election the Conservatives lost their overall majority and Labour, with Liberal acquiescence, formed a short-lived minority government under the leadership of Ramsay MacDonald. Given the political constraints, the government achieved little—its main domestic success was the passage of a Housing Bill—and lasted less than ten months. A second minority Labour government was formed following the 1929 general election. Its domestic program was largely crippled either by the Liberals in the Commons or the Conservatives in the Lords. In response to the Depression, it sought international loans, but these were dependent on financial cutbacks at home. The cabinet was divided on the issue and MacDonald tendered the government's resignation, subsequently accepting the King's invitation to form a coalition, or "National," government incorporating Conservative and Liberal MPs. The new government, though led by MacDonald, was dominated by the Conservatives. Within the Labour party, MacDonald's action was seen as a betrayal of the party's cause and only a handful of Labour MPs followed him into the new government. The majority of the parliamentary party, along with the trade unions, disavowed his action, and he and his supporters were subsequently expelled from the party. The National government, with MacDonald and his supporters standing as National Labour candidates, won a landslide victory in a quickly called general election. The Labour party was returned with only 52 MPs and, though the number increased to 154 in the 1935 general election, spent the 1930s in a political wilderness.

The Second World War, as we have seen (Chapter 3), had a significant impact on the fortunes and the appeal of the party. There had been a shift in popular attitudes, conducive to some form of social welfare program, and the party had proved itself a responsible partner of government in the wartime coalition. In 1945 it was returned with a large overall majority. In office, it implemented its election manifesto "Let Us Face the Future," bringing into public ownership various public utilities and introducing a comprehensive social security system and national health service. Much of its program was soon implemented, perhaps too soon. By the end of the Parliament, the party had begun to lose its impetus and there were growing doubts as to the direction in which it should be going. In the general election of 1950 it was returned with a bare overall majority, and in the general election called the following year it lost that majority altogether (despite receiving more votes than any other party), the Conservatives being returned to office.

The 1950s proved to be a period of bitter dispute within the party. The left wing within the party continued to press for greater control of the economy and the taking into public ownership of important industries: it remained committed to clause four of the party's constitution. Revisionists within the party, influenced by Anthony Crosland and his 1956 seminal work, *The Future of Socialism*, argued that public ownership was no longer necessary because of the absence of large-scale unemployment and primary poverty. Rather, they argued, one should accept the mixed economy and seek instead the goal of equality—equality of opportunity, especially in the sphere of education. Such a goal was possible in an affluent managerial society. Public ownership was seen as largely irrelevant. The dispute between the two sides culminated at the turn of the decade, when party leader Hugh Gaitskell sought to remove clause four from the constitution. The major unions swung against him and he was defeated at the party's 1960 Conference. He then turned his attention to the issue of the British nuclear deterrent, vigorously opposing attempts to commit the party to a policy of unilateral nuclear disarmament, and in so doing instigating another serious internal party dispute.

Conservative unpopularity in the early 1960s and the election of Harold Wilson as party leader in 1963 following the sudden death of Gaitskell helped restore a sense of unity to the Labour party as it sensed electoral victory. The party was returned to office in 1964. However, its periods of office from 1964 to 1970 and later from 1974 to 1979 were not successful ones. The attempt at a national plan in the first Wilson government was effectively stillborn, and both periods of government witnessed generally orthodox attempts to respond to economic crises. The period of Labour government from 1974 onward, in particular, appeared to lack any clear direction, being pushed in different directions by international pressures and the domestic problems associated with trying to stay in office while lacking an overall parliamentary majority. The period witnessed a growing tension within the party between those who adhered to a gradual approach to the achievement of socialist goals, recognizing the constraints imposed by prevailing conditions, and those on the left who pressed for more immediate action and the taking into public ownership of key industries such as the banks. This tension effectively emerged onto the political stage as open and violent political warfare following the election defeat of 1979. It was not only to take the form of a policy dispute but also to be fought largely and ostensibly on the question of the party's constitution.

The left within the Labour party argued that the social democratic consensus policies of the 1950s had been tried and had failed. What was needed was a socialist economic policy, one not seriously tried before by a Labour government. The left sought to increase its influence within the party by arguing for (1) the election of the party leader by a wider franchise than the parliamentary Labour party (the left was much stronger within constituency parties than it was in the parliamentary party); (2) the compulsory reselection of MPs—that is, for MPs to be subject to a full reselection process by local parties during the lifetime of a Parliament rather than the usual process of automatic readoption when an election was called; and (3) the vesting of the responsibility for writing the election manifesto in the party's National Executive Committee (the NEC), where the left was strong, rather than jointly by the NEC and the parliamentary leadership. At the party's 1980 conference the left was successful in achieving two of these three objectives: the widening of the franchise for electing the leader, and MPs being subject to compulsory reselection procedures. At a special conference in January 1981 the party adopted a formula for the election of the leader by an electoral college, the trade unions to have 40% of the votes, constituency parties 30%, and the parliamentary Labour party 30%. (This new method was employed for the first time in 1983 following the resignation of party leader Michael Foot.)

For a number of politicians on the right of the party, already bitterly opposed to the party's policy to withdraw from the European Community, the changes in the party's constitutional arrangements constituted the final straw. They responded by creating the Council for Social Democracy and then, in March 1981, broke away from the party completely, forming their own party: the Social Democratic party. Others in sympathy with their views remained within the Labour party to fight the battle there.

In terms of the ensuing dispute within the party, it would probably be fair to summarize the position as one in which the party's socialist wing won (up to 1987) the policy war but lost the organizational battles. Compulsory reselection, as we have seen (Chapter 4), had a limited effect on sitting MPs, and at the party conference in 1982 the party's right wing gained a majority on its National Executive Committee. It was also successful in persuading the conference to vote for immediate action to be taken against a left-wing group within the party, the Militant Tendency, which a party report earlier in the year had found to be "a party within the party," with its own organization and program contrary to the party's constitution. In January 1983 the NEC voted to expel from the party five leading members of the Tendency. Earlier, in 1981, the left had been unsuccessful, albeit narrowly, in seeking to get their leading figure, Tony Benn, elected to the deputy leadership of the party.

The policy program of the party nonetheless remained left wing, and in 1983 the party fought the general election on a platform that included withdrawal from the European Community, a non-nuclear defense program, a "massive" rise in public spending, a wealth tax (to catch "the richest 100,000"), and the return to public ownership of assets privatized by the Conservatives. The party entered the election campaign in a weak position; the Conservatives had achieved ascendancy in the opinion polls after the Falklands conflict, and the publicity generated by the rifts within Labour's ranks appeared to be resulting in a significant defection of former Labour supporters to the ranks of the Social Democratic party. In the campaign, Labour suffered from poor management, public clashes between some of its leading supporters, and a leader—Michael Foot—whom the mass media refused to take seriously as a potential prime minister. On election day, Labour suffered its worst result since 1918 in the percentage of the vote obtained. It received 28% of the votes cast, only marginally ahead of the share obtained by the Liberal-SDP Alliance.

In the wake of the election defeat, Michael Foot resigned the leadership of the party, and the party elected Neil Kinnock, a 41-year-old Welshman with no ministerial experience. Despite his projecting a more effective public image than his predecessor, and despite his achieving more effective control of the party's organizational machinery, he failed to dent the position established by the Conservative party. He was criticized for lacking impact in the House of Commons and for his failure to make full use of the opportunity offered by the Westland crisis; at the height of the crisis he made a lengthy speech in the House of Commons which, instead of bringing the government to its knees, failed to have any impact on the packed House. Though his performance in the general election of 1987 was recognized as highly effective—according to a Gallup poll, 43% of respondents felt he had campaigned most impressively, compared with 20% so rating Mrs. Thatcher—the party's manifesto remained an electoral liability. Its defense policy, in particular, was a source of Conservative criticism. The party committed itself to the replacement of a nuclear defense with a conventional defense force; if arms reductions talks failed to achieve removal of nuclear weapons, then the United States would be told to remove them from British bases (see Table 6.2). An exit poll on election day found that 52% of respondents felt that Labour's defense policy had made them "less likely" to vote Labour. The party made some gains in the election, especially in Scotland, but still went down to a significant defeat.

Conservative ascendancy was maintained in the wake of the 1987 election and throughout 1988. However, the picture improved notably for Labour in 1989, because of the confluence of two developments. One was the difficulties being faced by the Conservative government. The other was the growing reputation of the Labour party as a viable alternative government. Immediately after the 1987 election defeat, the party had set up seven policy groups to review party policy. Their work came to fruition in 1988, producing a broad review of policy, and in 1989 producing more specific policy recommendations. The policy review moved the party some way from the policies that had dented its electoral appeal. In particular, on defense it moved in the direction of a multilateral disarmament policy, displacing its previous unilateralist preference. Neil Kinnock was able to use his control of the NEC and an increasing body of support within the party to achieve endorsement by the party conference of the recommendations. What was of special importance, though, was the impression generated by the review rather than the specifics of it. In 1989 Labour drew ahead of the Conservatives in the opinion polls. Some of its previous supporters who had defected in or after 1981 to the Social Democratic party began to return to the fold, partly because of disarray within the ranks of the SDP. The Labour party had raised itself substantially from its low point of 1983 and was again a serious challenger for government.

Party Organization. The basic structure of the party is shown in Figure 6.2. Formally, the party stresses the concept of intraparty democracy. In the Labour party, unlike in the Conservative party, the leader is not the fount of party policy. The body formally responsible for determining the party program is the party conference, which meets each year in the autumn. Under the party's constitution, a proposal that receives two-thirds or more

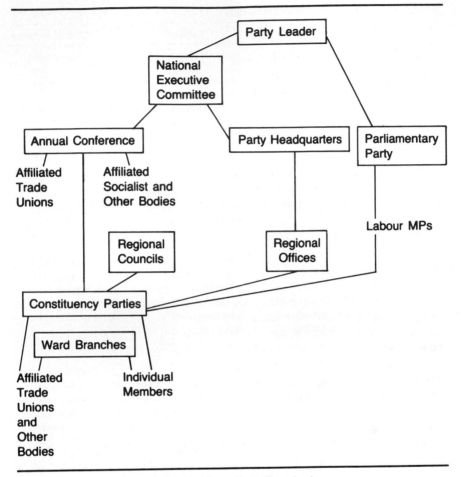

Figure 6.2. Labour Party Organization

of the votes cast at conference is adopted as part of the program. Between conferences, the body responsible for party organization and policy discussion is the party's National Executive Committee, which will normally bring policy documents forward for approval by the Conference.

Complicating the picture, however, is the fact that the party's program is not the same as its election manifesto. Under the party's constitution, the NEC in conjunction with the leaders of the parliamentary party decide which items of the program are to be included in the manifesto. In 1983 the program and the manifesto were synonymous, but in practice this has not always been the case. In 1979, for example, the party leader, James Callaghan, was criticized within the party for effectively blocking inclusion

TABLE 6.2. MANIFESTO PROMISES, 1987

	Conservative	Labour	SDP/Liberal Alliance
Economy	Conquest of inflation "our first objective"; cut income tax—reduce basic rate to 25p; reduction in public expenditure.	National Economic Summit as beginning of National Economic Assessment; reverse Conservative extra tax cuts; wealth tax.	Capital investment program; incomes strategy; reserve powers for counterinflation tax on companies.
Defense	Retain independent nuclear deterrent; modernize it with Trident; develop conventional forces.	Concentrate resources on non-nuclear needs; decommission Polaris, cancel Trident; work toward removal of U.S. nuclear weapons from	"Maintain . . . minimum nuclear deterrent until it can be negotiated away"; cancel Trident; seek battlefield-nuclear-weapon-free zone in Central Europe.
European Community	Press for opening of market in financial and other services; strict controls on EC budget; defend national trading interests.	"Work constructively with EC partners to promote economic expansion and combat unemployment"; reform Common Agriculture Policy.	Reform EC institutions to make them more accountable; reform CAP; extend common rights of citizenship.
Industry	Continue program of privatization; free trade; develop low-cost supplies of nuclear energy.	Capital repatriation scheme; create British Industrial Investment Bank; extend social ownership through a variety of means; implement a regional policy.	Introduce Industrial Investments Bonds; 25% cut in employers' National Insurance contribution; favor greater employee participation.
Employment	Extension of existing programs: Community Program, Job Clubs, Youth Training Scheme (YTS), Restart.	Reduce unemployment by one million in two years via public investment in infrastructure and reducing employers' National Insurance contributions in targeted areas.	Building and investment program; recruitment incentives to companies; crash program of education and training.
Trade Unions	Secret ballots before strikes; limitations on union "closed shops"; union governing bodies to be elected by secret ballot at least	Replace Conservative legislation; improve protection against unfair dismissal; law to ensure unions can organize effective	Committed to union reform; aim to make unions "democratic and accountable"; support system of referring disputes to

	Conservative	Labour	SDP/Liberal Alliance
	once every five years; safeguards on use of union funds.	industrial action.	independent arbitration.
Health and Welfare	Improve health service; complete 125 new building schemes; emphasis on prevention of diseases; introduce tax incentives to personal pensions; maintain value of state retirement pension.	Reduce hospital waiting lists; improve family doctor service; develop local health centers; network of Well-Women Clinics; end privatization in National Health Service; increase pensions, child benefit; restore maternity grant; strategy to abolish low pay.	Increase National Health Service budget; new innovation fund to tackle inequalities in health care; increase voluntary effort; increase pensions, child benefit, and work toward new basic benefit entitlement.
Law and Order	New Criminal Justice Bill, with statutory right to compensation for victims; allow lenient sentences to be referred to Court of Appeal; increase number of police and protect their operational independence; national organization to promote best practices in local crime prevention.	Introduce a victim support program; help local councils to implement Safer Streets and Safer Estates policies; lay down crime prevention standards for buildings, open spaces, and vehicles.	Target "crime crisis areas" for special measures; increase number of police; create new Ministry of Justice; appoint Royal Commission on the Presentation of Violence in the Media.
Constitution	Work toward devolved government in Northern Ireland; new method of local government finance.	Introduce elected Scottish Assembly; Freedom of Information Act; parliamentary scrutiny of security services; state aid for political parties; elected strategic authority for London; Ministry for Women; Ministry for Environmental Protection; Ministry for Arts and Media.	Electoral reform; Freedom of Information Act; Bill of Rights; devolution in Scotland, Wales, and English regions; reform of Whitehall, House of Commons, and House of Lords; establish Human Rights Commission; introduce local income tax; UK/Irish Parliamentary Assembly and devolved power to power-sharing body in Northern Ireland.

of the commitment to abolish the House of Lords. Furthermore, when it comes to implementing the party's program, some latitude is given to the parliamentary leadership, which is expected to give effect to the party's principles "as far as may be practicable." In office, Labour ministers have sometimes found it not "practicable" to implement party commitments, and on occasion the policy of a Labour government has not been congruent with that of the Labour party. Some of the foreign policy of the Labour government in the late 1960s, for instance, failed to gain approval at the party conference.

At party conferences, voting has been based on an organization's membership, not on the individual votes of those present. Thus the trade unions, with large affiliated memberships, have cast the most votes. In the 1950s the so-called bloc votes of the unions used to be cast regularly in support of the party's right-wing leadership. In the 1960s the leadership of some major trade unions changed and they became less predictable in their conference behavior. In the early 1980s they supported the moves against the Militant Tendency (union leaders were reputedly dismayed by the internal wranglings of the party) while supporting the policy documents brought forward for conference approval. After 1987 most, but by no means all, supported Neil Kinnock and the review of party policy. In 1990, they indicated their willingness to see the demise of the conference bloc vote.

Labour conferences differ markedly from Conservative conferences. The latter are purely advisory (and often criticized as stage-managed affairs), votes are cast by those attending in an individual capacity, and voting is extremely rare. Labour conferences are lively, often unpredictable gatherings, with ballots being frequent.[25] There are also significant differences between the parties in terms of membership. The Conservative party, as we have seen, recruits members directly. The Labour party, by contrast, has a large indirect membership in addition to a small direct membership. The indirect membership derives from trade unions and other organizations affiliated with the party. Members of unions pay, as part of their annual subscription, a "political levy" (unless they formally opt not to do so) and thus become affiliated members of the party. This affiliated membership provides the party with much of its income as well as a large paper membership: it has over 5.5 million affiliated members. In contrast, the number of direct members is small. At the beginning of the 1980s it had approximately 350,000 dues-paying members (though one source put it at less than 250,000);[26] by 1987 the number had fallen below 290,000. A modest increase was achieved by a membership drive in 1989. Membership nonetheless is roughly a quarter of that enjoyed by the Conservative party. Part of the explanation for this low membership may lie in the dependence for support on affiliated groups and an absence of professional staff to build up local organizations; the party's internal problems in the first half of the 1980s would appear also to have contributed to the decline in membership.

For its income, the party nationally is heavily dependent on the trade unions. Though contributions from constituency parties to central funds have increased in the past decade, they still constitute less than £1 million a year. Trade unions now contribute £4 million ($6.6 million) or more a year.[27] The unions also contribute the bulk of the party's election funds. (The unions also provided the capital expenditure for the new headquarters the party now occupies south of the Thames; previously the headquarters were housed in Transport House—close to Conservative Central Office—owned by the Transport & General Workers Union.) Most of the income, as with the Conservatives, is spent on routine management. However, the party has had problems raising sufficient funds to meet its expenditure. In 1988 a number of staff were made redundant and efficiency auditors were brought in. With a running deficit of more than £1 million, trade union affiliation fees were increased in order to boost income.

Income raised by constituency parties varies considerably. Some are poorly resourced and there exist a little over 50 full-time party agents in the whole country. Some local parties receive support from trade unions as a result of candidate sponsorship. Unions can sponsor parliamentary candidates, which means essentially that the candidate has the backing of the union and the union contributes a certain sum toward the local party's expenses. As with the Conservatives, most local income is spent on routine functions such as maintaining a local office. However, a greater proportion of funds tend to be allocated to fighting local elections than is the case on the Conservative side.

THIRD PARTIES

In postwar years, from 1945 to 1970, the principal third party in Britain, and the only one to enjoy parliamentary representation throughout the period, was the Liberal party. Its parliamentary strength was small, but as *the* third party it had no obvious competitors. The picture was to change markedly in the 1970s and more dramatically, in the 1980s.

In the 1970s the Scottish and Welsh Nationalist parties grew in strength: they had both gained a parliamentary toehold in the 1960s (one seat each) but that grew markedly in 1974. In 1972 the Ulster Unionists in Northern Ireland, previously affiliated with and, in parliamentary terms, subsumed within the Conservative party, broke away (in protest at the imposition of direct rule in the province) to sit as a separate parliamentary party.

The situation became more complicated in the 1980s. In 1981 a new party was formed, the Social Democratic party (SDP), drawing its parliamentary strength from defecting Labour MPs (and one defecting Conservative). It then formed an alliance with the Liberal party, and it was as an alliance that the two parties contested the 1983 and 1987 general elections. Following the 1987 election and the failure of the alliance to increase its parliamentary representation, the two parties voted to merge and in 1988 the Social and Liberal Democratic party (SLD party) was formed. However, not all within the SDP had supported the merger and they maintained themselves as a separate party, the continuing SDP. In the 1987 election the sole Social and Democratic Labour party MP from Northern Ireland was joined by two more colleagues, thus establishing another new parliamentary party. In 1989 the Green party—so named since 1985 and successor to the Ecology party—achieved significant support in the European Parliament elections in Britain, drawing more than twice as much support as the SLD. By 1990 the field of "third" parties was a crowded one. Figure 6.3 gives some shape to that field.

The Social and Liberal Democratic Party

The Social and Liberal Democratic party was formed in 1988 by a merger of the long-established Liberal party and the relatively new Social Democratic party. By virtue of its age and parliamentary representation, the Liberal party was the senior partner in the merger.

The Liberal party had had a relatively short history as a major political party, spanning less than 60 years. Succeeding the Whigs in the 1860s, it was a major force on the British political scene until the 1920s, when it went into rapid decline. Like the other parties, it was a coalition of interests. The main tenets of Gladstonian Liberalism in the nineteenth century were free trade, home rule for Ireland, economy wherever possible, and social reform where necessary. Within the party there was a radical wing, which placed more emphasis on social reform, as well as an imperialist wing.[28] Returned to government in 1906, the party enacted a number of social reforms, but it proceeded on the basis of no coherent program and was divided on a number of important issues. The second decade of the century proved a disastrous one. The party was beset by such problem as division in Ireland, the suffragettes, and the First World War.[29] It was also rent asunder by a rift between Asquith, the party leader until 1916, and Lloyd George, who successfully displaced him. The rift was never really healed successfully. The party's internal problems and its declining electoral appeal were to reduce its parliamentary numbers. In

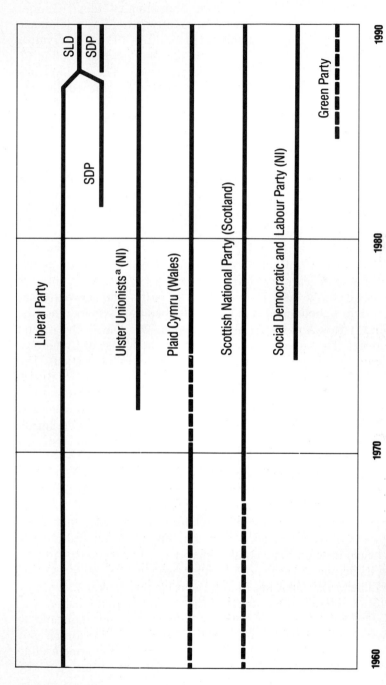

Continuous line indicates parliamentary representation; [a]Part of Conservative party until 1972; NI = Northern Ireland;
SDP = Social Democratic party; SLD = Social and Liberal Democratic party

Figure 6.3. A Growing Field: Third Parties, 1960–1990

1918 the election was won by a coalition consisting of Lloyd George Liberals and the Conservatives. The Conservatives were the dominant partner, though Lloyd George remained as premier. In 1922, Conservative MPs brought the coalition to an end. In the ensuing general election 62 National Liberal and 54 Liberal MPs were returned. The position improved temporarily in 1923, when 159 Liberal MPs were returned. In 1924 the number returned was only 40. In subsequent elections the number returned was 59 (1929), 33 (1931, 41 Liberal National MPs also being returned),[30] and 20 (1935). In the general elections between 1945 and 1979 the number of Liberal MPs elected varied from 6 to 14. The only occasion in postwar years when it came close to government was during the period of the Liberal–Labour (known as the Lib–Lab) Pact from 1977 to 1978, when it achieved some concessions and the opportunity to consult in return for sustaining the minority Labour government in office.[31] The Pact proved unpopular with party activists and was short-lived.

The fortunes of the party appeared to improve in 1981, when it entered into an alliance with the newly formed Social Democratic party. The Social Democratic party was formed in March 1981 when a number of Labour politicians broke away from the Labour party. The new party was led by four former Labour cabinet minsters, dubbed by newspapers as "the Gang of Four": Roy Jenkins, Shirley Williams, Dr. David Owen, and William Rodgers. The latter two were already in the House of Commons. The other two, both former MPs, were to return later in by-elections. The party was created with the ostensible aim of "breaking the mold" of British politics.[32] It wanted to get away from the adversary relationships that had characterized British politics, favoring instead consensus government that would represent the center ground of British politics. It favored decentralization, equality, electoral reform, a pay-and-prices policy, and especially membership in the European Communities.

The new party attracted support both within the House of Commons and within the country. By the end of 1981 a total of 27 Labour MPs (and one Conservative) had defected to join it. It attracted over 70,000 members, and by December its support in the Gallup Poll exceeded that of any other party. It formed an alliance with the Liberal Party, and alliance candidates began to score some notable victories in by-elections: Croydon North-West in October, Crosby in November (won by Mrs. Williams), and Glasgow, Hillhead the following March (won by Mr. Jenkins). Within a year of its formation, it posed a threat to the two main traditional parties.

During 1982 it began to develop its internal organization and to formulate policies. It also witnessed a decline in support. The former may provide a partial explanation for the latter. As the party committed itself to specific policies and as it selected a leader with a distinctive leadership style and appeal, so it began to shed its "catchall" appeal. A contest for the party leadership and a dispute with the Liberals over the allocation of Alliance candidatures produced some loss of support. The Falklands campaign also served to rob it of much-needed publicity.

A consequence of these developments was that the alliance entered the 1983 election campaign in third place in the opinion polls. As the campaign progressed and the Labour campaign faltered, alliance support increased. It became a topic of media speculation as to whether Labour or the alliance would come in second to the Conservatives in the number of votes cast. In the end, despite its worst share of the poll for almost seventy years, the Labour party retained second place in the polls and benefited from the concentration of its support. The alliance obtained 26% of the votes but suffered from the broadness of its support: only 23 alliance MPs were returned, 17 of them Liberals and 6 SDP.

In the wake of the election, SDP leader Roy Jenkins resigned and the party elected Dr. David Owen. The two parties remained in alliance but, with a limited parliamentary base, failed to make a dent on public consciousness during the new Parliament. Both alliance partners entered the 1987 election campaign hoping to improve on their 1983 result: the two party leaders—known as "the two Davids" (David Owen and David Steel)—toured the country together to rally support. However, the two parties, and their leaders, failed to make much impact and both parties were showing internal unease by the end of the campaign. In the election, alliance candidates garnered just under 23% of the vote and 22 seats.

Immediately following the 1987 election, Liberal leader David Steel pressed for a merger of the two parties, believing that such a move was necessary if the alliance were to maximize its impact. The move was opposed by David Owen, who decided to step down as SDP leader; he was replaced by SDP MP Robert Maclennan, who began negotiations with Liberal leaders. Agreement was reached eventually on a merged party: in January 1988 a special Liberal Assembly voted, 2,099 to 385, in favor of a merger. The Council of the SDP followed suit by a vote of 273 to 28. Both parties then held a mail ballot of all members: Liberals voted in favor by 46,376 to 6,365 and the SDP, less decisively, by 18,722 to 9,929. Many SDP members, including David Owen, abstained. The new party was formed with the support of all 17 Liberal MPs but only 2 SDP MPs; the remaining 3 SDP MPs refused to join.

The new party immediately encountered a problem of nomenclature: Liberals were insistent that the name "Liberal" should not be lost. Finally the party chose the name of the Social and Liberal Democratic Party. It was not a popular choice, especially with Liberal MPs, and the name was believed to contribute to confusion on the part of electors about the nature of the party. The new party also proceeded to elect a leader. David Steel decided not to stand and David Owen was no longer available. The party elected a relatively new MP, Paddy Ashdown, a candidate with a reputation for dynamism (and some degree of erraticism), in preference to a longer-serving MP, Alan Beith, regarded as solid and reliable but lacking in charisma.

A combination of new name and new leader appeared to leave electors confused as to what precisely the SLD was and what it had to offer. The party fared badly in local elections in 1988 and 1989 and was overshadowed in the 1989 European Parliament elections by the Green party. In constituency after constituency, the Green candidate came third and the SLD candidate usually a poor fourth. The Greens achieved 15% of the votes cast, the SLD a little over 6%. In the wake of the poor results, pressure built up within the SLD for a change of the party's name. There was a recognition that the intended electoral impact had not been achieved. In 1981 David Steel had told delegates to the Liberal conference to go "and prepare for government." By the end of the decade, survival rather than government was the principal goal.

The Continuing SDP

Not all members of the Social Democratic party supported a merger with the Liberal party in 1988. Among opponents, as we have seen, was David Owen. He advised other like-minded SDP members to abstain in the merger vote. With two other SDP MPs (Rosie Barnes and John Cartwright), he maintained a "continuing SDP". Owen argued that the SDP was distinct from the Liberals; though they shared many common aims, the SDP was not the same as the Liberal party: it had a different emphasis and different traditions, attracting supporters—many new to politics—that the Liberals had been unable to attract. Hence the need to keep the SDP in existence.

The continuing SDP, led by Owen, faced obvious difficulties in achieving a significant political impact. It had only three MPs—the same number as the Welsh Nationalists—and had difficulty raising sufficient funds, resources, and candidates to maintain itself as a national party. When the SDP was first created in 1981, it attracted over 70,000 members. The continuing SDP, after a year of existence, probably had fewer than 10,000. It did badly in local elections in 1988 and 1989, and in 1989 announced that it would not be in a position to contest all the British seats in the European Parliament elections: in the 16 seats it did contest, it amassed a total vote nationally of 0.5%. Its best result was to come in fourth place in one seat: in fourteen it came in fifth and in the one Welsh seat it contested it came sixth. In the wake of this disastrous performance, some members of the party began to talk about joining the Labour party; a number who had previously been Labour supporters did so. The party ceased to be taken seriously as a force in British politics.

Scottish and Welsh Nationalists

Prior to the 1960s the nationalist parties in Scotland and Wales had not proved to be politically important. Their main achievement had been "simply to survive."[33] In the 1960s they began to have some electoral success: the Plaid Cymru (Party of Wales) won a seat at a by-election in 1966, and the Scottish National Party won one in 1967. Their achievements were to be greatest in the 1970s. Favoring independence for Scotland, though being prepared to accept an elected national assembly as a step on that path, the Scottish National party was able to exploit dissatisfaction with Westminster government and to make use of an issue that became salient during this period: North Sea oil. It argued that the oil was Scottish oil and that revenue from it could make an independent Scottish government viable. In the February 1974 election it won 7 seats. In the October 1974 election it won 11 and came second in 35 out of 41 Labour-held seats. In Wales, the Plaid argued more for self-government than for independence and was able to play on the fears of the indigenous Welsh population, which felt its heritage to be threatened by English encroachment. In the 1974 elections it won 2 seats in February (out of 36 Welsh seats) and 3 in October. Responding to the nationalist threat, especially in Scotland, the Labour government introduced a scheme for elected assemblies in the two countries, which was subsequently put to the peoples of Scotland and Wales in referendums. The Welsh referendum resulted in an overwhelming vote against the government's proposals. In Scotland 1,230,000 people voted for the scheme and 1,153,000 voted against it. Under the rules laid down by Parliament, the "yes" vote was not sufficiently large for the scheme to be implemented (see Chapter 9).

The referendum results and apparent decline of interest in devolution took much of the wind out of the sails of the nationalist parties, though both retained significant support among a fraction of the electorate. In both the 1979 and 1983 general elections the Scottish National party won 2 seats, as did Plaid Cymru. In 1987 each increased its representation to 3 seats, the SNP achieving a fourth seat in 1988—at a time of an apparent upsurge in its strength—in a by-election at Glasgow Govan.

SNP strength in the highlands and islands resulted in its winning a European Parliament seat in 1979, retaining the seat in both 1984 and 1989. It is the only third party to hold a seat on the British mainland. Despite its small number of seats, it remains a significant political force in Scotland. In the 1989 European Parliament elections the party not only retained its one seat but also came second in five of the remaining seven seats.

The Green Party

The Green party was founded as the People's party in 1973, changed its name to the Ecology party in 1975, and took its present name in 1985. Before 1989 it was not regarded as a third party of any real significance. As the Ecology party, it had fought 109 seats in the 1983 general election, amassing a total of only 54,000 votes, and as the Green party it contested 133 seats in 1987, achieving a little over 89,000 votes. At the beginning of the 1980s it was believed to have about 3,000 members.

It came to prominence in 1989 in the elections for the European Parliament. It appeared to benefit from the confluence of two independent developments: the disarray within the ranks of the newly formed SLD, and a growing public awareness on the issue of the environment. Essentially perceived as *the* party of the environment, it attracted considerable support, though its performance in the Euro-elections took the other parties by surprise. It contested all 78 seats in Britain, doing especially well in England and Wales: of the 70 English and Welsh seats, it took second place in six and third place in 61. (It came fourth in each of the eight Scottish seats.) In all, it amassed 14.9% of the total vote. Its performance was particularly strong in the east and southeast of England, where it achieved more than 20% of the poll; only in Scotland did its support dip below 10%. By considerably outperforming the SLD, it achieved immediate national prominence.

Its new prominence immediately made it a target for its opponents. It was criticized especially for its policies. Though it focused on the environment, its policy program was attacked for being left wing: the party favors withdrawal from the North Atlantic Treaty Organization (NATO), unconditional nuclear disarmament, a levy on land values, the replacement of private banks with "community banks," and the disengagement of the United Kingdom from international money markets. It also considers the European Community to be "fundamentally flawed" in its objective of economic growth. In the period following the European elections the party's position in the opinion polls failed to match its election performance, vying instead with the SLD for third place. It had nonetheless established itself as a third party.

The party is unusual in terms of its internal structure: it claims to be nonhierarchical and each year elects three "co-chairs," elected from a 30-member Council. It also elects six "Speakers" to act as party spokesmen. By the time of the 1989 Euro-elections it was believed to have about

8,000 members; following the elections, that figure increased to 15,000, a membership in excess of the continuing SDP.

Northern Ireland Parties

In Northern Ireland the main party is the Unionist party, which stands for the maintenance of the Union with Britain. Originally a united party tied to the British Conservative party, it dissociated itself (though in organizational terms not totally) from the Conservative party following the 1972 imposition of direct rule in the province. It also divided within itself, the two main Unionist parties today being the Official Unionists, holding 9 of the province's 17 seats at Westminster, and the Democratic Unionist party, holding 3 seats and led by fundamentalist protestant clergyman Ian Paisley. The Official Unionists tend to be more middle-class and Anglican and Methodist, whereas the Democratic Unionists appeal more to working-class Protestants and are more heavily Presbyterian. There is also a predominantly Catholic party within the province, the Social Democratic and Labour Party (the SDLP), which in the 1987 election increased its parliamentary representation to 3 seats. The Alliance party (not connected with the former British SDP/Liberal Alliance) seeks to bridge the divide between the two communities: it has never won a parliamentary seat and won only 10% of the votes in the province in 1987. Sinn Fein, the political wing of the Provisional IRA (see Chapter 9), contested seats in the 1983 election, capturing 1 seat, retaining it in 1987; in 1983 it got 13.4% of the votes cast in the province, and in 1987 11.4%. The elected Sinn Fein Member (Gerry Adams) has refused to take his seat in the House of Commons.

Other Parties

Other parties in Britain include the National Front and the Communist party. Founded in 1967, the National Front is a right-wing neofascist party that attracts support largely on the basis of opposition to immigration by black and other nonwhite people. It has proved something of a disruptive influence, having more success in staging demonstrations and having skirmishes with opposing groups than in the electoral arena. In the 1979 election it contested more than 300 constituencies, losing its deposit in all of them and obtaining but 0.6% of the votes cast nationally. Following a split within its ranks, it contested only 60 seats in 1983, again losing its deposit in all of them and picking up but 0.1% of the vote nationally. (The breakaway British National party contested 53 seats and suffered a similar fate, its candidates garnering less than 0.1% of the poll.) In 1987 the Front fielded no candidates at all, giving as its reason the increased deposit for candidatures.

The British Communist party, formed in 1921, has had little significant impact in electoral terms. One Communist MP was elected in 1924, one in 1935, and two in 1945. Since then the party has achieved no parliamentary representation and has not really come close to doing so. In the 1987 election it contested 18 seats, down from 35 in 1983, and lost its deposit in every one. It has had greater influence at times within certain intellectual circles, notably in the 1930s, and in the trade union movement. A significant fraction of trade union officials are believed to be party members. According to a study by Robert Taylor, the party has succeeded in recent years in dominating one section of the Amalgamated Union of Engineering Workers (AUEW).[34]

Other minor parties include the Workers Revolutionary party (the WRP) and a host of fringe groups, none of which has any appreciable electoral impact; as was already noted in Chapter 5, all but one of the fringe candidates in the 1987 general election lost their deposits. Among them, they garnered less than 0.5% of the poll.

DECLINE IN PARTY SUPPORT

The past two decades have witnessed significant changes in electoral behavior and in support for the two main parties. Both parties have witnessed a decline in support. How extensive has that decline been? And—a topic of more than academic debate—what has caused it? Is the cause to be found in the *system* of party competition? Or is it the product of the particular performance and policies of each party?

That there has been a decline in party support is demonstrable at three levels: voting support, party identification, and membership. Both the Conservative and Labour parties have witnessed declining support under all three heads.

The decline in voting support for both parties has been sketched in the preceding chapter. Ever since the peak of two-party support reached in the 1950s, electors have shown a relative desertion of both of them. In the gneral elections of 1983 and 1987, one voter in four stayed away from the polling booths and of those who did vote more than 25% voted for parties other than the Conservative or Labour parties; in 1950 the figure had been less than 2%. As we have noted, the Labour share of the poll in 1983 was the lowest since 1918, and in 1987 it still failed to poll as many as 30% of the votes cast. Though achieving victory, the Conservative party received a lower share of the poll in 1979, 1983, and 1987 than it had in any of its previous postwar election victories.

A decline in party identification was detected in the 1970s by the research of Ivor Crewe and his associates.[35] What was termed partisan dealignment became especially marked among Labour supporters. The proportion of "very strong" identifiers among those who identified themselves with the Labour party declined from 50% in 1966 to 27% in 1979.[36] Low and declining levels of party identification have also been a feature of the 1980s. Table 6.3 shows that a majority of Conservative and Labour supporters consider themselves to be merely sympathizers or not close to any party at all. Thus, fewer people are voting for the two parties, and of those that do continue to support them fewer feel strongly committed to the party of their choice. As Table 6.3 reveals, though, low levels of strong partisanship are not confined to the two largest parties.

Figures for a decline in party membership are less well chronicled, in large part because no definitive membership figures are available. However, what data are available suggest that both main parties have been losing members since the 1950s. The Conservative party, as was already noted, probably has a membership in the region of 1.0 to 1.5 million, in itself not a poor figure but much less than the peak membership of nearly 3 million that it claimed in 1953. The party's youth movement, the Young Conservatives, showed an even greater decline in membership; by the end of the 1970s it had less than a quarter of the membership it had claimed in 1949. The Labour party achieved a peak in its individual membership at about the same time as did the Conservatives, with a membership on paper of just over a million in 1952; today, as we have seen, it has approximately one-third of that membership. Somewhat optimistically, Labour leader Neil Kinnock has set the party the target of restoring a membership of one million by the turn of the century.

Clearly, on all three indicators the two parties have witnessed a decline in support in recent years though the decline under all three heads

TABLE 6.3. PARTY AFFINITY, 1982 AND 1985

Q: Do you consider yourself to be close to any particular party? If yes: Do you feel yourself to be very close to this party, fairly close, or merely a sympathizer?

	August 1982			September 1985		
Response	Cons. %	Labour %	Lib/SDP %	Cons. %	Labour %	Lib/SDP %
Very Close	10.6	13.2	5.6	7.7	9.8	3.0
Fairly close	26.0	25.4	15.2	20.0	21.0	9.4
Merely a sympathizer	22.1	20.0	19.0	17.7	17.8	15.2
Not close to any party	40.5	40.0	59.3	54.0	50.9	71.5

Source: G. Heald and R. J. Wybrow, The Gallup Survey of Britain (Croom Helm, 1986), p. 14.

obviously did not commence at the same time; party membership, on the face of it, appears to have dropped prior to a drop in voting support, and voting support declined prior to a marked decline in partisan identification. Also, declining support for the two main parties is not a phenomenon peculiar to Britain. It has been witnessed elsewhere, including in the United States. Both main parties in the United States have witnessed a decline in terms both of the number of votes cast and party identification. (Given the absence of party membership on a scale similar to that in the United Kingdom, a strict comparison of membership decline is not possible.) The proportion of Americans turning out to vote for Republican and Democratic candidates at presidential elections has declined steadily and consistently from 63.8% in 1960 to 50% in 1988. This decline has taken the form not so much of voting for third parties (though independent candidates siphoned off a considerable fraction of the vote in the elections of 1968 and 1980) as of staying at home. British citizens not wishing to support the Conservative or Labour parties either stay at home *or* vote for third parties, while in the United States, citizens not wishing to vote Republican or Democrat tend to stay at home. (Third parties in the United States face considerably greater legal hurdles in getting candidates' names on the ballot than is the case in the United Kingdom.) The net effect in both countries is the same. Of the adult citizens in each country, fewer than before are now turning out to vote for the traditional two main parties.

Identification with the Republican and Democratic parties in the United States has also declined. There has been a decline both in the number identifying with one or other of the parties and in the number identifying themselves as "strong" Republicans or Democrats; by the mid-1970s less than two-thirds of citizens identified themselves with either party (compared with 75% in 1964) and only 24% claimed to be "strong" identifiers (compared with 37% in 1964). About a quarter of electors now register as Independents, and furthermore Republican and Democratic registration figures mask a proportion of voters who are following family tradition but have no partisan preference. Indeed, in U.S. presidential elections a significant proportion of those who vote do so not in order to support their chosen party but in order to vote against a candidate. According to survey data, in the 1988 presidential election half of each candidate's supporters voted more to stop the other ticket than because they genuinely approved of their choice.[37]

Both countries, then, have witnessed two-party decline. The decline is relative, however. Of those who do vote, three out of four in the United Kingdom, and nine out of ten in the United States, vote for one of the two main parties. The decline also is not identical in the two countries—the comparison cannot be pushed too far—nor is it exclusive to them.

Though two-party decline is not peculiar to Britain, explanations of that decline tend to be. The explanations correlate closely with the partisan preferences of those who advance them. We have considered already (Chapter 5) explanations of changes in voting behavior in Britain. Those explanations focused upon the decline of the class–party nexus and what may have replaced the influence of class. However, while these factors may help explain greater electoral volatility, they do not necessarily explain the *decline* in two-party voting. The fact that the two parties may not be able to rely on a core base of class support as in the past does not necessitate voters defecting from those parties. Spatial analyses may help us understand a realignment in party voting but again do not necessarily provide an explanation of two-party decline. Similarly, why should issue voting necessarily produce a decline in support for *both* main parties? Essentially, the changes identified help facilitate a decline in the two-party vote but they do not explain why it has declined. The principal explanations for two-party decline may be subsumed under the headings of *structural dealignment* and *policy orientation*. The structural analysis tends to be advanced by members of center parties such as the SLD and by a few within each of the main parties. The policy-orientation thesis is advanced predominantly by protagonists *within* the two main parties.

Structural Dealignment

The structural thesis is one we have touched upon already (Chapters 3 and 5). The contention is that the decline in support for the two main parties is the product of the structure of the two-party system. The two parties dominate the political agenda, taking positions that are not congruent with the wishes of most electors. Such a stance is dictated by the electoral system, forcing the parties to compete for the all-or-nothing spoils of electoral victory and, in so doing, to compete vigorously with one another in an adversary relationship. Once in office, a party reverses the measures of its predecessor and pursues wildly different policies, policies it often must modify or abandon when it discovers the resources do not exist to meet the more extravagant of its promises (made in order to outbid its opponent party). There is thus a poor fit between what electors want and what the parties actually provide. Britain, in short, has a dysfunctional party system.[38] As the economic resources to meet manifesto promises have declined, in inverse relationship to the growth of such promises, so voter disenchantment with the two parties—one in government, the other forming the alternative government—has grown. Such voters then have the option of voting for a third party or, given that the electoral system works against third parties, of staying at home on election day. That, on this argument, is what they have been doing for the past ten to twenty years.

Given that the party system cannot be separated from the workings of the nation's electoral arrangements, it is not surprising that proponents of this thesis advance reform of the electoral system as a primary means of resolving the problem. Reform of the electoral system, with the introduction of a form of proportional representation (PR), would allow voters to choose more precisely those candidates whose policies they agree with and, as no one party on current voting patterns would achieve an overall parliamentary majority, also produce some form of center-coalition government, allowing for a return to the consensus politics that electors seek. Such an improvement in fit between voters' wants and policies would encourage greater support for the political system and, in common with many other countries with systems of proportional representation, produce a higher turnout on election day.

The problem with this argument, as Nevil Johnson has observed, is that a decline in support for one or both of the two main parties does not of itself demonstrate a decline in support for the two-party system.[39] Voters may support a particular third party because they wish it to replace one of the existing major parties in a two-party framework. There is no objective data to suggest that electors wish to dispense with what supporters view as the fruits of a two-party system: a clear choice between parties, and a party government with an overall majority. Indeed, there are data that demonstrate the opposite. In an *Economist*/MORI poll in June 1986, respondents were asked: "If no party achieves an overall majority in the next general election so as to the able to carry out its policies without the support of other parties, do you think it will be a good or a bad thing for the country?" Fifty percent of respondents replied that it would be a bad thing for the country and only 28% answered that it would be a good thing. (Six percent said neither and 15% replied "Don't Know.") Even among supporters of the Liberal/SDP Alliance—the principal proponent of this thesis—less than half felt it would be a good thing and as many as 39% considered it would be bad for the country.[40] Such an unwillingness to lose the benefits of party government appears to underpin the volatility of responses to surveys carried out on voters' attitudes toward electoral reform. Support for PR on grounds of fairness is generally strong but tempered by fears of what may happen once it is implemented. In an ITN/Harris exit poll during the 1987 general election, voters were asked if the system of electing MPs should be changed to a form of proportional representation. Forty-six percent of respondents favored a change to PR, but 49% wanted to retain the present system.[41] The final objective data are voting figures. In the 1987 general election, only one in four electors who went to the polls cast a vote for an alliance of parties that advocated consensus politics and a reform of the electoral system; and, as we have seen, survey data would suggest that not all of them favored losing the fruits of the existing two-party system.

Policy Orientation

This thesis about the two-party decline takes different forms, largely dependent upon where one stands within the political milieu. One form, which may be described as the *consensus thesis*, attributes decline in party support to the consensus politics of the 1950s and 1960s, when the two parties appeared to converge and follow similar Keynesian economic policies. This was the era of the social democratic consensus, or what Samuel Beer termed the "Collectivist" era.[42] Increasingly, especially as the 1970s progressed, socialists within the Labour party and neoliberals within the Conservative party argued that the policies pursued during this era of consensus had failed to solve Britain's fundamental problems. More radical policies were needed, policies that offered a clear choice to the electorate: on the Labour side, this entailed more socialist measures (extension of public ownership, greater control of the national economy, import controls), while on the Conservative side it entailed pursuit of a free-market economy. As we have seen, pressure built up within both parties, resulting in a shift of policies in the 1970s and 1980s. The Labour party fought the 1983 and 1987 general elections on a socialist program, and the Conservatives, under Margaret Thatcher, committed themselves to a continuation of the policy introduced following their return to office in 1979. Thus in the decade of the 1980s critics of consensus politics were able to argue that the electorate was being offered a very clear choice. Neoliberals within the Conservative party were able to argue that the party's electoral success was the product of the neoliberal policy being pursued by the government. Socialists within the Labour party claimed that failure to win the elections was the result of poor communication and divisions within the party's ranks. More fundamentally, they contended that it was a result of the party's poor performance when it had been in office and pursuing essential centrist policies. Voters were continuing to vote on their evaluation of past performance rather than on an evaluation of future performance. As Paul Whiteley, who developed a sophisticated form of this thesis, put it: "If centrist policies fail, as they have done for the most part during Labour's tenure in office, no amount of moderation will bring electoral success."[43]

Both the socialist and neoliberal arguments encountered opposition in the 1980s. In the Labour party, members on the center and right ascribed the party's loss in both the 1983 and 1987 elections—in each case it achieved a worse result than in 1979—to the party's radical policies. After the 1983 defeat, pressure built up within the party for some of the more radical policies to be jettisoned: one leading figure, Roy Hattersley, pressed for the commitment to withdraw from the European Community to be abandoned; another argued that the party's non-nuclear defense policy was "fatally flawed."[44] As we have seen, in the wake of the 1987 election defeat the party established a review of policy, producing policies two years later that conveyed a more moderate image. By the end of the decade, socialists within the party were in a position to argue that, yet again, radical policies would not be implemented by a Labour government and thus the party was consigned to a cycle of defeat. Moderates within the party argued that without the new policy, the party would never witness electoral success.

In the Conservative party, the critics of neoliberalism variously argued that the government's economic policy was destroying the nation's manufacturing base and jeopardizing the party's claim to the Disraelian inheritance of "One Nation."[45] Electoral success they ascribed not to economic policy but to the good fortune of winning the Falklands conflict and of the disarray within the ranks of its opponents; the party won not because of positive support but because the anti-Conservative vote was split. Hence, according to the "Wets" within the party, electoral success in the future will be dependent upon their adopting more centrist—and hence electorally appealing—policies. Advocates of such an approach have been marginalized in the Cabinet by the Prime Minister—the key economic ministries remaining in the hands of neoliberal ministers—but they continue to advocate their case, and a number of possible contenders for the party leadership are known to be sympathetic to it. Such critics also take some comfort from the fact that, since taking office, Mrs. Thatcher has, as we have noted, variously found herself having to depart from strict monetarist policies and that by the end of the decade the conflict over economic policy within the party was less pronounced than in the first Parliament of Thatcher government. Though chronologically some way behind, it is possible that neoliberals within the Conservative party may find themselves in a position analogous to that of socialists within the ranks of the Labour party. In such an event, it is likely that they will make a not dissimilar claim, namely the necessary policies were never given an adequate opportunity to prove themselves.

There is thus a fundamental disagreement within both main parties as to the cause of two-party decline. Socialists and neoliberals ascribe the cause to the consensus politics of the 1950s and 1960s. Labour moderates and Conservative "Wets" ascribe the decline to the more recent pursuit of nonconsensus politics by both parties in the 1980s. Consequently, prescriptions differ. Resolution of the dispute within the two parties will depend on the political strength of the different groupings within each. For those in third parties, the dispute is doubtless one that points to the continuing ills of a two-party system.

NOTES

1. See C. O. Jones, "Can Our Parties Survive Our Politics?" in N. J. Ornstein (ed.), *The Role of the Legislature in Western Democracies* (American Enterprise Institute, 1981) pp. 20–23.
2. See L. Hartz, *The Liberal Tradition in America* (Harcourt, Brace and World, 1955).
3. As, e.g., J. M. Burns, *The Deadlock of Democracy* (Prentice Hall International, 1963)". See also above, Ch. 2.
4. L. D. Epstein, "What Happened to the British Party Model?" *American Political Science Review*, 74 (1), 1980, pp. 9–22.
5. R. H. S. Crossman, "Introduction" to Walter Bagehot, *The English Constitution* (Fontana ed., 1963), p. 39.
6. See J. Vincent, *The Formation of the British Liberal Party 1857–68* (Penguin, 1972).
7. P. Norton, "The Organisation of Parliamentary Parties" in S. A. Walkland (ed.), *The House of Commons in the Twentieth Century* (Oxford University Press, 1979), pp. 7–68.
8. R. Blake, *The Conservative Party from Peel to Churchill* (Eyre and Spottiswoode, 1970), p. 2.
9. See C. E. Bellairs, *Conservative Social and Industrial Reform*, rev. ed. (Conservative Political Centre, 1977).
10. P. Norton and A. Aughey, *Conservatives and Conservatism* (Temple Smith, 1981), Ch. 2.
11. See R. Rose, "Parties, Factions and Tendencies in British Politics," *Political Studies*, 12, 1964, pp. 33–46.
12. See P. Norton, *Conservative Dissidents* (Temple Smith, 1978), Ch. 4.
13. The epithet *Wet* has different meanings and uncertain origins. In the present context, it derives from Mrs. Thatcher's habit of annotating papers with the word when she wished to indicate that a particular proposal or comment was indecisive, bland, and poorly argued.
14. *The Economist*, May 21, 1983.
15. For a good account of the affair, see H. Young, *One of Us* (Macmillan, 1989), pp. 431–58.
16. *Gallup Political Index*, Report 322, June 1987. Respondents by 46% to 27% judged the Conservatives to have better leaders than Labour and, by 37% to 27%, to have the better policies.
17. Norton and Aughey, pp. 241–43.
18. M. Pinto-Duschinsky, "British Party Funding 1913–87," *Parliamentary Affairs*, 42 (2), April 1989, p. 210.
19. Ibid.
20. D. Butler, *British General Elections since 1945* (Blackwell, 1989), p. 78.

21. Pinto-Duschinsky, p. 197 and n. 2.
22. C. F. Brand, *The British Labour Party* (Stanford University Press, 1965); see also F. Williams, *Fifty Years March* (Oldham, n.d.), Part 1.
23. S. H. Beer, *Modern British Politics*, rev. ed. (Faber & Faber, 1969).
24. H. Pelling, *A Short History of the Labour Party*, 5th ed. (Macmillan, 1976), p. 44.
25. See F. W. S. Craig, *Conservative and Labour Party Conference Decisions 1945–81* (Parliamentary Research Services, 1982).
26. P. Whiteley, "The Decline of Labour's Local Party Membership and Electoral Base, 1945–79," in D. Kavanagh (ed.), *The Politics of the Labour Party* (George Allen & Unwin, 1982), p. 115.
27. Pinto-Duschinsky, p. 200.
28. P. Rowland, *The Last Liberal Governments* (Macmillan, 1969), p. 34.
29. See T. Wilson, *The Downfall of the Liberal Party 1914–1935* (Fontana, 1968), p. 20.
30. The Liberal National MPs became allied with and were eventually absorbed into the Conservative party.
31. See A. Michie and S. Hoggart, *The Pact* (Quartet, 1978).
32. See I. Bradley, *Breaking the Mould?* (Martin Robertson, 1981); and P. Zentner, *Social Democracy in Britain* (John Martin, 1982).
33. H. M. Drucker and G. Brown, *The Politics of Nationalism and Devolution* (Longman, 1980), p. 167.
34. R. Taylor, *The Fifth Estate* (Pan Books, 1980), p. 325.
35. I. Crewe, B. Sarlvik, and J. Alt, "Partisan Dealignment in Britain 1964–1974," *British Journal of Political Science*, 7 (2), 1977, pp. 129–90.
36. I. Crewe, "The Labour Party and the Electorate," in Kavanagh, *The Politics of the Labour Party*, pp. 15–17.
37. *The Independent*, November 10, 1988.
38. See S. E. Finer, *The Changing British Party System 1945–1979* (American Enterprise Institute, 1980).
39. N. Johnson, book review, *The Times Higher Education Supplement*, July 22, 1983.
40. *The Economist*, July 5, 1986.
41. *The Independent*, June 13, 1987.
42. Beer, *Modern British Politics*.
43. P. Whiteley, "The Decline of Labour's Local Party Membership and Electoral Base, 1945–1979," in Kavanagh, *The Politics of the Labour Party*, p. 132. See also P. Whiteley, *The Labour Party in Crisis* (Methuen, 1983).
44. *The Times*, August 2, 1983.
45. See, e.g., Sir I. Gilmour, *Britain Can Work* (Martin Robertson, 1983); and F. Pym, *The Politics of Consent* (Hamish Hamilton, 1984).

CHAPTER 7

Interest Groups
Pluralist or Corporatist?

Interest groups have commonly been defined as bodies that seek to influence government in the allocation of resources without themselves seeking to assume responsibility for government. This definition is usually employed to distinguish such groups from political parties, which do seek, through electoral success, to form the government. The distinction, though not watertight, is nonetheless a useful one.

Interest groups have been variously subdivided for analytic purposes. The two most common categories employed are those of *sectional* interest groups and *promotional* groups. The former, as the name implies, are formed to defend and pursue the interests of specific sections of the community, sections usually defined on an economic basis. (Indeed, to emphasize the point, some writers distinguish between economic or producer groups and promotional groups.) Promotional groups exist to promote particular causes, which may draw their support from disparate individuals and are not based on economic divisions within society. There are a number of recognizable interest groups that fall somewhere between the two categories (for example, the Automobile Association) and others that do not easily fall into either category.

Sectional interest groups are usually permanent bodies formed for a purpose other than that primarily of influencing government. Most are created to provide services of one form or another to their members: for example, negotiating on their behalf; providing legal, social, and insurance facilities; offering advice and information; and providing a forum in which matters of common interest can be discussed and policy determined. Such groups are numerous. Obvious examples would be trade unions (of which there are over 300, such as the National Union of Mineworkers, the Association of University Teachers, the Transport and General Workers Union), the Law Society, the National Farmers Union, the Royal College of Nursing, the Police Federation, the British Medical Association, and various employers' associations. Membership in such bodies is normally exclusive, and actual membership is often close to the potential membership. In some instances, membership in a professional body is a requirement for pursuing a particular vocation. Many have their counterparts in the United States: the AFL–CIO, for example, is the rough equivalent of the Trades Union Congress in Britain (see below), and the American Medical Association the equivalent of the British Medical Association.

Whereas sectional groups seek to promote the interests, normally the economic interests, of their membership, promotional groups seek to promote a cause or causes that are not usually of direct economic benefit to their members. The motivation for joining a sectional group is economic, and for joining a promotional group, often moral or ideological. Promotional groups may seek to promote and defend the interests of particular categories of individuals within society (for example, the Child Poverty Action Group, Shelter, Age Concern, the National Council for One-Parent Families), of particular rights (the National Council for Civil Liberties), or of shared beliefs (the Lord's Day Observance Society). Some seek to achieve a specific objective, one often embodied in their title (for example, the Abortion Law Reform Society, the Campaign for Homosexual Equality). A number are essentially defensive groups formed to counter the campaigns mounted by reform movements: for example, the Society for the Protection of the Unborn Child (SPUC) was formed to oppose the pro-abortion lobby, and the British Field Sports Society was created to defend hunting against the activities of the League Against Cruel Sports. A number of such groups, by their nature, are little concerned with public policy and rarely engage in political activity. The Royal Society for the Protection of Birds, for example, will have little reason to make demands of government. Others, by contrast, often exist for the purpose of pursuing a public campaign to achieve a modification of public policy and the enactment of legislation.

Interest-group activity and the study of it has been more apparent in the United States than in Britain. This difference is explicable largely in terms of the different political systems. The United States has been characterized as enjoying a "multiple access" system. A group can seek to influence a particular department or bureau. If that attempt fails, it can lobby the White House. It can lobby Congress. The separation of powers and the relative weakness of political parties—in essence, depriving representatives and senators of a protective party shield to hide behind—make members of Congress worthwhile targets for group pressure. Such pressure is applied continuously on Capitol Hill; well over 20,000 lobbyists are retained by groups of some sort to lobby congressmen. If pressure in Washington fails, a group can always turn to the congressman's district to try to rouse support there. Rallies may be organized. A mass mailing to Congress may be instigated. Not surprisingly, such visible activity and its apparent effect have been the subject of serious study and much academic debate. The United States has been the breeding ground of group and pluralist theory.

The position in the United Kingdom in terms of group activity has been somewhat different. For groups seeking to influence government decisions, the principal focus of activity is the executive: the ministers and officials occupying the government departments. As we shall see, for sectional groups such contact is often institutionalized. Attempts to lobby Parliament or to maintain regular contact on a scale analogous to that maintained on Capitol Hill have been notable for their rarity. Many groups maintain friendly contact with members of Parliament; as we shall see, an increasing number make use of professional lobbyists, but their number is small at present. What lobbying of Parliament does take place is conducted usually, though not exclusively, by promotional groups. Lobbying of MPs is an admission that attempts to influence ministers and their officials have failed. It is often an unprofitable exercise: failure to influence ministers will frequently be replicated in a house dominated by those same ministers. Interest group activity, certainly that of the well-entrenched sectional interest groups, is thus not as visible as it is in the United States. Only relatively recently has it begun to attract significant academic attention. A pioneering article by W. J. M. Mackenzie in 1955 was later followed by other studies.[1] Only in the past 30 years has group activity become an important topic of study in British political science: even then it has often been much overshadowed by the study of more conventional topics.

The relative lack of visibility of group activity and the attention accorded it by students of politics should nonetheless not be misconstrued. Lack of attention accorded such activity is explained by the difficulty of studying it. Group activity in Britain has been difficult to study because it has not been conducted as obviously and as openly as in the United States. And the lack of such obvious public conduct may be indicative of group influence, not weakness. Only if groups fail to influence ministers or officials do they need to go public and concentrate on Parliament and the media. For much of the postwar period, in which group pressure increased, government was able to satisfy the wants of those groups making demands of it as well as of consumers: there was little need for the more influential sectional groups to mount campaigns. In recent years, especially following the return in 1979 of a Conservative government committed to a neoliberal economic policy, important groups have become far more visible in their attempts to influence government. And as group activity has become more visible, the role played by particular groups in the political arena has become a topic of controversy, both academic and political.

GROUP TYPES

Sectional Interest Groups

Sectional groups in one form or another have existed for many years. Some existed in the fifteenth and sixteenth centuries—for example, various merchant guilds. The earliest, according to R. M. Punnett, was the fourteenth-century Convention of Royal Burghs in Scotland.[2] There was considerable group activity in the nineteenth century, but the phenomenon of a large and diverse body of permanent, well-organized sectional groups making demands of government is a relatively recent one, largely associated with the growth of government activity, especially in the years after the Second World War. "This surely was inevitable," wrote Robert McKenzie. "Once it had been largely agreed by all parties that the government (national and local) should collect and spend over a third of the national income, tremendous pressures were bound to be brought to bear to influence the distribution of the burdens and benefits of public spending on this scale."[3] Those pressures were channeled through and articulated by the sectional interest groups. Groups needed government in order to ensure that their members got the share of the economic cake that they desired. Conversely, government needed the groups—for advice, for information, and for cooperation. The relationship became one of mutual dependence.

As government extended its activities into the economic and social life of the nation, and especially as it began to utilize Keynsian techniques of economic management, it came to depend on information on which it could base both particular and macroeconomic policies. Such information could often be supplied only by sectional interest groups. The groups were also in a position to offer advice. The nearer the actual membership of a group came to its potential membership (all solicitors are members of the Law Society, for example, and 75% of full-time farmers are members of the National Farmers Union of England and Wales), the closer the group came to enjoying a monopoly of the expertise and understanding peculiar to that section of society. "If doctors are powerful," writes one observer, "it is not just because of their characteristics as a pressure group but because of their functional monopoly of expertise."[4] Government also became dependent on such groups for cooperation in the implementation of policies. If groups are ill-disposed toward a government proposal that affects them, they have the sanction of withdrawing their support in the carrying out of that proposal. A policy of noncooperation may cause grave and sometimes insurmountable difficulties for government. In 1949, for example, steel producers refused to cooperate with government in the nationalization of the industry. Their actions seriously weakened the ability of the new public corporation to achieve adequate control over the policy and operations of the publicly owned companies.[5] The 1971 Industrial Relations Act failed largely because of the refusal of trade unions both to register under its provisions and to recognize the National Industrial Relations Court it created. The act was subsequently repealed. Such instances of noncooperation are rare, a sign not of group weakness but of political strength. Anticipation of opposition from affected groups will frequently induce government to refrain from pursuing a particular policy or, more likely, to seek some modification acceptable to the groups concerned; in 1989, for example, the Conservative government modified proposals for reform of legal services following opposition from the legal profession.

The growing interdependence of government and groups led some observers to view sectional groups as central to policy making. They saw the ideological gap between the parties as having narrowed, with government acting primarily as arbiter between competing group demands, seeking to meet the demands of groups while meeting the expectations of consumers. It was seen as the age of what Beer referred to as the "new group politics." Whereas the electoral contest between parties may appear to emphasize an adversary relationship, the relationship between government and groups was perceived as a consensual one. In order to proceed with a given policy, government and the affected groups had to reach some measure of accord: one had to influence the other. In the formulation of public policy, government and groups could be seen increasingly as being inseparable.

As the relationship between government and sectional groups developed, political scientists formulated and applied various models in order to further understanding of that relationship. The three most important are the pluralist, the rational action, and the corporatist. These I shall discuss in looking at the current debate. As a preliminary to study of that debate, two important features of sectional groups and of their relationship with government need to be drawn out. One is the diversity of the groups themselves, and the other is the extent of the institutionalization of their relationship with government.

Diversity. There are at least several thousand bodies in Britain that constitute sectional interest groups. It is common to look at such groups under the three sectoral headings of labor, business, and agriculture. Although the business and labor sectors have "peak," or umbrella, organizations, they are notable for the number of groups that exist within them.

The groups within the labor sector comprise primarily trade unions. As was already mentioned, there are just over 300 of these. Some are extremely small and specialized, while others are large and not confined to a particular industry or trade. Over half the unions have memberships of under 1,000. The eight largest unions account for more than half of all union membership. The only union with a seven-figure membership is the Transport and General Workers Union (T & GWU), with just over one million members. Within the union movement, the older unions representing manual workers (such as miners) have suffered a decline in membership, and those representing white-collar workers (scientists, teachers, technicians, and other professional employees) have grown rapidly in recent years. The growth of white-collar unions, along with increasing employment after 1986, appears to have helped slow a decline in union membership. Total union membership in 1987 stood at just over 10 million, following a continuous decline from over 12 million in 1979. Among unions reporting increases in membership were the bank workers union (BIFU), civil servants (NUCPS), scientific and technical workers (MSF), and shopworkers (USDAW).

The income of each union comes primarily from membership subscriptions and from interest on invested capital. (Union pension funds are among the major investors in Britain.) Annual subscriptions vary from union to union, ranging from a few pounds a year to £20 or £40. In return, unions provide a variety of services to members, such as insurance schemes, benevolent funds, discounts on purchases at certain stores, help with house purchases, strike funds, wage negotiations with employers, and the compiling and publishing of information useful to members. More than two-thirds of union expenditure is on working expenses (paying the salaries of full-time officials, rent, and running of headquarters), and most of the remaining one-third is spent on providing various benefits to members.

The "peak" organization for trade unions is the Trades Union Congress (TUC). In 1989 there were 82 unions affiliated with it. Although a majority of trade unions are not affiliated, it is a far more inclusive body in terms of the large and important unions than is its equivalent in the United States, the AFL–CIO (the American Federation of Labor–Congress of Industrial Organizations). A number of the largest unions in the United States, such as the auto workers, are not affiliated with the American body. In Britain, the largest unions are in the TUC. Indeed, the 82 affiliated unions represent more than 88% of all trade unionists.

The TUC coordinates the activities of its members and represents them in dealings with government, of which more later. It has a number of specialist departments on topics such as employment, economic matters, social matters, and education; these departments research and compile data and help various specialist committees of the TUC formulate policy. It provides a service of trade union education and it provides, as we shall see, members to serve on various advisory and quasigovernmental bodies. It has an executive body, the General Council, which, following a 1989 rule change, has 53 elected members and a general secretary. Membership used to be based on industrial groupings, such as railways and mining; this arrangement, which had favored the old trades unions, was changed in 1983 following pressure from white-collar unions that considered themselves underrepresented. Council membership since then has been determined by the size of union membership. Under the 1989 rules, the Council comprises 31 members elected by unions with 200,000 or more members, 10 elected by unions with memberships of between 100,000 and 199,999, 8 elected by unions with memberships of less than 100,000, and 4 women drawn from unions with memberships of less than 200,000.

Three pertinent points can be made about trade unions. First, they are largely decentralized. The TUC conference represents at best a federal body. Individual unions are largely autonomous and often have difficulty in asserting their wishes over local branches. Most industrial stoppages, for example, are unofficial, that is, they take place without the official sanction of the union. (Since the relevant statistics on strikes began to be collected in 1960, unofficial strikes have accounted for more than 90% of strikes.) However, in terms of the number of strikes and days lost through such stoppages, Britain is not unusual in international comparison. It is in the remaining two features that unions are unusual. Politically, the trade unions have a close relationship with the Labour party, much closer than is the case between any union and party in the United States or most other European countries.[6] As we have seen (Chapter 6), the trade unions were the largest sponsoring element when the Labour Party was formed, and they continue to be its main provider in both income and affiliated membership. This relationship may in part help explain the third feature. Although unions may and do seek to influence government policy on such issues as employment and the economy, union militancy and strikes are used to pursue wage claims rather than political ends. Overtly political strikes or "days of action" are rare; unions rather look to the Labour party to achieve their political goals.

In the business sector, sectional groups are equally if not more diverse. Although there is a well-known peak body for firms in industry, the Confederation of British Industry, it is far from all-encompassing. According to Wyn Grant and David Marsh: "There is . . . a large and complex system of associations which look after the interests of individual industries or, in some cases, the interests of manufacturers of particular products, and many large firms deal directly with government."[7] Finance and the retail sector have their own structures and arrangements with government that are separate from those of the industry sector. "The City," the name given to the interests and institutions that inhabit the square mile of the City of London (Bank of England, the Stock Exchange, the Discount Market, the London Bankers' Clearing House, the commodity markets, insurance companies, and the like), is essentially a separate interest with its own structures and concerns, the latter not always compatible with those of business organizations. There are chambers of commerce throughout the country, though they tend to be most active and effective at regional and local levels than on a national scale. In 1967 an attempt was made to create a peak organization for the retail trade with the formation of the Retail Consortium, a loose confederation of the Multiple Shops Federation, the National Chamber of Trade, the Retail Distributors' Association, and the Cooperative Union. Only gradually did it establish itself as an influential body in its relations with government.[8] In addition, there is a host of trade associations, important ones being bodies such as the Society of Motor Manufacturers.

These examples give some flavor of the diversity of business organizations. The most important body, that which receives most academic and media attention, is the Confederation of British Industry (the CBI). It was formed in 1965 as a result of the amalgamation of the Federation of British Industries (known, confusingly to Americans, as the FBI), the British Employers' Confederation, and the National Association of British Manufacturers. It sought to bring together the resources of the amalgamated bodies in order to form a more efficient servicing body and a more effective representative of industry's needs in discussions with government. Indeed, its two primary functions are not dissimilar to those of unions: it provides various services to its members and its seeks to represent them in negotiations with government departments and with government generally. It provides advice and assistance on industrial problems, it provides information on such things as technical translation services and conditions in foreign countries, it produces its own economic reports, and, in practice, it provides a medium through which firms and associations can make new and useful contacts. It seeks to act as a spokesman for the needs of industry, not only through making representations directly to government and through appointing representatives to various advisory bodies, but also now through its own annual conference, a relatively recent innovation. (The TUC, by contrast, has been holding annual conferences since the last century.) A survey by Grant and Marsh found that the smaller firms in the CBI joined particularly because of the services it offered, whereas the larger industrial giants tended to join because of its position as a lobbying body on behalf of industry.[9]

Membership in the Confederation is broad, though industrial companies are predominant. In 1989 more than 250,000 public and private companies, most nationalized industries, and more than 200 trade associations, employer organizations, and commercial associations were members. Of the company members, approximately half had fewer than 200 employees. Most small firms, though, are not members; the smaller the firm, the less likely it is to be a member. (The Smaller Businesses Association claims to speak for such firms.) The biggest companies are more strongly represented, with about 80 of the top 100 companies in the United Kingdom being members. More than half of the CBI's income comes from the companies with more than 1,000 members (subscriptions being based on a company's salary bill and its United Kingdom turnover), and more than three-quarters comes from industrial companies. In 1988 the Confederation had an income of almost £13 million (just over $21 million), used primarily to finance its staff of just over 300, headquarters in London's Centre Point, 13 regional offices, and an office in Brussels.[10] The organization has an increasingly active seminar and conference program, which in 1988 generated more than £2 million.

The main body within the CBI is its council, a large body comprising up to 400 members nominated by the trade associations, CBI Regional Councils, and the CBI General Purposes Committee. The council meets several times a year but most of the work is conducted through a variety of committees, particularly the formulation of policy on industrial and economic questions. Within the council, the two most prominent and influential figures are the president, usually an industrialist drawn from one of the major companies, and the director-general, the full-time chief executive, usually drawn from a senior position in industry.

Politically, the CBI has no formal link with any political party but it is closely associated with the Conservative party and tends to be sympathetic to its policies. In 1981, when the director-general of the CBI, Sir Terence Beckett, made some critical comments about Conservative government policy, a number of firms withdrew or suspended their membership; there has been no similar gaffe since. Although the CBI itself makes no contribution to Conservative party funds, a number of its members are contributors to party funds and, as we have seen (Chapter 6), a significant proportion of Conservative party income nationally derives from business donations.

Although not an inclusive peak organization, the CBI nonetheless is more extensive than any similar body in the United States. Similarly, in the agriculture sector the National Farmers Union of England and Wales (NFU) is the predominant body; in the United States there are more obviously competing bodies in the form of the Farmers' Union, the

National Grange, and the American Farm Bureau Federation. The NFU in 1988 had a membership of 106,415, constituting approximately three-quarters of all full-time farmers in England and Wales. (There are separate NFUs in Scotland and Northern Ireland.) It is by no means the only body seeking to represent farming interests. The Farmers' Union of Wales, for example, is now recognized by the Ministry of Agriculture as a representative body for the purposes of discussions on the annual farm price review. There are also bodies representing more specialized interests within the broad sector of agriculture, such as dairy producers.

Like its union and business counterparts, the NFU provides various services to members (notably advice and information) and also represents the interests of members in discussions with government. Unlike the two other sectors, the agriculture sector is covered primarily by one government department, the Ministry of Agriculture, Fisheries and Food, and so the relationship with government is more concentrated and, in many respects, more structured and discreet than is the case with the TUC and the CBI. The ministry and the NFU discuss on a regular basis the annual review of farm prices, and the union is represented on a host of advisory bodies.

Rather like the CBI, the union has a large national council, with the most influential members being the president and the general secretary. Below national level, the main unit of organization is the county branch, an often active and well-organized body, particularly in the large agricultural counties. Although farmers are traditionally strong supporters of the Conservative party, the union nationally as well as at county level tends to adopt a strict political neutrality, though this is essentially of postwar origin. Before 1945 (the union was founded in 1908), it was more closely associated with the Conservative party, despite formal assertions of nonpartisanship.[11]

Institutionalization. As its responsibilities expanded, government came to have greater need of what groups could offer, and the groups, in turn, looked to government for the satisfaction of their demands. This relationship often necessitated frequent contact and increasingly became institutionalized. Groups not only were asked for advice on an informal or nonroutine basis, they became drawn into the processes of government by being invited to appoint representatives to serve on advisory bodies, tribunals, and committees of different sorts. This in itself is not a recent phenomenon. The National Health Insurance Act of 1924 provided for the functional representation of specific interests, such as the medical profession, on various committees appointed to administer the system of social insurance. Analogous provisions had appeared in the Trade Board acts of 1909 and 1918. By the late 1950s, more than 100 advisory bodies existed under statutory provision. The 1960s and 1970s witnessed the growth of bodies that comprised representatives of the peak organizations of the CBI and the TUC as well as representatives of the government. Examples of such bodies were the National Economic Development Council (the NEDC, known as "Neddy"), created in 1961 to provide a forum in which representatives of the three could meet to discuss the economy; the Manpower Services Commission (since disbanded) to promote training and job creation schemes; the Health and Safety Commission, to help regulate and supervise safety and health at work; and the Advisory Conciliation and Arbitration Service (known as ACAS), to help resolve industrial disputes. At the same time, various bodies at a lower level proliferated in number, to consider more specialized topics and to bring together representatives of the various core (as opposed to peak) groups. Between 1974 and 1978, for example, 11 new governmental bodies were created in the sector covered by the Department of the Environment: these included an advisory group on commercial property development and an advisory board of constructions experts.[12] A report on such bodies in 1978 identified more than 1,560 advisory bodies and nearly 500 similar bodies with executive powers (to issue regulations, dispense funds, and carry out similar functions), such as the Manpower Services Commission.[13] The Scottish Office alone had more than 60 advisory bodies, ranging from the Scottish Industrial Development Advisory Board to the Scottish Food Hygiene Council. Methods of appointment to these disparate bodies have varied. In some cases there are statutory requirements to include representatives of particular groups, and in other cases the power is vested with the relevant minister, who may appoint people in a representative capacity (on behalf of a group) or in an individual capacity (drawn from but not officially representing a particular group). What is significant for our purposes is the number of such bodies and the extent to which they are manned by, and indeed would be unable to function without, members of affected interest groups.

It is important to remember that such bodies constitute the formal, institutional embodiment of the close relationship between groups and government departments. Over and above these, there is regular contact between groups and departments through formal and informal meetings, sometimes through formal or informal social gatherings. At the level of regular contact, for example, the National Farmers Union and the Ministry of Agriculture follow fairly well-established procedures each year in discussing the annual price review. Throughout the year the two are in constant touch with one another, "almost hourly contact," according to one study.[14] There is similar contact between other departments and groups within their sphere of responsibility.

What emerges from even this brief review of the institutionalization of group–departmental relationships is its range and diversity, which should not be surprising. Groups, as we have seen, are remarkably diverse, with peak organizations being at best federal or confederal bodies. Government departments are not dissimilar in diversity. Usually a department is divided into a number of functional units. A given unit will have contact with the relevant unit—comprising civil servants—and if agreement is reached, the none has the luxury of being able to negotiate with one inclusive outside group. It is at this level that most policy changes, or adjustments, will be discussed. The relevant outside groups will discuss a proposal with the relevant unit—comprising civil servants—and if agreement is reached, the proposal is then "sold" to the department itself before, if necessary, it is put forward for approval at a higher level. Only major policy decisions percolate up to the cabinet for discussion and approval. Most policy is made at departmental and subdepartmental levels. There are functional and legal, as well as cultural, reasons encouraging this practice. The range and extent of government policy making is such that the cabinet is able to deal with only a fraction of it. Formally, legal powers are vested in individual ministers (not the cabinet), and for a proposal to be authoritative and enacted, it is often sufficient for a minister to give it formal approval. Furthermore, the political culture favors consensus within these small policy communities of officials and group representatives. Disputes are neither sought nor encouraged. It is to the advantage of both group and civil servants to avoid dissent. Each needs the other, and disputes could jeopardize their relationship as well as pass the problem on for others to resolve. A desire to decide the issue for themselves impels civil servants and the groups to seek agreement. One of the characteristics of the British policy style, according to Jordan and Richardson, is that of "bureaucratic accommodation."[15] Such accommodation ensures that the public gaze is not so much on the relationships involved but instead tends to be fixed on the more public relationship of government to employers and unions.

A combination of this diversity and institutionalization has important implications for the nature of policy making in Britain, for it favors incrementalism. Policy has been—and largely remains—subject to minor or at least not fundamental change. This situation creates problems for any government seeking to impose a comprehensive new policy on both its own departments and affected groups. Departments or their various units often become so closely associated with the groups with which they deal that they tend to represent the interests of the groups to the government rather than (or in addition to) representing the interests of government to the groups. This position, sometimes referred to as a form of "clientelism," results in departments speaking on behalf of different interests and often competing among themselves where those interests are not compatible. Thus, a government determined to cut public expenditure has the task of imposing cuts upon departments that are keen to resist them and that come up with plausible arguments for their own exemption, arguments that have the backing of the department's clientele groups. For example, cuts in the defense budget are likely to be resisted by officials, sometimes the minister (if persuaded by department officials), as well as by the armed services and the various industries that help manufacture and maintain military hardware and equipment. This is precisely what has happened on more than one occasion under the present Conservative government, leading in one instance to the dismissal of a junior minister. Similarly, cuts in other departments would be resisted on analogous grounds, ministers competing to defend their own departmental budgets. For government to impose a comprehensive policy, it has to persuade a variety of policy communities to agree to that policy. While a party manifesto might provide a government with its plan of action, achieving that plan is a task for which neither the manifesto nor control of a party majority in the House of Commons may be sufficient.

Promotional Groups

Promotional groups generally lack the political clout enjoyed by sectional interest groups. They rarely have a monopoly of information and expertise, certainly not information and expertise that is needed by government. A feature of promotional groups is that normally anyone sympathetic to their aims is welcome to join them. There is no exclusive membership. Their potential membership, technically, constitutes the adult population. They have few if any sanctions that they can employ against government if it proves unresponsive to their overtures. In short, they are without the attributes enjoyed by the sectional interest groups in achieving leverage in their relationship with government. Since departments are not dependent on promotional groups for advice, information, or cooperation, they will not usually maintain regular or institutionalized contact with such groups. Indeed, given the causes promoted by some groups, a government may be keen to keep some of them at arm's length. To achieve their goals, promotional groups often find themselves compelled to seek support outside the corridors of government departments.

Failure to influence ministers or their officials results usually in the groups turning their attention to Parliament, either directly or indirectly. Direct contact with MPs takes the form of letters or pamphlets sent to all MPs or, in the case of better-organized groups, to MPs likely to be sympathetic to their cause and, increasingly, through lobbying of members by group supporters. Sympathetic MPs, some of whom may hold office in the groups (quite often as honorary vice presidents), may arrange for delegations from a group to meet with other MPs or even a minister. All such contact, though, is less systematic, less professional, and less obvious than in the United States, and it often attracts little publicity.

Indirectly, groups seek to influence MPs through mass demonstrations, marches, public meetings, and press releases. Similar activities are often pursued by sectional groups when they have failed to achieve their goals through contact with ministers and officials. In the absence of extremely large numbers or violence, attracting publicity by such means can be an uphill struggle.

Through persuading MPs of the justice of their case, promotional groups seek some parliamentary action, such as a parliamentary question or a debate, in the hope that it will arouse parliamentary interest in the subject and, if persistent and widespread, will influence government to act. On some issues, government action may not even be needed. A private member's bill on an issue about which the government would prefer not to take a stand (for instance, a moral issue that cuts across party lines) may make it to the statute book with government acquiescence rather than support. Indeed, even when a government has sympathy for a particular cause, it may prefer to leave the matter for determination by private members' legislation, thus avoiding responsibility for the measure and any public resentment that may result from its passage. This reticence was a feature of the period from 1964 to 1970, when several major measures of social reform—on divorce, abortion, homosexuality, the death penalty, and theater censorship—were enacted as private members' bills.[16]

The success of groups varies considerably. Some enjoy the respect and sympathy of the public, MPs, and ministers (especially those of charitable status, such as the Royal National Institute for the Blind). Some have proved effective because of the dedication of their supporters, albeit limited in numbers, in mounting campaigns and lining up a number of committed MPs. The Lord's Day Observance Society, for example, has been especially able in obstructing attempts to reform the law governing activities on Sundays, and entertainment laws. In 1986, in conjunction with the Church of England and various unions, it proved remarkably successful in obtaining the defeat of a government bill designed to extend opportunities for trading on Sunday. Such obstruction can prove effective—as in this 1986 example— despite popular support for reform. Conversely, some groups have proved effective in persuading MPs of the need for change despite popular resistance to reform. This was notable in the case of a number of conscience issues in the 1960s, such as abolition of the death penalty for murder.

Other groups have not proved so successful. Some groups fail or have limited impact because their cause arouses little popular interest (for example, the Temperance Alliance); because they are viewed as politically suspect bodies by certain parties (Conservatives in particular look on the

National Council for Civil Liberties-as a front organization for the Labour party); because they pursue a cause unpopular at both the mass and elite levels (for example, EXIT, favoring voluntary euthansia); because they pursue contentious issues that arouse strong feelings across party lines, often encountering well-organized opposition groups; because they make financial demands that government is unable or unwilling to meet; because they make demands that run counter to those made by well-placed sectional interest groups (on legal matters, for example, the National Council for Civil Liberties against the Law Society); or because for one reason or another they are not taken too seriously (the National Viewers' and Listeners' Association, concerned with moral standards in broadcasting, has tended at times to fall into this category). In most such cases, MPs and ministers tend to prefer to leave well enough alone.

Many of the features of British promotional groups, and indeed the causes pursued, are not dissimilar to those of American promotional groups. Both have benefited from the development of television, which gives them more visual impact through their public demonstrations and lobbies. British groups, though, are arguably more limited than their American counterparts by virtue of the strength of party. On an issue about which a party stance is taken, an MP can hide behind his party's position in responding to group pressure. It is an effective shield. Promotional groups present no significant threat to a sitting MP. They stand no chance of persuading electors to vote the MP out at the next election, because party label will normally determine whether the MP stays or goes. Groups will have no leverage through campaign donations: donations go to parties and, as we have seen, campaign expenditure is limited and strictly controlled. Contributions from promotional groups would be considered impolitic. Occasionally, issues become divisive within parties—for example, capital punishment in the Conservative party or abortion in the Labour party—but rarely do they impinge upon an MP's chosen behavior or continuance as a party candidate. Even where they do, it is not because of group activity. A good constituency MP who remains loyal to party will have little difficulty in ignoring any promotional groups that he or she chooses to ignore. Indeed, many MPs are so tired of the mass of material sent them by promotional groups that it is filed automatically in the wastepaper basket.

This is not to argue that MPs do not align themselves with or are not persuaded by promotional groups. Many are associated with such groups and not infrequently serve as active advocates of their cause. The point is that MPs are in a much stronger position than are congressmen to resist pressure from groups with which they are not in sympathy. MPs do not need such groups and rarely could groups be considered a threat to their political survival. Congressional victims of the Moral Majority or of the

National Rifle Association would probably concede that a similar point could not be made by an MP's counterpart in the United States.

THE CURRENT DEBATE

The activity of interest groups in the political process in Britain is clearly significant. Since at least the late 1960s it has also generated controversy. In the 1960s and 1970s the influence of certain groups on government was criticized for being too direct and extensive. Since 1979 the focus has shifted to the largely indirect means that many groups have chosen in order to affect public policy.

In order to give some shape to group activity, various models have been constructed. In this section I will first outline briefly each of these models and then assess its utility for explaining the changes of recent years.

Groups and Models

The three most important models are the pluralist, the rational action, and the corporatist. The three are not mutually exclusive. Nor, as we shall see, are they free of criticism.

The Pluralist Model. The basic framework of the pluralist model is that there is a consensus on the nature of the political system, on "the rules of the game," and that the role of government is to act as independent arbiter among the competing demands of groups. Within the political process, the essential element is the group, and the political system is characterized by individuals having the opportunity to join groups and then, through those groups, enjoying access to government. Pluralists emphasize the extent and range of groups, their access to government, and the competition among them.[17] There is presumed to be something of a balance among groups, no one group enjoying supremacy, and the balance and institutionalized relationship between groups and government provides for both stability in the political system and incremental policy making.

Like all models, the pluralist one constitutes an ideal. However, according to proponents, it is a model to which both American and British experiences have provided a reasonably close fit. The importance of groups in Britain has been emphasized by a number of writers, and from our brief survey of sectional and promotional groups we can discern substantial empirical evidence to support a pluralist analysis. Clearly there is a wide range of interest groups, a large proportion of the population are members of groups (over 10 million are members of trade unions, for example), and there are groups with mutually countervailing goals. In most spheres, the government could be characterized as serving as arbiter. Incrementalism has been a predominant feature of policy making. Thus pluralism would seem an adequate description of policy making in Britain.

The pluralist model is a far from perfect fit, however, and a number of weighty objections have been leveled against it. Marxists and elite theorists would dispute the role of government, conceiving it as a subjective rather than a neutral actor.[18] For groups, there are problems with pluralist analysis in terms of their membership, their internal organization, and their impact on government. Although many people in Britain are members of groups, a great many are not. Only about half the workforce, for example, belong to trade unions. Furthermore, group membership, and especially group activity, is much more notably a feature of the middle class than of the working class. For example, a study of planning decisions found that those who participated were generally middle class and had both the time and the knowledge to be involved; the poor and the inarticulate tend not to be heard. The exception to this generalization is the trade unions, and even there, as we have seen, the emphasis is shifting from the old manual to the newer white-collar unions.

Many groups, as Reginald Harrison has pointed out, also lack developed democratic structures and extensive member participation.[19] Practices within groups vary, but the number with extensive consultative procedures designed to inform group representatives of members' opinions does not appear extensive. In the case of some groups there may not even be procedures for election and consultation. The Automobile Association, for example, claims to speak on behalf of motorists yet has no developed procedures for consulting its members.

In policy impact, pluralist theory is criticized for emphasizing a balance among competing groups. While few pluralists would contend that there is perfect balance among groups, the concept of some measure of balance is central to their thesis. There are presumed to be potential countervailing groups to existing ones, and the potential groups will be realized by the activities of the existing ones. An example given would be the creation of the CBI as a counterweight to the TUC. Yet from the preceding study one can glean material that throws doubt on the thesis. Obviously, the concept of balance is difficult to apply in any comparison between sectional and promotional groups: the latter are clearly the weaker brethren. Within sectional interest groups, some have far more extensive wealth and resources than others and are more needed by government, and thus they tend to wield disproportionate influence in their relations with government. For instance, insofar as it represents one coherent interest, the City of London is a powerful body that has few obvious and comparable countervailing groups.

Finally, critics state that pluralist theory fails to acknowledge the impact of political parties and of elections in policy making. Political parties help provide a framework for government action, since a government is elected with the intention of implementing a particular manifesto. Although Richard Rose in his study of political parties found that the particular party in office did not make a great difference in terms of various economic indicators, he nonetheless contended that parties did make *some* difference: the fact that one party was in office, rather than another, was important.[20] A party in office adopts a particular approach, it adheres to a particular program, and it may adopt a specific style of government. Clearly, a Labour government under Neil Kinnock would behave very differently from the Conservative government under Mrs. Thatcher. In any study of public policy, political parties cannot be left out of consideration.

The Rational Action Model. This model, deriving in large part from the work of Mancur Olson,[21] interprets group strength as a function of the members' reasons for joining. It may thus serve to explain some disparities among groups. This model contends that people join a group only if a rational calculation of costs and benefits shows that their personal welfare would be improved if they became a group member.

Groups that are all-encompassing—that is, are able to negotiate benefits intended only for their members—are in a strong position to recruit members. These groups include professional bodies in which membership is necessary to remain and progress in a given profession—for example, the British Medical Association and the Law Society. They are well-organized and powerful bodies, enjoying influence in relation both to their members and to government.

Groups that are not all-encompassing, on the other hand, that negotiate benefits to be enjoyed by members and nonmembers alike (for example, wage rises), are in a weaker position to recruit members. These include most promotional groups; generally, what they can offer to their members exclusively is advice and information. Such groups tend to be weak and are often poorly organized.

The model is helpful in understanding the "pluralist stagnation" argument advanced by Samuel Beer and others. The absence of all-encompassing groups militates against the ability of government and groups to formulate and impose policies in the public interest. The range of groups, pursuing the interests of members who have joined to benefit their own and not the public interest, results in a lack of agreement, each group recognizing that by itself it cannot produce the end desired by government for the public good. One group's accepting the need for moderation in wage demands, for example, will have little effect if all other groups do not follow suit. The consequence, according to Beer's analysis (see Chapter 3), is pluralist stagnation.

This model tends to draw attention to inequalities among groups and hence is not strictly compatible with the pluralist model. Like pluralism, however, it has been subject to a number of important criticisms. For example, it fails to offer an explanation for the existence of well-organized and influential promotional interest groups. The welfare of a promotional group member may not benefit from membership, but the moral or ideological stance of the group moves some people to commit both their time and their money to a particular cause. The Campaign for Nuclear Disarmament, to take a recent example, became an important "cause" group in the 1980s in Britain, yet few of those who went on marches and demonstrations would claim to have done so for their own welfare (rather, justification tends to be expressed in terms of the welfare of others). Similarly, a well-organized environmental conservation group, Greenpeace, has attracted much useful publicity, yet many of its members risk personal injury in their attempts to prevent the slaughter of animals. Nor does this model explain extensive membership of sectional groups that negotiate benefits that can be enjoyed by nonmembers. For example, the study of the CBI by Grant and Marsh found that many members, particularly a number of large and medium-sized firms, were aware that nonmembers could receive some of the benefits (such as research reports) they received as members and that, as members, they did not receive value for money.[22] Many firms had not even attempted to do a costs–benefit analysis of membership.

The model thus has its uses, but one of its important contributions to a study of groups lies in its failure to provide a comprehensive explanation— that is, it points attention to the need for more extensive studies of why people join groups. The rationality model provides but a partial explanation.

The Corporatist Model. Of all the models, this is probably the most contentious. Corporatism has been subject to various definitions but basically it entails a system in which government directs the activities of industry, which remains predominantly in private hands, through the representatives of a limited number of singular, compulsory, noncompetitive, hierarchically ordered, and functionally differentiated interest groups.[23] *Societal* corporatism exists where government tends to be but one participant in a complex of negotiations with such groups. Where government is dominant in the relationship, there exists a form of *state* corporatism.[24]

Britain, on these definitions, has never enjoyed a pure form of corporatism. However, various writers have identified corporatist trends, based primarily on a tripartite relationship of government, employers, and trade unions. They have discerned that in practice this relationship has taken two forms: the co-option of representatives of employers and unions onto various bodies concerned with resolving disputes and discussing economic policy, and informal discussion between ministers and representatives of the CBI and TUC. The 1960s, as we have noted, saw the emergence of structured tripartite bodies such as the National Economic Development Council; discussions between ministers and leaders of unions and employers' bodies were already a feature of political life. The extent to which "tripartism" has been, and remains, a feature of political life is still a point of some contention, as we shall see. Taken to its logical conclusion, tripartism would, as Edward Heath observed, be a relationship in which government, employers, and unions "share fully . . . the benefits and obligations of running the country";[25] in other words, societal corporatism.

Many writers on corporatism are divided on its merits. Some see it as a threat to existing representative institutions, with decisions being taken by unelected bodies rather than by the citizens' elected representatives.[26] Adherents to a free-market economy regard corporatism as a direct threat and are vigorous in their condemnation of it. In contrast, some economists and political scientists consider that some form of tripartism, or a more full-blooded form of corporatism, would offer the best way of dealing with Britain's economic problems.[27] They feel that corporatism would allow government to persuade or induce groups to give up the pursuit of narrow goals in favor of the national interest. Marxists provide a somewhat different interpretation: they see corporatism as a device used to defend capitalism and, according to some Marxist analyses, to incorporate the working class into a system dominated by business interests.[28]

How relevant, then, are these models to helping us understand the role of groups in contemporary Britain?

Groups and Political Influence

In relation to government and the making of public policy, groups have gone through two distinct periods since 1960: one of co-option and one of exclusion. The period of co-option lasted until the return of a Conservative government in 1979. Since then, *particularly at the higher levels of policy making*, exclusion has been more the order of the day.

The co-option of groups into the policy-making process developed especially in the latter years of the Macmillan government, particularly with the creation of the NEDC. The process grew apace under the Labour governments of the 1960s (1964–1970) and the 1970s (1974–1979) and was also to become a feature of the later years of the Conservative government of Edward Heath (1970–1974). Insofar as Britain has experienced a form of corporatism in postwar years, it was during these years that the term "tripartism" was generated to describe the relationship.

During this period, as we already noted, representatives of the CBI and the TUC were co-opted onto a range of bodies, from the NEDC to the Health and Safety Executive. Informal negotiations with government, often at prime ministerial level, were common; Labour Prime Minister Harold Wilson was keen to consult with the two peak organizations—in 1966, he told the House of Commons it was the government's *duty* to consult with them—and, as we have already seen (Chapter 6), Edward Heath sought to arrange a voluntary prices-and-pay policy with both bodies in 1972. For the relationship that developed, tripartism would seem an adequate description.

However, the concept of tripartism is inadequate to explain fully the relationships that developed. Some negotiations were essentially multipartite: for example, the Labour government of 1974–1979 had, in effect, to negotiate with the TUC, the International Monetary Fund, the CBI, the City of London, and (if not negotiate, at least take into account) the House of Commons in order to achieve the economic policy it wanted. More frequently, the relationships were bipartite. And the most important of those bipartite relationships in the late 1960s and 1970s was the one between government and unions.

In 1969 the Labour government introduced proposals for the reform of trade union law in Britain. The trade unions opposed the proposals and, following discussions between TUC leaders and Prime Minister Wilson, they were withdrawn. Their withdrawal encouraged a popular perception of union power and of the dependence of a Labour government on its union allies. The perceptions of union power were reinforced when Edward Health felt constrained to call a general election in 1974 in the face of a threatened national coal strike, and they reached new heights in the latter half of the 1970s. In 1976 the chancellor of the exchequer, Denis Healey, made a 3% reduction in income tax conditional on the acceptance of pay restraint by trade unions. The decision invoked a political storm, Conservative and Liberal politicians asserting that the final say on the levying of taxation was being transferred from Parliament to the trade unions.[29] The government also negotiated with the TUC a "social contract" that entailed the government's introducing various measures (on employment law, for example) favored by the unions, in return for which the unions moderated wage demands. The relationship that developed between government, and especially certain trade union leaders, was seen as an intimate one. By the end of the 1970s opinion polls demonstrated that the unions—and particular union leaders—were considered "too powerful." There were fears that other groups, as well as the public interest, were being excluded from the process; a pluralist system was being stifled by corporatist tendencies.

Though the concept of tripartism is descriptively inadequate, the period of the mid- to late 1970s clearly witnessed the basic feature of negotiation intrinsic to societal corporatism. The unions in particular, but by no means exclusively, were co-opted into the process of determining public policy. This was in part institutionalized—and much of the institutionalization was on a tripartite basis—and in part based on *ad hoc* gatherings as occasion demanded. Indeed, the nature and frequency of meetings at 10 Downing Street involving union representatives became popularized in the term "beer and sandwich" meetings, implying talks while beer and sandwiches were brought in to sustain the participants. Union as well as business leaders became used to being consulted by government.

The Conservative government that returned in 1979 was opposed to anything that smacked of corporatism. However, corporatist tendencies in the form of tripartism had failed before Mrs. Thatcher entered No. 10. Though tripartism was highly visible and, in the eyes of critics, too strong an influence on public policy, it failed because of its intrinsic weakness. This is where the rational action model is useful in helping us understand what happened. The TUC and CBI were, and remain, loose umbrella organizations, lacking the power to enforce discipline on their members. Not all unions were affiliated with the TUC, and those that were put the interests of members first and the interests of the TUC second. In the autumn and winter of 1978, wage claims were pressed for the benefit of members; a wave of strikes in the public sector followed. Far from being able to exert pressure from the top, TUC leaders were forced by pressure from activists below to repudiate renewal of a national pay policy. Though public opinion was clearly hostile to the industrial action that occurred, individual unions pursued their claims. According to Robert Taylor, workers were striving "through fragmented and localised bargaining, to hold their position relative to workers in other work-places and other industries," seeking at most "to climb a rung or two above those whose pay they traditionally compare with their own."[30] The result was "the Winter of Discontent" and the return of a Conservative government.

Under a Conservative government, there were significant changes. However, tripartism, especially in its institutionalized form, did not disappear altogether. Though the Manpower Services Commission was eventually disbanded and the role of the NEDC was downgraded, the tripartite bodies created in the 1960s and 1970s remained largely intact: the Health and Safety Executive, ACAS, the NEDC itself, and, less centrally as tripartite bodies, the Equal Opportunities Commission and the Commission for Racial Equality. And at the lower levels of policy formulation—or, more appropriately, adjustment—the relationship between civil servants and group representatives has remained more or less as it was. Groups are still consulted about secondary legislation and incremental policy changes. It is at the level of high and medium policy making that the changes have been significant.

In order to achieve its neoliberal economic policy, the government has had to disengage itself from corporatist relationships and carve out for itself an autonomous position. The realization of a free-market economy necessitates not negotiation but imposition. The goal of government economic policy is non-negotiable, and bodies such as the trade unions are seen as obstacles to its realization. Like other bodies deemed to adopt restrictive practices, they have been the subject of reform. The Conservative government has introduced a series of trade union reform acts and has sought to break up monopolistic practices in other sectors. "Beer and sandwiches" at No. 10 have become taboo. Allowing high levels of unemployment has served also to reduce the bargaining power of the unions. By the end of the 1980s they were in a relatively weak position; during the decade they reached the nadir of their fortunes compared with the period from 1974 to 1979.

By withdrawing from bipartite and tripartite relationships, the government has removed an obstacle to the realization of goals by other groups. However, by virtue of its free-market orientation, it is also less responsive to group demands. A pluralist analysis is now more relevant—a growing number of groups compete with one another to influence government, the latter in a position of some autonomy—but government is less amenable to group influence. Though government is now more autonomous of groups, it has not assumed a position of independent arbiter; policy making, especially at the level of economic policy, is a "top-down" rather than a "bottom-up" process. Hence the problem that has confronted such groups since 1979 has been to determine the most effective way to get their voice heard by government.

The answer, for many groups, has been to engage in more extensive, and more professional, lobbying. Two developments have facilitated this move. One has been the greater realization that Parliament is a more influential actor in the policy cycle than was previously assumed; since the early 1970s MPs have proved more willing to take an independent line on particular issues, thus forcing government to take notice and, on occasion, make concessions. Hence lobbying of Parliament has been recognized as a worthwhile course of action. The second development has been the growth of professional lobbyists. Known as political consultants, such lobbyists grew in number throughout the 1980s. Relative to the number in the United States, there are few of them; however, compared with the position in 1979, they have constituted a major growth area.

Many large companies, such as BP (British Petroleum), now have their own in-house lobbyists, responsible for relations with both government departments and Parliament. Others hire independent political consultants. There are at least thirty firms now offering their services as lobbyists. A 1985 survey of 180 sizable United Kingdom companies found that 41% of them used political consultancy firms and 28% used public relations firms for work involving government.[31] Works on lobbyists have now started to appear, as well as "how to" guides for those wishing to lobby; among those producing such a guide is the CBI.[32]

For larger groups, especially the well-entrenched sectional interest groups, such lobbying serves as a supplement to rather than a substitute for their existing, institutionalized relationship with government departments. As was already noted, the basic institutionalized relationship sketched above remains intact, particularly for discussion of policy detail. If such contact fails to elicit the desired response, then the groups have the option of lobbying potentially sympathetic MPs (and, indeed, peers, since the House of Lords also serves as a magnet for lobbying activity). Lobbyists working for City (and other financial) institutions, for example, were especially active during the passage of the Financial Services Bill in 1986, which introduced self-regulating mechanisms in the City. The government had discussed the measure with outside interests, but not until the bill was published did these interests see the specifics of the measure, and so they lobbied to achieve amendments that they favored.

For small groups, the availability of lobbyists has added a new dimension to their activities. Despite limited resources, a number now employ either political consultancy firms or, more likely, free-lance political consultancies. Such activity serves to reinforce the pluralist model, giving a greater number of groups access to the political system. Through the use of consultants, small groups can target potentially sympathetic parliamentarians. Doing this may be sufficient to initiate parliamentary action. Group influence often derives not from the scale of group resources but from the force of the case being advanced. Animal welfare organizations, for example, have limited resources but can often mobilize support in the House of Commons as a result of the information they supply.

Though still modest by the standards of the United States, lobbying in Britain is, then, becoming more extensive—and visible. It has also resulted in some notable instances of policy modification or even withdrawal. The most visible instance of effective lobbying came in 1986 when, as we have noted already, the government was defeated in its attempt to reform the law on Sunday trading. The various groups opposed to the measure hired a lobbying firm, which focused its activities at the constituency level; opponents of the measure were encouraged to write to their local MPs.[33] The campaign proved stunningly effective: 72 Conservative MPs joined Labour members to vote against the bill, sufficient to ensure the bill's defeat. The campaign also fits within a pluralist framework in that a countervailing campaign was being waged, lobbyists having been hired by retailing firms that favored a change in the law.

From a pluralist perspective, there is thus a positive side to the activity of lobbyists. However, their activity has also come in for criticism, including from many MPs. The use of lobbyists has been regarded by some critics as, in effect, "buying influence." Groups that can afford lobbyists can achieve an input into the policy cycle; those lacking such resources, however worthy they may be, are denied such access. This criticism has been fueled by the fact that many Members of Parliament themselves serve as political consultants or are hired to act as advisers to firms of political consultants. Some of these firms also supply MPs with research assistants, who then enjoy privileged access to the House because they have parliamentary passes. These developments, according to *The Observer* in 1989, constitute "worryingly corrosive influences."[34] As a result of such criticisms, the Select Committee on Members' Interests of the House of Commons has twice investigated the activity of lobbyists. Research assistants and journalists are now required to register outside interests. (MPs were already subject to registering such interests, although, in the case of those undertaking consultancy work, they are not required to list their clients.) There is also pressure, including from some lobbyists, for lobbyists themselves to be subject to some form of registration; at present, none exists, and anyone can set up as a political consultant.

Such criticisms, however, are probably misplaced. MPs, as well as civil servants, are well able to recognize, and to resist, lobbying. As was already detailed, MPs have the protective cloak of party; if they choose to do so, they can resist the blandishments of lobbyists and, as the 1980s progressed, they showed signs of becoming increasingly bored with the more ostensible forms of lobbying employed (such as expensive dinners and receptions). Rather, if there is a problem, it lies with what a colleague and I have elsewhere termed consumer accountability: it is the client, not the politician, that may be in need of protection from an amateurish (and overpaid) lobbyist.[35] However, where a group with a case to make comes together with a professional lobbyist or firm of lobbyists, then this combination may produce a desired outcome. The growing availability of free-lance lobbyists also serves to fulfill the pluralist ideal of more groups having access to the political system; they may not achieve the desired outcome, particularly if they are not compatible with known government policy, but at least they have the opportunity to make their views known.

Though a pluralist analysis may thus be employed, the activity of lobbyists, as in the United States, is likely to remain a point of controversy. Part of the problem derives from the activity being at least partially observable; part also derives from the fact that payment now takes place for such activity. Some regulation of lobbyists may emerge in the 1990s, but the decade is likely also to witness a growth of political lobbying. Whatever the ethics of lobbying, groups are not likely to want to be left behind in the rush to influence government.

CONCLUSION

Pressure groups in Britain are numerous and diverse. Many, especially sectional interest groups, enjoy a frequent and fairly well-institutionalized relationship with civil servants. For peak organizations, the relationship with government became especially close, and structured, in the 1960s and 1970s, when tripartism became a feature of policy making. Since 1979, government has pursued an economic policy largely independent of group pressure and negotiation. Increasingly, in order to influence policy, groups have resorted to lobbying both government and Parliament. The features of government–group relationships established earlier remain largely in place, especially for discussion of policy detail and incremental changes, but an extra dimension has now been built onto them. By Capitol Hill standards, the development is an extremely modest one, but it is growing and likely to continue to do so. It offers the prospect of a more, rather than less, pluralistic system of policy making.

NOTES

1. W. J. M. Mackenzie, "Pressure Groups in British Government," *British Journal of Sociology*, 6(2), 1955, pp. 133–48. Several other studies appeared in the following decade.
2. R. M. Punnett, *British Government and Politics* (Heinemann, 1970 ed.), p. 134.
3. R. T. McKenzie, "Parties, Pressure Groups and the British Political Process," *Political Quarterly*, 29 (1), 1958.
4. R. Klein, "Policy Making in the National Health Service," *Political Studies*, 22 (1), 1974, p. 6.
5. S. H. Beer, *Modern British Politics*, rev. ed. (Faber & Faber, 1969), p. 326.
6. See C. Crouch, "The Peculiar Relationship: The Party and the Unions," in D. Kavanagh (ed.), *The Politics of the Labour Party* (George Allen & Unwin, 1982), pp. 175–77.
7. W. Grant and D. Marsh, *The CBI* (Hodder & Stoughton, 1977), p. 55.
8. Ibid., pp. 61–68.
9. Ibid., pp. 44–50.
10. *CBI: Annual Review and Report for 1988* (CBI, 1989); other material is drawn from *CBI: Britain's Business Voice* (CBI, 1989).

11. P. Self and H. Storing, "The Farmer and the State," in R. Kimber and J. J. Richardson (eds.), *Pressure Groups in Britain* (Dent, 1974), pp. 58–59.
12. J. J. Richardson and A. G. Jordan, *Governing Under Pressure* (Martin Robertson, 1979), p. 61.
13. *Report on Non-Departmental Public Bodies*, Cmnd. 7797 (Her Majesty's Stationery Office, 1980), p. 5.
14. G. K. Wilson, *Special Interests and Policy Making* (Wiley, 1977), quoted in Richardson and Jordan, p. 114.
15. A. G. Jordan and J. Richardson, "The British Policy Style or the Logic of Negotiation?" in J. Richardson (ed.), *Policy Styles in Western Europe* (George Allen & Unwin, 1982), p. 81.
16. See especially P. G. Richards, *Parliament and Conscience* (George Allen & Unwin, 1970).
17. The main works on pluralism are American, most notably those of Dahl and Truman. See especially R. A. Dahl, *A Preface to Democratic Theory* (Chicago University Press, 1956), and *Who Governs*? Yale University Press, 1961). See also D. Truman, *The Governmental Process* (Knopf, 1962).
18. For a Marxist analysis, see R. Miliband, *The State in Capitalist Society* (Quartet, 1973). The classic American elite study is that of C. Wright Mills, *The Power Elite* (Oxford University Press, 1956).
19. R. J. Harrison, *Pluralism and Corporatism* (George Allen & Unwin, 1980), Ch. 5.
20. R. Rose, *Do Parties Make a Difference*? 2nd ed. (Macmillan, 1984). See also A. King, "What Do Elections Decide?" in H. Penniman (ed.), *Democracy at the Polls* (American Enterprise Institute, 1980), pp. 304–8.
21. M. Olson, *The Logic of Collective Action* (Schocken Books, 1968). See also, by the same author, *The Rise and Decline of Nations* (Yale University Press, 1982).
22. Grant and Marsh, pp. 50–52.
23. See A. Cawson, "Pluralism, Corporatism and the Role of the State," *Government and Opposition*, Spring 1978, p. 197.
24. P. C. Schmitter, "Still the Century of Corporatism?" *The Review of Politics*, 36 (1), 1974, pp. 85–131. See also R. Pahl and J. Winkler, "The Coming Corporatism," *New Society*, October 10, 1974.
25. Quoted in Richardson and Jordan, *Governing Under Pressure*, p. 50.
26. See P. Norton, *The Constitution in Flux* (Martin Robertson, 1982), pp. 2, 179, 275, and 282.
27. See A. Cox, "Corporatism and the Corporate State in Britain," in L. Robins (ed.), *Topics in British Politics* (Politics Association, 1982), p. 128.
28. Ibid., p. 129.
29. Norton, pp. 272–75.
30. Quoted in S. H. Beer, *Britain Against Itself* (Faber & Faber, 1982), p. 57.
31. *The Financial Times*, December 23, 1985.
32. See I. Greer, *Right to Be Heard* (Greer, 1985); C. Miller, *Lobbying Government* (Blackwell, 1988); and, for a good review of parliamentary lobbying, C. Grantham, "Parliament and Political Consultants," *Parliamentary Affairs*, 42 (4), 1989. The first major academic work on the subject is M. Rush (ed.),

Parliament and Pressure Politics (Oxford University Press, 1990).

33. See P. Regan, "The 1986 Shops Bill," *Parliamentary Affairs*, 41 (2), 1988; and F. A. C. S. Bown, "The Shops Bill," in Rush, *Parliament and Pressure Politics*.
34. *The Observer*, April 9, 1989.
35. P. Norton and C. Grantham, "The Hyphen in British Politics? Parliament and Professional Lobbying," *British Politics Group Newsletter* (USA), 45, Summer 1986, pp. 4–8.

PART III

Governmental Decision Making

CHAPTER 8

The Executive
Government at the Center

The formal process of determining public policy in Britain is dominated by the executive. Once the executive has agreed on a measure, the assent of Parliament can usually be ensured. Parliament is essentially a policy-ratifying rather than a policy-making body. Once the measure is enacted in legislative form, it will be enforced by the courts: it cannot be struck down on grounds of being contrary to the provisions of the constitution. In the United States, by contrast, the executive enjoys no such dominance. The president cannot proceed on the basis that any proposals he makes can be ensured the assent of Congress. Once enacted, legislative measures can be and occasionally are struck down by the courts as contrary to the provisions of the Constitution. The American political system has been described as a "multiple access" one. It may also be characterized as a "multiple check" system. A proposal emanating from one branch of government can be checked—that is, negated—by another. Congress has negating powers that it is prepared to and not infrequently does use; Parliament has negating powers that it can but hardly ever does use. The executive in Britain can make assumptions about legislative support that few American presidents would dare to make.

Viewed in terms of Constitution and the relationships governed by conventions, the policy-making process in Britain may appear clear and effective. An executive is formed and proceeds to implement a party program with the support of a parliamentary majority. That has been a popular perception, in Britain itself as well as elsewhere. In practice, the process has proved to be more complex and constrained than this picture suggests. An executive has to work within an increasingly intricate political environment shaped by public expectations, group pressures, party commitments, limited resources, the global economy, and an often volatile milieu of international relations. The international constraints have become more pronounced as a consequence of membership in the European Community. Domestically, Parliament has become a more active scrutineer of executive actions. Within Parliament, the executive continues to face a critical body unknown in U. S. politics: the alternative government. The second largest party in the House of Commons forms the official Opposition and in recent decades its leaders have formed a "Shadow Cabinet." For every cabinet minister sitting on the government front bench, there is usually a "shadow" minister on the Opposition front bench. The executive in Britain may achieve the legislative enactments it wants, but those measures may be the product of external pressures and, in being passed, are subject to a process of more organized criticism than exists in the United States.

THE STRUCTURE

It is not only the environment external to the executive that is complex and not always (if ever) harmonious. The same may be said of the executive itself. It comprises an entangled web of bodies, powers, and relationships that, in practice, are not easy to discern and that confuse any attempt to delineate clearly how policy is formulated and where power lies within government. At the apex of government stands the cabinet, headed by the prime minister, and below that the individual government departments headed by ministers and staffed by civil servants. But even within the cabinet there exist a complex infrastructure and sometimes shifting relationships. As government has grown, it not only has become more complex but also has experienced problems of political accountability. Over the course of the century, the civil service has variously grown. At the edges of government, nondepartmental public bodies have burgeoned. For the cabinet, maintaining control of the government body itself has become an awesome task.

In terms of the structure of the executive and the lines of responsibility to Parliament, the formal position is outlined in Figure 8.1. For the purposes of analysis, it is necessary to identify the essential features of the different elements of the executive. The main elements may be subsumed under the headings of the prime minister, the cabinet, ministers, departments, civil servants, and nondepartmental public bodies, known popularly as "quangos." The powers, structure, and composition of each element

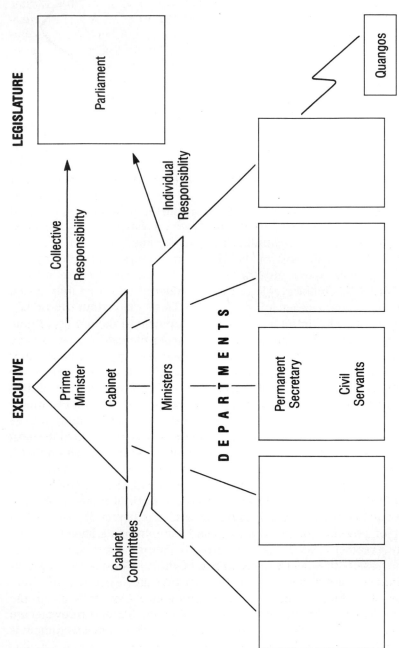

Figure 8.1. The Executive in Britain

and the relationships among them have become increasingly a matter of some controversy.

The Prime Minister

The prime minister stands at the apex of government. The position is a powerful and highly visible one and has achieved even greater prominence in recent years, especially since Margaret Thatcher ascended the steps of 10 Downing Street, the prime minister's official London residence, on May 4, 1979. In the 1960s there was a largely academic debate as to whether or not Britain had "prime ministerial government." Over the past decade the concept has been resuscitated and become the subject of a much wider debate.

In the sixteenth and seventeenth centuries, monarchs were often dependent on particular ministers. However, it was not until the eighteenth century that a recognizable first, or "prime," minister began to emerge. George I, the first of the Hanoverian kings, had little interest in British politics, spoke little or no English, and spent six months of each year on the continent. He left the conduct of affairs entirely to the Cabinet, his chosen group of ministers. "This," as Arthur Berriedale Keith observed, "led inevitably to the development of the office of Prime Minister; for, once the King was removed from the cabinet, the natural tendency was for some minister to take his place as a unifying influence."[1] The first minister to be considered—at least by historians—as prime minister was Sir Robert Walpole, from 1721 to 1742. The term itself had been used before and Walpole himself disclaimed it. It came eventually into colloquial but not formal use. Not until the twentieth century was the position to be referred to in a statute. The official position held by most "prime" ministers was that of First Lord of the Treasury, a position that is still retained by holders of the office. Over time, however, the position of prime minister grew in recognition and in powers. The growth of party government acted as a particular spur to the growth of prime ministerial power. The nineteenth century, as we have seen (Chapter 3), witnessed a transfer of power from the monarch and later from Parliament to the cabinet, a cabinet headed—and chosen—by the prime minister.

The powers that inhere in the office of Prime Minister are considerable. They are also remarkable for the fact that they exist by convention and not by statute or common law. Prerogative powers, such as the appointment of minister, reside in the monarch. Statutory powers are vested in individual ministers. The most powerful person in government is the one who wields no legal powers at all.

The best-known as well as the most important of the prime minister's powers are those of appointment and dismissal. The monarch formally appoints ministers, but by convention she does so on the advice of her prime minister. The reality of who does the choosing is well recognized. Announcements of ministerial appointments are made direct from Downing Street. The prime minister not only chooses who the ministers will be, she can also decide when they are no longer to be ministers. Ministerial reshuffles are used by prime ministers to make changes and bring new blood into the cabinet, or the ranks of noncabinet ministers, and are sometimes controversial, as in July 1962 when Harold Macmillan dismissed one-third of his cabinet and in July 1989 when Margaret Thatcher moved a very unwilling Sir Geoffrey Howe from the Foreign Office to the position of Lord President of the Council and Leader of the House of Commons. The extent of prime ministerial patronage is considerable: there are now over a hundred ministers and all owe their positions to the prime minister. Nor does the patronage end with ministers. The prime minister in effect chooses new members of the House of Lords, decides other honors (such as the award of knighthoods), and can appoint individuals to a range of public positions. She even has the final say, should she choose to exercise it, over the appointments of archbishops and bishops in the established church, the Church of England.

The power to appoint ministers is not unfettered. By convention, ministers must normally be drawn from Parliament and, by convention, predominantly from the House of Commons. (There is no legal requirement that ministers be MPs or peers, and occasionally one post in particular—that of the solicitor general for Scotland—is filled by a lawyer outside Parliament.) Partisanship dictates that the ministers will be drawn from the prime minister's own party. It is also deemed politically prudent to ensure a reasonable balance of ministers, in terms of both geography—drawing ministers from different constituencies across the country—and the different wings of the party. There are also likely to be senior figures with considerable support among MPs whom the prime minister would find it difficult to exclude, not least because they could become dangerous critics from the back benches. Nonetheless, the extent of the balance is sometimes a little skewed—Edward Heath in particular was accused of selecting a personally loyal cabinet—and there are few who are willing to challenge the prime minister's judgments. The appointing—and dismissal—power wielded by the prime minister serves to ensure loyalty on the part of ministers and of those MPs who would like to be ministers.

The power to choose ministers is important not only in ensuring ministerial loyalty to the prime minister; it is also a major tool in influencing the direction of public policy. As Maurice Kogan has observed, the authority to appoint, transfer, or dismiss enables the prime minister to allocate values and thus change or confirm an individual minister's policies.[2] Mrs. Thatcher has ensured that supporters of a neoliberal economic policy have been appointed to key enconomic ministries. Her removal of Sir Geoffrey Howe from the Foreign Office in 1989 was seen as a rejection of the approach he had taken toward European economic integration.

Power to determine the direction of policy is not confined to the blunt weapon of appointment and dismissal. It derives also from the prime minister's position as chairman of the cabinet. In the nineteenth century John Morley described the prime minister as *primus inter pares* (first among equals) in the cabinet. In practice, the premier's position has always been much more than that. The prime minister determines when the cabinet will meet and what it will discuss. She also sums up discussion in cabinet. Very few prime ministers have resorted to taking votes. Richard Crossman, a cabinet minister in the 1960s, claimed that minutes of cabinet meetings contained what the prime minister wanted to be done rather than a record of what had, on his recollection, been agreed to. The prime minister also determines the extent and composition of cabinet committees, appointed to save cabinet time by discussing particular topics or areas of government responsibility.

There is no Prime Minister's Department as such. The size of the staff in Downing Street is small.[3] However, the prime minister, as chairman of the cabinet, has at her disposal the secretary to the cabinet (who is also usually head of the civil service), the cabinet secretariat (which records and monitors cabinet decisions), and a policy unit. The policy unit was first brought into being in the 1970s, following the return of a Labour government in 1974, and was maintained by Mrs. Thatcher when she took office in 1979. It now comprises seven or eight experts on particular subjects (economic policy, industry, and so on); they are politically committed individuals, usually seconded from outside bodies. The unit exists to advise on and propose future policy. It is, significantly, the *No. 10* policy unit. When it was established, it supplanted to some extent the Central Policy Review Staff (CPRS, known colloquially as the Think Tank), an advisory body set up in 1970 by Edward Heath; comprised of seconded civil servants as well as political appointees, it ranged widely over areas of policy and advised the cabinet in addition to the prime minister. The policy unit was designed to provide a more party-oriented body working directly with the prime minister. The CPRS was gradually overshadowed, and in 1983 Mrs. Thatcher disbanded it.

Unlike members of the policy unit, members of the cabinet secretariat are permanent civil servants. The prime minister's control over the governmental machine is enhanced by the fact that she is also minister for the civil service: the permanent head of the service reports directly to her and, indeed, as secretary to the cabinet, sees her usually on a daily basis. Power over the appointment of senior civil servants—primarily the permanent secretaries, the civil service heads of each department—rests with the prime minister, not the ministers in whose departments they serve.

The powers that inhere in the position of Prime Minister are thus considerable. They are reinforced by the fact that the prime minister is an obvious focus of media attention—election campaigns are seen increasingly as gladiatorial contests between the prime minister and the leader of the Opposition (the alternative prime minister)—and by the fact that the prime minister is party leader. The confluence of the two positions, party leader and prime minister, the former being the basis for achieving the latter, makes for a powerful head of government. This is especially the case under a Conservative prime minister. As we saw in Chapter 6, the party leader is the fount of all party policy and appoints the heads of Conservative Central Office. All party bodies are advisory, not policy making, and loyalty within the party normally flows to the leader. Consequently, a Conservative prime minister is normally in a position to determine the direction of public policy; that direction, as Margaret Thatcher has demonstrated, can sometimes constitute a radical departure.

The prime minister's powers, then, are extensive. The use to which they are actually put depends upon the person occupying the office. Britain has experienced 18 prime ministers since 1900 (see Table 8.1), and their approach to the office has varied considerably. In terms of the purpose for which they seek the office, it is possible to identify four types:

Innovators. They seek power in order to achieve a future goal of their own creation and are prepared, if necessary, to bring their party kicking and screaming in their wake in order to achieve that goal.

Reformers. They seek power in order to achieve the implementation of a particular program, but one drawn up by the party rather than by the premier.

Egoists. They seek power for the sake of power; they are concerned with enjoying the here and now of office rather than with future goals, and they fight to keep power.

Balancers. They fall into two categories: those who seek power in order to achieve balance, within society and within party, and those who share the same goal but, rather than seeking power, have it thrust upon them, usually as compromise choices for leader; the latter may be described as conscripts in the office.

These four are ideal types. Some premiers have straddled categories. Others have changed over time: Winston Churchill was essentially an innovator as wartime prime minister but a balancer in peacetime. Nonetheless, the categories are useful for assessing and distinguishing prime

TABLE 8.1. PRIME MINISTERS SINCE 1900

Took Office	Prime Minister	Party
June 25, 1895	The Marquess of Salisbury	Unionist (Conservative)
July 12, 1902	Arthur James Balfour	Unionist (Conservative)
December 5, 1905	Sir Henry Campbell-Bannerman	Liberal
April 8, 1908	Herbert Henry Asquith	Liberal[a]
December 7, 1916	David Lloyd George	Liberal[b]
October 23, 1922	Andrew Bonar Law	Unionist (Conservative)
May 22, 1923	Stanley Baldwin	Unionist (Conservative)
January 22, 1924	J. Ramsay MacDonald	Labour
November 4, 1924	Stanley Baldwin	Conservative
June 5, 1929	J. Ramsay MacDonald	Labour
August 24, 1931	J. Ramsay MacDonald	National Labour[c]
June 7, 1935	Stanley Baldwin	Conservative[c]
May 28, 1937	Neville Chamberlain	Conservative[c]
May 10, 1940	Winston S. Churchill	Conservative[d]
May 23, 1945	Clement Attlee	Labour
October 26, 1951	Sir Winston Churchill	Conservative
April 6, 1955	Sir Anthony Eden	Conservative
January 10, 1957	Harold Macmillan	Conservative
October 19, 1963	Sir Alec Douglas-Home	Conservative
October 16, 1964	Harold Wilson	Labour
June 19, 1970	Edward Heath	Conservative
March 4, 1974	Harold Wilson	Labour
April 5, 1976	L. James Callaghan	Labour
May 4, 1979	Margaret Thatcher	Conservative

[a] Coalition from May 1915
[b] Coalition Government
[c] National Government
[d] Coalition Government May 1940–May 1945; National Government May–July 1945.

ministers. Table 8.2 categorizes the twentieth-century premiers. The past quarter century has seen power-seeking balancers (Macmillan, Callaghan), a conscript balancer (Douglas-Home), an egoist (Wilson), an obvious innovator (Thatcher), and a premier who straddled the categories of innovator and egoist (Heath).[4] The quest to occupy the office thus draws many different politicians. Which one actually reaches the top of what Disraeli described as "the greasy pole" will affect significantly how the powers of the office are used. Had William Whitelaw been elected leader of the Conservative party in 1975 instead of Margaret Thatcher, he would almost certainly have used the powers of the office in a very different way than has Mrs. Thatcher (always assuming, of course, that he was able to

TABLE 8.2. TYPOLOGY OF PRIME MINISTERS

Innovators	Reformers	
Churchill	Campbell-Bannerman	
(wartime)	Asquith	
Heath?	Chamberlain	
Thatcher	Attlee	

Egoists	Balancers	
	Power-Seeking	*Conscripts*
Lloyd George?	Salisbury	Bonar Law
MacDonald?	Balfour?	Douglas-
Eden	Baldwin	Home
Wilson	Churchill	
Heath?	(peacetime)	
	Macmillan	
	Callaghan	

Source: P. Norton, "Prime Ministerial Power," Social Studies Review, 3 (3), 1988, p. 110.

lead his party to victory in 1979). Mrs. Thatcher has wielded the levers of power in a distinctive manner. According to one former cabinet minister, she has used her power to sum up cabinet discussions in a novel way: she sums up at the beginning!

However determined a prime minister, wielding the powers of the office will not necessarily achieve a desired outcome. Prime ministerial success depends in part upon the skills of the individual in the office: some are able to mold a united cabinet, some to utilize powers at a time likely to maximize their effectiveness, some to judge what will and what will not prove politically acceptable (a particular skill of Mrs. Thatcher's), and some to assess likely outcomes. It depends in part upon external circumstances over which the prime minister can have little or no control, such as crop failure, the U.S. economy, and Third World debt. It also depends in large part upon something over which the prime minister can exert considerable influence: the immediate political environment, encompassing not least the cabinet and the rest of the executive. The prime minister is powerful but not all-powerful. The prime minister's time and resources are limited. The cabinet, individual ministers, and civil servants are not lacking in powers of their own to influence the making of public policy.

The Cabinet

The cabinet is the collective decision-making body of British government. Today it comprises between 20 and 25 members (see Table 8.3), constituting the ministerial heads of all the principal government departments as

TABLE 8.3. THE CABINET: JANUARY 1990

Prime Minister, First Lord of the Treasury and Minister for the Civil Service—The Rt. Hon. Margaret Thatcher, F.R.S., M.P.

Lord President of the Council and Leader of the House of Commons—The Rt. Hon. Sir Geoffrey Howe, Q.C., M.P.

Lord Chancellor—The Rt. Hon. Lord Mackay of Clashfern

Secretary of State for Foreign and Commonwealth Affairs—The Rt. Hon. Douglas Hurd, C.B.E., M.P.

Chancellor of the Exchequer—The Rt. Hon. John Major, M.P.

Home Secretary—The Rt. Hon. David Waddington, Q.C., M.P.

Secretary of State for Wales—The Rt. Hon. Peter Walker, M.B.E., M.P.

Secretary of State for Defense—The Rt. Hon. Tom King, M.P.

Secretary of State for Trade and Industry and President of the Board of Board—The Rt. Hon. Nicholas Ridley, M.P.

Chancellor of the Duchy of Lancaster—The Rt. Hon. Kenneth Baker, M.P.

Secretary of State for Health—The Rt. Hon. Kenneth Clarke, Q.C., M.P.

Secretary of State for Education and Science—The Rt. Hon. John MacGregor, O.B.E., M.P.

Secretary of State for Scotland—The Rt. Hon. Malcolm Rifkind, Q.C., M.P.

Secretary of State for Transport—The Rt. Hon. Cecil Parkinson, M.P.

Secretary of State for Energy—The Rt. Hon. John Wakeham, M.P.

Lord Privy Seal and Leader of the House of Lords—The Rt. Hon. Lord Belstead

Secretary of State for Social Security—The Rt. Hon. Anthony Newton, O.B.E., M.P.

Secretary of State for the Environment—The Rt. Hon. Christopher Patten, M.P.

Secretary of State for Northern Ireland—The Rt. Hon. Peter Brooke, M.P.

Minister of Agriculture, Fisheries and Food—The Rt. Hon. John Gummer, M.P.

Chief Secretary to the Treasury—The Rt. Hon. Norman Lamont, M.P.

Secretary of State for Employment—The Rt. Hon. Michael Howard, Q.C., M.P.

well as a number of ministers without departmental responsibilities (for example, the chancellor of the Duchy of Lancaster). By convention, as we have seen, its members are drawn from, and remain within, Parliament. A minimum of two peers (the Lord Chancellor and the leader of the House of Lords), and rarely more than four, are appointed to the cabinet. Most members have served a parliamentary apprenticeship, having moved up from the back benches to junior ministerial office and then to minister of state level before being considered for cabinet appointment. It is rare for cabinet ministers to be appointed from the ranks of back-benchers or from people outside the House. There have been rare exceptions: in the Second World War, for example, union leader Ernest Bevin was brought straight into government. In such cases, the normal practice is for the new minister to be created a peer or to be found a safe seat to win in a by-election.

The cabinet, like the position of prime minister, developed in importance in the eighteenth and nineteenth centuries. However, as the monarch's principal body of advisers, it was not particularly efficient. It often had little to do, decisions were frequently leaked by waiters (it met for dinner at the home of one of its members), members sometimes slept during meetings, and there was no agenda. In the twentieth century, as the demands on the cabinet grew—public policy becoming both more extensive and more complex—it developed in terms of its political significance and its organization. The second decade of the century witnessed a particular improvement in organization as well as an authoritative clarification of what its role was. In 1916 the cabinet secretariat came into being, responsible for circulating agenda, papers, and minutes and for monitoring the implementation of cabinet decisions; previously, implementation had been very much dependent on the memories of ministers, some of whom forgot what had been decided. In 1918 the Machinery of Government Committee delineated the functions of the cabinet to be (1) the final determination of the policy to be submitted to Parliament, (2) the supreme control of the national executive in accordance with the policy prescribed by cabinet, and (3) the continuous coordination and delimitation of the authorities of the several departments of state. This delineation remains extant. It has not been superseded but what has changed has been the cabinet's mode of fulfilling its functions. As the functions became more onerous for a single body meeting once or twice a week, it developed a complex infrastructure. Consequently, there are two vehicles through which the cabinet now operates: cabinet committees and the full cabinet.

Cabinet committees have burgeoned, particularly since 1945. They are formed from the ministers relevant to the area covered by the committee as well as some ministers free of departmental responsibilities. The committees' creation, membership, and chairmanship are determined by the prime minister. They are serviced by the Cabinet Secretariat, which, among other things, provides briefing papers for the chairmen. The committees are shrouded in secrecy. Neither their existence nor their membership is officially supposed to be revealed, though Prime Minister Mrs. Thatcher did break with tradition in 1979 to admit their existence.[5] The committees comprise a number of standing committees, designated by letters of the alphabet (E committee, for example, designates the economic strategy committee), and others created on an ad hoc basis to cover particular problems. Mrs. Thatcher announced that she had established four standing committees: economic strategy, defense and overseas policy, home and social affairs, and legislation, the first two being under her chairmanship. Although she did not reveal the number of subcommittees, they are believed to be numerous. (There were about 100 subcommittees during Harold Wilson's premiership.) Decisions emanating from the committees have the same authority as full cabinet decisions, and since 1967, disputes within committees can be referred to the full cabinet only with the approval of the committee chairman. When important issues are under discussion, it is usual for the designated members to attend, though on other occasions senior ministers can and do replace themselves with their junior ministers.[6] Richard Crossman, subsequently a cabinet minister himself, took the view that the committees detracted from the power of the cabinet,[7] though the more general view is that they serve as a useful complement to cabinet, lightening its workload, clarifying issues for it, and allowing it to concentrate on the more central and general matters of government.

The full cabinet usually meets every Thursday morning in the Cabinet Room at 10 Downing Street. In addition to the cabinet ministers, the government chief whip attends the meetings. He is the minister responsible for ensuring the support of the parliamentary party in parliamentary votes and he acts as a channel of communication between the cabinet and its parliamentary supporters. He advises on likely parliamentary reaction to proposed measures. The cabinet secretary attends and sits on the prime minister's right. Meetings usually last for one to three hours, with additional meetings, if necessary, on Tuesdays and sometimes other days as necessary. As prime minister, Margaret Thatcher has tended to rely on the regular Thursday meeting, with few additional meetings being called.

The cabinet remains important as the central forum for the resolution of disputes between departments, particularly in the allocation of public expenditure. Ministers usually defend their particular department, often supported on a reciprocal basis by ministers representing other spending departments. Much depends on the personalities involved, not least that of the PM. Some PMs tend to involve themselves in a wide range of items being brought forward by ministers, while others content themselves with concentrating on central issues of the economy and foreign affairs, leaving other departmental ministers to get on with their jobs unhindered. The process by which a cabinet determines policy thus varies from PM to PM and, depending on changing political circumstance, may vary during the tenure of office of one PM. The cabinet remains the forum for the resolution of most major issues of public policy, but a number of those issues may effectively be resolved elsewhere, either in cabinet committee or by a meeting of senior ministers. Less central issues usually do not reach the cabinet at all.

As with the position of prime minister, no formal powers are vested in the cabinet: it exists and operates by convention. The most important convention, one that in part governs its behavior as well as its relationship to Parliament, is that of collective responsibility. This convention, which developed during the eighteenth and nineteenth centuries, prescribes that members of the cabinet accept responsibility collectively for decisions made by it. Ministers may argue in cabinet, but once a decision has been made they are required to support that decision publicly. Any minister failing to support a cabinet decision in public once it had been announced would be expected to resign: failure to do so would result in the PM's requesting that minister's resignation.

The convention is deemed also to dictate the necessity for secrecy to attach to cabinet discussions. The authority of the cabinet and of particular ministers could be undermined if cabinet disputes were made public. Ministers publicly defending decisions with which they are known to have disagreed in cabinet would weaken the cabinet in trying to ensure implementation of those decisions. A minister's authority and influence could be undermined if it were known that he was implementing a policy against which he had fought in cabinet. Nonetheless, recent years have witnessed a weakening of this aspect of the convention, with ministers engaging in semipublic and, for all intents and purposes, public leaks and disagreements, and with some ex-ministers recording cabinet discussions in their memoirs. On two occasions in the Labour government of 1974–1979 the convention was actually suspended in order to allow ministers to vote against government policy in the House of Commons. Both occasions concerned the issue of British membership in the European Communities, on which cabinet members were bitterly divided. To avoid the possibility of resignations or the cabinet falling apart, the PM (Harold Wilson in 1975, James Callaghan in 1977) decided to suspend the convention. Although the convention remains extant, it is becoming a difficult one for PMs to enforce.

One other condition dictated by the convention of collective responsibility continues to be followed. A government defeat in the House of Commons on the motion "that this House has no confidence in Her Majesty's Government" necessitates the government's resigning or requesting a dissolution. On March 28, 1979, when the minority Labour government was defeated on a vote of confidence, the PM immediately went to Buckingham Palace to request a dissolution. This requirement stipulated by the convention is one of the few about which it remains possible to generalize with confidence.

The cabinet remains at the heart of British government, but its capacity to make the final determination of government policy is limited. In some sectors, power has passed upward to the prime minister (sometimes in conjunction with senior ministers) and to the institutions of the

European Community. Because of the sheer workload, power over much nonessential policy has passed downward to individual ministers. The departmental responsibility of ministers makes it difficult for the cabinet to act as a truly collective decision-making body; most ministers are concerned with fighting for their departments and, where matters do not affect their departments, they take no interest. Yet despite this limitation, the cabinet remains a powerful body. No prime minister, however hard he or she may try, can ignore it. The cabinet can constitute an important constraining influence. On occasion it may actually go against the wishes of the PM. Even Churchill at the height of his wartime powers could not always get the cabinet to agree to what he wanted. The same has been true of Mrs. Thatcher. Though it has little opportunity to be proactive in the policy-making process—the initiative for policy comes from below or above—the cabinet nonetheless still forms a significant reactive body. Despite being hand-picked by the prime minister, the cabinet is not always predictable in its actions.

Ministers

When a PM forms an administration, he or she is called on to select not only the senior ministers to head the various departments of state, as well as senior ministers without portfolio, but also a host of junior ministers. In addition to a ministerial head, who is usually of secretary of state rank, each department normally has one and sometimes more ministers of state and one or more undersecretaries of state. The PM also appoints a chief whip and 12 or 13 other whips in the Commons as well as a chief whip and 5 or 6 other whips in the House of Lords. In total, a little over 100 ministerial appointments are now made (see Table 8.4). Despite the demands made of

TABLE 8.4. NUMBER OF GOVERNMENT MINISTERS, OCTOBER 1989

Rank	House of Commons	House of Lords	Total
Cabinet ministers (including PM)	20	2	22
Ministers of state[a]	25	8	33
Law officers	2	1	4[b]
Undersecretaries of state	22	4	26
Whips (including chief whips)	14	6	20
Total	83	21	105[b]

[a] Includes Financial and Economic Secretaries to the Treasury.
[b] Includes the Solicitor General for Scotland, Alan Rodger, who is not a member of either House.
Note: Three nonpolitical Household appointments (officers of the Royal Household, traditionally listed as part of the government) are excluded here.

government, the increase in the number of ministers during the course of the century has been a modest one.

Of the ministers appointed, the most important are, as one would expect, those appointed to head the various departments (see Table 8.3). The significance of junior ministers tends to vary. In past decades, many parliamentary undersecretaries had little to do and often were regarded as constituting something of an insignificant life form within the departments. To some extent, that remains the case today for a number of undersecretaries, known in Whitehall circles under the acronym PUSS (parliamentary undersecretaries of state). The influence of junior ministers within departments tend to depend on the ministerial head. There is a growing tendency for ministers to assign greater responsibility for certain functions to their ministers of state and undersecretaries; when junior ministers attend cabinet committees, they gain some knowledge of the workings of the higher echelons of government. Nonetheless, disputes between junior ministers and the chief civil servant, the permanent secretary, in a department can be resolved only by the ministerial head, and there remains a tendency for interested bodies to try to influence the senior minister even on matters delegated to junior ministers.

The heads of departments have tended to become even more important decision makers than they were hitherto. Indeed, there is a case for arguing that, far from having prime ministerial or cabinet government, Britain has a form of ministerial government. As demands on government have increased, only the most important matters have percolated up to the cabinet for resolution. Most important decisions affecting a department are taken by the minister. The relationship between a minister and the House of Commons and between the minister and his or her department is governed by the convention of individual ministerial responsibility. The convention is important not only for determining who is responsible to whom (civil servants to minister, minister to Parliament), but also for determining who is responsible for what. The cabinet as a body has no legal powers; powers are vested in ministers. When government takes on new responsibilities by statute, powers to fulfill those responsibilities are granted to a minister. "The Secretary of State shall have power to. . . ." According to Nevil Johnson, "the enduring effect of the doctrine of ministerial responsibility has been over the past century or so that powers have been vested in ministers and on a relentlessly increasing scale."[8]

Ministers, then, are very much at the heart of the government process. Major issues are resolved in cabinet as is battle for departmental budgets. Other issues are usually but not always resolved at the departmental level. Two former education ministers, Edward Boyle and Anthony Crosland, both asserted that "the individual Minister of Education rather than the Cabinet is the focal point of political initiatives and decisions in Education."[9] Crosland himself took only two matters concerning education policy to the cabinet.

Nonetheless, ministers operate within the context of a number of significant constraints. Because of parliamentary, constituency, and various public duties, the time they have to devote to the job is limited. They are dependent largely on their departments for advice. They have few independent channels for obtaining advice and information: a number of ministers in recent years have appointed political advisers, but their numbers are limited (on prime ministerial instructions), they have no institutional resources of their own, and on occasion civil servants have worked around them rather than with them. Ministers have little time to get to know a department before moving on to another post. Few ministers serve in the same post for the lifetime of a Parliament. Since 1944, the average tenure of office of a minister of education has been a little under two years. When Mrs. Thatcher appointed a new Secretary of State for Northern Ireland in July 1989, it was her fifth in ten years; her turnover of Trade and Industry secretaries has been even greater. Turnover in junior ministers is sometimes even more rapid. Furthermore, and perhaps most important, because of the number of decisions that a minister is now called on to make, many have to be delegated to officials to make in the minister's name. Even matters that do come before a minister for a personal decision may be heavily weighted by the advice of officials and by the manner in which the issue is brought to the minister's attention. Such decisions also have to be taken within the context of increasingly limited resources. The minister has to battle with treasury ministers to try to get what share of the government cake he can. Given economic cutbacks, it is rarely likely to be enough to meet a department's self-perceived needs.

Departments

Ministers are appointed to head departments. The way those departments are structured and the responsibilities vested in them can affect the nature of policy making. If departments are small and are allocated responsibility for very specific subjects, particularly those subjects that have been the responsibility of government for many decades, there is a problem of achieving coordination on matters that touch on the responsibilities of other departments and that may recently have come onto the political agenda. Interdepartmental coordination has tended to be dominated by officials rather than ministers and hence it has been viewed as reinforcing the influence of the civil service. Attempts to solve the problem of divided responsibilities by creating large departments may help improve the quality of decision making, since an issue can be dealt with more efficiently within one department, but they may also generate difficulties in trying to keep the departments under ministerial control. In Britain, these difficulties have been realized as a result of various restructurings of the different departments.

The number of major departments has fluctuated during the twentieth century. Sir Richard Clarke listed 18 as being in existence in 1914, 23 in 1935, 30 in 1951, 27 in 1964, 18 in 1973, and 21 in 1974.[10] There are currently 20 main functional departments, plus 2 with no major functions (Table 8.5). Following his return to office as prime minister in 1951, Winston Churchill attempted to achieve some greater degree of coordination through the appointment of a number of departmental "overlords," ministers with responsibility for a broad range of departments. The experiment was not successful, in part because a number of the overlords were indeed Lords and hence were sitting in the Upper House away from the scrutiny of MPs. Since then, there has been a tendency instead to amalgamate departments. In 1964 the Defense Department was expanded to encompass the three service departments, and in 1968 the Foreign Office and the Commonwealth Office were merged to form the Foreign and Commonwealth Office. Following the return of a Conservative government under Mr. Heath in 1970, two so-called "super departments" were created. The Department of Trade and Industry (DTI) encompassed the former Board of Trade and the Ministries of Technology and Power. The Department of the Environment incorporated the former Ministries of Housing and Local Government, Transport, and Public Buildings and Works. The government made a conscious effort to improve its machinery. It designed the amalgamations to reduce the need for interdepartmental compromise, to enable a single strategy to be pursued within one department, to create the capacity to manage larger resource-consuming programs, and to allow more direct identification to the public of ministers responsible for defined functions. These intentions were not to be wholly fulfilled. Because of the oil crisis of 1973–1974, Mr. Heath sliced off part of the DTI to form the Department of Energy. In any event, there had been problems in maintaining ministerial control of the DTI. Under the subsequent Labour government, the concept of "super ministries" did not find such strong support. Transport was reinstated as a separate department and the DTI was broken up into the Departments of Trade, Industry, and Prices and Consumer Affairs. When Mrs. Thatcher came into office in 1979, Prices and Consumer Affairs was put back under the Department of Trade, and the Departments of Trade and Industry subsequently merged again; in 1988 the Department of Health and Social Security (DHSS), the biggest spending domestic ministry, was broken up into its two components.

Of remaining departments, a number have remained largely unchanged in terms of title and responsibilities throughout the century.

TABLE 8.5. THE PRINCIPAL GOVERNMENT DEPARTMENTS HEADED BY MINISTERS IN 1989

Department	Responsibilities
Agriculture, Fisheries and Food	Agriculture, horticulture, fishing, food
Defense	Defense policy, control and administration of armed services
Education and Science	Education, fostering development of civil science
Employment	Manpower policy, unemployment benefits
Energy	Energy, government relations with nationalized industries, Atomic Energy Authority
Environment	Wide range of responsibilities covering the physical environment, including housing, construction, land use, regional planning, new towns, countryside, and local government structure and finance
Foreign and Commonwealth Office	International relations; protecting British interests overseas; certain administrative responsibilities in dependent territories
Health	Administration of National Health Service (in England); certain aspects of public health
Home Office	Covers domestic functions not assigned to other departments; includes administration of justice, police, immigration, public morals and safety, broadcasting policy, and prisons
Law Officers' Department	Law officers are chief legal advisers to the government; appear on behalf of the Crown in major court cases; attorney-general has ultimate responsibility for enforcement of criminal law
Lord Advocate's Department	Equivalent in Scotland to the Law Officers' Department in England
Lord Chancellor's Department	Assists Lord Chancellor in the administration of the courts and the law
Management and Personnel Office	Responsible for civil service management (minister in charge is the prime minister)
Northern Ireland Office	Exercises executive powers in Northern Ireland on behalf of United Kingdom government: encompasses agriculture, commerce, education, community relations, finance, environment, health and social services, housing, and manpower
Privy Council Office	Minor functions (e.g., for arranging making of Royal Proclamations); office often occupied by minister with responsibility for government's legislative program in House of Commons

Department	Responsibilities
Scottish Office	Governmental functions in Scotland, including agriculture, education, economic planning, Home and Health, and development
Social Security	Social services
Trade and Industry	National and regional industrial policy, aerospace policy, overseas trade policy, information technology
Transport	General transport policy, railways, ports, freight movements, road safety, inland waterways
Treasury	Economic strategy, public expenditure, fiscal policy, foreign currency reserves, international monetary policy
Welsh Office	Within Wales, agriculture (jointly with Ministry of Agriculture), primary and secondary education, town and country planning, water, roads, tourism, new towns, forestry, urban grants
Chancellor of Duchy of Lancaster	Administration of royal estate of Duchy of Lancaster; primarily occupied by minister with no specific portfolio

Note: There are a number of other bodies classed officially as departments but not headed directly by a minister. These include the Cabinet Office (under the cabinet secretary), responsible to the cabinet as a whole; the Board of Customs and Excise (parliamentary responsibility for which is exercised by Treasury ministers); and the Board of Inland Revenue.

Others have lost some of their functions to other or newly created departments. For example, the Welsh Office, created in 1964, and the Northern Ireland Office, created in 1972, took over responsibilities previously vested in the Home Office. Such changes may serve certain purposes, such as improved coordination or more clearly defined responsibility for a particular subject, but they may also be costly in resources and manpower, especially where there is a frequent change in a ministry's status and responsibilities. They also can lead to confusion as well as competition, when certain groups demand the recognition of having their area of interest made the responsibility of a separate department, headed preferably by a minister of cabinet rank. Given the differences in the size and responsibilities of departments, only broad generalizations can be made about their internal structures. Each department, as was mentioned in Chapter 7, is normally divided into functional units. The hierarchical structure in each department is basically as shown in Figure 8.2. Each functional unit, the division, is headed by a civil servant of assistant undersecretary of state rank. Above the units are deputy undersecretaries, and above them, the civil servant responsible for the running of the department, the permanent undersecretary of state (known as the permanent secretary). He (rarely she) is in effect the chief executive officer of the department and answers directly to the minister.

Figure 8.3 shows the organization within a relatively small department, the Department of Employment, chosen because it provides a manageable and not too complex diagram but still indicates the basic structure of each department. For the larger departments, the figure would have to be greatly expanded to encompass all the functional units. In the Foreign and Commonwealth Office, for example, there are more than 50 functional units. The Scottish Office, with responsibility for matters covered in England by separate departments, actually has bodies titled Department of Agriculture, Home and Health Department, and Education Department (see Chapter 9).

Departments are clearly complex and diverse bodies, and they are likely to become more so as a result of the creation of executive agencies. In 1988, following a report from an efficiency unit set up by the prime minister, the government decided that to the greatest extent practicable the executive functions of government should be carried out by operationally distinct agencies, each with clearly defined tasks and managerial responsibility for carrying out those tasks. Each agency was to have a chief executive who would also be the accounting officer. Various bodies within departments were identified as potential agencies, and by the beginning of 1989 three of them—the Vehicles Inspectorate, Companies House, and Her Majesty's Stationery Office—had been given agency status. Another thirty were also planned, ranging from the Civil Service College to the Patent Office. Agencies remain within departments, and responsibility for day-to-day operations rests with the chief executive, who works within policy objectives and a resources framework set by the responsible minister in consultation with the Treasury.

Structures are not neutral in their effect. Though some management

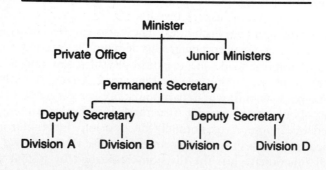

Figure 8.2. Department Structure.

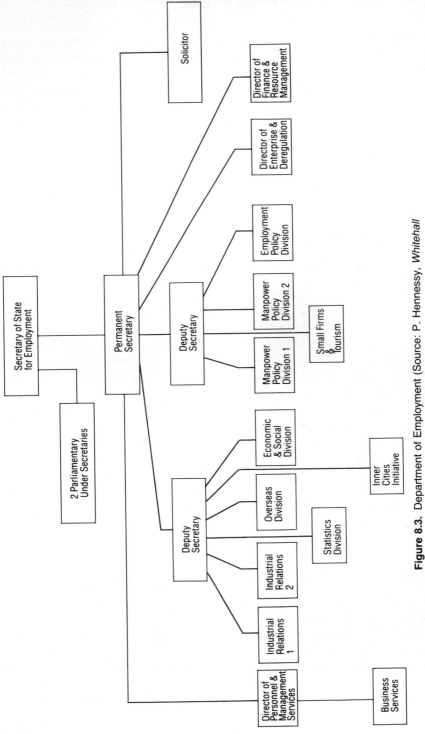

Figure 8.3. Department of Employment (Source: P. Hennessy, *Whitehall* [Secker & Warburg, 1989], p. 451.)

consultants criticized the agency proposal for not being sufficiently radical (none of the proposed agencies covered core functions, such as defense procurement), its implementation will nonetheless significantly affect the shape of government departments. By the end of the century a significant fraction of government responsibilities will rest with operationally independent agencies, which will absorb approximately one-third of government employees. Hence a more complex—and, if government intentions are fulfilled, more managerially efficient—departmental structure will result.

Civil Service

Ministers stand at the political apex of government. They head departments that are staffed by a body of permanent public employees, known collectively as the civil service. At the turn of the century there were a little over 100,000 civil servants. Their numbers reached a peak in 1979, when there were over 700,000; by 1988, following government cutbacks and some transfers of bodies such as the Royal Ordnance to the private sector, there were approximately 577,000. (The figure does not include employees of nationalized industries or local government, or members of the judiciary or the armed forces.) They serve to provide ministers with advice and information, to carry out their decisions and to administer the business of government. The relationship between them and ministers is governed by the convention of individual ministerial responsibility. The minister is answerable to Parliament for his or her department and alone is formally responsible for that department and its activities. The civil service head of each department (the permanent secretary) is answerable to the minister for the administration of officials within the department and serves usually as the minister's principal adviser. The convention of ministerial responsibility provides a cloak of anonymity to departmental activities. The advice a minister receives from officials and the manner of its formulation and presentation are kept from public gaze. Knowledge of what goes on in a department, certainly at the higher levels, may be made available only by the minister or by officials acting on his or her behalf.

Most civil servants carry out the routine tasks of government, administering various government programs and everyday matters for which government has responsibility. The largest department is Defense, with more than 90,000 civilian officials. The civil servants involved in advising ministers are comparatively few, comprising essentially the 3,000 or so of permanent secretary, deputy secretary, assistant secretary, senior principal, and principal rank (i.e., the most senior ranks within the service, ranked now by grades, G1, G2, and so on). They advise ministers, prepare briefs for them, and ensure that their decisions are carried out. Officials take great care to study parties' election manifestos, and an incoming government will find the civil service ready with advice on how to implement its program. According to Bruce Headey, civil servants prefer ministers who are capable of taking decisions, of winning cabinet battles, and of defending their departments from parliamentary criticism.[11] Ministers, for their part, look for officials who will provide them with a range of options from which to choose, expert advice, and the loyal implementation of ministerial objectives and policies.

As a rule, civil servants behave as their political masters expect them to behave. A number of former prime ministers and ministers have praised officials for their loyalty and their ability. Nonetheless, various criticisms of the civil service have been heard. One concerns the recruitment and training of civil servants. Although selected by open, competitive examination, those recruited to the senior ranks of the service have been and are predominantly public-school- and Oxford-educated applicants, despite attempts to widen the intake.[12] Recruitment also tends to favor generalists over specialists; that is, there has been a tendency to select graduates in the arts and humanities rather than those in the pure or applied sciences. The presence of generalists has been a point of some contention, some observers considering it to be responsible in large measure for poor advice to ministers and poor appreciation of new developments in science and technology. Once an applicant is in the service, most training is on-the-job training. Senior civil servants are geared to assisting ministers in the formulation and implementation of policy; they have little training as managers, even though they have extensive responsibilities for personnel and finance.[13] The government's decision in 1988 to create executive agencies within departments was made in order to improve management in the civil service; improved management training was also introduced. Other criticisms are directed at the relationship between ministers and civil servants. There is a school of thought tending toward the view that Britain has, if anything, not a cabinet or ministerial form of government, but rather a form of rule by civil servants.

The argument advanced by this school of thought is that civil servants are able to exert undue influence over decisions nominally taken by ministers. The body of civil servants is able to exert such influence because of its permanence, size, expertise, coordination, anonymity, and control of information as well as, to a large extent, the ministers' timetables. Furthermore, it is argued, this influence has grown in recent years, not only because of the increase in the number of decisions needing to be made by ministers (the greater the number, the less time a minister has to devote to each one), but also because of Britain's membership in the European Community (EC) and the uneven implementation of the Report of the Fulton Committee (of which more below). Civil servants' influence in the 1970s was also enhanced, according to Tony Benn, by their access to the Central Policy Review Staff, which existed until 1983, officials using it as a vehicle for getting their views injected into cabinet committees.

Civil servants effectively enjoy tenure in their appointments, and once they are recruited to the service they tend to make a career of it. Most permanent secretaries have spent more than 25 years in the service. While ministers will come and go, their senior officials remain in place. Ministers will look to their permanent secretaries for knowledge of how their departments work. They will look to their officials for briefing documents and advice on the merits and demerits of available options. They will look to their private offices to control the flow of paperwork that reaches their desks. Officials, if so inclined, may seek to influence a minister's decision by the content of the papers they submit to him or her, or by the manner of presentation of such papers. By submitting papers at the last minute and forcing a speedy decision, or by inserting the relevant documents in a mass of paperwork in the minister's file so that their significance may not be obvious, officials may get the response they favor. Similarly, ministers may have little time to give to important decisions because of the schedule prepared for them by their private offices.

If decisions that are reached run counter to those preferred by the senior civil servants within a department, various techniques are still available to them to try to delay or negate those decisions. They may reach their counterparts in other ministries to persuade them to brief the other ministers against their own minister's decision, they may try internal delaying tactics (including nonimplementation, in the hope that the minister will neither notice nor raise the matter again), they may try to inject their views into cabinet discussion, or they may try to stall until a new minister takes over. "Oh, in another year or so he won't be minister here anyway" is a phrase that has been heard from the lips of some civil servants in unguarded moments, including in the hearing of this writer. A new administration provides even greater scope for officials to refight old battles. By tradition, incoming ministers do not see the papers of their predecessors. This system provides senior civil servants with an almost clean ministerial canvas on which to try their persuasive brushwork.

Many of these techniques will be familiar to anyone with experience in bureaucratic machinery. In recent years, civil-service influence has been enhanced by other developments. Membership in the EC has been identified as being one of the most important. Not only has it entailed greater demands on ministerial time in attending meetings of the Council of Ministers, but most of the matters discussed are based on extensive preliminary work done at official level both within the EC itself and between EC officials and civil servants in the member states. Officials, it has been argued, have benefited also from the implementation of the Report of the Fulton Committee, published in 1968. The report argued for a more specialized, more open, and better-trained civil service and made various recommendations for achieving that. It recommended also the provision of independent policy advice to ministers through the appointment of political advisers and the creation of policy units within each department. In effect, the civil service achieved the implementation of those elements of the report that strengthened their position. For example, a recommendation that civil servants should constitute a majority on service selection boards was readily accepted, as was a proposal for the committee that advises the prime minister that senior appointments within the civil service include a number of senior officials (the committee now includes no one else). In contrast, policy units never saw the light of day, and civil servants, if they so choose, effectively work around rather than with political advisers.

A combination of these factors has helped to produce an influential breed of senior civil servants, sharing a common background and experience and meeting together regularly for lunch and other social occasions. Insofar as they consciously exert influence over ministerial decisions, they do so not in pursuit of a particular party bias but rather in furtherance of what they perceive to be some "national interest," seeking to steer ministers toward what one permanent secretary referred to as "the common ground."[14] That common ground is geared to a longer-term perspective than the more short-term perspective usually taken by ministers. It is a somewhat amorphous concept but one that tends to favor incremental change carried out within the context of departmental norms and that appears to militate against proposals that might limit civil service influence or undermine the status of individual departments. The dividing line between the perceived national interest and departmental interest is not always a clearly perceptible one.

Against the arguments adduced in support of the contention that civil servants exert undue influence in policy making must be set some countervailing points. Officials are guided by ethics that lead them to carry out a minister's wishes and, as we have mentioned, they prefer a minister who is capable of making decisions to one who is not. Nor do they constitute a monolithic entity. Civil servants differ in their approaches, both in style and in substance. The ethos of a particular department may differ from that of another (the Environment Department has a reputation for being a fairly open one, for example, and the Home Office one of excessive secrecy), and the perception of the national interest may differ from one department to another.

In the relationship between ministers and civil servants, a determined minister capable of winning cabinet battles and defending his or her department in the House of Commons will normally enjoy mastery of that department. Even so, that mastery will extend primarily to the important issues drawn to the minister's attention or to the specific policy goals which he or she has set. Other matters, of necessity, will be dealt with at lower levels. On occasion, a forceful minister may run into conflict with his or her officials (Barbara Castle at the Ministry of Transport in the 1960s, for example, and Tony Benn at the Department of Energy in the 1970s), in which case prime ministerial support may be necessary for a minister to prevail (and such support is not always forthcoming). Less forceful, less energetic, or less intelligent ministers may be content to be guided by the papers and recommendations put before them by their officials. Joel Barnett records one occasion when a senior cabinet minister attended a cabinet committee and "studiously read out one line from his brief: 'I agree with the Chief Secretary.'"[15] (Unfortunately for the minister's officials, the Chief Secretary to the Treasury had taken the line opposite to what they had expected.) In the days before he became a minister, Ian Gilmour estimated that "only about one Minister in three runs his Department."[16] When queried about this estimate after he had served as a cabinet minister, he replied that "on reflection, I think it was probably an overestimate."

Quangos

The term *quango* is used to denote what in American terminology would be referred to as an off-line governmental agency (for example, the Environmental Protection Agency). It is supposed to be the acronym for quasi-autonomous nongovernmental organizations, though it has confusingly been assumed to denote quasi-autonomous national government organizations. An official inquiry into quangos concluded that the term was inappropriate, preferring instead to refer to nondepartmental public bodies.[17] The latter is a more accurate description of the bodies concerned. They comprise various public bodies set up either by administrative act or specifically by statute in order to carry out various executive actions or to operate in an advisory capacity on a particular subject. Although they may be associated with a particular department, they do not form an official part of that department and are not under the day-to-day control of a minister or permanent secretary. Advisory bodies are usually formed to provide government with advice that it cannot obtain from within its own ranks. Such bodies will normally comprise representatives or appointees of interested groups (see Chapter 7). Bodies with executive powers are often formed in order to facilitate an arm's-length relationship between government and a particular concern.

A number of nondepartmental public bodies are long-standing and are not confined to the twentieth century.[18] The number has shown a considerable increase in this century, especially after the Second World War and again after 1968. The Report of the Fulton Committee on the Civil Service (1968) recommended the creation of accountable units of management within departments and raised the possibility of separating, or "hiving off," autonomous units from departments. Although admitting that such hiving off would raise parliamentary and constitutional issues, it commented, "We see no reason to believe that the dividing line between activities for which Ministers are directly responsible, and those for which they are not, is necessarily drawn in the right place today." Among those activities that they thought could be hived off were the work of the Royal Mint, air traffic control, and parts of the social services. The concept of hiving off found favor with the Labour government, fitted in well with the managerial revolution that the Conservative government of Edward Heath sought to achieve, and was continued under the Labour government of 1974–1979. Among the more important creations were those of the Manpower Services Commission, the Health and Safety Commission, and the Advisory, Conciliation, and Arbitration Service (see Chapter 7). In 1980 the report on nondepartmental public bodies, conducted by Sir Leo Pliatzky, identified the existence of over 2,000 such bodies. It identified 489 executive bodies ("between them these carry out a wide range of operational or regulatory functions, various scientific and cultural activities, and some commercial or semi-commercial activities") and 1,561 advisory bodies. The report recorded that the executive bodies in 1978 were the channel for expenditure on capital and current account of nearly £5,800 million (about $9,570 million) and had staff of about 217,000. The top spending bodies were the Regional Water Authorities, the Manpower Services Commission, the New Town Development Corporations, and the Housing Corporation.

Support for quangos and the policy of hiving off came to an end with the return of a Conservative government under Mrs. Thatcher in 1979. The government took the view that there were too many quangos, that they constituted too heavy a drain on the public purse, that they were not sufficiently accountable to Parliament, and that, in the case of some with quasi-judicial functions, they were a threat to the rule of law. As a government committed to a free-market economy, it was keen to reduce the number of interventionist and unaccountable quangos, especially those with significant expenditure powers.

The government initiated a process of abolishing quangos wherever possible. In January 1982 the Prime Minister listed a total of 441 nondepartmental public bodies that had been abolished since 1979, and 109 more scheduled for abolition. As for quangos that were not abolished, it was decided that ministers would be responsible for those coming under their department's sponsorship and that they would have the duty to ensure that the quangos were run effectively and efficiently. In this way, quangos would come within the scope of parliamentary scrutiny, including that of the new select committees.

Quangos still remain a significant feature of public activity. The government has made clear that those doing valuable and necessary work will continue. The number in existence remains a four-figure one, and ministers continue to announce in the House of Commons the setting up of advisory bodies on particular topics of current concern. A prominent example in the latter half of the 1980s was a body to monitor broadcasting standards. Some quangos are replaced by others: in 1989, for example, the University Grants Committee, which was responsible for allocating public funds to universities, was replaced by a University Funding Council. However, such bodies are created on an "as and when necessary" basis rather than as part of a conscious, encouraged strategy. A number of prominent quangos, most notably the Commission for Racial Equality, are the target of campaigns waged by a number of Conservative MPs for their abolition. Quangos are in existence but not in favor.

THE CURRENT DEBATE

For anyone seeking to identify the genesis of a policy that emerges from the executive, the task is a formidable one. Once in office, a government has a program that it proposes to implement. The extent to which the various proposals contained in that program are actually carried out in legislative or other form will be influenced by civil-service advice, by the reaction of affected groups, and by extraneous events, such as the discovery of North Sea oil, a Middle East crisis, or a downturn in world economic conditions. The form that a proposal takes will be affected by the process by which it is considered and applied. How officials interpret and apply a policy may not coincide precisely with the intentions of those responsible for its initiation. How a nondepartmental public body responds to a government policy may not be in line with government expectations. The response of groups and individuals affected by a policy may be vastly different from that which the government expected. Such reactions may in turn influence and modify government policy. Over and above its original program, government will be faced with numerous demands and the task of continuing the day-to-day business of governing, of administering inherited programs and commitments, of maintaining essential services, and of engaging in diplomatic relations with other governments. The level at which and manner in which such matters are dealt with in government will vary from issue to issue, from government to government, and from prime minister to prime minister, as well as over time. As society has become more specialized, as government has accepted greater responsibility for the control and allocation of a large part of the national wealth, and as more and more demands have been made of it, government has developed a complex infrastructure. The elements of that have been identified above, and in the identification process, the complexities of government emerged. Government does not operate in a vacuum. It has had to exist within and respond to an increasingly confused environment. And the government that responds to that environment is itself a complex web of bodies, powers, and relationships. For the political scientist seeking to explain governmental policy making, a case-study approach is often the most useful.

The complexity of government has been seen as part of the problem by those who have sought to identify government itself as being chiefly or partially responsible for Britain's poor economic performance in recent decades. There is a perception that government policy and the manner in which it is formulated and the body that formulates it have not served the nation as well as they might: hence a need for reform. But which element of government should be changed? And how? Does the problem lie with the civil service? With the cabinet? Or with the whole structure and mass of relationships that go to form the British government?

Since 1960, the government has made various attempts to improve decision making in a way that would enable it more efficiently and effectively to raise and allocate resources and, in some instances, to maintain or increase consent for its activities. In the 1960s, government went in for a form of economic planning and introduced the Public Expenditure Survey exercise. Previously, each item involving public expenditure had been judged on its merits and not considered in terms of the government's overall priorities or of the long-term consequences. The "forward look" form of quinquennial planning introduced by Selwyn Lloyd as Chancellor of the Exchequer was designed to rectify this state of affairs. Under the new exercise, each department costed the items on which government money was spent, doing so at current prices, and then entered into negotiation with the Treasury at official—that is, civil-service—level in order to agree on the figures and the effect of existing policy commitments over the coming years. The figures so agreed on were then assembled and submitted to the Public Expenditure Survey Committee (PESC), a high-level committee of civil servants under Treasury chairmanship. The committee next presented a report to ministers showing where existing policies would lead in terms of public expenditure at constant prices over a period of five years. The ministers then considered the report and made decisions on issues affecting the amounts to be spent by each department, on each public expenditure program, and on the total figure. The final figures required cabinet approval, and the cabinet was the forum for resolving disputes between ministers.

The PESC system had the attraction of helping establish relative priorities and of helping ministers to see where present policies would lead. Ministers could weigh the demands of the policies against the resources needed to fulfill them. However, the system did not prove to be the panacea that had been hoped for. It tended to favor incremental change (because priorities and commitments were established on a rolling five-year basis, immediate changes could be wrought only at the margin), and cabinet battles tended to result in conceding more to departments than had been recommended. It was also only as good as the projected figures on which it was based. In the Labour government returned in 1964, the exercise was undermined by exaggerated estimates of growth rates, and in the 1970s it was largely vitiated by the effects of high inflation rates. By 1974–1975, actual expenditure exceeded planned expenditure by £5 billion ($8.25 billion). To try to deal with this problem, the government introduced cash limits in 1976. Today the government makes an estimate of the likely rate of inflation and then translates spending plans into "cash" terms, allocating to each department the amount of money it can actually spend. Although not fulfilling initial expectations, the PESC exercise remains useful for providing a framework in which priorities may be established.

Other attempts since 1960 to reform government have included, as we have seen, the hiving off from departments of manageable units of account and a limited attempt to create a more open and specialized civil service. From a somewhat different perspective, the period also witnessed attempts, eventually successful, to join the European Community (see Chapter 10). The Heath government also undertook various reforms of the governmental machine. Apart from the policy of hiving off elements of departments that could be separated from ministerial line control, there was the creation of the "super departments" and also of the Central Policy Review Staff. In addition, a system of Program Analysis and Review (PAR) was instituted. This was designed to provide for an independent body of analysts to review particular programs within a department and to ensure that the best means were being employed to achieve the desired end. In practice, the PAR exercise comprised officials as well as outsiders and soon came under Treasury control. Because of the demands it made on limited resources, it could be employed only very selectively. Departments tried to use such surveys to lay claim to extra resources, in effect negating the purpose of the exercise. In November 1979, PAR was phased out. And, as we have seen, the Central Policy Review Staff was disbanded in 1983.

At the end of the 1980s the emphasis shifted to executive agencies. Instead of hiving off *from* departments, the policy became one of hiving off *within* departments. The purpose of the exercise was—and remains—to improve management in the civil service. Civil servants in agencies, according to a government statement, "will be better able to tailor management structures and practices to the specific needs of their work, will have better defined jobs and objectives, and greater personal responsibility and accountability for achieving them. The aim is better value for money and better service to the public."[19] Several agencies were established in 1989, but some observers criticized the exercise for being insufficiently radical and the official responsible for it conceded that it would "take a very long time to come about."[20]

Various reforms of government structures and procedures have thus been undertaken in an attempt to improve the quality of government in Britain. None has served to still the criticisms leveled at how the country is governed. I earlier outlined the argument advanced by some writers that Britain has a dysfunctional political system, a consequence of the adversarial party system induced by the plurality method of electing MPs. There is also an argument, variously advanced, that the country has also a dysfunctional governmental structure.

Of the criticisms leveled at the structure and operation of government, a number have been of government as a whole, while others have been directed at specific elements of government. The most prominent criticisms have been directed at the civil service and at increasing centralization of power within government, especially in the hands of the prime minister.

For most of this century the civil service in Britain has been highly praised as an efficient body of highly able public servants. That perception gave way in the 1960s to the view that the nation's problems were not best solved by a privileged elite of gifted amateurs. Hence the establishment of the Fulton Committee. As we have seen, its recommendations were in effect implemented selectively to the benefit of the civil service. The basic nature of the service remains unchanged, and hence the focus of critical attention. The preference for the generalist and for the socially privileged strata from which civil servants are drawn continue to draw criticism, as do civil servants' manner of operation and their relationship with ministers. According to Peter Hennessy, in his massive 1989 study of the service, *Whitehall*, civil servants as a breed are intellectually able, often dedicated, but lacking in the appropriate training and skills to inject dynamism and efficient management into the machinery they run. The heart of Hennessy's thesis, which echoes William Ryrie, is that the civil service "constitutes a government machine designed for nineteenth century needs."[21] The secrecy in which officials operate, according to several critics, also creates problems of accountability and consent. Civil servants work behind a screen of anonymity, working on documents that often are classified, from "Restricted" to "Top Secret." An anonymous body of powerful bureaucrats, believed to enjoy a degree of mastery over their nominal masters, is not considered conducive to public confidence in and support for government. Secrecy in government, according to Labour MP Tony Benn, works only in the interests of weak ministers and strong civil servants, "both of whom prefer to keep the public in the dark."[22] Neither wishes to be found out.

The thesis of greater centralization was sketched in Chapter 3. According to this thesis, power has become more and more concentrated in government and especially in the hands of the prime minister. A number of writers have claimed that Britain now witnesses a form of prime ministerial government. The concentration of power in the hands of the prime minister, according to Benn, has gone too far "and amounts to a system of personal rule in the very heart of our parliamentary democracy."[23] This, it is argued, denies a sense of responsibility to electors. The public, Parliament, and even the cabinet are presented with decisions that cannot be changed. Consequently, parliamentary democracy is undermined.

The argument surrounding prime ministerial power became more intense as the 1980s progressed. Longevity in office, large parliamentary majorities, and a radical program of public policy combined, in the eyes of many critics, to provide Britain's most extreme peacetime example of prime ministerial government. They said that Margaret Thatcher ensured that supporters occupied key ministries, she kept discussion of economic policy in cabinet to a minimum, she used bullying tactics in cabinet—described by one cabinet minister as "Stalinist"—in order to get her way, and she used her powers to "handbag" any institution, including the civil service, that constituted an obstruction to the realization of her goals. (The concept of "handbagging" derives from the observation of one of Mrs. Thatcher's back-benchers that "she cannot see an institution without hitting it with her handbag.")[24] In the wake of her third election victory in 1987 she was seen by many, including some within her own party, as politically invulnerable, capable of achieving what amounted to a system of one-woman rule. Texts analyzing the creation of "the strong state" grew in number, claiming that traditional safeguards were being eroded as more and more power became concentrated in the Thatcher government.[25] In a lecture in 1976, Lord Hailsham had identified the emergence of what he termed "an elective dictatorship."[26] The term referred to government; a decade later it was more frequently applied to one particular part of government—the office of Prime Minister.

Many of these criticisms are exaggerated and, as applied to the

Thatcher premiership, misleading. The best example of prime ministerial government in recent British history was the premiership of Edward Heath; he chose a compliant cabinet and had little difficulty getting them to accept whatever he wanted, including major reversals of existing policy. Mrs. Thatcher's tactics in dealing with her cabinet—bullying, summing up at the beginning, holding as few meetings as possible—are signs of weakness, not of strength. Also, since the rules for electing the leader were changed in 1975, she is the first Conservative leader to be subject to annual election by her parliamentary party. Rumors of a possible challenger— or an actual challenger—emerge at times of apparent vulnerability (as in 1981 and 1989) and act as a spur to greater responsiveness to back-bench feeling. However, her highly visible personal style, and the radical goals of her premiership, have reinforced perceptions of prime ministerial hegemony. Critics, including some within the ranks of the Conservative party, have argued the case for restraints to be placed on that power.

Given these various problems identified with government in Britain, it is not surprising that more than one solution is offered. Indeed, the main changes that have been suggested can be grouped under four headings:

1. Changing the relationship within the political apex of government
2. Changing the structure of government
3. Changing the relationship between ministers and civil servants
4. Changing the civil service in terms of composition and procedures

Changing the Relationship within the Political Apex of Government. This recommendation concerns primarily limiting the powers of the prime minister and takes different forms. Tony Benn has suggested reforms that are particularly, though not wholly, Parliament-based. These include electing the cabinet by the parliamentary party when Labour is in office, extending the select committee system in the House of Commons, abolishing the House of Lords, and making public appointments subject to confirmation by the House of Commons. He also favors a freedom of information act, designed to remove the secrecy surrounding the operations of the premier and the civil service. "Strong leadership there must be," he wrote, "But it must be open, collective, and accountable, and must learn to exercise its necessary powers by persuasion and, above all, through the development of a constitutional premiership."[27]

Not all of these proposals enjoy widespread support. That of electing the cabinet has been variously criticized, including within the Labour party, and in any event would apply only when Labour is in office. As we have recorded, Conservative prime ministers are usually in a stronger position than their Labour counterparts. Other critics have proposed a more fundamental restructuring of government; less radical critics have pressed for a change in the ethos of PM–cabinet relations. The radical proposals are for a decentralization of power—to regional assemblies and local councils—and for strengthened powers in the case of those bodies designed to protect the rights of citizens: principally Parliament and the courts. Basically, what is intended is a reversal of the momentum, identified by Hailsham, toward centralization. By dispersing power, no one body—and certainly not the prime minister—can become all-powerful. Less radical reformers see the problem as much in terms of personalities as of structures. What is needed, on their argument, is a reassertion of cabinet government; cabinet ministers must be willing to act collectively and to constrain an over-mighty prime minister. In 1989, following the party's poor showings in the European Parliament elections and the removal of Sir Geoffrey Howe from the Foreign Office, various ministers made comments to the effect that it was necessary for them to ensure a more prominent role for cabinet in determining policy.

There are problems with both sets of proposals. The latter is open to the obvious criticism that it does not go far enough and, in any event, rests on the willingness of a fluctuating body of individuals to act against the person who has appointed them. The former, more radical approach has been criticized for basing its argument on a false premise and recommending changes that could undermine the capacity of government to govern. The prime minister may be powerful but is by no means all-powerful, operating within a political milieu that makes it difficult to achieve particular, especially radical, policies.[28] The process of government is a complex one, the prime minister has limited resources to oversee the whole operation, and government operates within an increasingly crowded political environment, both domestically and internationally. Mrs. Thatcher, on this argument, may be seen as having had to fight to achieve policies that earlier might have been achieved without such effort. Government may not be stronger, just more difficult.

Changing the Structure of Government. Attempts in this direction have taken various forms. In the early 1970s the emphasis was on a rationalization of government departments as well as the hiving off of various departmental activities to the burgeoning quangos. By the latter half of the decade, the attraction of "super departments" had worn off and, with the return of a Conservative government in 1979, the approach toward nondepartmental public bodies was put into reverse.

The Conservative government, as we have seen, now favors hiving off within departments, making civil servants more clearly responsible for designated managerial tasks. However, in the 1970s and again toward the end of the 1980s, a far more radical proposal for changing the structure of government was advanced. In effect, the proposal was to create a new tier of government by devolving government powers to elected assemblies. The creation of "super departments" was intended not only to contribute to efficiency in policy making but also to strengthen the link between government and the individual by identifying clear ministerial responsibility for particular functions. That intention was not fully realized. Proponents argued increasingly that the intention could be realized if certain functions of government were devolved to elected assemblies in Scotland and Wales as well as the English regions. The argument concerning devolution we shall consider in more detail shortly (Chapter 9). For the moment, it is important to record that an attempt to introduce devolution to Scotland and Wales was made in the 1974–1979 Parliament but failed in the face of parliamentary opposition and the results of referendums in the two countries.

Although interest in devolution waned in the wake of the referendum results of 1979, it emerged again on the agenda of political debate as the 1980s progressed. The argument for it dovetailed with that of centralization. Devolution is favored by all the parties in the House of Commons, with the exception of the Conservative party. It figured prominently in the constitutional reforms emerging from Labour's policy review in 1989. Devolution, it is argued, would not only increase government effectiveness, since decision makers would be able to act with a greater knowledge of and concern for local conditions, but would also increase consent for government. It would allow decisions to rest with the people, not with central government in London.

Critics of devolution have argued that it would most likely add another burdensome layer to government, would be expensive (thus adding to the costs of industry and the taxpayer), and could result in a greater degree of economic disparity among the regions. It would create problems in trying to ensure an equitable distribution of national resources. There would also be potential for friction between national and regional governments. Hence the outcome would be less, not more, effective government.

Changing the Relationship between Ministers and Civil Servants. This proposal is concerned primarily with attempts to ensure that the reality matches the formality, with ministers being able to enjoy control of their own departments. The two main changes recommended to achieve this are for ministers to have alternative sources of advice to those of their officials, and for them to have power to dismiss their permanent secretaries. For alternative advice, as we have seen, there has been the innovation of ministers appointing political advisers. Various Labour politicians and, more recently, Sir John Hoskyns, a former head of Mrs. Thatcher's policy unit, have also advocated the creation of advisory bodies similar to the

French *cabinets*, allowing ministers to bring together a small group of handpicked specialists and thus offering the twin benefits of expert knowledge and independence of the civil service.[29] Some former Labour ministers have also indicated that they would prefer to have had more control over the appointment, transfer, or dismissal of their permanent secretaries, a power that rests with the prime minister. To achieve the removal of a permanent secretary, a minister needs the support of the prime minister, and when it has been sought it has not always been forthcoming. Tony Benn and a number of his supporters have variously argued about the need for such changes. "We need to ensure that ministers are able to secure compliance with the policies that they were elected to implement," he has written. "Proposals to this end have been widely discussed and would certainly involve making the most senior officials in each department more responsible to the ministers whom they serve."[30]

Various arguments have been deployed against such proposals. Giving ministers hire-and-fire power over permanent secretaries would raise the potential for senior officials to become more partisan in their orientation, as ministers select those most in tune with their own views. The use of *cabinets* would raise the potential for conflict between advisers and departments. There may also be a practical problem in recruiting high-caliber experts to serve ministers whose tenure in a particular office may be short. It is also doubtful whether such changes would have the desired effect, since civil servants are adept at working around rather than with such bodies. Finally, it is unlikely that the prime minister would readily give up the power of appointment and transfer of senior officials. Mrs. Thatcher in particular has taken an interest in senior appointments and used the power probably more than any of her immediate predecessors.

Changing the Civil Service in Terms of Composition and Procedures. As we have seen, the civil service has been criticized for consisting of Oxford-educated generalists. Since the late 1950s, various critics have attacked the inherent attitude of effortless superiority displayed by senior civil servants who are confident in their ability to deal with the nation's problems but lack any real knowledge of the changing world and its problems. These criticisms were sufficient to prompt the appointment of the Fulton Committee, which reported in 1968. As we have seen, its recommendations were designed to achieve a more open, specialized, and trained civil service, but its intentions were largely vitiated by the skilled machinations of the civil service. "The real difficulty," as one member of a committee set up to implement the Fulton proposals put it, "is that you are trying to solve a problem with people who are themselves part of the problem."[31] The civil service continues to favor Oxford-educated generalists, and selection committees tend to favor candidates molded in their own image. Various calls have been made for the intentions of the Fulton Committee to be realized. The problem remains one of how to achieve that in the face of inherent civil-service reluctance.

Among various proposals put forward have been for posts in the service to be publicly advertised and for the number of new entrants to the higher levels of the service to be reduced, thus forcing the service to recruit more skilled outsiders.[32] An allied proposal is to allow those who have left the service to return at a higher grade than they left it. (At present, anyone returning to the civil service joins it at precisely the same rank as he or she left it, regardless of what the person has done in the interval.) It is argued that implementation of these proposals would help open up the service and make it more responsive to outside skills and advice. The problem remains one of implementation. Even if posts are advertised, the selection procedures would need to be changed, and there is the danger that experts brought in from outside would be ignored. To a large extent, the problem is not just one of changing procedures but rather one of changing a particular and well-entrenched culture.

The other main reform advocated is to open up the civil service by ridding it of the shroud of secrecy in which it buries itself. Various attempts have been made to introduce a freedom-of-information bill similar to that enacted in such other countries as the United States, Sweden, Denmark, and Norway. The Fulton Committee asserted that "the public interest would be better served if there were a greater amount of openness."[33] More openness on the part of the civil service, it is argued, would most likely improve decision making, since decision makers would be more careful and responsive knowing that the reasons for their decisions would be subject to public scrutiny, and they would remove much public suspicion of civil-service activity. Keeping material hidden unnecessarily from public gaze does nothing to increase public confidence in government.

So far, attempts to achieve passage of a freedom-of-information bill have been unsuccessful, though such a bill now enjoys support from a wide body of MPs. More success in reducing civil-service anonymity and secretiveness has been achieved by the departmental select committees in the House of Commons, though officials appearing before them still remain protected by the doctrine of ministerial responsibility, which has on occasion been used in order to deny information to the committees. Defenders of the existing system argue that more openness would undermine the convention of ministerial responsibility, would inhibit officials in tendering advice to ministers, and would cost too much to implement. Proponents point out that the first two consequences need not necessarily flow from the release of official documents and that the third argument does not necessarily detract from the merits of the case for more openness. It could be argued that it would not cost too much for officials to give up responding to queries with a noncommittal answer and to spend less time imprinting papers with the designation of "Restricted." The essential difficulty is persuading civil servants of that.

CONCLUSION

Although it is common to refer to the executive in Britain, the executive is not a monolithic body. It consists of a sophisticated infrastructure, and relationships that are not static or easy to discern. There is no one part of the executive that can be identified clearly and unambiguously as the body for the making of public policy. Policy is formulated and agreed upon at different levels. What can be called high policy (determining economic strategy, for example) is usually made at the level of prime minister and cabinet, medium-level policy (a new initiative on transport safety, for instance) tends to be made at the ministerial level within a department, and low-level, or day-to-day, incremental policy adjustments more often than not have their genesis at the civil-service level, often in conjunction with representatives of affected bodies (see Chapter 7). The boundaries are far from clear-cut. Some prime ministers may allow economic policy making to be shaped by the Chancellor of the Exchequer and Treasury officials; others will take a more proactive stance. Some minor issues may achieve political prominence and hence move up the decision-making ladder. However, only a small number of policy issues will percolate beyond the level of cabinet committees. At any one time, there is a significant two-way flow of policy recommendations and decisions taking place within government, with various proposals flowing up from departments to ministers and cabinet committees, and various policy decisions flowing down from the prime minister and from the cabinet. Given the prominent style of Margaret Thatcher and the particular set of policy goals she has set, there has been a tendency in recent years to focus upon the high policy and the mechanisms for its resolution. There is the danger in so doing of overlooking the other policy processes operating within government. These processes are extensive and, given the degree of secrecy, often obscure.

NOTES

1. A. B. Keith, *The British Cabinet System*, 2nd ed. by N. H. Gibbs (Stevens and Sons, 1952), p. 14.
2. M. Kogan, *The Politics of Education* (Penguin, 1971), p. 35.
3. See especially G. W. Jones, "The Prime Minister's Aides," in A. King (ed.), *The British Prime Minister*, 2nd ed. (Macmillan, 1985), pp. 72–95.

4. P. Norton, "Prime Ministerial Power," *Social Studies Review*, 3 (3), 1988, p. 110; see also P. Norton, "Prime Ministerial Power: A Framework for Analysis," *Teaching Politics*, 16 (3), 1987, pp. 325–45.

5. *House of Commons Debates* (*Hansard*), Vol. 967, col. 179.

6. J. Barnett, *Inside the Treasury* (Andre Deutsch, 1982), p. 27.

7. R. Crossman, Introduction to W. Bagehot, *The English Constitution* (Fontana, 1963 edition).

8. N. Johnson, *In Search of the Constitution* (Methuen, 1980), p. 84.

9. Kogan, p. 38.

10. Sir R. Clarke, "The Machinery of Government," in W. Thornhill (ed.), *The Modernization of British Government* (Pitman, 1975), p. 65.

11. B. Headey, "Cabinet Ministers and Senior Civil Servants: Mutual Requirements and Expectations," in V. Herman and J. Alt (eds.), *Cabinet Studies* (Macmillan, 1975), pp. 131–35.

12. See P. Kellner and Lord Crowther-Hunt, *The Civil Servants* (Macdonald Futura, 1980), pp. 119–23; and G. Drewry and T. Butcher, *The Civil Service Today* (Blackwell, 1988).

13. See J. Garrett, *Managing the Civil Service* (Heinemann, 1980), and P. Hennessy, *Whitehall* (Secker & Warburg, 1989).

14. Sir A. Part, speaking on the Independent Television program, "World in Action," January 7, 1980.

15. Barnett, p. 17.

16. I. Gilmour, *The Body Politic*, rev. ed. (Hutchinson, 1971), p. 201.

17. *Report on Non-Departmental Public Bodies*, Cmnd. 7797 (Her Majesty's Stationery Office, 1980), pp. 3–4.

18. See. P. Holland, *The Governance of Quangos* (Adam Smith Institute, 1981), pp. 10–12.

19. *House of Commons Debates* (*Hansard*), Written Answer, Vol. 146, col. 238.

20. *The Times*, February 19, 1988.

21. Hennessy, p. 192.

22. T. Benn, "Manifestos and Mandarins," in *Policy and Practice: The Experience of Government* (Royal Institute of Public Administration, 1980), p. 75.

23. T. Benn, "The Case for a Constitutional Premiership," *Parliamentary Affairs*, 33 (1), 1980, p. 7.

24. J. Critchley M.P., *Westminster Blues* (Futura, 1986), p. 126.

25. Thus, for example, A. Gamble, *The Free Economy and the Strong State* (Macmillan, 1988); C. Graham and T. Prosser (eds.), *Waiving the Rules* (Open University Press, 1988); P. McAuslan and M. J. McEldowney (eds.), *Law, Legitimacy and the Constitution* (Sweet & Maxwell, 1985).

26. Lord Hailsham, *Elective Dictatorship* (BBC, 1976).

27. T. Benn, *Arguments for Democracy* (Penguin, 1982), pp. 39–41.

28. See P. Norton, "The Constitution in Question," *Contemporary Record*, September 1989.

29. See "New Style Aides for Labour Ministers," *Tribune*, July 10, 1981, p. 6, and *Reskilling Government* (Institute of Directors, 1986).

30. Benn, *Arguments for Democracy*, p. 66.

31. Quoted in B. Page and I. Hilton, "The 'Reformers' Who Made Sure Nothing Changed," *Daily Express*, April 6, 1977, p. 11.
32. Hennessy, conclusions.
33. *Report of the Committee on the Civil Service*, Cmnd. 3638 (Her Majesty's Stationery Office, 1968), para. 177.

CHAPTER 9

Subnational Government
Government below the Center

The United States enjoys, or at any rate labors under, three distinct tiers of government: national, state, and local. Because the nation is federal rather than unitary, Congress can legislate only on those matters enumerated or implied in the Constitution: all remaining powers are reserved to the states or to the people. The position in the United Kingdom is significantly different: as a unitary nation, it lacks the equivalent of state governments. Although, as well shall see, attempts have been made to introduce an intermediate level of government in the form of national assemblies in Scotland and Wales and regional assemblies in England (Northern Ireland, for 50 years, had its own provincial Parliament), such assemblies would be able to exercise only those powers delegated to them by Parliament. This is the case with local government in Britain. Parliament enjoys legislative sovereignty and can both give and remove as it chooses delegated powers to subordinate units of government. Even in the case of the European Community, the legislation that emanates from the Community is applied by virtue of the provisions of the 1972 European Communities Act, an act that Parliament retains the power to amend or, should it so choose, to repeal.

Subnational government (see Map 9.1) within the United Kingdom can be discussed under two headings: actual and proposed (see Table 9.1). The first of these, existing subnational government, comprises local government, regional government, and administrative devolution in Scotland, Northern Ireland, and Wales. The only level of elected government below national level in Britain is local government. There is no government

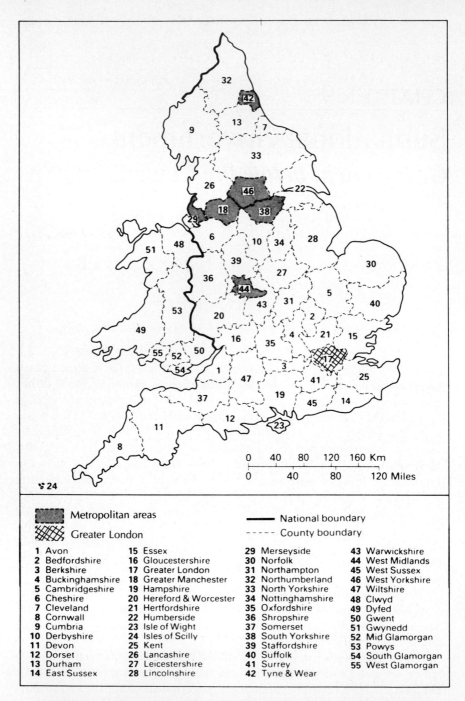

Map 9.1. England and Wales: Metropolitan and Nonmetropolitan counties. (Source: A. Alexander, The Politics of Local Government in the United Kingdom (Longman, 1982). Copyright 1982 Alan Alexander. Reprinted by permission.)

The legend and labels within the map:

Metropolitan areas
Greater London
National boundary
County boundary

1 Avon
2 Bedfordshire
3 Berkshire
4 Buckinghamshire
5 Cambridgeshire
6 Cheshire
7 Cleveland
8 Cornwall
9 Cumbria
10 Derbyshire
11 Devon
12 Dorset
13 Durham
14 East Sussex
15 Essex
16 Gloucestershire
17 Greater London
18 Greater Manchester
19 Hampshire
20 Hereford & Worcester
21 Hertfordshire
22 Humberside
23 Isle of Wight
24 Isles of Scilly
25 Kent
26 Lancashire
27 Leicestershire
28 Lincolnshire
29 Merseyside
30 Norfolk
31 Northampton
32 Northumberland
33 North Yorkshire
34 Nottinghamshire
35 Oxfordshire
36 Shropshire
37 Somerset
38 South Yorkshire
39 Staffordshire
40 Suffolk
41 Surrey
42 Tyne & Wear
43 Warwickshire
44 West Midlands
45 West Sussex
46 West Yorkshire
47 Wiltshire
48 Clwyd
49 Dyfed
50 Gwent
51 Gwynedd
52 Mid Glamorgan
53 Powys
54 South Glamorgan
55 West Glamorgan

TABLE 9.1. SUBNATIONAL GOVERNMENT IN THE UNITED KINGDOM

Level	Existing Governmental Bodies	Proposed Governmental Bodies
Territorial		
England	No specific countrywide English bodies	
Scotland	Scottish Office (United Kingdom government department)	Elected assembly with legislative/ executive powers
Northern Ireland	Northern Ireland Office (United Kingdom government department) Elected assembly (no executive powers)	Elected assembly with executive powers; power sharing
Wales	Welsh Office (United Kingdom government department)	Elected assembly with limited executive powers
Regional	Regional offices of government departments Disparate public bodies, e.g., regional health authorities	Elected regional assemblies
Local (counties and towns)	Elected councils	Some modification to existing structure

elected at an intermediate level, either at a regional level or for the whole of Scotland or Wales. However, though not elected, there are governmental bodies operating at these levels. The most important of these are the Scottish Office, the Northern Ireland Office, and, to a lesser extent, the Welsh Office, enjoying executive powers that for the rest of the United Kingdom are exercised in London. The carrying out of these powers by government departments is essentially a substitute for their exercise by elected bodies. Various proposals have been put forward for the creation of such bodies, in Scotland and Wales as well as in Northern Ireland. A measure to establish elected assemblies in Scotland and Wales was introduced in 1976 but failed for reasons to be explored shortly. Several schemes have been put forward for constitutional change in Northern Ireland, none of which has yet proved successful. Such proposals remain on the political agenda. Their importance is such that they deserve attention.

ACTUAL: LOCAL GOVERNMENT, REGIONAL GOVERNMENT, AND ADMINISTRATIVE DEVOLUTION

Local Government

Structure. For the first six decades of the twentieth century the structure of local government in England and Wales remained largely unchanged. That system, based on a system created in the nineteenth century, was essentially a two-tier one. The first tier consisted of county boroughs, exercising control over all local government services within their boundaries, and county councils, each exercising control over certain local government services within the county (though not over any county borough within the county). Below the county councils was the second tier: municipal boroughs, urban districts, and rural districts, all exercising limited functions. Within rural districts, there was also an additional layer of local government in the form of parish councils, each exercising very limited responsibilities.

As demands on government grew and the responsibilities of local government expanded, the structure of local government appeared increasingly inappropriate. Allowing county boroughs to exercise functions that seemed more suitable to a larger authority (such as control of planning and roads) came in for criticism, while many municipal boroughs exacerbated the problem by applying for county borough status. Reform came on to the political agenda. After a period of little change, local government came to witness a period of rapid change, with significant reforms in succeeding decades.

Reform began in the 1960s with the creation of the Greater London Council (GLC). Established under the 1963 London Government Act, the GLC was vested with responsibility for planning, roads, traffic, overspill housing, and other needs affecting the whole of the Greater London area. Responsibility for education in the area covered by the old London County Council was vested in an Inner London Education Authority (ILEA). However, responsibility for personal health services (except ambulances) and for most local authority housing was retained by the 32 borough councils within the GLC area.

The most significant reform took place in the 1970s, when local government in the rest of England and Wales was completely reorganized. The 1972 Local Government Act, which took effect on April 1, 1974, created a new two-tier system. A Royal Commission on Local Government in England, which had reported in 1969, had recommended a single-tier, with the creation of all-purpose local authorities. The Conservative government that was returned in 1970 decided against this, ostensibly for fear that the new authorities would be too distant from the local communities they served. Its position was also heavily influenced by the fear that unitary authorities would fall predominantly into the hands of its Labour opponents. The result, under the 1972 act, was the creation of 47 county councils, each with responsibility for education, transport, highways (except motorways and unclassified roads), planning, housing, personal social services, libraries, police, fire service, refuse disposal, and consumer protection. Below them was established a second tier of more than 300 district councils, each with responsibility for town planning, environmental health, building and housing management, and various registration and licensing functions. The act also created six separate metropolitan counties (see Map 9.1). Each metropolitan county council was given the same functions as the other county councils with the exception of education, personal social services, and libraries. Below the metropolitan counties was created a second tier of 36 metropolitan districts which, because of their population density and some ministerial reluctance to give metropolitan counties too much power, were given control of education, personal social services, and libraries, as well as the other functions given to district councils. In addition, the metropolitan counties and districts were to share responsibility for certain matters, principally parks, museums, and airports. Below the two tiers, provision for parish councils was also retained. In Scotland, under the provisions of the Local Government (Scotland) Act passed in 1973, a two-tier division was created between nine large regional councils and district councils. Because of the concentration of population in the western lowlands of Scotland, one region— Strathclyde—contained more than half of the country's population.

The reforms did not prove lasting, at least not in their entirety. The aim of the reorganization had been to achieve a more rational system of local government. The emphasis was on an efficient managerial approach. Whereas the chief permanent officials of the old borough councils had been titled town clerks, the chief appointed officials of most of the new authorities were titled chief executives and the approach to administration was that of corporate management. The chief executive was seen as a coordinating head, advised and supported by a team of management officers. Councils continued to exercise their functions largely through committees (in marked contrast to the form of government at national level), though each council was given greater latitude than before in deciding what committees they wished to establish. (Certain committees were and remain mandatory, principally police, education, and social services committees.) Especially popular was the creation of a policy committee to establish priorities and monitor resources and policy implementation. By the end of the decade, though, the corporate approach had not proved as worthwhile as many councils had hoped, and a number reverted to the more traditional approach, doing away with the concept of the chief executive and redrawing committee responsibilities based on established services rather than expenditure functions.

The reorganization also proved costly and did little to enhance consent for government: there was little apparent increase in citizens' awareness of local authority responsibilities. As Anthony King observed, "things are not working out quite as expected."[1] Certain features of the reorganization created resentment. Inhabitants of counties that had been dismembered or abolished were often vehement in their vocal opposition to the changes. So too were former councillors and other citizens in the boroughs that were reduced to parish council status. Within some of the new counties, a number of boroughs resented and continue to resent the dominance of larger conurbations. Dissatisfaction with the new structure found expression in the Labour party manifesto in 1979, which committed the party to restoring to the larger district councils in England the responsibility for education, personal services, planning, and libraries. The party repeated the commitment in 1983.

However, of greater significance was the attitude toward local government adopted by the Conservative government returned in 1979. It clashed with many local authorities, expecially the Labour-controlled GLC and metropolitan counties. The government wanted to limit public spending, and local government spending was one of the major features of public spending that exceeded government targets. In 1983–1984, for example, GLC spending exceeded grant-related expenditure (the amount government considered it should spend) by 81%. The need to limit public spending was accorded priority over the commitment to the principle of local autonomy, and various measures were introduced to limit the spending of local councils. However, the GLC and many other Labour-controlled councils also constituted an additional thorn in the government's flesh as a result of campaigns that they waged on particular political issues. Though councils are statutorily constrained in what they can spend money on, they have some limited latitude: under the 1972 act, they could spend up to a 2p rate on almost anything, a sum that in some cases could amount to several million pounds. The GLC, under its leader Ken Livinstone, used this power to fund campaigns on a wide range of issues—usually opposed to government policy—and to fund organizations (such as feminist and gay groups) that the government regarded as inappropriate recipients of public funds. By 1983, because of the government's annoyance at such activities, it promised to introduce a bill to abolish the GLC and the six metropolitan councils. The commitment was embodied in the party's 1983 election manifesto and was carried through two years later in the 1985 Local Government Act. The GLC and the metropolitan county councils ceased to exist on March 31, 1986. The councils' functions were dispersed to metropolitan boroughs (and joint authorities to run police, fire, and passenger transport services) in the metropolitan counties, and to the 32 London boroughs. The councils, according to the government, had proven to be a superfluous layer of local government—there was little for them to do—and abolition constituted a significant saving in public funds.

The structure of local government, in what are known as "shire counties" (those with county councils), is now under the system established by the 1972 Local Government Act (county councils, district councils, parish councils); the metropolitan areas have metropolitan district councils, with more extensive functions than those vested by the 1972 act, and in addition some joint authorities administer certain countywide functions; as in shire counties, parish councils also remain, though serving little purpose. The structure, which is outlined in Figure 9.1, remains a topic of partisan debate. Having made the structural changes of the 1980s, the Conservative government has announced that it sees no reason to make any further changes in local government structure. The Labour party has committed itself to review the structure that now exists.

Election and Members. Local government, as we have had cause to note already, differs significantly from government at the national level. Not only is local government subordinate to national government, its approach to administration (committee-based, emphasis on professional administrators) is essentially the opposite of that adopted at the national level (not committee based, emphasis on the generalist). It differs also in that elections to local councils take place, as in the United States, on a fixed-term basis; elections to the House of Commons, in contrast, take place on a flexible basis.

Councillors are elected for four-year terms, with no limit on the number of terms one can serve. All county councils, London borough councils, and about one-third of district councils are elected in their

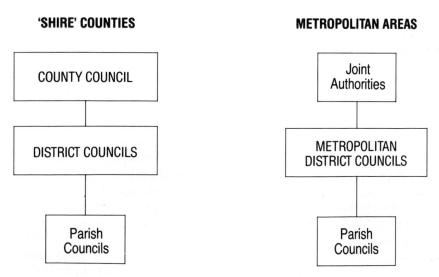

'SHIRE' COUNTIES   **METROPOLITAN AREAS**

COUNTY COUNCIL

Joint
Authorities

DISTRICT COUNCILS

METROPOLITAN
DISTRICT COUNCILS

Parish
Councils

Parish
Councils

Figure 9.1. Local Government Structure in England and Wales since 1986. (Principal local government authorities in capital letters.)

entirety every four years. In the remaining districts, and in all the metropolitan districts, one-third of the councillors are elected in each of the three years between county council elections.

The franchise to vote in local elections is essentially the same as that for national elections: citizens aged 18 or over who are resident in the area on the qualifying date. (Members of the House of Lords, who cannot vote in elections to the House of Commons, can vote in local elections.) Candidates in local elections must be citizens aged 21 or over and be resident in the local authority area or have resided in premises in the area for the preceding 12 months or, in that 12 months, have had their principal place of work in that area. No one may be elected to a council of which he or she is an employee. This prohibition was extended in 1988 by an act prohibiting senior council officials from being elected as councillors in any authority.

Election procedure is essentially the same as that for national elections. (In May 1979 the two actually coincided, a general election taking place the same day as local elections.) Although elections are fought ostensibly on local issues, candidates at other than parish council level now usually stand under a party label, a tendency that increased in postwar years and was given added impetus by the reorganization of 1972. Large authorities are now such significant bodies of public expenditure and policy making that the national parties cannot afford to ignore them. Party is now the most important variable influencing the voting behavior of those few electors who bother to cast a vote (turnout, as in local elections in the United States, is low, rarely reaching 40% of eligible voters); local elections are viewed as an annual opportunity to pass judgment on the incumbent national government. The governing party is expected to lose council seats during the mid-term of a Parliament; a net gain of seats would be hailed as a considerable victory.

Although councillors are elected on party labels and usually operate within coherent party groupings, with elected officers and whips, they behave differently depending on local circumstances. Given that the needs and demands of communities vary, local parties temper their responses accordingly. The councillors themselves tend to be disproportionately male and drawn from nonmanual occupations. The likelihood is greater now than it was prior to the mid-1970s that they will have university educations. In the opinion of two observers, "The rise in the proportion of councillors with higher educational qualifications suggests that local-authority service is attracting its fair share of the best-educated sections of society—although a fall in the number of manual workers elected might make some voters feel that local authorities might be remote from them and so unresponsive in their needs."[2] One innovation introduced in 1972 to increase the attractiveness of local government service to able and economically in active citizens (many councillors were retired persons) was attendance allowances for councillors. The introduction of such allowances may also have been encouraged by the desire to lessen the incentives for corruption, an occasional unfortunate feature of local government life not usually witnessed at a national level.[3] In order to consider cases of alleged maladministration, a number of local government ombudsmen (known as local commissioners) were established under the Local Government Act of 1974.

Once elected, councillors devote much time to casework and also tend to specialize in their committee work. Very few appear interested in helping formulate authority-wide policy.[4] What motivates individuals to seek election to local councils is not at all clear. Some appear to see it as a stepping-stone to higher things (though only a few are subsequently selected as parliamentary candidates); some do it out of a desire to further the aims of their party; some do it out of a sense of civic responsibility (to be found also in the performance of a wide range of other local activities, such as serving on the local magistrates' bench and doing voluntary social work); some do it to enhance their status in the community; and some, possibly a majority, do it for the simple reason that they were inveigled into running by friends or local party activists. One writer with several years' council experience summarized the position succinctly: "Most of us stand in the first instance by accident or because we are bullied into it but then we discover that Council work is interesting and worthwhile, although hard, so many councillors stay in local government for a lifetime."[5] Because of the number of councillors to be elected and the level of public indifference toward local government, local parties sometimes have difficulty recruiting candidates to contest elections. In some areas, it might be described as a seller's rather than a buyer's market.

Powers and Finance. Local councils enjoy no constitutionally protected autonomous powers and can exercise only those powers vested in them by law. Their scope for branching out into areas of activity for which they have no specific statutory authority is limited: under the 1972 Local Government Act, they could levy up to a 2p rate for generally whatever purpose they wished; under the 1988 Local Government and Housing Act, this amount was replaced by a per-adult limit (£5 per adult, for example, in the case of London borough and metropolitan district councils). In addition to having to work within statutorily defined limits, councils are also constrained within the confines of powers held and policies pursued by national government. Ministers have various statutory powers to make orders as well as to issue circulars to local authorities giving guidance on the implementation of government policy. The limitations upon local government are considerable and in recent years these have grown.

Local authorities are nonetheless major spenders and employers in the United Kingdom. Nearly 3 million people are employed by councils in Great Britain. In 1987–1988 expenditure by councils was some £41 billion, a little under one-quarter of general government expenditure. Education accounted for one-third of the total, and most of the remainder was spent on health and social security, law and order, and the environment. Local authorities thus constitute significant economic units.

Until 1990, local authorities derived their revenue from three main sources: a central government grant, known as the rate support grant; local rates (an annual tax on real estate, based on property value); and income from services provided by the authority. The central government grant has been the largest element, though it declined since 1979 from about 60% to just under 50%. The extent of local government expenditure has been subject to various restrictions and these have increased since 1979. In order to restrict high-spending (usually Labour) councils, the Conservative government in the first half of the 1980s introduced several rate-levying restrictions. In 1981 the block grant to councils exceeding the government's expenditure targets was reduced; in 1982 the power of councils to raise supplementary rates (that is, additional rates levied after the rate for the year had already been decided) was abolished; and, after the government was returned for a second term in 1983, power was also taken to impose a maximum limit on the rates that could be levied by big-spending authorities. However, the most significant reform came in the Local Government Finance Act of 1988, which implemented the government's long-standing pledge to abolish the rating system.

The government took the view that the rating system was inherently unfair; a single person in a house paid the same rate as did a large family living in the next house, the former in effect helping subsidize the services consumed by the latter. The system they chose to replace the rating system was based on a Community Charge, known popularly as the "poll tax." Under this system, a charge is levied on individuals rather than on property. The government argued that the new system was inherently fairer as well as more likely to increase local accountability: since almost everyone would pay all or part of the Community Charge (very few people are exempt), they would have a greater interest in how the council spent their money. The system was introduced first in Scotland, in 1989, and then in England and Wales in 1990. It was accompanied by a uniform business rate (UBR), set centrally by government, replacing the business rate that was set by councils and that had varied significantly in the amount levied.

The introduction of the Community Charge was the most significant of many local government reforms introduced by the Conservative government in the 1980s. Indeed, in the first ten years of Conservative government, fifty measures affecting local government were introduced in Parliament. In the first and second Parliaments of the decade many of these dealt with local government finance. In the third Parliament, returned in 1987, the emphasis shifted to making local government services more competitive. Competitive tendering was encouraged; under this system local government services are put out to tender, and private firms are able to compete for the contract. Under the provisions of the 1988 Local Government Act local authorities are required to submit six services to competitive tendering: refuse collection, street cleaning, cleaning of buildings, ground maintenance, vehicle maintenance and repairs, and catering services (including school meals). It was felt that this system would ensure greater efficiency in local government and ensure better value for public money.

The purpose of the changes introduced by the Conservatives in the decade was summed up by Environment Secretary Nicholas Ridley. Local authorities, he declared, would no longer be universal providers. They would, according to one party publication, "increasingly become regulators not suppliers, guarantors not participants, enablers not providers."[6] The past decade has thus witnessed a major change in the role and powers, and to some extent the structure, of local government in Britain. It remains a major spender and employer, but one operating under greater statutory control than before.

Regional Government

In Britain, there are no directly elected governmental bodies between the local and the national level. There are, though, a number of governmental or quasi-governmental bodies that operate at a regional level. They are significant not only for being nonelected but also for being disparate, not integrated with one another, and decreasing rather than increasing in number. Nonetheless, they constitute an important level of government in Britain.

Various factors have contributed to governmental functions being fulfilled at a regional level. Among the more important pressures have been administrative convenience, the need to involve more local authorities, technical advantages, the desire to dissociate central government from certain decision-making activities, and pressure from groups and professional bodies seeking some degree of regional autonomy in their sphere of activity.[7] The reason the number of government or public bodies operating at such a level has decreased in recent years has been the knock-on consequence of the Conservative government's privatization policy. Various public utilities, which previously had an extensive regional organization (the Regional Water Authorities being the most extensive), are no longer in the public sector.

Among public bodies with some degree of regional organization are the BBC and British Railways. Eight government departments have some organization at the regional level, either as an integral part of the department or as part of a service for which the department is responsible. The Prison Department in the Home Office, for example, has a regional organization. Within the Lord Chancellor's Department, courts are organized on a regional (circuit) basis (see Chapter 13). Both the Department of the Environment and the Department of Trade and Industry have regional offices, each under a director. The regional offices in the DTI have responsibility for administering the department's regional development policy; about £200 million to £300 million are channeled each year, on a selective basis, to firms in areas that are designated as Assisted or Development Areas. However, the most extensive regional organization is that of the Regional Health Authorities in the Department of Health.

The Regional Health Authorities (RHAs) were created under the Health Service Reorganization Act of 1973, replacing regional hospital boards. This act also created a second tier of 90 Area Health Authorities. Each level had planning functions and below them were the main operational units, the District Management Teams. The reorganization did not work out as government had intended: it proved costly, with an increase in the size of administrative and clerical staff; the RHAs had little impact on the work of the permanent officers (members of the Authorities were part-time); and both Regional and Area Health Authorities achieved a degree of autonomy that put them almost beyond ministerial control.[8] Following the report of a Royal Commission on the National Health Service, which endorsed the view that there was one too many tiers of administration, the Area Health Authorities were abolished in 1982, and District Health Authorities replaced the District Management Teams (Figure 9.2). Management structures were reorganized, with general managers brought in to replace consensus management by teams of officers.

The National Health Service is thus administered now essentially at two levels: at the local level, where the District Health Authorities have responsibility for the planning and organizational control of all health services in their areas (though under government plans announced in 1989, larger hospitals are being given the opportunity to become essentially self-governing units); and at the regional level, where the RHAs have responsibility for regional planning, resource allocation, major capital building work, and certain specialized hospital services that are more appropriately administered on a regional basis. Regional organization thus continues to constitute a central feature of the National Health Service.

There is thus an important layer of government operating at regional level in Britain. However, that regional layer has no common pattern. The various regional forms of organization just identified differ in size and

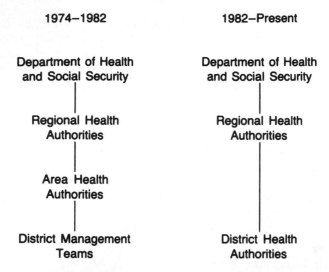

Figure 9.2. The Structure of the National Health Service (England). Family Practitioner Committees and Community Health Councils are not included. (Source: C. Ham, Health Policy in Britain [Macmillan, 1982]. Copyright 1982 Macmillan. Reprinted by permission.)

authority. Part of the problem stems from the spatial disparity in population and resources and also from the absence of clearly acknowledged regions in England. The boundaries of regions vary, depending on which government department, public body, or political organization is responsible for defining them.[9] Map 9.2 shows the 14 Regional Health Authorities in England. Other public bodies organized on a regional basis would not usually have a separate Mersey region nor divide the Southeast into Thames regions. The creation of Oxford and, to some extent, Wessex regions is not altogether common practice. There is an RHA for East Anglia. The Department of Trade and Industry has an Eastern region. The Department of the Environment has neither. This lack of standardization not only provides a muddled picture in any discussion of regional government, it also points to an important problem in any attempt to create a structured and elected tier of regional government in England. One would first have to determine the number of regions and their boundaries. The existing confusion reinforces an indistinct picture of what they might be.

Administrative Devolution

In England the various functions of government are carried out by a number of functionally differentiated departments (agriculture, education,

Map 9.2. Regional Health Authorities.

energy, and so on). In Scotland those functions are vested in one single department. The same is true of Northern Ireland and, to a lesser extent, Wales. This concentration of functions in territorially defined departments has been given a number of labels, the most common and probably the most appropriate being *administrative devolution*. Instead of being governed by London-based departments, Scotland and Northern Ireland are in effect governed largely by single departments based in Edinburgh and Belfast, respectively.

The Scottish Office (SO) is a government department that has existed for some time. The first secretary for Scotland was appointed in 1885. However, not until 1939 did the department absorb many important functions affecting Scotland that had previously been carried out by other bodies. At the same time, the bulk of the department was moved from London to St. Andrew's House in Edinburgh.[10] Since then, the department has expanded and acquired new responsibilities. In the immediate postwar period it was given responsibility in Scotland for the National Health Service, assistance to agriculture, and town and country planning. More recently it has acquired responsibility for economic development.

The SO is divided into functional units known as departments. There are currently five principal departments (see Table 9.2), plus a central services unit, which is in effect a sixth department and is responsible for personnel and finance, and four smaller departments (the Scottish Record Office, Scottish Courts Administration, General Register Office for Scotland, and the Department of Registers for Scotland). At the political apex stands the secretary of state for Scotland, assisted by two ministers of state (one drawn usually from the House of Lords) and two parliamentary undersecretaries. Because the number of departments in the SO exceeds the number of junior ministers, one minister will often be given responsibility for more than one department. Below the ministers, at the civil-service level, there is a management group made up of departmental heads, with a secretariat and regular meetings.

Despite this concentration of functions in one department and the attempt at coordination, the heads of each department retain considerable

TABLE 9.2. SCOTTISH OFFICE DEPARTMENTS

Department	Responsibilities
Agriculture and Fisheries for Scotland	Most agricultural and fisheries matters
Scottish Development	Housing, local government, roads, land-use planning, environmental protection and the countryside, historic buildings, certain transport functions
Industry for Scotland	Industrial and regional economic development, energy, tourism, urban regeneration, new towns
Scottish Education	Education outside the universities, libraries, social work services, the arts, sport, museums
Scottish Home and Health	Police, criminal justice, legal aid, NHS, prisons, fire service, home defense

autonomy and, as two observers write, "departmental interaction resembles the independence of Whitehall ministers."[11] The individual departments in conjunction with outside interest groups would appear to form the policy communities within the SO. Which outside group raises an issue will normally determine which department will deal with it, and apparently groups rarely refer to the Scottish Office as such, talking instead of individual departments.[12] Once a policy has been agreed on by the SO, cabinet or cabinet committee discussion and agreement are often influenced by the nature of the issue. Where a proposal falls clearly within the scope of the SO and affects Scotland solely, it is often approved without any debate.[13] A proposal that has wider United Kingdom implications is considered in the same way as proposals emanating from other government departments.

The picture that emerges is thus one of a government department that operates in a particular territory almost as a minigovernment. It is a government department and yet in many respects is more than a government department. The same is true of the Northern Ireland office. It is of more recent origin than is the SO. For the 50 years prior to 1972, Northern Ireland had its own parliament, granted to it by the United Kingdom Parliament. It was organized on the model of the United Kingdom government, with departments and ministers, and with members elected to it known as members of Parliament. For reasons to be discussed shortly, it was suspended in 1972 and replaced with direct rule from the United Kingdom government. This entailed the creation of the Northern Ireland Office, which was formed as a government department under a secretary of state and a number of junior ministers. Its civil-service staff was drawn largely from the Northern Ireland civil service, and the bulk of the department was based at Stormont, just outside Belfast, the home of the old Northern Ireland Parliament.

The department is similar to the SO in the scope of its responsibilities and the functional separation of its responsibilities into departments. These departments encompass health and social services, finance, environment, education, economic development, agriculture, and Northern Ireland Office responsibilities specific to the province. As with the SO, the number of departments exceeds the number of junior ministers and so one minister may be given responsibility for more than one department. At the moment, the secretary of state is assisted by one minister of state and four parliamentary undersecretaries. In addition, he has an executive committee, comprising these ministers and the civil-service heads of department. It serves as a coordinating committee and has been likened by one minister to a cabinet.[14]

The department is unlike the Scottish Office in that the ministers do not sit for seats in the province. Also, though it is usually very successful in obtaining money from the Treasury, it is less of a lobbying department for its territory in London. Rather, it is more concerned with the task of administration and with carrying out United Kingdom government policy in the province. Much of its time has been taken up with bringing the law in the province in line with that of the rest of the United Kingdom. For the secretary of state, the task is one of heading an administrative department while at the same time seeking a political solution to the problems peculiar to the province. It places him in a unique position. When first introduced, direct rule in Northern Ireland was intended as a temporary expedient. So far, it has survived the various attempts to introduce new forms of government for the province.

The Welsh Office constitutes something of a hybrid department. It is much smaller than the Scottish Office and the Northern Ireland Office—with a secretary of state, one minister of state, and one parliamentary undersecretary—and it does not enjoy quite the same degree of autonomy. Nonetheless, it has multifunctional responsibilities. Within Wales, it has responsibility for health, primary and secondary education, town and country planning, housing, local government, new towns, roads, water, forestry, tourism, national parks, and historic buildings. It shares with the Ministry of Agriculture responsibility for agriculture in the principality. It also has a general duty to supervise the carrying out of government policy in Wales. Like its other territorial counterparts, it is based mainly in the territory itself, with its headquarters in Cardiff. It maintains only a small office in London.

To reiterate, the government of the United Kingdom fulfills various functions. In England these are carried out by different, functionally based departments, whereas in Scotland, Northern Ireland, and, to a lesser extent, Wales they are carried out by single, territorially defined departments that operate largely as minigovernments. However, such an arrangement has not met with the overwhelming approval of the inhabitants of the territories concerned. Direct rule in Northern Ireland, as I have noted, was intended as a temporary expedient. In Scotland and Wales, government by nonelected and, despite their location, United Kingdom government departments has generated calls for change. In recent years, proposals for reform have been on the agenda of political debate.

PROPOSED: DEVOLUTION

Of reforms proposed in subnational government in recent years, the most prominent have been those for the devolution of executive and legislative powers to some form of elected assemblies in Scotland and Wales, and, in a somewhat different format, Northern Ireland. Various schemes have been proposed and received parliamentary approval but none has yet proved successful.

Scotland and Wales

The proposal for devolving some executive and legislative powers to national assemblies in Scotland and Wales is not new. The Liberal party advocated the somewhat more radical proposal of federalism during most of its history,[15] and the Scottish National party favors complete independence for Scotland, though it is prepared to accept some form of devolved government in the interim. Only in the past twenty years, however, has devolution become a significant issue of political debate.

Some form of home rule for Scotland and Wales has been advocated by the Scottish National (SNP) and Plaid Cymru (PC) parties, respectively, since their formation earlier this century, but the main achievement of the two parties prior to the 1960s was simply to have survived. This situation was to change somewhat in the 1960s, when each party won one seat at a by-election and also made gains in local elections. The apparent growing strength of nationalist sentiment was sufficient to encourage the Labour government to establish a Royal Commission on the Constitution; announced in 1968, it was appointed in 1969 and reported in 1973. The nationalist parties had not done well in the 1970 general election, with the SNP winning only one seat. Four years later the picture had changed significantly: the Royal Commission had reported in favor of some form of devolved government and there had emerged what A. H. Birch has referred to as the "eruptive factor,"[16] North Sea oil. The SNP was able to play on the argument that the location of the off-shore oil fields meant that the oil was Scotland's as much as anyone's and that revenue from it would be sufficient to make a Scottish government viable. By playing on the expectation of a rising middle class in Scotland, whose expectations had been left unfulfilled by the Westminster government, the SNP began to make electoral inroads into the strength of both main parties. By playing on the cultural fears of the Welsh people, the PC also achieved a somewhat more limited impact in Wales. In the February 1974 general election, the SNP won 7 of the 71 Scottish seats and the PC won 2 of the 36 Welsh seats. In the October general election, the SNP increased the number of seats won to 11 and the PC to 3. Of the SNP's 11 seats, 9 were won from the Conservatives but the party had come second in 35 out of 41 Labour-held seats. In total number of votes received, it was the second largest party in Scotland.

The Labour government that returned in 1974 saw the prospect of the SNP developing into the dominant political party in Scotland and, in so doing, ruining Labour's chances of winning future elections (both Scotland and Wales constitute important electoral bases for the party; see Chapter 5). In order to respond to the nationalist challenge, the government put forward proposals for a form of devolved government in both Scotland and Wales and in 1976 introduced a Scotland and Wales bill. The bill provided for an elected assembly in each of the two countries, each with a fixed term of four years, with responsibility for countrywide concerns such as health, land use, and tourism, though with Scotland having more devolved power than Wales. Neither assembly was to have powers of taxation; money was to be provided by means of a block grant voted by Parliament as well as through local authority taxation and borrowing by local authorities and public corporations.

The bill ran into serious parliamentary opposition. The Conservative Opposition did not like the provisions and decided to vote against it. Many Labour members also found it unpalatable. A number were opposed to devolution, seeing it as a step on the road to eventual independence. Some MPs from the North of England disliked it because they felt that it would effectively discriminate against regions that were not to have similar assemblies. In order to facilitate the bill's passage, the government announced its agreement to the devolution proposals being submitted to referendums in Scotland and Wales. The bill achieved a second reading (see Chapter 11) but ran into sustained opposition from both sides of the House in committee (taken on the floor of the House), and the government decided to introduce a motion to limit debate (a guillotine motion). The vote on the guillotine maximized the opposition to the measure and, with 22 Labour MPs voting with the Opposition (a further 21 abstained from voting), the government suffered an embarrassing defeat.[17]

The government decided not to proceed with the bill as it stood. Instead, it introduced two new bills, the Scotland bill and the Wales bill. The Scotland bill largely retained the proposals incorporated in the original bill, while the Wales bill provided only for a very limited form of devolution to the principality. On this occasion the government achieved passage of both bills, though only after a number of amendments had been carried against the government's wishes. The most important of these stipulated that if 40% of eligible voters did not cast a "yes" vote in the referendum in Scotland, the government was to bring forward a motion for the repeal of the act. A similar provision was inserted in the Wales bill. In this way, MPs created an important and unprecedented hurdle to the achievement of devolved government.

The referendums in Scotland and Wales were scheduled to be held on March 1, 1979, and were preceded by vigorous campaigns in the two countries. In Wales, it appeared that the prospect of devolved government aroused suspicion among non-Welsh-speaking inhabitants and was not gaining overwhelming support. In Scotland, the debate was keenly fought between pro- and antidevolutionists. Some opponents feared devolution would constitute the thin end of the wedge, leading to an eventual breakup of the United Kingdom; supporters argued that it was necessary in order to maintain the unity of the kingdom. On March 1, 950,330 voters in Wales voted "no" to the devolution proposals: only 243,048 voted "yes." The result in the principality was clearly a decisive rejection. In Scotland, the result was a close one: 1,230,937 people voted "yes," and 1,153,502 voted "no." Although a slight majority of those who voted had opted for the devolution proposals, the number voting "yes" did not constitute 40% of all eligible voters. As a consequence, the cabinet decided not to proceed with devolution, a decision that precipitated Nationalist MPs' withdrawing their support from the government. This loss of Nationalist support deprived the government of a majority in a vote of confidence on March 28, 1979. The result was a general election and the return of a Conservative government. In the new Parliament, the government introduced the relevant motions for the repeal of the two acts and both motions were carried.

In the wake of the 1979 general election, it looked as if devolution was no longer an important issue on the political agenda. The SNP won only two seats in the election, as did Plaid Cymru. The new government was not keen to pursue the issue—Prime Minister Thatcher being a notable opponent of devolution—and other issues came to the fore. However, from the early 1980s onward, the subject began to reemerge as a feature of debate. Initially, much of the running was made by the Liberal party and then the newly formed SDP. In alliance, the two parties pressed for elected assemblies in Scotland, Wales, and the English regions. This manifesto commitment was reiterated in 1988, when the two parties merged to formed the SLD. The Labour party, which had maintained a commitment to some form of devolution throughout the decade, also committed itself— following its policy review of 1987–1989—to support ten regional assemblies in England as well as assemblies in Scotland and Wales. There was also some pressure within Conservative ranks for some devolution of power to a Scottish assembly. Calls for such a policy became more pronounced from Scottish Conservatives following the party's disastrous showing in Scotland in the 1987 general election (the party lost 11 of its 21 seats). In the wake of the election, Scottish Secretary Malcolm Rifkind, himself a prodevolutionist in the 1970s debate, conceded that changes might be necessary "in respect of some policies."[18] However, official Conservative policy remains opposed to devolution—Mrs. Thatcher rejected legislative devolution "unequivocally" at the 1988 conference of the Scottish Conservative party—and the party is the only one represented in the House of Commons to take such a stance. All the other parties represented favor some form of devolution or, in the case of the SNP, independence for Scotland within the European Community.

The arguments advanced in favor of devolution have centered on both consent and effectiveness. Decisions taken in Scotland and Wales by elected government, it is argued, would be more efficient and effective because of a better appreciation of the area—its needs as well as its resources—and additionally, would enhance consent by being closer to the people. Devolving governmental responsibilities would also serve to reduce pressure on central government and on Parliament. Both government and people, it was felt, would benefit. Against this, Conservatives, as well as some Labour MPs, have expressed the fear that devolution could lead to a breakup of the United Kingdom. They have also opposed it on the grounds that it would introduce another expensive and unnecessary layer of government (people being more interested in their individual needs being met by government—any government—than in being able to elect another body of government) and that it would exacerbate economic inequality between the regions. Economically, it is argued, wealthy regions will wish to retain as much of their wealth as possible. Among the poorer parts of the United Kingdom to suffer would be Scotland; its small population and limited resources make it economically dependent on the rest of the United Kingdom. The argument, in short, is that more government is not necessarily better government.

The stance of the Labour party has ensured that devolution remains on the agenda of political debate. At a practical level, there is little likelihood of any measure of devolution being passed under the present Conservative government. In the event that the Labour party—or any party dependent on SLD support to form a government—is returned at a future general election, then the constitutional framework of the United Kingdom may witness a major reformulation. The principle of the unitary state would be maintained, but major powers could be devolved to newly elected assemblies throughout Great Britain.

Northern Ireland

The problems of Northern Ireland and its form of government are particular to the province. Those problems arouse perplexity, incredulity, and misunderstanding in other parts of the United Kingdom as well as abroad. (Indeed, the failure of some Americans to comprehend the problems of the province has been a bone of contention both within Northern Ireland and in government circles.) Whereas in Britain there is a consensus favoring a certain norm of political behavior—abiding by the rules of the constitutional game even if one favors a change of the rules (or even a new game)—there is no such consensus in Northern Ireland. There never has been. To Britons reared on solving or avoiding disputes by talk and compromise, the vehement and often violent pursuit by opposing communities of mutually exclusive goals is a vexing and near-incomprehensible phenomenon.

The history of Ireland has been a depressing and troubled one extending over many centuries and marked by bitter conflict between the English and the Irish and, within Ireland, between indigenous Catholic Irish and Protestant Scottish Presbyterian settlers. The Irish uprising in 1916 forced the United Kingdom government to recognize Irish demands for self-determination. In 1920 the Westminster Parliament passed the Government of Ireland Act, which provided for home rule in the country and created two Parliaments: one for the 6 northern counties, part of the region of Ulster, and one for the remaining 26 counties. The provisions for the southern counties were stillborn. The continuing troubles in the country resulted in the Treaty of Ireland of 1922, which realized the Irish Free State. Ireland was partitioned and the provisions of the 1920 act applied in the new province of Northern Ireland. A bicameral Parliament was established at Stormont, from which an executive was drawn. The new government of the province exercised a number of devolved powers and, in exercising those powers, was not much hindered by the Westminster government. British politicians were not keen to be drawn again into the infructuous bog of Irish politics.

The province of Northern Ireland was created at the forceful behest of the Protestant community of the North. Largely derived from Scottish Presbyterian stock, it had no wish to be engulfed within a Catholic Irish state. Within the new province, it was dominant. It was not, though, the only community within the province: one-third of the population was Catholic. The religious divide between the two communities was reinforced by social, economic, and educational differences as well as by centuries of ingrained animosity. Catholic children were educated in Catholic schools, were taught Irish history, played Gaelic games, and lived in Catholic communities. Protestant children were taught British history, played non-Gaelic games, lived in Protestant communities, and were taught to look down on Catholics as being lazy and threatening to the existence of the province. Catholics, in turn, looked on Protestants as being gravely in error. The divisions ran deep. The Protestants continued proudly to celebrate the victory of Protestant William of Orange in the Battle of the Boyne in 1690. Indeed, in the new province the anniversary of the victory was made a public holiday.

Northern Ireland after 1922 became for all intents and purposes a one-party province. The Unionist party, representing the Protestants, regularly won two-thirds of the seats at Stormont (there was little alternation of seats from one party to the other) and formed the government, enjoying uninterrupted power. Despite occasional violence by the self-styled Irish Republican Army (the IRA), which wanted a united Ireland and was prepared to engage in terrorist activities to achieve it, the Stormont government enjoyed sufficient coercive powers to impose its will and did so in a manner that favored the Protestants. Catholics were discriminated against in the allocation of houses and jobs and were forced to live in an environment where they felt themselves to be second-class citizens. There was little they could do about the situation within the existing political structure: unlike American blacks, they had no Bill of Rights or Supreme Court to call upon and the Westminster government preferred not to get involved.

The position in the province was to change in the latter half of the 1960s. A new, relatively liberal Unionist prime minister, Terence O'Neill, sought better relations with the Republic of Ireland, a move that caused consternation in the more traditional ranks of his party. On the Catholic side, the steps taken by the O'Neill government were seen as being too little and too late. A civil-rights movement sprang up in the province, inspired by the experience of the United States. The Civil Rights Association was formed in 1967 and was joined the following year by a more revolutionary organization, the People's Democracy. The two groups engaged in tactics designed to provoke a violent response in the hope that this would draw attention to the plight of the Catholic minority in the province. They organized demonstrations and marches. These resulted in a vigorous reaction from the police force, the Royal Ulster Constabulary, as well as from various Protestant groups. Clashes between protesters and their opponents erupted into civil disorder that the police and their auxiliary forces, the so-called B-Specials (despised in the Catholic community), were unable to contain. In August 1969, at the request of the Northern Ireland cabinet, the Westminster government introduced troops into the province to maintain order. In return for such action, the government insisted on phasing out the B-Specials and the introduction of full civil rights for Roman Catholics. Ensuring that the latter demand was complied with was another matter.

The arrival of troops was initially welcomed by Catholics in the province. However, the use of troops to support the civil authorities—in other words, the Protestant government and the police—and the searching of Catholic areas for arms produced a rapid dissipation of that support. A "shooting war" broke out between the IRA and the British army in February 1971. In August the British government decided to intern without trial suspected IRA leaders. Instead of lessening the violence, the action appeared to exacerbate it: internment aroused greater sympathy for the IRA cause among the Catholic community, and the interned leaders were replaced by more extreme followers. At the same time, tension increased between the Stormont and Westminster government, the former contending that the latter was not doing enough to counter the activities of the IRA. The Stormont government even made a request for troops in the province to be put under its control. The request was denied.

Violence in the province became more marked toward the end of 1971, with more than 100 explosions a month. In the first two months of 1972, 49 people were killed and another 257 injured as a result of gunshots and bombings. In an attempt to break the deadlock in the province, the Conservative government at Westminster decided to pursue some form of political initiative: pressure for such action had been building up for some weeks, both abroad and at home, including pressure from the Labour Opposition. The government's proposals included periodic plebiscites on the issue of the border, a start to the phasing out of internment, and the transfer of responsibility for law and order from Stormont to London. The last proposal proved unacceptable to the Northern Ireland cabinet, which made clear that it would resign if the proposal was implemented. In consequence, Prime Minister Edward Heath informed the House of Commons on March 24, 1972, that the British government was left with no alternative but to assume full and direct responsibility for the administration of Northern Ireland until such time as a political solution to the problem of the province could be achieved. In order to give effect to the government's decision, the Northern Ireland (Temporary Provisions) bill was quickly passed by Parliament, enjoying the support of the Labour Opposition as well as of the Liberals. The new act suspended the Stormont Parliament and transferred its powers to the Westminster government. A new Northern Ireland Office was established under a secretary of state. The first occupant of the office was William Whitelaw.

The tasks of the new secretary of state were twofold. He had to try to maintain security within the province, doing so in a way that would not alienate either community (the Protestant community by not doing enough, the Catholic community by doing too much), while at the same time seeking a political solution that was acceptable to both. The solution favored by the government, and supported by the Labour Opposition, was the creation of a power-sharing assembly in the province—that is, an assembly with devolved powers and with power shared among the different parties: in other words, the Catholics were to have some part in government. Mr. Whitelaw held a conference attended by parties from the province and then published a White Paper outlining proposals for an assembly elected by a form of proportional representation. Agreement was also reached with the government of the Irish Republic on the establishment of a consultative council of Ireland to provide what was commonly referred to as "the Irish dimension."

Elections to the new assembly, a unicameral body with 78 members, took place in June 1973. Unionists of different descriptions won 50 of the seats. The second largest number, 19, was won by the predominantly Catholic Social Democratic and Labour party (SDLP). In December, agreement was finally reached on the formation of an executive, comprising six members of the Official Unionist party, four members of the SDLP, and one member drawn from the nonsectarian Alliance party. The executive took office on January 1, 1974. The creation of the power-sharing executive and the council of Ireland was opposed by a large section of the Protestant community. In the February 1974 general election, 11 of the 12 seats in the province went to Unionists of one hue or another who were opposed to power sharing. A province-wide strike was organized by the protestant Ulster Workers Council. It proved devastatingly effective, for all intents and purposes virtually bringing the province to a standstill. The new Labour government in London was unwilling to employ its coercive powers to try to break the strike. The executive resigned. It had lasted four months.

With the collapse of the executive, the province reverted to direct rule from London. Two months later the government published a White Paper proposing an elected constitutional convention as a medium for political leaders in the province to seek an acceptable settlement. The White Paper made clear the government's own continuing commitment to the principle of power sharing. In elections to the convention, held on May 1, 1975, 46 of the 78 seats went to Unionists opposed to power sharing. Only 5 members representing the pro-power-sharing Unionist party of Northern Ireland were returned. The convention was a failure. It issued a report favoring a Stormont-type cabinet government—that is, a majority party exercising all governmental powers unhindered by any sharing of such powers with minority parties. The British government rejected the report and asked the convention to reconvene and reconsider. The reconvened convention failed to reach any new agreement. Recognizing that no further progress could be made, the British government introduced the necessary order to bring the convention to an end. It was dissolved on March 6, 1976.

For the next three years, the government pursued the approach of trying to maintain order in the province while encouraging its people and their leaders to reach agreement among themselves. Some modest proposals for a nonlegislative assembly were made, only to be rejected by the parties in Northern Ireland. Various attempts by the Conservative secretary of state appointed in 1979, Humphrey Atkins, to find some acceptable compromise among the parties failed. A conference he convened at the beginning of 1980 was boycotted by the Official Unionist party. The parties that did attend disagreed on the form of government they favored for the province. A proposal by Mr. Atkins to create an advisory council of elected officials drawn from the province, to fulfill advisory and reporting functions until such time as a more durable settlement could be reached, was stillborn. It was overshadowed by the hunger strikes of IRA prisoners in the Maze prison (demanding various concessions, including the reintroduction of "political status") and by a recommendation from former prime minister James Callaghan that the province develop into a "broadly independent State."[19] The problem of Northern Ireland remained intractable.

The government continued to pursue policies that sought to maintain order and move in the direction of a political settlement, but in so doing it ran the risk of alienating both communities within the province. Its refusal to give in to the demands of the IRA hunger strikers forced an end to the strike, but the strikers had aroused sympathy for the IRA cause among a large section of the Catholic community. One hunger striker, Bobby Sands, was elected MP in a by-election in Fermanagh and South Tyrone. He died a month later. Protestants for their part were extremely suspicious and dismayed by meetings between Mrs. Thatcher and her opposite number in the Irish Republic, meetings that resulted in the agreement on the formation of an Anglo-Irish intergovernmental council. The council was to involve regular meetings at ministerial and official level to discuss matters of common concern between the two governments. Protestants were also highly critical of the government's security policy in the province, considering it to be inadequate. In November 1981 a Unionist MP, Robert Bradford, was assassinated. The leader of the Democratic Unionist party, Ian Paisley, accused the prime minister of being a traitor to Northern Ireland. He also threatened to make the province "ungovernable." For the government, the problem appeared to be getting worse rather than better.

The government emphasis remained on achieving a political solution, and since 1982 the government has attempted two major initiatives. The first, "rolling devolution," was initiated in 1982; the second, the Anglo-Irish Agreement, was signed in November 1985. Under the first initiative, a 78-member assembly was to be elected, through a system of proportional representation. It differed from previous such assemblies by virtue of its internal organization: it was to have a committee system, each committee paralleling a government department. The committees were to have salaried chairmen and deputy chairmen, chosen to reflect the party composition in the assembly, and were to have powers to make reports to the assembly and to the secretary of state. The concept of "rolling devolution" allowed the assembly to propose at any time the transfer of executive responsibilities for any particular department to its own jurisdiction. The ultimate objective was full devolution, but to be achieved at a pace made possible by the assembly itself. In practice, the assembly proved short-lived. The elections to it, in October 1982, provided a publicity coup for Sinn Fein, the political wing of the Provisional IRA: it garnered one-tenth of the first-preference votes cast and saw five of its candidates elected. SDLP as well as Sinn Fein candidates elected to the assembly boycotted its sittings. Only Unionists attented. In March 1986 they decided not to fulfill the assembly's statutory functions in protest at the Anglo-Irish Agreement. Three months later the government decided to disband the assembly; like its predecessors, it had fallen foul of the lack of consensus that it was designed to counter.

The Anglo-Irish Agreement was the product of the discussions that had taken place under the aegis of the Anglo-Irish intergovernmental council. Signed at Hillsborough Castle in Northern Ireland on November 15, 1985, by the British prime minister, Mrs. Thatcher, and the *Taoiseach* (prime minister) of the Irish Republic, Dr. Garret Fitzgerald, the Agreement had three essential elements. Under Article 1, both governments recognized that "any change in the status of Northern Ireland would only come about with the consent of the majority of the people of Northern Ireland." This was the first time the Irish government had given legal recognition to Northern Ireland's right to self-determination. The British government hoped this part of the Agreement would help make the whole document acceptable to the Unionists. The second element was embodied in Articles 2 to 8, which established an Intergovernmental Conference, chaired by the secretary of state for Northern Ireland and the foreign minister of the Republic. Through the conference, the Republic was enabled to raise issues on the administration of the province that were of particular concern to the minority community. The committee was an advisory one, with a small secretariat. It became a particular target for Unionist opposition. The third element, covered by Articles 6, 7, and 9, provided for greater cross-border cooperation on security matters, and security became a subject regularly discussed at meetings of the conference. The Agreement also dealt with a number of other topics, including the creation of an Anglo-Irish parliamentary body, and this came into being in February 1989.

The first and third elements of the Agreement proved insufficient to make it acceptable to the Unionist parties. To them, the Intergovernmental Conference allowed a foreign government the opportunity to interfere in the affairs of the province and constituted a "thin end of the wedge," the first step toward forcing the province into a united Ireland. In protest, all fifteen Unionist MPs in the province resigned their seats in December 1985, fighting by-elections as a means of demonstrating popular opposition to the Agreement. The move was a partial success: one Unionist failed to achieve reelection; the rest were returned, including Enoch Powell in the highly marginal seat of Down South (he lost the seat in the 1987 general election). Their next step, as we have seen, was to refuse to fulfill the statutory functions of the Northern Ireland Assembly, in effect signing the assembly's death warrant. Their actions failed to dent the government's resolve to persist with the Agreement.

Three years after the signing of the Agreement, the British government could point to a notable increase in cross-border coordination on security matters and a notable decline in the number of deaths and injuries in the province; Unionists could point to the fact that the biggest decline predated the Agreement taking effect. (In 1972, the worst year for violence since 1969, there were 467 deaths, almost 5,000 injured, and more than 10,000 shooting incidents; in 1985 there were 54 deaths, 916 people injured, and 196 shooting incidents, these numbers increasing slightly in succeeding years.) There was greater contact between the two governments, and the Irish Republic proved willing to make some changes to its extradition policy, a contentious issue on which the British government had been pressing for significant changes for some years. On the British side, various measures were introduced to meet some of the fears or demands of the nationalist community: an independent commission for complaints against the police, a Fair Employment bill, the extension of the franchise for council elections, and the removal of special protection for the Union Flag. Relative to previous initiatives, the Agreement—in terms of substance and longevity—now constitutes the most successful initiative taken by a British government since the imposition of direct rule.

For the Unionists in the province, however, the Agreement goes too far; for the IRA it does not go far enough. This problem points to the essential dilemma for British government. It seeks, to a large extent, to reconcile the irreconcilable. The government is faced with factions within the province (and interests outside) that pursue mutually exclusive goals, feelings within the divided province being bitter and running deep. It pursues political initiatives against a backdrop of continuing violence. Though the incidence of murder and violent injury is much reduced compared with the early 1970s, bombings and tit-for-tat murders continue to mar the everyday life of the province.

For the British government, then, the situation continues to present a perplexing and irritating conundrum. The government seeks to find a constitutional settlement for the province, but there is none that is acceptable to the various bodies involved. There are at least nine different constitutional options that have been canvassed. Each one is unacceptable to one or more interested parties. *Direct rule* has little attraction to any party as a permanent solution: it is recognized for what it is—a temporary expedient. *Self-government* within the United Kingdom, akin to the pre-1972 position, is favored by a majority of the Unionists but not by the Catholics, the British and Irish governments, or for that matter, opinion within the United States. *Integration* within the United Kingdom, analogous to the position of, say, Scotland and Wales, finds favor among some Unionists but is unacceptable to a majority of Catholics as well as to the British government: the problems peculiar to the province are thought to require a constitutional framework distinct from that of the rest of the United Kingdom.

A *Power-sharing assembly* is supported by the British government but is opposed by a significant and influential fraction of Unionists, who object to sharing power with a minority not committed to the maintenance of the union with Britain, and it is unacceptable to the SDLP, unless created within the context of an "Irish dimension." *Unification* with the Republic of Ireland is sought by the Irish Government and by most Catholics in the North, and in the long term this has a certain appeal to the British government. It is totally opposed by the Protestant majority in the province, however. An absolute majority voted to maintain the union in a plebiscite in 1973: 99% of those who voted—58% of the total electorate—voted for retention.

A *federal Ireland* is unacceptable to the majority of Protestants, as it is to the IRA: the Protestants consider that such a solution would go too far, the IRA that it would not go far enough. A *redrawing of the boundary* between Northern Ireland and the Republic has been canvassed by some writers but is unacceptable to a majority of both Protestants and Catholics. A redrawing of the boundary would solve little and would almost certainly create new problems, including the possibility of a refugee problem (few Protestants would wish to remain in Fermanagh if it became part of the Republic). The creation of an *independent Northern Ireland* has been advocated by some politicians, notably James (now Lord) Callaghan, but finds little favor among Catholics, Protestants, the British and Irish governments, and other countries. It would be unlikely to be able to sustain itself as an independent entity.

The one other solution that has been raised is for the *withdrawal of British troops*, allowing the competing forces within the province to sort out, or rather fight out, the destiny of the province. It has a certain appeal to opinion within Britain, tired of the terrorist activities conducted by the IRA both within the province and on the British mainland; a 1987 MORI poll found that 61% of respondents favored withdrawing troops, either immediately or within a preset period.[20] Troop withdrawal is not acceptable to the government. Successive governments have accepted responsibility for the province, admitting the need to try to maintain order and to create the framework for a solution, and making clear a commitment to maintain the Union so long as a majority of the people of Northern Ireland wish to maintain it. There is also the realization that to withdraw troops could precipitate a bloodbath within the province, with the conflict spreading into the Republic and possibly onto the British mainland as well. As much as Britain would like to be rid of the problem, it accepts that it cannot just wash its hands of the difficulty.

In summary, then, Britain is faced with a problem that admits of no obvious or easy solution. It has tended to proceed on the basis of a settlement premised on traditional British assumptions, and for that very reason its efforts have tended to be unsuccessful: it is faced with a very non-British problem. It is a problem that annually takes more lives within the province and sometimes, in quite horrific attacks of violence, on the mainland as well. It is a problem that Britain would like to be free of but one that it is committed to resolve without giving in to violence. The one thing that prevents the IRA from achieving its goal of a united Ireland is the very violence they pursue in order to achieve it. The problem of Northern Ireland is one riddled with paradox.

CONCLUSION

Below the level of national government in Britain, the picture is a complex one. Scotland, Northern Ireland, and Wales each has a multifunctional government department largely responsible for the administration of the territory. At a regional level (which usually means regions within England, plus Scotland, Wales, and Northern Ireland), there are disparate and discrete public bodies, such as the regional health authorities, while at the level of counties and towns there are elected councils.

Despite this complexity, these bodies have one thing in common. They are subordinate units of government. What powers they enjoy are granted at the discretion of Parliament, which means in practice (or largely so) that of the government. As resources have diminished, central government has proved increasingly willing to rein in some of the activities of these subordinate units. Squeezed between the demands and expectations of local electors and those of central government, local government is not in an enviable position.

In terms of political authority, local government can be seen to be encountering problems in raising resources to meet its commitments to the local community, hemmed in by the demands of local citizens and the limitations imposed by central government, and to be having difficulty in maintaining the consent of citizens. Attempts to maintain political authority by the creation of national or regional assemblies, bringing some decision making closer to the people, have not come to fruition, or else, in the unique case of Northern Ireland, have failed. There is no consensus among political leaders as to what the next step should be.

NOTES

1. A. King, "The Problem of Overload," in A. King (ed.), *Why Is Britain Becoming Harder to Govern?* (BBC, 1976), p. 9.
2. M. Beloff and G. Peele, *The Government of the United Kingdom* (Weidenfeld & Nicolson, 1980), p. 267.
3. The functions and proximity of local councils make certain officials and committee chairmen more likely targets for attempts at corruption by bodies seeking preferential treatment than is the case at the more distant levels of central government; the problem has been exacerbated by the fact that some local authorities are dominated, more or less permanently, by one party.
4. See R. E. Jennings, "The Councillor as a Point of Access to Local Government," paper presented at the annual conference of the American Political Science Association, Washington, DC, 1980; and G. W. Jones, "The Functions and Organization of Councillors," *Public Administration*, 1973, pp. 140–41.
5. Professor Howard Elcock to author, July 18, 1989.
6. Conservative Research Department, *The Campaign Guide 1989* (Conservative Central Office, 1989), p. 414.
7. See B. W. Hogwood, "Introduction," in B. W. Hogwood and M. Keating (eds.), *Regional Government in England* (Oxford University Press, 1982), pp. 10–12.
8. See S. C. Haywood and H. J. Elcock, "Regional Health Authorities: Regional Government or Central Agencies?" in Hogwood and Keating, p. 131; and H. J. Elcock and S. C. Haywood, *The Buck Stops Where? Accountability and Control in the National Health Service* (University of Hull Institute for Health Studies, 1980).
9. See B. W. Hogwood and P. D. Lindley, "Variations in Regional Boundaries," in Hogwood and Keating, pp. 21–49.
10. M. Keating and A. Midwinter, *The Government of Scotland* (Mainstream Publishing, 1983), p. 14.
11. Ibid. See also P. Hennessy, *Whitehall* (Secker & Warburg, 1989), pp. 460–65.
12. Keating and Midwinter, p. 17.
13. Ibid.
14. D. Birrell and A. Murie, *Policy and Government in Northern Ireland* (Gill and Macmillan, 1980), p. 84.
15. David Steel refers to the commitment to such a policy as stemming from Gladstone's pamphlet of 1886 that argued for a reform of government consistent with the aspirations of the individual nations in Great Britain. D. Steel, "Federalism," in N. MacCormick (ed.), *The Scottish Debate* (Oxford University Press, 1970), p. 81.
16. A. H. Birch, *Political Integration and Disintegration in the British Isles* (George Allen & Unwin, 1977).
17. *House of Commons Debates (Hansard)*, Vol. 926, cols. 1361–66.
18. *Sunday Telegraph*, June 21, 1987; *Sunday Times*, June 21, 1987.

19. *House of Commons Debates (Hansard)*, Sixth Series, Vol. 7, col. 1050.
20. *Daily Express*, February 10, 1987. In terms of the future of Northern Ireland, the poll found that 29% believed it should remain part of the United Kingdom, 29% felt it should become independent, 27% thought it should become part of a united Ireland, and 15% replied "Don't Know."

CHAPTER 10

The European Community

Government beyond the Center

Prior to the 1970s, the United Kingdom had entered into various treaty obligations with other nations. It was a founding member of the United Nations Organization. It had joined the North Atlantic Treaty Organization (NATO). It signed, though did not incorporate into domestic law, the European Convention on Human Rights. At no time, though, did it hand over to a supranational body the power to formulate regulations that were to have domestic application within the United Kingdom and be enforceable as law.

This situation was to change on January 1, 1973. On that date the United Kingdom became a member of the European Community. Forty-two volumes of legislation promulgated by insitutions of the European Community were incorporated into British law and, under the provisions of the 1972 European Communities Act, future legislation emanating from the Community was to be incorporated as well. The United Kingdom entered into a relationship for which the United States has no parallel.

THE EUROPEAN COMMUNITY

The European Community comprises the European Steel and Coal Community, the European Atomic Energy Community (Euratom), and the better-known European Economic Community (the EEC). The Steel and Coal Community, formed in 1951 under the Treaty of Paris, placed iron, steel, and coal production in member countries under a common authority. Euratom and the EEC were created under the Treaty of Rome and came into being on January 1, 1958. Euratom was designed to help create a civil nuclear industry in Europe. The EEC formed a common market for goods within the community of member states. The three bodies were merged in 1967 to form the European Communities, known now by the singular term, the European Community (the EC).

Britain declined to join the individual bodies when they were first formed. The Labour government in 1951 found the supranational control of the Steel and Coal Community to be unacceptable. The succeeding Conservative government was not initially attracted by the concept of the EEC. The economic and political arguments for joining, which weighed heavily with the member states, did not carry great weight with British politicians. Britain was still seen as a world power. It was enjoying a period of prosperity. It had strong political and trading links with the Common-wealth. It had a "special relationship" with the United States. It had stood alone successfully during the Second World War. Lacking the experience of German occupation and the need to recreate a polity, Britain was not subject to the psychological appeal of a united Europe, so strong on the continental mainland.[1] Neither main political party was strongly attracted to the idea of a union with such an essentially foreign body. The Conservatives still hankered after the idea of Empire, something that had died as a result of the war (Britain could no longer afford to maintain an empire and the principle of self-determination had taken root) and something for which the Commonwealth now served as something of a substitute. Labour politicians viewed with distrust the creation of a body that they saw as inherently antisocialist, designed to shore up the capitalist edifice of Western Europe and frustrate any future socialist policies that a Labour government in Britain would seek to implement. It was one of the few issues on which the leader of the Labour party, Hugh Gaitskell, found himself in agreement with left-wingers within his own party.

The attitude of the British government toward the EEC, at both a ministerial and official level, was to undergo significant change in 1960. Britain's economic problems had become more apparent. Growth rates compared poorly with those of the six member states of the EEC (i.e., France, Germany, Italy, and the Benelux countries). There was a growing realization that having lost an empire, Britain had gained a Common-wealth. That Commonwealth, however, was not proving as amenable to British leadership as many Conservatives had hoped, nor was it proving to be the source of trade and materials that had been expected. Even the special relationship with the United States was undergoing a period of strain. The "special" appeared to be seeping out of the relationship. Some anti-Americanism lingered in Conservative ranks following the insistence of the White House that Britain abort its operation to occupy the Suez Canal zone in 1956, a distrust still not wholly dispelled. The sudden cancellation by the United States administration in 1960 of the Blue Streak, a missile that Britain had ordered and intended to employ as the major element of its nuclear defense policy, awakened British politicians to the fact that in the Atlantic partnership, Britain was very much the junior partner. The United States administration itself began to pay more attention to the EEC, and President Kennedy made clear to his friend and distant relative, Prime Minister Harold Macmillan, "that a British decision to join the Six would be welcome."[2] The option became one that had an increasing attraction to Britain.

Politically, the EEC was seen as a vehicle through which Britain could once again play a leading role on the world stage. Economically, it would provide a tariff-free market of 180 million people, it would provide the advantages of economy of scale, and it was assumed that it would encourage greater efficiency in British industry through more vigorous competition. Political and economic advantages were seen as inextricably linked. Economic strength was necessary to underpin the maintenance of political authority.[3] "If we are to meet the challenge of Communism, . . . " Macmillan wrote to Kennedy, "[we must show] that our modern society—the new form of capitalism—can run in a way that makes the fullest use of our resources and results in a steady expansion of our economic strength."[4] On July 31, 1961, he announced to the House of Commons that Britain was applying for membership.

The first application for membership was vetoed in January 1963 by the French president, General de Gaulle. He viewed British motives with suspicion, believing that Britain could serve as a vehicle for the United States to establish its dominance within the EEC. A second application was lodged in 1967, this time by the Labour government of Harold Wilson.[5] Agreement to open negotiations was reached eventually in 1969. Negotiations began under the newly returned Conservative government of Edward Heath in 1970. Relations between the British and French governments on the issue were now more amicable, de Gaulle having resigned the presidency in 1969, and no French veto was imposed. Negotiations were completed in 1971, and the British government recommended entry on the terms achieved. On October 28, 1971, following a six-day debate, the House of Commons gave its approval to the principle of membership on the terms negotiated. The vote was 356 in favor, 244 against.[6] Both parties were badly divided. Of Labour members, 69 voted with the Conservative government in favor of entry and a further 20 abstained from voting. Of Conservatives, 39 voted with the Labour Opposition against entry, and 2 abstained.[7] It was the most divisive vote of the Parliament.

At the beginning of 1972, the Treaty of Accession was signed, and the

European Communities bill, to give legal effect to British membership, was given a second reading on February 17. In order to ensure its passage, Prime Minister Heath made the vote one of confidence. Despite that, the majority for the bill was a slim one of only 8, since Opposition MPs had largely united against the measure.[8] The bill faced sustained opposition from Labour members and a number of dissident Conservatives, but it completed its remaining stages without amendment and was given a third reading on July 13.[9] The United Kingdom became a member of the European Community on January 1, 1973.

Britain's membership in the EC has been anything but uneventful. Following the return of the Labour government in 1974, the terms of Britain's membership were renegotiated, and the renegotiated terms were put to—and approved by—the electorate in Britain's first nationwide referendum, in 1975. Following the return of the Conservative party to government in 1979, Prime Minister Margaret Thatcher argued that Britain's contribution to the EC was too high and pressed for a reduction. After several often heated meetings with other heads of government, agreement was eventually reached in 1984; the United Kingdom received refunds for previous years' payments and a new system of payments operated for future years. In 1988 the Prime Minister again caused controversy within the EC, signaling her opposition to full monetary union within the Community and defining a role for the EC that was at odds with that envisaged by other member states. Mrs. Thatcher's views stand at the heart of the current debate concerning Britain's membership in the Community.

British membership has clearly not been trouble free. What have been the implications of membership? They may be considered under three heads: economic, political, and constitutional.

Economic Implications

The economic attractions for joining the EC were, as we have seen, a major influence in Britain's applying for membership. The Community offered, in trading terms, a "common market" (the popular name for the EEC), one which has assumed increasing significance for the British economy. In the first nine years of membership, British exports to EC countries increased by 27% a year, compared with a 19% average annual growth in the country's exports to the rest of the world. By the end of the 1980s, British dependence on EC was well established. By 1987, 49% of British exports went to other EC countries, and those same countries supplied 53% of British imports.[10] The United Kingdom's next biggest trading partner, the United States, accounted for only 16% of British exports and 11% of imports.

Britain has benefited considerably from what are known as the Community's "structural funds": those administered by the European Social Fund (ESF), the European Regional Development Fund, and the European Agricultural Guidance and Guarantee Fund. The Social Fund was established to assist with the training and retraining of workers. Since 1973 it has been used to help agricultural workers who are leaving the land, workers obliged to leave textile and other industries, migrant workers requiring language or vocational training, handicapped workers, and those who are unemployed or in need of some form of training. Since 1983, Britain has received either the highest or second highest allocation from the fund; in 1988 the amount totaled over £400 million (over $600 million), almost 20% of the money available from the fund. The Regional Development Fund came into being in 1975 to promote economic activity and the development of the infrastructure in the poorer regions of the Community. The fund can be used to contribute up to 50% of national expenditure on a given scheme if it is for the relief of agricultural poverty, for industrial change, or for the provision of infrastructure. Since 1985, it has adopted a more Community-wide focus.[11] Between 1975 and 1988 Britain received more than £2 billion (over $3 billion) from the fund, particularly for building the infrastructure in the north of England, Scotland, Wales, and Northern Ireland. The fund has been used to assist with building a reservoir, improving roads, building a new airport runway, and constructing new buildings, such as an enterprise center, in Northern Ireland. The Agricultural Fund has been more contentious. The guarantee part of the fund supports the Common Agricultural Policy (the CAP) for which the United Kingdom has sought, and achieved, various reforms. Britain has a highly efficient agricultural sector, especially in comparison with other member states. The CAP has favored price supports rather than cheap food, thus working to the benefit of countries with large farming communities, such as France. The guidance part of the fund, forming part of the structural funds, is designed to help finance the modernization of farming and to provide income support in rural areas. Britain's attitude toward the Agricultural Fund is thus somewhat mixed, but overall the United Kingdom has been a substantial beneficiary of the structural funds. Following a decision of 1988, the funds are scheduled to double in size by 1998.

The EC also administers a number of other funds and programs, such as one to provide assistance with energy research and development, and it also encompasses the European Investment Bank. Created under the Treaty of Rome, the Bank operates on a nonprofit basis to grant loans and guarantees that facilitate the financing of new investment and projects concerned with modernization. By 1988 the Bank had provided more funds than did the combined structural funds, lending almost £7 billion (over $11 billion). Private sector lending by the Bank in Britain in 1988 totaled £682 million (over $1.1 billion), more than three times the amount lent in the previous year.

As a result of membership, Britain also faces a major challenge—and opportunity—in the 1990s: completion of the Single European Market (SEM). Though the EC was formed in order to create a common market for goods and services, various physical and technical barriers have continued to exist, hindering the realization of a barrierless market. In order to achieve a single market, the Single European Act (the SEA) was implemented in 1987, designed to speed up the decision-making process within the EC so members could agree on measures to get rid of existing barriers. In 1985 the EC Commission identified approximately 300 measures that were necessary for achieving the SEM. December 31, 1992, was agreed upon as the deadline for completing these measures. By the end of 1988 almost half of the measures had been passed, plus over a hundred other measures designed to facilitate the single market.

For member states, the SEM constitutes a major challenge. The free flow of services and goods is expected to provide major benefits. According to the EC Commission's report on the economic benefits of the SEM (the Cecchini Report), it should produce almost 2 million new jobs in the medium term and possibly more than 5 million in the long term. The total economic gain was calculated at £120 billion at 1988 prices. However, what is not clear is how the benefits will fall. The SEM is designed to achieve greater competition, and the governments of the member states have been encouraging their industries, companies, and financial services to prepare for "1992." Many firms have a national base and orientation and are not geared to operate at a cross-national level. (Indeed, some U.S. firms that operate on a European rather than a country-specific basis, such as Ford, are somewhat better placed.) Competition at an international level will force the demise of inefficient and unprepared companies. To ensure that British business was well prepared, the British government in 1988 initiated a business awareness program (encompassing a mass of publications, seminars, television advertising, a computer database on measures taken to implement the SEM, and even a telephone hotline); so too did the Confederation of British Industry. By the end of 1988, 90% of British businessmen were aware of the coming of the SEM.[12] Not until at least the mid-1990s will it be apparent what they have done with that knowledge.

Political Implications

British membership in the Community, as we have seen, also had a political motivation. It was felt that, if all member states acted together, the Community could constitute a major power bloc. For Britain, such a prospect looked increasingly attractive as the other avenues for maintaining a world status (the Commonwealth, the "special relationship" with the United States) receded in significance.

The Community had already taken steps toward achieving some degree of political cooperation before Britain became a member. In 1970, EC foreign ministers approved the Luxembourg Report, which established the basic procedures for some form of cooperation on foreign policy. As a member, Britain has supported the development and formalization of this cooperation. In 1987, European Political Co-operation (EPC) was put on a formal treaty basis under the provisions of the Single European Act. EPC is "the process of information, consultation and common action" among the member states in the field of foreign policy.[13] Though now formalized, EPC remains distinct from the central structures and procedures of the Community.

Under EPC, there is direct contact between foreign ministers of the member states and there is a commitment to consult and cooperate on foreign policy issues and not to adopt a national position until having done so. The structure of EPC encompasses at least two meetings of foreign ministers per EC presidency (the presidency rotates among member states, each term lasting for six months), one meeting per presidency of the European Council (heads of government) to discuss Community and EPC subjects, and regular monthly meetings of the Political Committee, which comprises senior officials drawn from the foreign ministries and having responsibility for the day-to-day business of EPC. There also exists the Group of European Correspondents, made up of one official from each country's foreign ministry, to monitor the functioning of EPC, and there are fifteen to twenty Working Groups, drawing on experts, with each group meeting at least two or three times per presidency. The country holding the EC presidency is in charge of EPC and responsible for setting agenda and drafting common statements.

Through such cooperation between member states, a number of common positions have been agreed upon and links have been developed with other international organizations, such as the Gulf Cooperation Council, ASEAN, the Arab League, and the United Nations. In many cases, the agreement is essentially on a position, attracting little publicity and entailing no substantive action on the part of member states. In some cases, a common stance has been taken on major contentious issues. Agreement, albeit at the level almost of lowest common denominator, has been reached on pressing the South African government to dismantle apartheid, and a Code of Conduct has been introduced for EC companies operating in South Africa. Some restrictive economic measures, though limited, were also taken. The member states also took measures against Libya in 1986 and Syria later the same year following terrorist acts, for which responsibility was deemed to rest with the two countries. Member states have also had some success in agreeing on measures to combat terrorism generally.

Progress in the sphere of EPC is necessarily slower than in the economic sphere. There is no one agreed-upon goal analogous to the SEM, and satisfying national interests entails progressing at the level of the lowest common denominator. In a number of areas EPC has not resulted in action as extensive as some member states would wish. A further limitation is that defense policy is outside the terms of reference of EPC. Nonetheless, the process of cooperation is now formalized, has some degree of infrastructure (including a small secretariat in Brussels), and facilitates regular contact and discussion among those responsible for the formulation of foreign policy in each of the member states. The British government is keen to develop (and to take a lead in) such cooperation and takes the credit for proposing the treaty on EPC.

Constitutional Implications

As we have already had cause to note (Chapter 4), membership in the EC added a new dimension to the British Constitution. Under the provisions of the European Communities Act, existing EC law was to have general and binding applicability in the United Kingdom, as was all subsequent law promulgated by the Communities. Section 2(1) of the act gives the force of law in the United Kingdom to "rights, powers, liabilities, obligations and restrictions from time to time created or arising by or under the Treaties." Section 2(4) provides that directly applicable EC law should prevail over conflicting provisions of domestic legislation. The net effect of membership and the provisions of the act was to introduce two new decision-making bodies into the ambit of the British polity (the Council of Ministers and the European Communities Commission), to restrict the role and influence of Parliament in matters that came within the competence of the Communities, to inject a new judicial dimension to the Constitution (disputes concerning the treaties or legislation made under them to be treated by the British courts as a matter of law, with provision for their referral to the European court for a ruling), and to allow for British representation in the European Parliament, albeit until 1987 a body with very limited powers.

The constitutional implications were a matter of controversy at the time Britain joined the EC. Equally controversial were the implications of the Single European Act. Implemented in 1987, it was agreed upon by the United Kingdom under the provisions of the 1986 European Communities (Amendment) Act. The effect of the SEA, as we earlier observed, was to effect a shift in power relationships *within* the institutions of the EC as well as *between* the institutions of the EC and the member states. Under the SEA, the European Parliament not only was designated as a Parliament (its formal title previously was that of Assembly) but also was given a more powerful role in the formulation of EC legislation. To allow for the approval of the measures necessary to achieve the Single European Market, the procedures in the Council of Ministers for weighted majority voting were also extended, thus making it possible for more measures to be passed despite the opposition of a small minority of member states. By the end of the decade, British ministers had variously found themselves outvoted under this procedure on a number of issues.

The constitutional implications of the SEA became a matter of major political debate, though not so much during the passage of the 1986 bill as toward the end of the decade as the effects of the SEA began to realized. The debate was fueled by the increasingly critical comments of Prime Minister Thatcher, who saw it as a weapon in the hands of European integrationists for achieving a type of European Community that did not coincide with her view of how the Community should develop. The E.C. as it had been at the beginning of the 1970s, again became a major issue on the agenda of political debate.

INSTITUTIONS OF THE COMMUNITY

In addition to having responsibility for removing trade barriers and administering the agricultural, regional, and social funds, the EC is charged with seeking to ensure the free movement of persons, services, and capital within the Community and with generating policies on external trade, overseas aid, energy, and consumer affairs. In order to eliminate barriers to the development of a single market, it has power to adjust national legal rules through what is known as harmonization procedures—in other words, to ensure that the rules are standardized throughout the EC. It was in order to speed up the decision-making process in eliminating barriers that the Single European Act was introduced.

Within the EC, the main bodies are the European Council, the Council of Ministers, the EC Commission, the European Parliament, and the Committee of Permanent Representatives. In addition, there is the European Court of Justice, which ensures that EC law is observed in the interpretation and application of the treaties, and this court can itself interpret EC law. Its judgments are binding on member states and enforceable through the national courts. Under the SEA, the Council of Ministers may now attach to the court a new Court of First Instance, to help reduce the burden on the court in a limited number of areas.

The European Council, more commonly known as the "European Summit," comprises the heads of government of the member states.

Though already a regular feature of the EC, it was not until the passage of the SEA that it was given Treaty status. The SEA provides that the Council shall meet at least twice a year. However, though it is of central political importance, the body has no legislative powers. For its wishes to be enacted, action has to be taken by the Council of Ministers.

The Council of Ministers comprises the ministers from the member states whose portfolios cover the subject under discussion. Thus a proposal on agriculture will be considered by the council comprising agriculture ministers. (In practice, it would be more appropriate to refer to *councils* of ministers.) The demands made of the council vary according to the subject. The Council of Foreign Ministers and the Council of Finance Ministers meet more often than do the others. The council seeks to proceed on the basis of consensus and tacit agreement. Even before passage of the SEA, many matters could, under the EC treaties, be resolved by weighted majority voting. (Under this procedure, each of the larger countries—the United Kingdom, Germany, France, and Italy—has 10 votes; Spain has 8; Belgium, Greece, the Netherlands, and Portugal each have 5; Denmark and Ireland each have 3; and Luxembourg has 1. For a measure to be adopted, 54 votes are required.) Provision for such voting was extended by the SEA. Other issues are subject to simple majority voting (at least seven members voting in favor, each country having one vote) or to unanimity (or rather, "nobody against," since abstention is not sufficient to prevent adoption). Under the so-called Luxembourg Compromise of 1966, a country may veto legislation if "very important interests" are involved. However, this is a highly contentious provision, with no clear agreement on what is actually entailed. The British government takes the view that the Compromise is unaffected by the SEA. Others, including the House of Commons Select Committee on Foreign Affairs, have taken a more skeptical view.[14]

The EC Commission constitutes the bureaucracy of the EC. It is headed by a College of Commissioners. The seventeen commissioners are drawn from the member states (two each from the United Kingdom, Germany, France, and Italy; one from each of the smaller countries), though each takes an oath not to seek to represent national interests. Each is appointed for a four-year term. (Britain's two commissioners taking office in January 1989 were Sir Leon Brittan, a former Conservative MP and cabinet minister, and Bruce Millan, a former Labour MP and cabinet minister, both nominated by the Prime Minister.) From their number, the commissioners choose a president, who serves a two-year, renewable term. The commissioners head a sizable bureaucracy with a highly developed infrastructure. There are 23 Directorates-General, each responsible for different aspects of EC work (e.g., DGIV deals with competition, DGVI with agriculture, and DGXVI with regional policy), plus a number of specialized services. Commissioners formulate proposals within their area of responsibility aimed at implementing the treaties. The commissioners as a body then discuss the proposals and decide on the final form the proposals shall take. Decisions are taken by simple majority vote.

Until the passage of the SEA, the European Parliament was an advisory body in dealing with EC legislation. It did have two formal, but rather blunt powers: one was to reject the budget, a power it did employ, and the other was to force the resignation of the EC Commission *en bloc*, a power it did not use. In the legislative process, it ws called upon to offer an opinion on a proposal emanating from the commission. That opinion was then passed on to the European Council to consider along with the actual proposal. Under the SEA, there now exists a "cooperation procedure." After a proposal has gone through the traditional procedure (from commission to council, with an opinion offered by the Parliament), the council adopts a "common position." This then goes to the Parliament, which may reject or amend it by majority vote. The commission then reexamines and resubmits its proposal, taking account of the Parliament's views. The council can then adopt the resubmitted proposal by qualified majority but can only amend it or reinstate a proposal rejected by the Parliament by unanimity. The Parliament works primarily through committees, and the effect of the SEA has been to enhance the significance of both the Parliament as a whole and its committees. From July 1987 to March 1989 inclusively, the commission accepted 67% and the council adopted 50% of the amendments proposed by the Parliament on first reading (i.e., when giving its first opinion). The figures for second reading (amendments made under the new procedure) were 60% and 25%.[15]

The other principal body in the process is the Committee of Permanent Representatives (known as COREPER) which has responsibility for preparing the work of the Council of Ministers and for carrying out tasks assigned to the council. As the name implies, COREPER comprises official representatives (classified often as ambassadors) from the member states, each assisted by a staff of diplomats and officials seconded (released from regular duty and temporarily assigned elsewhere) from the national civil service. COREPER studies a proposal on behalf of the council, isolating any problems associated with it. If the committee reaches agreement, it is usual for the council to adopt the proposal without further discussion.

There is thus a major decision-making process within the EC, taking place essentially at one remove from national government. Following the passage of the SEA, there is increasing debate as to how far this process will develop and the extent of the decision-making capacity that it will come to embody. Though elite opinion within other member states tends to be favorable toward a development of EC powers and integration, elite (and popular) opinion within Britain is, as we shall see, divided.

TABLE 10.1. ELECTIONS TO THE EUROPEAN PARLIAMENT, 1989

Party	Number of Seats Won (change from 1984 in parentheses)	% of Votes Won
Conservative	32 (−13)	34.7
Labour	45 (+13)	40.1
SLD	0	6.2
Greens	0	14.9
SNP	1	3.4[a]
Total (Britain)[b]	78	99.3

[a] Includes votes of Plaid Cymru. The SNP won 25.6% of the votes in Scotland, Plaid Cymru 12.9% of the votes in Wales.

[b] Northern Ireland elected three members by a system of proportional representation, returning, as in 1984, one Ulster Unionist, one Democratic Unionist, and one Social and Democratic Labour member.

Elections to the European Parliament

With the passage of the SEA, elections to the European Parliament have taken on a new significance. Until 1979, members of the Parliament were drawn from the national Parliaments of the member states. Since 1979, they have been elected. The argument for election is that it enhances the legitimacy of the institution. In the British case, it also provides a more direct link between electors and the Parliament, members being elected— via the plurality, first-past-the-post method—for constituencies. However, one criticism leveled at the change was that it ended a useful linkage between the EP Parliament and the member Parliaments. The linkage that now exists between members of the EP Parliament and the Westminster Parliament is largely informal and tenuous.

Each Parliament sits for a fixed term of five years. There have thus been three elections to the Parliament: in 1979, 1984, and 1989. In the first two elections in Britain the Conservative party did especially well, benefiting in large measure from the fact that these were periods when the Conservative government was doing well in the opinion polls. In 1989 the party's fortunes were reversed: it lost 13 of its 45 seats to Labour candidates (see Table 10.1). The Scottish National Party held onto its one seat and the Green party polled unexpectedly well, largely at the expense of the Social and Liberal Democrats. Turnout, as in the previous two elections and in the 1975 referendum, was low. For every elector who went to the polls, approximately two stayed at home. Though low, the turnout was not exceptional. Within the EC as a whole, 100 million out of 240 million stayed at home. Though support for the Community appears to be broad, the results suggest it is not deep. European election campaigns have yet to attract attention on the same scale as national elections. For anyone traveling across Europe at the height of the European election campaign early in June 1989 (as this writer was), it was difficult to detect that there was an election taking place.

Within the Parliament, the British Labour members (MEPs) are members of the Socialist group, which has enjoyed increased influence since the 1989 elections; the effect of the elections was to transform a small center-right majority into a small center-left majority. Prior to the elections, the Conservative MEPs, along with 17 Spanish and 4 Danish MEPs, formed a European Democratic Group. Following the elections, the Spaniards withdrew from the group (disagreeing with the Conservative stance on European integration) and the Conservatives were too small in number to have much impact as a separate group. They thus began the process of seeking allies elsewhere.

THE CURRENT DEBATE

In the first half of the 1970s, debate on the European Community centered on whether or not Britain should be a member. After it became a member, various groups were formed to campaign for British withdrawal. The results of the 1975 referendum were taken as confirming that Britain was committed to remaining in the Community, and much of the debate had died down by the end of the decade. In the latter half of the 1980s, the issue of the EC returned. This time it was not so much a question of continued membership (though a number, especially on the left of the Labour party and the right of the Conservative party, remained opposed to membership), but rather what form the EC was to take in the future.

Toward the end of the 1980s the implications of the Single European Act began to be more clearly discerned. The 1986 European Communities (Amendment) Act had been motivated by economic considerations: the need to achieve the SEM. Constitutional considerations were seen as largely secondary or at least not entailing major changes to the existing constitutional arrangements. When it was apparent that the constitutional implications were significant, a public and—for the Conservative party— divisive debate erupted. From being if not a largely moribund debate at least a secondary one, it came to occupy a central place in political debate. At the heart of it was how the EC was going to develop, and it embodied two conflicting approaches. One approach was expressed by Prime Minister Margaret Thatcher. The other was expressed by the president of the EC Commission, Jacques Delors.

To Mrs. Thatcher, the EC constitutes a collection of sovereign nation states cooperating in order to achieve a single market. That process should not entail each member state's losing its particular culture and identity, nor should it entail the generation of a new layer of decision-making bureaucracy. "To try to suppress nationhood and concentrate power at the centre of a European conglomerate," she declared in a major speech at Bruges, "would be highly damaging and would jeopardize the objectives we seek to achieve."[16] The objectives, as far as she was concerned, were to achieve a free trade in goods, in services, and in capital. It was a means of reducing barriers, not creating new ones. She made clear that she was totally opposed to the creation of a supra-national government capable of imposing its will upon member states. "We have not successfully rolled back the frontiers of the state in Britain," she declared, "only to see them reimposed at a European level, with a European super-state exercising a new dominance from Brussels."[17]

To Mrs. Thatcher and those who took a similar view, the SEA provided a potential Trojan Horse through which European integrationists would seek to create the new layer of government to which they were opposed. They saw their fears being realized through the activities of the EC Commission and in particular through Jacques Delors. Speaking to the European Parliament in July 1988, Monsieur Delors declared: "My feeling is that we will not succeed in taking all the decisions which face us between now and 1995 unless under one formula or another we get the beginnings of European Government"; two months later, addressing the TUC, he argued, "It is essential to strengthen our control of our economic and social development, of our technology, and of our monetary capacity," the steps already taken to achieve this constituting part of an "irretrievable process."[18]

At the heart of the Delors approach was economic and monetary union. In 1988 the European Council authorized a study on the subject. The result—the Delors Report—outlined a three-stage process toward achieving such union. Stage I envisaged realization of the single market, liberalization of capital movements, freedom from exchange rate controls, and membership by all member states of the Exchange Rate Mechanism (ERM). Stage II envisaged the creation of a European System of Central Banks (ESCB). Stage III would entail the achievement of, especially, monetary union, plus controls on fiscal policy, with members setting "binding limits" on each other's fiscal deficits.[19] For the EC president, such union was a necessary and desirable goal. Mrs. Thatcher took a different view. For her Stage I was acceptable and, apart from failing to participate fully in the EMS (Mrs. Thatcher waiting "until the time was right"), Britain had fulfilled its essential conditions. However, Stages II and II were totally unacceptable, constituting a major threat to national sovereignty. She did not see Stage I as part of an "irretrievable process" and was determined to ensure that it did not become so. She took her opposition to the European Council in Paris in 1989, where she found herself in a public minority of one.

Within Britain, Mrs. Thatcher's stance divided the Conservative party between those who agreed with her and those who believed in European integration, or at least that Britain should not be isolated and hence should make appropriate positive noises, even if not intending fully to take all the steps proposed in the Delors Report. (Though other member states gave public backing to the Delors position, it was widely assumed that in practice they also would adopt such a stance.) The dispute appeared to split the parliamentary party down the middle. Both the Chancellor of the Exchequer, Nigel Lawson, and the Foreign Secretary, Sir Geoffrey Howe, appeared to lean toward a more cooperative approach (both favoring an earlier full membership of the ERM than favored by Mrs. Thatcher), a stance that was believed to precipitate Sir Geoffrey's removal from the Foreign Office in July 1989. The split within the government's ranks harmed the Conservative campaign in the European Parliament elections. The Labour party, though also divided on the issue, took advantage of the situation, focusing upon the government's difficulties and appearing more friendly toward the EC, an institution from which it had previously favored withdrawal. The party came increasingly to see the Community as a vehicle through which a number of its goals, such as on worker participation, might be achieved.

The Conservative party appears to have suffered particularly because of its appearance of disunity rather than because of the Prime Minister's specific stand on the issue of monetary union. In 1989 a Gallup poll conducted for the EC Commission found that 55% of respondents considered membership in the EC to be a "good thing" (the highest level since Britain joined the EC); only 18% thought it to be "a bad thing." More significantly in terms of the present debate, which is not about the value of membership but rather the direction in which the EC is going, were the findings of a separate EC-wide poll on the creation of a European government by 1992. Within member states, the average support for such a government was 77%. In the United Kingdom, respondents were more or less evenly divided: 52% were in favor, 48% against.[20] Only in Denmark was a more negative result obtained; all other member states were clearly in favor. Britain's membership in the Community has been an eventful, sometimes stormy one. There is every evidence that it will continue in that vein.

NOTES

1. See A. King, *Britain Says Yes* (American Enterprise Institute, 1977), pp. 2–7.
2. M. Camps, *Britain and the European Community 1955–1963* (Oxford University Press, 1964), p. 336.

3. See the comments of E. Heath, *Our Community* (Conservative Political Centre, 1977), p. 4.

4. H. Macmillan, *Pointing the Way* (Macmillan, 1972), p. 310.

5. On the first two applications, see R. J. Lieber, *British Politics and European Unity* (University of California Press, 1970); and U. Kitzinger, *The Second Try* (Pergamon, 1968).

6. *House of Commons Debates* (*Hansard*), Vol. 823, cols. 2211–18.

7. See P. Norton, *Dissension in the House of Commons 1945–74* (Macmillan, 1975), pp. 395–98; and U. Kitzinger, *Diplomacy and Persuasion* (Thames and Hudson, 1973), Ch. 13 and Appendix 1.

8. *House of Commons Debates* (*Hansard*), Vol. 831, cols. 753–58.

9. See P. Norton, *Conservative Dissidents* (Temple Smith, 1978), pp. 64–82.

10. For the country-by-country breakdown, see *Basic Statistics of the Community: 25th ed.* (Office for Offical Publications of the European Communities, 1988), pp. 270–71.

11. A. Daltrop, *Politics and the European Community*, 2nd ed. (Longman, 1986), p. 116.

12. *Campaign Guide 1989* (Conservative Central Office, 1989), p. 532.

13. *European Political Cooperation (EPC)* (Office for Official Publications of the European Communities, 1988), p. 5.

14. See *The Single European Act: Third Report from the Select Committee on Foreign Affairs, Session 1985/86*, HC 442 (Her Majesty's Stationery Office, 1986); and the Government's Response (Cmnd. 9858). The House of Lords Committee on the European Communities also took a skeptical view.

15. D. Millar, "The European Parliament," in *Study of Parliament Group Newsletter*, 5, Spring 1989, p. 11.

16. Margaret Thatcher, *Britain and Europe* (Conservative Political Centre, 1988), p. 4. The pamphlet constitutes the text of Mrs. Thatcher's speech.

17. Ibid.

18. House of Commons Library, *Brussels, Westminster and the Single European Act*, Background Paper No. 220 (House of Commons Library, 1988), pp. 21–22.

19. For a discussion of the report, and the position of the British government, see *The Delors Report: Fourth Report from the Treasury and Civil Service Committee, Session 1988/89*, HC 341 (Her Majesty's Stationery Office, 1989).

20. *The Independent*, June 15, 1989.

PART IV
Scrutiny and Legitimation

CHAPTER 11

Parliament
Commons and Lords

The United States has a bicameral legislature. In legislative matters, each house is the equal of the other.[1] Both houses are chosen by popular vote, albeit by differently defined constituencies. They are elected separately from the executive, and members of the two houses are precluded by the Constitution from holding any civil office under the authority of the United States. There is a formal separation between the executive and the legislative branches not only in personnel but also of powers. Congress displays the characteristics of what Michael Mezey has aptly termed an "active" legislature: its policy-making power is strong and it enjoys popular support as a legitimate political institution.[2] Each house is master of its own timetable and proceedings.

In their behavior, not least in their voting behavior, senators and members of the House of Representatives are influenced by party, more so than is sometimes popularly supposed.[3] Nonetheless, while party is an important influence, it is not an exclusive one. Members of Congress are responsive to other influences. The political landscape bears the bodies of senators and representatives who, regardless of party, fell to the wrath of their electors because of their neglect of their constituencies or because of their stance on a particular issue. Although the initiative in policy making has passed largely to the executive, Congress remains an important part of the policy-making process. As Professor Mezey writes, "Even though a decline in the power and authority of the Congress has been announced on several different occasions, it remains today one of the few legislative institutions in the world able and capable of saying no to a popularly elected president and making it stick."[4]

The United Kingdom has also a bicameral legislature, but there the similarity ends. Of the two houses, only one—the House of Commons—is popularly elected. Members of the Upper House, the House of Lords, serve by virtue of birth, by appointment for life, or because of the positions they hold. The two houses are no longer equal: the House of Commons as the elected chamber enjoys preeminence and can enforce its legislative will over the Upper House under the provisions of the 1911 and 1949 Parliament Acts (see Chapter 3). The executive, or rather the political apex of the executive (i.e., ministers), is drawn from Parliament—there is no separate election—and its members remain within Parliament. The executive dominates both the business program (deciding what will be debated and when) and the voting of Parliament, party serving as the means of that domination. Party cohesion is a feature of voting in the House of Commons. (The same is largely true of the House of Lords, though fewer votes take place there.) Party is the determining influence in an MP's election and it is normally the determining influence in his or her parliamentary behavior. Parliament exhibits the features of what Mezey has termed a "reactive" legislature: it enjoys popular support as a legitimate political institution but enjoys only modest power, if that, in policy making. Discussion of "the decline of Parliament" has been a characteristic feature of political discourse in Britain in recent years. Not surprisingly, MPs have on occasion been known to look with envy across the Atlantic at the power and influence of their American counterparts.

The reasons for executive dominance of the legislature in Britain have been sketched already (Chapter 3). For part of the nineteenth century, Parliament exhibited the characteristics of an "active" legislature. The 1832 Reform Act helped lessen the grip of the aristocracy and of the ministry on the House of Commons (seats were less easy to buy, given the size of the new electorate), allowing MPs greater freedom in their parliamentary behavior. Debates in the House could influence opinion and the outcome of votes was not a foregone conclusion. This period was short-lived. The 1867 Reform Act and later acts created a much larger and more demanding electorate. With the passage of the 1884 Representation of the People Act, a majority of working men were enfranchised. Electors were now too numerous to be bribed, at least by individual candidates. The result was that "organized corruption was gradually replaced by party organization,"[5] as one observer puts it, and both main existing parties were developed from small cadre parties to form mass-membership and complex organizations. Party organization made possible contact with the electors. To stimulate voting, candidates had to promise something to electors, and electoral promises could be met only if parties displayed sufficient cohesion in parliamentary organization to ensure their enactment.

Institutional and environmental factors combined to ensure that the pressures generated by the changed electoral conditions resulted in a House of Commons with low policy influence. Competition for the all-or-nothing spoils of a general election victory, the single-member constituency with a plurality method of election, and a relatively homogeneous population (relative to many other countries) would appear to have encouraged, if not always produced, a basic two-party as opposed to a multiparty system. One party was normally returned with an overall parliamentary majority. Given that the government was drawn from and remained within Parliament, the electoral fortunes of MPs depended primarily on the success or failure of that government. Government was dependent on the voting support of its parliamentary majority both for the passage of its promised measures and for its own continuance in office. Failure of government supporters to vote against a motion expressing "no confidence" in the government or, conversely, not to vote for an important measure that the government declared a "matter of confidence" would result in a dissolution. Within the House of Commons, party cohesion quickly became the norm.

Internal party pressures also encouraged MPs' willingness to defer to government. A member was chosen as a party candidate by his local party and was dependent on it for renomination as well as for campaign support. Assuming local party loyalty to the party leadership (an assumption that usually but not always could be made), local parties were unlikely to take kindly to any consistent dissent from "their" members. The norms of the constitution and of party structures also encouraged acquiescence. There were no career channels in Parliament alternative to those of government office, and a place in government was dependent on the prime minister, the *party* leader. Achieving a leadership position in the House meant, in effect, becoming a minister.

The nature of government decision making as well as the increasing responsibilities assumed by government also had the effect of moving policy making further from the floor of the House. The conventions of collective and individual ministerial responsibility helped provide a protective cloak for decision making within cabinet and within departments. Only the conclusions of discussions could be revealed. Furthermore, as government responsibilities expanded and became more dependent on the cooperation of outside groups (see Chapter 7), government measures came increasingly to be the product of negotiation between departments and interest groups, who then presented those measures to Parliament as packages already agreed on. As the demands on government grew, these "packages" increased in extent and complexity. The House of Commons was called on primarily to approve measures drawn up elsewhere and for which it had neither adequate time nor resources to submit to sustained and informed debate.

Parliament thus came to occupy what was recognized as a back seat in policy making. This is not to say that it ceased to be an important political body. The government remained dependent on Parliament for its support, and both houses continued to provide significant forums of debate and scrutiny. In an important article in 1975, Nelson Polsby distinguished between transformative legislatures (enjoying an independent capacity, frequently exercised, to mold and transform proposals into law) and arena legislatures (providing a formal arena in which significant political forces could express themselves).[6] The British Parliament can most appropriately be described as having moved from being a transformative legislative in the second third of the nineteenth century to an arena legislature in the twentieth. The United States Congress, by contrast, has remained a transformative legislature.

THE HOUSE OF COMMONS

The events of the nineteenth century that served to transfer power from Parliament to the executive served also to ensure the dominance of the House of Commons within the triumvirate of Monarch, Lords, and Commons. The Commons constitutes the only body of the three that is popularly elected. Indeed, its dominance has become such that there is a tendency for many to treat "House of Commons" and "Parliament" as almost synonymous terms. The attention accorded it by the media and outside observers is far more extensive than that accorded the House of Lords. It has a greater "working" membership and more importance is attached to the functions it is expected to fulfill.

Members

The House of Commons has a much larger membership than its U.S. equivalent. It has 650 members, each elected to serve a particular constituency (see Chapter 5). The size of the House has varied, ranging from a twentieth-century high of 707 members (from 1918 to 1922, subsequently reduced because of the loss of most Irish seats) to a low of 615 (from 1922 to 1945). Since 1945, the size of the House has increased gradually as a result of the recommendations of the Boundary Commissions.

There is no formal limit on the number of terms an MP can serve. It is not uncommon for MPs representing safe seats to sit in the House for twenty or thirty years, sometimes longer. In 1989, for example, Prime Minister Margaret Thatcher celebrated thirty years as the MP for the London constituency of Finchley. The MP with the longest continuous record of service is given the courtesy title of "Father of the House." Following the return of the new Parliament in 1987, the title fell to Sir Bernard Braine, an MP since 1950. He succeeded Sir James (now Lord) Callaghan, the former prime minister, an MP from 1945 until his retirement from the House in 1987.

The House elects one of its members as Speaker. By tradition, the Speaker is normally drawn from the majority party in the House, though he (never yet she) may continue in the position following a change in government. The Speaker, once elected, disclaims any party affiliation and serves as an independent presiding officer. Though enjoying important powers of discipline and some business management, much of his activity is governed by precedent, most of it embodied in the parliamentary "bible," known by the short title of *Erskine May*; he is also advised by the clerks, the full-time officers of the House.

Since 1945, MPs have become notably more middle class. Before the Second World War, and for a little time thereafter, the Parliamentary Labour party (the PLP) boasted a significant proportion of MPs from working-class backgrounds, often miners; the Conservative ranks were swelled by members of aristocratic families and very wealthy industrialists. As parliamentary work has become more demanding, and as salaries and resources have improved, more members drawn from the professions and from academia have entered the House. Today most MPs have university degrees and enter the House after a spell in business or the professions. Tables 11.1 and 11.2 show the backgrounds of members returned to the House in 1987. An increasing number are drawn from careers in the political world, either as party researchers or as representatives of groups making demands of government. Critics contend that such MPs have little knowledge of the world outside the political domain; their defenders point out that they enter the House well versed in the ways of government and hence are in a good position to influence government on behalf of their constituents.

MPs are more numerous than members of the U.S. House of Representatives. There is also another notable difference: MPs, compared with their U.S. (and indeed most Western) counterparts, are underpaid and under-resourced. The payment of salaries to MPs is a twentieth-century innovation, and even in 1964 an MP enjoyed a salary of only £3,250 (less than $5,400) and little else: most MPs had no offices (they had to make do with lockers) and for research and information were dependent on the facilities of the Commons' Library, a body with limited staff. There were

TABLE 11.1. THE EDUCATIONAL BACKGROUND OF MPs, 1987

	Conservative	Labour	Alliance	Other	Total
	%	%			%
A. Level of full-time education					
Elementary	—	3.5 (8)	—	2	1.5 (10)
Secondary	17.3 (65)	23.1 (53)	4	5	19.5 (127)
Elementary/ secondary+ [a]	9.6 (36)	15.7 (36)	2	10	12.9 (84)
Graduate	73.1 (274)	57.6 (132)	16	7	66.0 (429)
Total	100.0 (375)	99.9 (229)	22	24	99.9 (650)
B. Graduates					
Oxford	24.8 (93)	10.0 (23)	3	—	18.3 (119)
Cambridge	21.3 (80)	5.7 (13)	3	—	14.8 (96)
Other universities	22.1 (83)	40.2 (92)	9	6	29.2 (190)
Polytechnics	1.1 (4)	1.3 (3)	—	1	1.2 (8)
Overseas	1.6 (6)	0.4 (1)	1	—	1.2 (8)
Service colleges	2.1 (8)	—	—	—	1.2 (8)
Nongraduates	26.9 (101)	42.4 (97)	6	17	34.0 (221)
Total	99.0 (375)	100.0 (229)	22	24	99.9 (650)
C. Type of school attended					
Public school	62.7 (235)	12.7 (29)	10	3	42.6 (277)
Nonpublic school	37.3 (140)	87.3 (200)	12	21	57.4 (373)
Total	100.0 (375)	100.0 (229)	22	24	100.0 (650)

Note: [a]Elementary/secondary+ = elementary or secondary schooling plus technical, vocational, or similar nongraduate education. (Source: M. Rush, "The Member of Parliament," in M. Ryle and P. G. Richards (eds.), The Commons Under Scrutiny (Routledge, 1988), p. 24.)

no secretarial or research allowances. A number of MPs could not afford to hire secretaries and some replied to constituents' letters in longhand.

Conditions have variously improved since then. MPs now have offices, though in many cases these are shared and often very small, based either in the Palace of Westminster or in surrounding buildings. (The Norman Shaw Buildings on Victoria Embankment, former home of Scotland Yard, were taken over for MPs' use when the metropolitan police moved out.) A secretarial allowance has been introduced, along with allowances for living away from one's main residence and, for MPs representing London seats, a London supplement. Members also now have travel passes, and some provision is made for spouses as well. Library facilities have also been improved, including the provision of a computer retrieval system known as POLIS (parliamentary on-line information service). The secretarial allowance now proves sufficient to hire some research help, albeit often on a

TABLE 11.2. OCCUPATIONAL BACKGROUND OF MPs, 1987

Occupation	Conservative	Labour	Alliance	Other	Total
	%	%			%
Professions	33.3 (125)	41.0 (94)	12	13	37.5 (244)
Business	51.5 (193)	4.8 (11)	5	9	33.5 (218)
Workers	0.8 (3)	29.7 (68)	—	2	11.2 (73)
Miscellaneous	14.4 (54)	24.5 (56)	5	—	17.7 (115)
Total	100.0 (375)	100.0 (229)	22	24	99.9 (650)

Definitions: Professions: lawyers, doctors, dentists, school, university, and adult education teachers, retired officers of the regular forces, and all recognized professions.

Business: all employers, directors of public and private companies, business executives, stockbrokers, farmers and landowners, and small businessmen.

Workers: self-explanatory, but including all employed manual and nonmanual (or "white-collar") workers and full-time trade union officials.

Miscellaneous: housewives, professional politicians, welfare workers, journalists, professional party organizers, and miscellaneous administrators.

These definitions are the categories used by S. E. Finer, H. B. Berrington, and D. J. Bartholomew in *Backbench Opinion in the House of Commons, 1955–59*, (Pergamon, 1961) and in the Nuffield Election series, but following the formers' practice of classifying occupations according to the MP's principal occupation prior to election. Many MPs, especially on the Conservative side of the House, accept company directorships or develop other business or journalistic interests after their election, and an analysis based on such considerations would produce significantly different figures. *(Source: M. Rush, "The Member of Parliament," in M. Ryle and P. G. Richards (eds.),* The Commons Under Scrutiny *(Routledge, 1988), p. 25.)*

part-time basis. By 1984, just over half of all members employed research assistants, though very few on a full-time basis. MPs' pay is now linked to civil-service pay, rising when the latter does, and in 1989 it rose to £24,107 ($40,000), a figure still modest by professional standards, at the bottom end of middle-management pay levels. The secretarial and research allowance rose to £24,903 (just over $40,000). In terms of pay and resources, MPs tend to look with some envy at the position across the Atlantic (in Canada as well as the United States) as well as, in some instances, across the English Channel to bodies such as the West German Bundestag.

Functions

The House, like other legislatures, is a multifunctional body: that is, it fulfills a variety of tasks in addition to the one defining task of legislatures (that of giving assent). The most important twentieth-century functions of the House are those of providing the personnel of government, of legitimation, of debate, and of scrutinizing and influencing government. The list is not exhaustive, nor are the functions mutually exclusive.

Parliament provides the personnel of government—that is, ministers: by convention, most ministers, including the prime minister, are drawn from the Commons. This function is best described as a passive one. The House itself does not do the choosing. The outcome of a general election determines which party will form the government, and the prime minister, in practice, chooses who will fill which ministerial posts.

The most important functions requiring action on the part of the House are those of legitimation and of debate. Government requires the formal assent of Parliament both for the passage of legislation and for the grant of money. Given the government's control of a parliamentary majority, such assent is normally forthcoming. The giving of this assent, however much it may be taken for granted, fulfills an important symbolic role. First, it constitutes the elected assembly giving the seal of approval on behalf of the electoral populace. It remains significant also because the House retains the formal power to deny its assent. It may hardly ever use that power, but the option to do so remains.

The function that occupies the most time of the House and is the most obvious manifestation of its position as an arena legislature is that of debate. As a representative assembly, the House provides an authoritative forum in which the views of the political parties can find expression. It also provides a forum in which MPs individually can raise the concerns and specific problems of constituents.

Through debate, the House or elements of it can seek to influence government. Formally, it retains the sanction of denying assent to measures. In practice, the publicity accorded debates provides the House with its greatest leverage. Governments are sensitive to the subjection of their measures or specific actions to criticism. If that criticism is effective, especially if it comes from government supporters, then ministers may respond to it. The House provides the forum for their response—hence its importance.

The House, through debate, can thus seek to subject government to a process of scrutiny and influence. The means of "debate" available to the House to achieve this are varied. They can be divided into those used to discuss and scrutinize legislation and those employed to discuss and scrutinize executive actions.

Legislation

Legislation is subject to a well-defined procedure once it has been submitted to the House (see Table 11.3). First reading constitutes the formal introduction of a bill. At this stage it is not debated. Indeed, it does not even exist in printed form. Once formally introduced, it is set down for its second reading. Compared with the analogous legislative procedure in the United States Congress, the second reading is distinct in two significant respects. First, it is the government that determines when the debate will

TABLE 11.3. LEGISLATIVE STAGES IN THE HOUSE OF COMMONS

Stage	Where Taken	Comments
First Reading	On floor of the House	Formal introduction only. No debate.
Second Reading	On floor of the House (noncontentious bills may be referred to a second reading committee)	Debate on the principle of the measure.
Committee	Standing committee (constitutionally important measures and certain other measures may be taken in Committee of the Whole House)	Considered clause by clause. Amendments can be made.
Report	On floor of the House (there is no report stage if the bill reported is unamended from Committee of the Whole House)	Reported to the House by the committee. Amendments can be made.
Third Reading	On floor of the House	Final approval of the bill. Debate confined to bill's content.
Lords Amendments	On floor of the House	Any amendments made by the House of Lords are considered, usually on a motion to agree or disagree with them.

take place. (On all days, with the exception of certain Fridays, 3 Estimates Days, and 20 "Opposition days," the government has control of the parliamentary timetable, deciding what will be debated.) Second, the debate precedes the committee stage. On second reading, the principle of the bill is debated and approved. Only after it has received its second reading is it referred to a committee for consideration of its specific provisions.

At committee stage, bills are considered by standing committees. The name is a misnomer: they are appointed on an ad hoc basis. A committee will be appointed to consider a specific bill and then, having completed its deliberations, ceases to exist in that form. (Committees are known by letters of the alphabet, such as Standing Committee A, and once a committee with the letter A has finished its deliberations, a new Standing Committee A will be appointed to consider another bill—but the members of the committee will be different.) Each committee has a membership of between 16 and 50 members, usually now 18 members for all but the largest and most contentious bills. They meet to discuss bills clause by clause. In practice, their ability to amend and influence the content of measures is circumscribed. Once the House has approved the principle of the measure, a committee cannot make any changes that run counter to the principle embodied in the bill. The greatest constraints, however, are political. The format adopted at committee meetings is an adversarial one: government MPs sit on one side, Opposition MPs on the other. Debate is usually along party lines, as is voting. The result is that the amendments that are carried are almost always those introduced by ministers. (The relevant minister is invariably appointed to the committee.) Usually less than 5% of amendments tabled by Opposition MPs or government back-benchers are accepted.[7] Since most bills discussed by standing committees are introduced by the government, the main purpose of introducing government amendments is to correct drafting errors, improve the wording, or, more substantially, to meet points made by outside groups or meet points made by MPs that the government finds acceptable.

Standing committees thus differ considerably from their American counterparts. They have no power to summon witnesses or evidence, they are presided over by an impartial chairman (an MP drawn from a body of MPs appointed for their ability to chair such meetings), and they are confined in their deliberations solely to the content of bills. They have no power to undertake inquiries or to discuss anything other than the bill before them. The government's majority on a standing committee is in proportion to its majority in the House as a whole. Hence, as long as it has a majority in the House, it is ensured a majority on such committees. The result is that bills usually emerge from committees relatively unscathed. Unlike United States congressional committees, standing committees are not a burial ground for bills. Rather, they serve as temporary transit points in their passage.

Once a standing committee has completed its deliberations, a bill is then returned to the House for the report stage, during which the House may make further amendments. This stage is not dissimilar to the committee stage and the government may use it to introduce amendments that it had not been able to introduce in committee (for example, to meet points raised in committee but for which it had not had time to formulate a precise amendment). The outcome of votes on amendments is the same as in committee. Government amendments are normally carried. Amendments introduced by private members are usually defeated, unless they find favor with the government. The acceptance rate is similar to that in committee.[8]

All bills considered in standing committee go through a report stage. Certain important bills, such as those introducing constitutional change (for example, reform of the House of Lords), have their committee stage on the floor of the House. If they emerge from this stage without amendment, there is no report stage. In 1972, for example, the European

Communities bill was taken on the floor of the House and was not amended. It thus proceeded directly to the final stage, that of third reading. At third reading, the House gives its final approval to a measure. Debate at this stage is usually shorter than on second reading, and it must be confined to the content of the bill. Suggestions for amendments are out of order.

Once the House has approved third reading, the bill is sent to the House of Lords. (The exceptions, of course, are any bills that originate in the Lords.) If the Lords make any amendments, these are then sent to the Commons. The House debates these amendments, usually on a motion to agree or disagree with them. If the House disagrees with a Lords amendment, this fact—along with the reasons for the disagreement—is communicated to the Upper House. The House of Lords then usually concurs with the Commons and does not press its amendment. Once a bill has passed both Houses, it proceeds for the Royal Assent.

Government bills dominate the legislative timetable. This is hardly surprising given the onus placed on government to initiate measures and the fact that the government controls the timetable. Between 50 and 70 government bills are introduced and passed each year. Opportunities for private members to introduce bills of their own are extremely limited. Certain Fridays each session (usually 10) are set aside to discuss private members' bills. So limited is the time available and so great the number of members wishing to introduce bills that a ballot is held each parliamentary session (that is, each year), and the resulting 20 top members have priority in introducing bills. In practice, only about the first six whose names are drawn out will stand much chance of getting their bills discussed, and even then there is no guarantee of the bills being passed. The opportunities available for a bill to get through all its stages during private members' time on Fridays are small. A substantial bill will normally need more time than is available and will be dependent on government's finding time in its own timetable. The government is thus in a position to determine the fate of most private members' bills. It can deny such bills the necessary time to complete the required legislative stages or it can persuade its supporters to defeat them in a parliamentary vote. As a result, most private members' bills cover matters that are not politically contentious and are unlikely to arouse the opposition of government. (Consequently, a modest number of bills are passed; 68 in the 1983–1987 Parliament.)[9] A further important constraint is that such bills cannot make a charge on the public revenue: only ministers can introduce bills that make such a charge.

Hence, the scope for legislative initiative by private members is extremely limited. Nonetheless, it is not nonexistent. Occasionally, a private member may introduce a bill on an important issue toward which the government is sympathetic and for which it is prepared to find time.

This was the case notably with a number of social reform issues in the 1960s. Because the Labour government did not wish to take responsibility for certain reforms that might prove politically unpopular, possibly with some of its own supporters, the Labour government left it to back-bench MPs to introduce private members' bills on subjects such as abortion, divorce, homosexuality, and the death penalty. Where necessary, the government found time to allow the House to reach a decision on these measures, but it otherwise adopted a "hands off" approach. The consequence was that a number of substantial social reforms were introduced through the medium of private members' legislation.[10] Such occasions, however, are rare.

The number of days the House spends in session each year is shown in Table 11.4. About one-third of its time is taken up with debate on government bills. Less than 4% of its time is spent discussing private members' bills.[11] Most of the remainder of parliamentary time is given over in one form or other to debate and scrutiny of government actions.

Executive Actions

Ministers and civil servants spend most of their time pursuing and administering policies and programs for which legislative authority has already been given or for which such authority is not necessary (for example, policies pursued under prerogative powers). Hence, the formal approval of

TABLE 11.4. THE HOUSE OF COMMONS: SITTINGS AND PARLIAMENTARY QUESTIONS, 1984–1988

	Parliamentary Session			
	1984–85	*1985–86*	*1986–87[a]*	*1987–88[b]*
Number of days sitting	172	172	109	218
Number of hours sitting	1,566	1,536	930	1,978
Average length of sitting day	9 hrs., 6 mins.	8 hrs., 57 mins.	8 hrs., 32 mins.	9 hrs.
Parliamentary Questions:				
Oral[c]	14,800	18,139	12,766	24,940
Written	31,523	31,808	21,331	47,726

[a] Short session as a result of the calling of the 1987 general election
[b] Long session
[c] Most questions tabled for oral answer, because of lack of time, received written answers.
(Source: Data derived from House of Commons Sessional Information Digest, *1984/5–1987/8.)*

Parliament is not required. Nonetheless, the House of Commons seeks to subject such executive actions to scrutiny and debate. There are various procedural devices available. These may be identified as Question Time, debates (of different types), and, away from the floor of the House, select committees, correspondence, and the submission of Early Day motions.

Question Time is a feature of the House of Commons for which there is no United States parallel. It entails the regular appearance of ministers and the head of goverment in the House to answer questions submitted by back-bench MPs. (The rough equivalent in the United States would be for cabinet secretaries and the president to appear regularly on the floor of the House or Senate to answer questions, such sessions taking place several times a week.) Question Time in the House of Commons takes place each parliamentary sitting day, Monday to Thursday. It occupies between 45 and 55 minutes at the beginning of each day (the House commences its business at 2:30 P.M. with prayers) and is subject now to well-defined procedures.[12] Ministers answer questions on a rotating basis, the more important ministers coming up for a Question Time about once every three weeks. The prime minister has a regular twice-weekly slot in Question Time, answering questions for 15 minutes between 3:15 and 3:30 P.M. on Tuesdays and Thursdays. Each MP is restricted in the number of questions he or she can hand in (eight in any ten sitting days and no more than two on any given day), though the number submitted remains substantial (see Table 11.4). After being submitted, questions are published on the Order Paper of the House (see Figure 11.1). At Question Time, the MP who has the first question rises and says to the Speaker "Number one, sir." The relevant minister then rises to answer the question. Having been sent a copy of the question immediately after its submission, the minister is armed with relevant information compiled by his or her department and will normally give a prepared answer. Once the answer has been given, it is normal practice for the Speaker to call the member who asked the question to put a supplementary, or follow-up question. It is at the Speaker's discretion as to how many such supplementaries are permitted. Having allowed one or more supplementary questions, the Speaker then calls the MP in whose name the second question on the Order Paper appears. The MP rises, says "Number two, sir," and the process is repeated. This continues until 3:30 P.M., when questions automatically cease, regardless of how many remain on the Order Paper. Questions not answered during Question Time receive instead written answers that are published in *Hansard*, the official report of proceedings that also includes the verbatim transcript of debates as well as of Question Time.

MPs have the option also of tabling (that is, submitting) questions for written answer. These are more numerous than questions tabled for an oral answer at Question Time (see Table 11.4). The answers, along with the

ORDER PAPER

QUESTIONS FOR ORAL ANSWER

★1 **Mr Roger King** (Birmingham, Northfield):   To ask the Secretary of State for Foreign and Commonwealth Affairs, what efforts the United Kingdom is making in international fora to prevent the return to power in Kampuchea of Mr Pol Pot.

★2 **Mr Tim Boswell** (Daventry):   To ask the Secretary of State for Foreign and Commonwealth Affairs, if he will make a statement on recent political developments in the Warsaw Pact countries.

★3 **Mrs Gwyneth Dunwoody** (Crewe and Nantwich):   To ask the Secretary of State for Foreign and Commonwealth Affairs, if he will make a statement on British-Israeli, relations in the light of the recent visit to Israel by the Minister of State the honourable Member for Bristol West.

★4 **Mr Bernie Grant** (Tottenham):   To ask the Secretary of State for Foreign and Commonwealth Affairs, what discussions he has had with other governments in order to resolve the problem of Vietnamese refugees in Hong Kong.

★5 **Mr Harry Greenway** (Ealing North):   To ask the Secretary of State for Foreign and Commonwealth Affairs, if he will make a statement on the current situation in Afghanistan.

★6 **Mr John Maples** (Lewisham West):   To ask the Secretary of State for Foreign and Commonwealth Affairs, if he will make a statement on the recent visit by the Minister of State, the honourable Member for Bristol West, to Israel.

★7 **Mr Simon Burns** (Chelmsford):   To ask the Secretary of State for Foreign and Commonwealth Affairs, what co-operation is being achieved through the United Nations to tackle the threats from international trafficking in cocaine.

★8 **Mr Alistair Burt** (Bury North):   To ask the Secretary of State for Foreign and Commonwealth Affairs, if he will make a statement on the Middle East peace process.

★9 **Mr David Martin** (Portsmouth South):   To ask the Secretary of State for Foreign and Commonwealth Affairs, if he is satisfied that the Nicaraguan Government is committed to introducing democracy.

★10 **Mr Ian Gow** (Eastbourne):   To ask the Secretary of State for Foreign and Commonwealth Affairs, if he will make a statement on current Anglo-French relations.

★11 **Mr William McKelvey** (Kilmarnock and Loudoun):   To ask the Secretary of State for Foreign and Commonwealth Affairs, if he will make it his policy to make a positive commitment to the social dimension in the European Community.

★12 **Mr David Evans** (Welwyn, Hatfield):   To ask the Secretary of State for Foreign and Commonwealth Affairs, how many British citizens detained abroad required consular help in 1988; how many of these faced criminal charges; and what was the total cost of providing assistance.

★13 **Mr Michael Colvin** (Romsey and Waterside):   To ask the Secretary of State for Foreign and Commonwealth Affairs, if he will make a statement on the implementation of United Nations Security Council resolution 435.

★14 **Mr Steve Norris** (Epping Forest):   To ask the Secretary of State for Foreign and Commonwealth Affairs, if he will make a statement on Anglo-Israeli relations.

Figure 11.1. Questions on the House of Commons' Order Paper, March 8, 1989. Questions continue on subsequent pages of the Order Paper. (*Copyright 1989 by the Crown. Reprinted by permission of the Controller of Her Majesty's Stationery Office.*)

questions, are published in *Hansard*. Tabling written questions is popular especially as a means of eliciting statistics and other material that cannot easily be given in oral form. Oral answers, by contrast, are used to elicit statements and comments on government policy and matters that MPs think might embarrass (or, if the MP is on the government side, help) government or generate favorable attention back in the constituencies.

There are various types of *debate* held on the floor of the House. The most important can be classified as general debates, held to discuss particular government policies. These can be between three and seven hours in duration. They take place on motions tabled by the government (for example, on motions to take note or approve particular policies or government policy documents) or, on 20 "Opposition days," by opposition parties (the official Opposition decides topics on 17 days, the third largest party—presently the SLD—on the other 3 days). General debates are also held at the beginning of the parliamentary session on the Debate on the Address. Following the Queen's Speech at the beginning of each session, outlining the government's program for the year, a debate extending over several days is held. Ostensibly the debate is on an address to the Queen, thanking her for her gracious speech, but in practice it covers particular government policies: one day, for example, is normally given over to a discussion of foreign policy.

The other main type of debate is the adjournment debate. In practice, there are two forms of adjournment debate. One is the same essentially as a general debate; the only difference is that no substantive motion is before the House. Instead, a motion to adjourn is put down as a way of allowing debate to range freely on a topic for which the governmet has no specific policy or action that it wishes to be approved. In short, it is a useful means of sounding out the opinion of the House. At the end of such debates, the motion to adjourn is generally negatived without a vote. The other type of adjournment debate is known as the half-hour adjournment debate and is held at the end of each day's sitting, usually from 10:00 to 10:30 P.M. on Mondays through Thursdays (2:00 to 2:30 P.M. on Fridays). These debates allow an MP, chosen usually after a ballot, to raise an issue, usually of constituency interest, for about 15 minutes, and allow the relevant minister (traditionally a junior minister) about 15 minutes to respond to the points made. After exactly 30 minutes have elapsed, the House is automatically adjourned. These short debates take up little time but are extremely popular with back-bench MPs, allowing them to raise constituency problems or important but nonparty issues (for example, problems such as gambling, drug misuse, or the transferability of pensions). MPs raising the issues normally give ministers advance information of the points they intend to raise, thus allowing for a full reply to be prepared.

There are one or two other forms of debate, the most important but rarely employed being that of the emergency debate. A member can ask leave to move the adjournment of the House "for the purpose of discussing a specific and important matter that should have urgent consideration." If the MP can convince the Speaker that the matter (1) deserves urgent attention, (2) falls within the responsibility of government, and (3) cannot be raised quickly by another procedure, then the debate may be granted. If the debate is granted, it takes place the next day (or the following Monday if granted on a Thursday) or, if the Speaker considers that the urgency of the matter justifies it, that same evening at 7:00 P.M. In practice, the Speaker tends to dislike the interruptions to scheduled business caused by such debates, and few are granted: on average, only about four a session. They nonetheless constitute a useful safety valve function, allowing members to discuss an important topic on occasion that the government had not proposed to have discussed.

Of these various types of debate, general debates take up the most time. About 10% of the House's time is taken up with debates on government motions. The format of such debates is similar to that of second reading debates. A government minister moves the motion, an Opposition front-bench spokesman speaks (each probably for half an hour or more, the minister in particular reading from a prepared brief), then back-bench MPs speak, called alternately from each side of the House, then an Opposition front-bench spokesman winds up for the Opposition and a minister concludes for the government. Ministers and Opposition front-bench spokesmen tend to dominate not only in terms of the time they take but also in the audience they attract. Few MPs remain to listen to the speeches of back-bench MPs. Instead, they tend to leave the Chamber, returning when the final front-bench speeches are being made and in time for the vote (if there is to be one). In practice, any debate thus takes place among very few members. Indeed, it is a misnomer to refer to "debates." Most speeches are delivered from prepared notes and often have little relevance to the speeches that have preceded them. Nonetheless, any member wishing to have a speech appear in *Hansard* has to be present, catch the Speaker's eye, and deliver it. There is no procedure in debate analogous to the United States' practice that allows for material to be inserted in the official record without it having been presented verbally in the Chamber.

Away from the floor of the House, the most important device employed for the scrutiny of the executive is that of *select committees*. These committees have responsibility for maintaining scrutiny of particular departments or sectors of government responsibility, though they have no responsibility for the formal scrutiny and approval of legislation (that is the function of the separate standing committees, unlike the procedure in the United States, where the two responsibilities are combined in congressional standing committees). Select committees have been variously utilized in past centuries[13] but not on any consistent or comprehensive basis. Only two such committees have existed as important committees for any length of time. One is the Public Accounts Committee, first appointed in 1861 to ensure that public expenditure was properly incurred on the purpose for which it had been voted. Over time the committee has interpreted more widely its terms of references, conducting value-for-money exercises and investigating possible negligence. The committee has developed a reputation as a thorough and authoritative body, its recommendations resulting either in government action to implement them or to provide a reasoned response to them. Traditionally, the committee is chaired by an Opposition MP. The other important committee was the Estimates Committee: unlike the Public Accounts Committee, it no longer exists. It was first appointed in 1912 and, after being suspended from 1914 to 1921, existed until 1971. It was appointed to look at the annual estimates and to consider ways in which policies could be carried out more cost-efficiently. It was not supposed to consider the merits of policies but after 1945 began to venture into areas that could not be described as solely administrative. However, it was hampered by limited resources both in staff and in terms of the information presented to it by government. In 1971 it was replaced by a larger committee, the Expenditure Committee, itself divided into functional subcommittees. This committee disappeared in 1979, when a new system of committees was introduced.

The Select Committee of Nationalized Industries was established in 1955 and a number of similar committees were established in the late 1960s and early 1970s. This latter development began in 1966, when Labour politician Richard Crossman was appointed as leader of the House (i.e., the minister with responsibility for the government's business program in the House). Encouraged by a number of reform-minded Labour MPs, he instigated the creation of a Select Committee on Agriculture and another on science and technology. Later committees included ones to cover education, overseas development, Scottish affairs, and race relations. The committees had limited impact on government. The Agricultural Committee encountered opposition from the Foreign Office when it wanted to go to Brussels to pursue an inquiry and, after it had operated for only two years, Richard Crossman decided not to put forward the necessary motion to renew its existence. The new committees, as one observer recorded in 1970, "have so far exerted only the most minor influence on policy-making and administration."[14] In 1978 a Commons' procedure committee recommended that if Commons' scrutiny of the executive was to be effective, a new system of committee was necessary, created on a systematic and continuing basis. Pressure for the creation of such a committee system built up within the House, and in 1979 the new Conservative leader of the

House, Norman St. John-Stevas, brought forward motions for the appointment of the recommended committees. By 248 votes to 12, the House approved the creation of 12 committees to "examine the expenditure, administration, and policy of the principal Government Departments . . . and associated public bodies." In addition to the 12 committees approved, it was agreed subsequently to establish also a Committee on Scottish Affairs and another on Welsh Affairs. The committees are listed in Table 11.5.

The new committees have faced a variety of problems. Of necessity they have had to be selective in their choice of topics for investigation (and whether or not to opt for long- or short-term studies, whether to concentrate on the estimates or on policy, and so on), they have had limited resources (usually one full-time clerk each and up to four specialist advisers paid on a per-diem basis), they have had no formal powers other than the power to send for "persons, papers and records" (a power that does not

TABLE 11.5. DEPARTMENTAL SELECT COMMITTEES IN THE HOUSE OF COMMONS, SESSION 1987–1988

Committee	Chairman	Number of Substantive Reports Issued During the Session[a]
Agriculture	Jerry Wiggin (Con)	2
Defence	Michael Mates (Con)	8
Education, Science and Arts	Timothy Raison (Con)	1
Employment	Ron Leighton (Lab)	3
Energy	Sir Ian Lloyd (Con)	5
Environment	Sir Hugh Rossi (Con)	3
Foreign Affairs	David Howell (Con)	4
Home Affairs	John Wheeler (Con)	4
Scottish Affairs	not appointed[b]	
Social Services	Frank Field (Lab)	5
Trade and Industry	Kenneth Warren (Con)	3
Transport	David Marshall (Lab)	3
Treasury and Civil Service	Terence Higgins (Con)	8
Subcommittee[c]	Giles Radice (Lab)	
Welsh Affairs	Gareth Wardell (Lab)	1

[a] Excludes Government Observations on committee reports and committee responses to such observations.
[b] The small number of Conservative MPs returned for Scottish seats in the 1987 general election made it difficult to get a sufficient number of Conservative Members to sit on the committee; consequently the committee was not reappointed for the Parliament.
[c] Three committees are empowered to appoint subcommittees (Foreign Affairs, Home Affairs, Treasury and Civil Service) but only the Treasury and Civil Service Committee now uses this power.
Con = Conservative
Lab = Labour

extend to cabinet ministers and cabinet papers), and they have had problems in determining their relationship with the House as such. There is no automatic provision, for example, for a committee report to be debated by the House. Yet despite these limitations, the committees have proved to be major improvements on their predecessors. They have proved to be more extensive and more thorough in their scrutiny, have operated as identifiable units, and have attracted the enthusiasm of Members: they are well-attended and there is demand to join them. They have also proved to be prolific. In the first Parliament of their existence (1979–1983) they issued 193 reports; in the second Parliament (1983–1987) they issued 306. (Examples of committee reports are given in Table 11.6.) They have attracted more extensive media attention than their predecessors and they have become the target of representations from outside groups, something that never happened before. As bodies of scrutiny, they not only have served as independent critics of government but also, by issuing reports with or without comment, they have helped inform debate on particular subjects. In a parliamentary written answer in 1986, the Prime Minister listed 150 recommendations from select committees that had been accepted by the government in the twelve-month period from March 1985 to March 1986. By examining witnesses and receiving evidence, they have provided authoritative forums in which outside groups can make their views known (especially useful to promotional groups; see Chapter 7). By their questioning of civil servants, they have served also to open up a little more to public scrutiny the activities of government.

TABLE 11.6. SELECT COMMITTEE REPORTS, 1987–1988: DEFENCE AND FOREIGN AFFAIRS COMMITTEES

Committee	Substantive Reports
Defence	1. Ethnic monitoring and the armed forces
	2. Business appointments: acceptance of appointments in commerce and industry by members of the armed forces and officials in the Ministry of Defence
	3. Progress of the Trident program
	4. The defence requirement for merchant shipping and civil aircraft
	5. The procurement of major defence equipment
	6. Future size and role of the Royal Navy's surface fleet
	7. Statement on the Defence Estimates 1988
	8. British forces in Belize
Foreign Affairs	1. Famine in the Horn of Africa
	2. Current UK policy toward the Iran/Iraq Conflict
	3. Political Impact of the process of arms control and disarmament
	4. Foreign and Commonwealth Office/Overseas Development Administration expenditure 1988–1989

The remaining two devices, available to all members, are those of *correspondence* and submitting or signing Early Day motions. Members can and do write to ministers, normally for the purpose of eliciting information or action in pursuit of some constituency casework. On average, a member may write 5 to 25 such letters a week (ministers are among those writing, sending letters in their capacity as constituency MPs); in the 1988–1989 session, members wrote more than 100,000 letters to ministers.[15] Letter writing is a popular device for pursuing casework, undertaken free of party considerations, and often evokes the desired information or response from departments. In many cases, all that members and their constituents are after is an authoritative explanation of a particular official action. Such letter writing provides, in conjunction with the letters written by MPs to constituents, the most structured and direct contact that many citizens have with government. About 11% of constituents communicate with their MPs.[16] Of these, according to one survey, about 75% reported a "good" or "very good" response. Of citizens in the United States communicating with their congressmen, a somewhat higher 90% reported a "good" or "very good" response.[17]

Early Day motions are motions put down by members, technically for debate "on an early day." In practice, there is no available time to debate them. Rather, given that they are published, they serve as means of expressing a written opinion. Members can and do add their signatures to such motions and the number of names a motion attracts serves as some indication of opinion within the House.[18] Their impact is limited by the large number tabled, now more than a thousand a year, and by the range of topics covered. Some are essentially flippant or congratulatory (congratulating some prominent figure on a recent achievement, for example), while others express opinions on important issues of policy. Members are free to submit and to sign as many motions as they like. Some rarely do so; others have a reputation for signing every motion with which they have some sympathy. (At least one has been known to sign two motions that were mutually exclusive.) As a result, the significance of such motions is limited.

These, then, constitute the primary devices available to members of Parliament to debate and scrutinize the actions of government. Most such devices are long-standing ones, though used more often in recent years than they were previously. Others are of recent origin. Indeed, the House has witnessed significant developments in recent years which, in the view of some observers, have made it a more effective instrument of scrutiny and influence. Others, as we shall see, consider the changes inadequate as a means of ensuring that the House can constrain an ever-growing executive.

Recent Developments

Over the past 20 to 25 years, the House of Commons has seen a number of changes. They have not proved sufficient to render it, in Mezey's terminology, an "active" legislature, but they have helped make it a more effective "reactive" legislature. The changes themselves are interrelated and can be described under three heads: behavioral, structural, and representational.

Behavioral. Before 1970 the voting cohesion of MPs was so close to 100% that Samuel Beer suggested that there was no longer any point in measuring it.[19] MPs voted loyally with their party; no postwar government ever lost a vote as a result of its own supporters voting with the Opposition. After 1970, MPs displayed greater voting independence: commencing in the 1970–1974 Parliament, during the premiership of Edward Heath, Conservative MPs voted against their own side more often, in greater numbers, and with much more effect than before. On six occasions, the government was actually defeated as a result of cross-voting by its own back-benchers. This sudden change in behavior I have attributed elsewhere to the leadership style of Edward Heath: the policies he pursued, the unbending manner in which he pursued them, and his refusal to listen—or even explain his decisions—to his own supporters generated such resentment that MPs, frustrated and ignored by the Prime Minister, found that the only way to express disagreement was to vote against their own side.[20] (Previously they would have abstained from voting or would have voted loyally after being listened to by their leaders.) The action of Conservative dissenters set a precedent for subsequent Parliaments and was followed by Labour MPs. From 1974 to 1979 the Labour government was also vulnerable to defeat because for most of the period it lacked an overall parliamentary majority (being dependent on third-party support). It was defeated 17 times in the short 1974 Parliament (the result of opposition parties combining against it) and 42 times in the subsequent 1974–1979 Parliament (23 of the defeats resulting from Labour MPs voting, sometimes in sizable numbers, with the Conservatives, and 19 attributable to opposition parties combining against a minority government). From April 1972 to April 1979 there were 65 government defeats in the House of Commons. For a similar number of defeats in a seven-year period one has to go back to the 1860s.

The defeats were important not only in themselves—they took place on a range of important issues, including the government's economic policy and its most important constitutional measure of the Parliament (the Scotland and Wales Bill: see Chapter 9)—but also because they induced a change of attitude on the part of many MPs. Their old deferential attitude was replaced by what Beer termed a participant attitude toward government.[21] They wanted to be more involved in scrutinizing government and were more prepared now to use their political muscle in order to do so.

This change of attitude had two results. One was to generate sufficient pressure for the House to insist on various structural and procedural reforms, of which more in a moment. The second was to allow behavioral independence to remain a feature of parliamentary life. Since the return of a Conservative government in 1979, with strong parliamentary majorities, government back-benchers have continued to display a degree of independence that would have been unthinkable in pre-1970 Parliaments. At times, this independence has been highly visible—most notably in April 1986, when 72 Conservative members voted against the second reading of the Shops Bill. As we have recorded already (Chapter 7), this produced a major defeat for the government, the first time this century a government with a clear working majority has lost a second reading vote. However, most of the intraparty dissension has been less visible than in the 1970s. In part, this has been a sign of weakness: cross-voting by a few MPs is more easily absorbed than before, given the size of the government's overall majority. In part, though, it is also a sign of strength: when back-bench dissent has looked serious, the government has made concessions in advance of the issue reaching the floor of the House. These have included the withdrawal of at least two government bills and the withdrawal or modification of a number of government proposals in each Parliament. Mrs. Thatcher has conceded that she has not been as radical in her economic policy as she would like to be, because she does not believe she would have been able to get her measures approved by Parliament. Despite large majorities, the government in each of the three Parliaments returned since 1979 has found itself having to make concessions. In April 1988 alone, dissent by Conservative MPs on the issues of nurses' pay, the Community Charge, and housing benefits led the government to make concessions totaling £240 million (almost $400 million). Though such activity is necessarily reactive and sporadic—MPs normally voting with their own side at least 99 times out of 100—it nonetheless creates a parliamentary situation unknown prior to 1970. Though government is usually ensured the passage of whatever measure it wants, it cannot now take that approval for granted. It has to anticipate parliamentary reaction to a greater extent than before.

Structural. The behavioral changes of the 1970s emboldened MPs to use their political strength to generate new structures, and to improve their procedures, in order to facilitiate more consistent and more effective scrutiny of government. Foremost among these changes were the departmental select committees. Unlike earlier committees, which were established on the initiative of government (and dispensed with on the initiative of government), the new committees were essentially the creation of the House itself. Members of the cabinet were hostile or agnostic toward their creation but were not prepared to go against the wishes of an assertive House.

The select committees were the most important of the changes achieved by the House but they were by no means the only change. Initially against the wishes of government (ministers had opposed the bill on second reading), the House passed the National Audit bill; enacted in 1983, it established the National Audit Office, responsible for efficiency audits of government departments. Against the wishes of government, the House variously voted to raise Members' salaries (by more than that recommended by ministers) and in 1986, again against government advice, increased by 50% the secretarial and research allowance. Back-benchers in 1983 also insisted on their choice of Speaker, in preference to the candidate favored by the Prime Minister. Other procedural changes approved in the 1980s included power to appoint special standing committees (standing committees with power to examine witnesses—a useful reform but one little used since) and the creation of three Estimates Days each session: under the latter, a senior committee of the House (comprising primarily select committee chairmen) decides which estimates to debate on each of these three days, and in practice selects estimates on which select committees have issued reports. However, the most significant change approved by the House toward the end of decade came in 1988 when the House voted, by 318 votes to 264, to approve the televising of the House on an experimental basis, thus following the lead of the House of Lords, which has been televised since 1985. The Prime Minister was among those voting against the proposal. Televising of the Commons began on November 21, 1989. As a consequence, reports from the House achieved greater prominence in news bulletins and programs reporting on events in the House became regular items in TV schedules. The reaction from both viewers and MPs was favorable and the live broadcasts of prime minister's Question Time achieved a seven-figure audience.

Many MPs believe that the 1990s will witness further changes in the structures and procedures of the Commons, not least as a consequence of television. Televising committee proceedings gave new life to the select committees. The 1990s are also likely to witness a greater pressure within the House for more extensive means of scrutinizing developments in the European Community. Following the Bruges speech by Mrs. Thatcher in 1988 (see Chapter 9), MPs began to express concern about the constitutional implications of the Single European Act. Various members proposed reforms designed to enhance parliamentary scrutiny of Community lawmaking. At the end of 1989, the Select Committee on Procedure recommended the creation of a series of special standing committees to scrutinize EC documents in particular sectors. It also urged select committees to develop closer links with both the EC Commission and with members of the European Parliament.

Representational. This refers to the constituency activity of members. Before the 1960s, constituencies appeared to expect little of their MPs. Many members did not live in their constituencies and in some cases paid what amounted to annual visits. Constituents rarely troubled their MPs with correspondence or meetings. This has changed significantly since then, developing a particular momentum in the 1980s.

MPs are now notably constituency-active. In part, this change appears to be demand-led, as constituents are making more demands of Members than before. In part, it is supply-led, with members, and especially new members, being particularly energetic in seeking out and pursuing constituency casework. Demand and supply appear to have reinforced each other. A member is now estimated to spend on average about 2 to 3 hours a day on constituency work, primarily correspondence, and to spend most weekends in the constituency. A 1984 survey found that most members spend eight or more days a month in the constituency while the House is sitting; one in five spend thirteen or more days in the constituency. Most hold constituency "surgeries," constituency meetings at which citizens can come to discuss problems privately with the member. Most communication, though, takes place through correspondence (and, increasingly, through telephoning). In pursuit of casework, MPs write regularly to ministers; the number of letters written has grown by approximately a quarter from 1982 to 1989; as we have seen, more than 100,000 letters a year are now sent. Generally members get the response sought by constituents. In the event of an inadequate response, members can table parliamentary questions, seek a meeting with the minister, and put in for a half-hour adjournment debate; a keen member may pursue all these courses in pursuit of a particular case.

Members attach importance to their constitutency work, traditionally regarding it as "a part of the job" for which they received no tangible (but some psychological) reward. Increasingly, there is evidence that such activity may generate some electoral reward. In the 1987 general election, Conservative new members—those first returned in 1983 and with a reputation for being especially active in constituency work—achieved an increase in their share of the poll, achieving better results than other Conservative candidates; the achievement was consistent.[22] In a marginal seat, the member's "personal vote" may make the difference between political life and death.

These developments are important and have made for a busier and more effective House of Commons. However, they have not proved sufficient to still pressure for more radical reform.

THE HOUSE OF LORDS

The House of Lords was gradually forced in the nineteenth and early twentieth century to accept a subordinate position in its relationship with the House of Commons. The reason for this is clear. It was well stated by the Earl of Shaftesbury during debates on the 1867 Reform Act. "So long as the other House of Parliament was elected upon a restricted principle," he declared, "I can understand that it would submit to a check from a House such as this. But in the presence of this great democratic power and the advance of this great democratic wave . . . it passes my comprehension to understand how an hereditary House like this can hold its own."[23] Although not altogether swept away by this "great democratic wave," the House was at least to be swamped by it. It could not maintain a claim to equal status with the elected House, a House elected on an ever-widening franchise.

It is clear that the House of Lords cannot sustain a claim to being a representative chamber. Peers represent no one but themselves: their writs of summons are personal. No member serves by virtue of election. A peer is a member of the Upper House either by virtue of birth (hereditary peers), by virtue of appointment by the Crown on the advice of the prime minister (life peers and hereditary peers of first creation), or by virtue of position (Lords of Appeal in Ordinary, the Archbishops of Canterbury and York, the Bishops of London, Durham, and Winchester, and 21 other Bishops of the Church of England in order of seniority). They are divided into the Lords Temporal and the Lords Spiritual. The Lords Temporal are the hereditary and life peers, comprising (in order of seniority) the ranks of Duke, Marquess, Earl, Viscount, and Baron. There are hereditary peers of all ranks, life peers being created only as Barons. The Lords Spiritual comprise the Archbishops and the senior Bishops representing the established Anglican Church, the only members of the House who may be deemed to sit in some albeit tenuous form of representative capacity.

Currently there are more than 1,000 members of the House (1,185 in 1989), making it the largest legislative assembly in the world. In practice, many peers do not bother to attend. About 800 attend one or more sittings of the House a year, and the average daily attendance is just over 300 (see Table 11.7). As a proportion of their total number, life peers are more active than hereditary peers. Life peerages were introduced under the provisions of the 1958 Life Peerages Act and made possible the introduc-

TABLE 11.7. INCREASED ACTIVITY OF THE HOUSE OF LORDS, 1959–1986

Session (at approximately 4-year intervals)	Total number of Peers on Roll	Total Number Who Attended	Total Number Who Spoke	Average Daily Attendance	Number of Days House Sat	Total Number of Hours Sat	Average Length of Sittings (hours)	Number of Sittings after 10:00 P.M.
1959–60	907	542	283	136	113	450	4	1
1963–64	1,012	525	289	151	110	534	4¼	3
1967–68	1,061	679	424	225	139	803	5¾	31
1971–72	1,073	698	419	250	141	813	5¾	28
1975–76	1,139	752	486	275	155	969	6¼	39
1981–82	1,174	790	503	284	147	930	6⅓	41
1985–86	1,171	798	529	317	165	1,213	7⅓	93

Source: D. Shell, The House of Lords (Philip Allan, 1988).

tion of new blood to the Upper House, especially that drawn from the ranks of those who disliked the hereditary principle (notably Labour party supporters). Life peerages also served to prevent the inflation of membership, since the title—and eligibility to sit in the Lords—dies with the holder. There are approximately 350 life peers, and elevation to the House of Lords is in practice now usually by the conferment of a life peerage. Labour Prime Minister Harold Wilson suspended the conferment of hereditary peerages in 1964, a suspension continued by his successors until 1983. Since then, Mrs. Thatcher has created three hereditary peerages.

Given that it is not an elected body and it occupies a subordinate position in relation to the House of Commons, what functions are performed by the House? For one thing, as we have seen, it provides some of the personnel of government. No fewer than two but usually no more than four peers are chosen to be cabinet ministers. Up to ten more may be chosen as junior ministers, with an additional six or seven being appointed as government whips.

The other functions may be subsumed under the broad rubric of scrutiny and influence (of legislation and of executive actions), of providing a forum for public debate, and, formally, of legitimation. The House also has a unique judicial function as the highest domestic court of appeal, a function in practice now exercised by a judicial committee (see Chapter 13). These may be identified as the main functions of the House. Of them, one—that of legitimation—has been circumscribed both by the provisions of the Parliaments acts and by the acceptance by peers of their politically surbordinate status.

Recognizing their undemocratic nature, as well as their one-party dominance (the House has a permanent Conservative predominance—see Table 11.8), the Lords has refrained from seeking to challenge the House of Commons. There have been occasional periods of bad feeling between the two houses, notably in the period of Labour government from 1974 to 1979, but the Upper House rarely seeks to press an amendment—let alone delay a measure—when it is clear that the Commons is not prepared to support it. As a result of an agreement between the two front benches in the 1945–1950 Parliament, the official Opposition in the Lords does not force a vote on the second reading of any bill promised in the government's election manifesto. A government is usually ensured of the Upper House's approving the principle of any measure it proposes.

Given the Lords' reluctance to challenge the government on the principle of measures, the House concentrates instead on scrutinizing the specific provisions of such measures. Bills pass through the same legislative stages as in the Commons, though committee stage is taken on the floor of the House rather than in standing committee. Consideration of a bill in the Lords allows for discussion of many provisions that may not have been

TABLE 11.8. POLITICAL AFFILIATION OF PEERS, 1970–1984

Party/Group	1970		1984	
	N	%	*N*	%
Conservative	468	43.4	460	38.6
Labour	120	11.1	133	11.2
Liberal	38	3.5	39	3.3
Social Democrat	–	–	38	3.2
Communist	2	0.2	2	0.2
Independent—	110	10.2	209	17.6
Crossbench[a]	51	4.8	50	4.2
—non-party[b]	289	26.8	259	21.7
No declared affiliation[c]				
Total	1,078	100.0	1,190	100.0

[a] Those in receipt of the independent crossbench "notification of business"
[b] Law lords, Archbishops, Bishops and (some) Royal Dukes
[c] Those peers about whose party allegiance no information is available *(Source: N. Baldwin, "The House of Lords: Behavioural Changes," in P. Norton (ed.), Parliament in the 1980s (Blackwell, 1985), p. 109.)*

debated fully in the Commons, for what may be termed technical scrutiny (ensuring that the specifics of a measure make sense and that they are correctly drafted), and for the introduction of further amendments. Of amendments made to bills during their passage through the House, the majority are initiated by the government. Not surprisingly, therefore, most amendments made by the Lords prove acceptable to the Commons. Of those that do not, the Lords rarely seeks to press any.

Under the rubric of scrutiny of legislation may now be included scrutiny of draft legislation emanating from the European Community (see Chapter 10). It is a function shared with the House of Commons, but one that the Lords is generally credited with fulfilling most effectively. The function is fulfilled primarily through the Select Committee on the European Communities and its seven subcommittees. The subcommittees cover different subjects and make greater use than does the Commons of specialist advisers and outside witnesses. Peers who are not members of the subcommittees may attend to offer the benefit of their knowledge and experience in particular cases. These factors, coupled with the fact that the Lords concentrates on the legal and administrative (as opposed to the political) implications of draft proposals and can comment on their merits, has meant that the House has achieved a more formidable reputation than its Commons' counterpart in scrutinizing EC legislation.[24]

Apart from scrutinizing bills introduced by government (and draft EC legislation), the House seeks also to scrutinize the actions of the executive. The procedures available to do this are similar to those employed in the Commons: debates and questions. The House spends about one-fifth of its time on general debates, though not all are confined to discussion of government actions and policy. The procedure for asking questions differs somewhat from Commons' procedure. At the start of the day's business, only four oral questions may be asked, though supplementary questions are permitted. At the conclusion of a day's business, what are termed "unstarred questions" are taken (see Figure 11.2). These are questions (previously submitted, like all questions) on which a short debate may take place before a minister replies. As in the Commons, written questions may also be put down, and the answers are published in the Lords' *Hansard*. In the Lords, unlike the Commons, all questions are addressed to Her Majesty's government and not to individual ministers.

NOTICES AND ORDERS OF THE DAY

Notices marked † are new or have been altered.

TUESDAY THE 23RD OF JANUARY

At half-past two o'clock

*The Lord Campbell of Croy—To ask Her Majesty's Government what impact they expect the new E.E.C. quotas for catches of sea fish will have on the British fishing fleet.

*The Viscount Mountgarret—To ask Her Majesty's Government whether it would be desirable to have a fixed date for the State Opening of Parliament other than for the first after any General Election.

*The Lord Dean of Beswick—To ask Her Majesty's Government under what circumstances the present chairman of the Trafford Park Development Corporation will not continue in that post, and what are their future plans for the Corporation.

*The Lord Rochester—To ask Her Majesty's Government whether they are satisfied with the present arrangements for determining the pay of ambulance workers.

Penzance Albert Pier Extension Bill—Third Reading.

Courts and Legal Services Bill [H.L.]—House to be again in Committee.
[THE LORD CHANCELLOR]

Co-operative Development Agency (Winding up and Dissolution) Order 1989—THE LORD STRATHCLYDE to move, That the draft Order laid before the House on 30th November 1989 be approved. *[2nd Report from the Joint Committee]*

European Communities (Privileges of the European School) Order 1989—THE LORD REAY to move, That the draft Order laid before the House on 21st November 1989 be approved. *[2nd Report from the Joint Committee]*

European Communities (Definition of Treaties) (European School) Order 1989—THE LORD REAY to move, That the draft Order laid before the House on 6th December 1989 be approved. *[3rd Report from the Joint Committee]*

Figure 11.2. Questions on the House of Lords' Order Paper, January 23, 1989. (Copyright 1989 by the Crown. Reprinted by permission of the Controller of Her Majesty's Stationery Office.)

Except for its work in the sphere of EC draft legislation, the House makes little use of committees. It has a number of what may be termed domestic committees, covering the internal administration of the House and its privileges, but it has rarely employed select committees as tools of scrutiny. Nonetheless, it has recently made some tentative moves in the direction of such committees. In 1979 it appointed a Select Committee on Unemployment, "to consider and make recommendations on long-term remedies for unemployment"; the committee reported in 1982. It has a sessional (i.e., permanent) committee on science and technology with a general brief to consider the topic. More recently, it has appointed a committee to consider murder and life imprisonment.

The other main function that may be ascribed to the House is that of providing a forum for debate of important public issues. A similar function, of course, may be ascribed to the Commons. The difference between the two is that the Lords allows greater scope for the discussion of important topics that are not the subject of contention between parties. The Commons concentrate on partisan issues, with little time for discussion of subjects outside the realm of party debate.

The Upper House has not only the time and the inclination to debate important but essentially nonpartisan issues, it can also claim the expertise to do so. Whereas MPs are essentially professional politicans (even though they may have expertise derived from preparliamentary employment), many peers hold—indeed are often ennobled on the basis of holding—

TABLE 11.9. OCCUPATIONAL EXPERIENCE OF PEERS, 1981

		Percentage of Peerage in Category	
Occupation	N	Hereditary	Created/ Appointed
Full-time trade union official	20	—	4.9
Civil/diplomatic service	114	6.2	16.1
Legal (judge, barrister, solicitor)	120	5.9	18.3
Banking/insurance	121	11.6	7.8
Engineer	25	1.6	3.2
Accountant/economist	25	1.9	2.4
Scientist	9	0.4	1.5
Medical (surgeon, doctor,	19	0.6	3.4
Teaching (school, university)	103	3.4	18.8
Industry	208	15.6	21.5
Politics	166	3.0	34.9

Source: N. Baldwin, "The House of Lords: Behavioural Changes," in P. Norton (ed.), Parliament in the 1980s (Blackwell, 1985), p. 105.

leading positions in industry, the trade unions, finance, and the arts (see Table 11.9 for peers' principal occupations). Being a member of the House of Lords is usually a secondary pursuit to another activity or interest. Indeed, given that peers are paid only an expense allowance and receive no salary, there is little incentive for them to be full-time members of the House. The consequence is that there are frequently a number of peers who are experts in a particular field and who will attend debates only on those occasions when their subject of expertise is under discussion. The result, according to some observers, is informed and interesting debate. Many view favorably this perceived combination of expertise and lack of party bickering. Detractors would draw attention to the fact that Lords' expertise in certain areas is not replicated in other fields, producing superficial and often dull debate, and, more significantly, calling into question what attention is paid to Lords' debates by government and outside bodies.

Possibly the most significant role played by the House in acting as a forum of debate is as a safety valve. By avoiding replication of the party debate in the Commons, it allows for the occasional public debate on topics that might otherwise not receive an airing in an authoritative public forum. For some outside interests, making their voices heard through such a forum is all that they desire. The House of Lords has achieved a reputation especially for discussing important social issues (notably in the 1960s) and for helping ease onto the political agenda topics that might otherwise have been kept off. In recent years, for example, it has proved a valuable forum for those seeking to introduce a bill of rights.[25]

Recent Developments

Like the House of Commons, the House of Lords in recent years has witnessed something of a revitalization. In the 1950s and for much of the 1960s, the House sat at a very leisurely pace and very few peers attended; it came close to being a moribund institution. The position changed significantly in the latter half of the 1960s and even more in the years since then. Peers became more active, attending in greater number: between 1963 and 1983 the average daily attendance doubled. More peers took part in debates and the House sat for longer: whereas the average length of a daily sitting was less than 5 hours in 1963–1964, the average length by 1985–1986 was more than 7 hours (Table 11.7); since the latter half of the 1980s, late-night sittings (those going beyond 10.00 P.M.) have become frequent. Peers have also shown themselves more independent in their voting behavior. The Labour government from 1974 to 1979 suffered a total of 362 defeats in the Upper House. Given the Conservative preponderance in the House, the defeats were not unduly surprising; a number caused tension between the two Houses, but in most cases the defeats were on noncontentious amendments and acceptable to the government. What has been surprising has been the degree of independence shown by the House during a period of Conservative government. In the ten years of Conservative government from 1979 to 1989, the government suffered more than 115 defeats in the Lords' division lobbies. Some of the issues have been contentious, including the 1984 bill paving the way for the abolition of the Greater London Council. The House has proved unpredictable, and Conservative MPs who dissent on particular issues in the House of Commons will often now send what amount to political signals to the Lords encouraging dissent there. Though the parties in the House have whips, there is no sanction they can employ against dissenting peers; peers come and go as they wish, and they sometimes vote as they please. Party voting predominates but, even more so than in the Commons, the government cannot take the assent of the House of Lords for granted.

The reason for this behavioral change has been attributed by Nicholas Baldwin to the convergence of two developments. One is the introduction of life peers. They have provided new blood, introducing many from political life who have an interest in remaining active in public affairs. As the number of life peers increased, so the House gained a larger body of active peers. The other reason was the failure to reform the House in 1969. Following the failure of the Parliament (No. 2) Bill, of which more shortly, peers realized there was little likelihood of their chamber being reformed in the foreseeable future; hence it was a case of making the existing House work effectively.[26] The consequence has been a more active and, from the government's point of view, more troublesome Upper House.

Attempts at Reform

The House of Lords not only debates political topics, it is itself a topic of political dispute. The debate about the House has centered not on whether it fulfills the functions outlined above, or on whether they are the functions most appropriate to a British second chamber, but rather on whether the House of Lords is the body that should constitute the second chamber and discharge those functions. At the heart of the problem is the hereditary basis of the House. It is seen by many as the remnant of a feudal age, one that can no longer be justified in a political system based on rational–legal rather than traditional authority. It is often seen as a wonderful anachronism that has survived by dint of inertia and by a failure to agree on what, if anything, should replace it.

Schemes for reform of the House are common. "On summer evenings and winter afternoons, when they have nothing else to do, people discuss how to reform the House of Lords," wrote Janet Morgan. "Schemes are taken out of cupboards and drawers and dusted off; speeches are composed, pamphlets written, letters sent to the newspaper. From time to time, the whole country becomes excited."[27] The problem has been one of translating the desire for reform into a tangible and generally acceptable measure. The most important attempt at reform since the passage of the Parliament acts was that made by the Labour government in 1968 and 1969. The government introduced the Parliament (No. 2) Bill, which sought to reform rather than replace the existing House. It proposed a two-tier House with voting members (life peers) and nonvoting members (hereditary peers), the House having a six-month delaying power over nonmoney bills. Nonvoting membership was to be confined to the existing hereditary peers, their successors not being entitled to seats in the House. As a result, the hereditary element was to be slowly removed. Under the bill's provisions, the government of the day would be provided with a working majority. The result, according to the White Paper that preceded the bill, would be a move in the direction of ensuring that the Upper House played a role "complementary to but not rivalling that of the Commons." It was envisaged that closer cooperation between the two Houses and a review of the Lords' functions would follow once the changes were implemented.

In any event, the bill was not enacted. Although support for it in the House of Commons was broad—the bill followed interparty talks on the issue—it was not deep. There was bitter opposition to it from a number of Labour MPs, led by Michael Foot, who wished to abolish the House of Lords altogether, and from a number of Conservative MPs, led by Enoch Powell, who wished to leave it as it was. This unholy alliance, as it was generally described, fought to delay the bill, and that delay proved successful. The government appeared to lose heart in the measure and many MPs who favored reform found fault with its specific provisions. The committee stage of the bill was taken on the floor of the House, and the government whips had increasing difficulty keeping sufficient MPs present in order to carry closure motions. Debate began to eat into time that the government preferred to utilize for other measures. In April 1969 the government decided not to proceed with the bill.

The experience of the 1969 bill deterred succeeding governments from seeking to tackle the problem. Nonetheless, debate surrounding the future of the House of Lords was not stilled. Various Labour politicans sought to keep it on the agenda of political debate, proponents of root-and-branch reform becoming more vocal in recent years. The House of Lords remains an issue of political debate.

THE CURRENT DEBATE

In historical perspective, debate on parliamentary reform has tended to be more intense—and to generate the introduction of more measures of reform—when focused on the House of Lords. In recent years, however, both Houses have become targets of radical proposals for change.

The House of Commons

In the 1960s a number of Labour MPs and academics, notably Professor Bernard Crick, were active in pressing for parliamentary reform and especially for procedural change. The dominance of the government over Parliament, they argued, was too great. The House of Commons lacked the facilities to subject the government to sustained scrutiny; MPs were too badly paid, lacked adequate research facilities, and were constrained by archaic procedures.[28] Even as an arena assembly, the House was performing badly. What was needed, they argued, were reforms that would allow the House to engage in more effective scrutiny through investigation and debate. To such an end, they advocated the greater use of select committees, longer sittings of the House, better pay and research facilities for members, modernization of parliamentary procedure, the broadcasting of debates, and more opportunities for emergency debates. Such reforms, it was contended, would allow the House the opportunity to subject government to public scrutiny and to keep it responsive to public feeling, thus maintaining consent for the political system (the House doing the job expected of it) without jeopardizing the effectiveness of government (the government retaining its parliamentary majority). A strong government, declared Professor Crick, was compatible with a strong Opposition.

In the 1970s pressure for limited internal reform of the House began to give way to calls for more radical change. A convergence of two developments may help explain why this happened. One was the failure of a number of internal reforms implemented in the latter half of the 1960s and early 1970s. The extended use of select committees had little impact on government and on policy making. As an experiment, the House began to meet in the morning on two days a week. However, votes could not be held during these sittings and members, especially Conservative members (many of whom had outside interests), showed little interest in them and rarely attended. The morning sittings were abandoned. Pay for MPs was increased and more offices were made available, but the improvements were relative: MPs remained poorly paid and had little by way of research facilities. The relationship between the House and the part of it that formed the government remained essentially unchanged—hence an impetus for more far-reaching reform. This was reinforced by a second development. The 1970s witnessed greater economic and political turmoil than had existed in the previous decade. The country's economic position worsened, and the two general elections of 1974 produced governments elected with less than 40% of the votes cast and an apparent and significant shift away from the two main parties (see Chapters 5 and 6). A combination of these developments fostered more rigorous and critical analyses of the House of Commons and its relationship to the country's economic and political malaise.

The radical reformers, led by academics such as S. E. Finer and S. A. Walkland, were intent on ripping away what they saw as the inaccurate and misleading gloss that previous writers had placed on the role of the House.[29] They assailed the House as having clung to nineteenth-century practices and beliefs during a period that witnessed major economic and social change (the welfare state and the managed economy), the swelling of bureaucracy, and the trend toward a corporate economy. It had failed to adapt and to keep pace with such developments. The electoral system encouraged the return of one party with a majority of seats, and party discipline within the House assured the resulting party government of a parliamentary majority for whatever it proposed. The result was a malfunctional parliamentary system. It was a system that undermined rather than reinforced political authority. The House was incapable of subjecting government to scrutiny, let alone having any tangible impact on public policy.

Such an analysis led reformers to advocate electoral reform, a move supported by academics such as Professors Finer and Walkland, by the Liberal party, by the SDP, by a number of Conservative MPs, and by some Labour Members. The basis of their argument and its implications was discussed in Chapter 5. Electoral reform would produce, according to its exponents, a more representative House of Commons. On the basis of existing voting behavior, no one party would achieve an overall majority, thus forcing a coalition of the political center or a minority government responsive to other parties in the House. The House of Commons would continue to provide most of the personnel of government, to subject government to (more effective) scrutiny and influence, and to legitimate the government and its measures. The most significant difference would be that the House itself would have a greater claim to legitimacy in fulfilling those functions and would, in its behavior, be more consensual.

Despite a swelling of their ranks in the latter half of the 1970s and in the 1980s—electoral reform became a central plank of the manifesto of "Charter '88," a constitutional reform movement formed in 1988—electoral reformers have not yet found themselves in a position to implement such a measure. As we have seen (Chapter 5), they are opposed by a majority of MPs in both main parties. They have been opposed also, on less self-serving grounds, by a number of writers. Some have contended that such change is not necessary. Indeed, a number have argued against any substantial change. In the 1960s Ronald Butt argued that, through party, Parliament continued to keep government responsive to the wishes of the electorate. If the government went too far, its own back-benchers would prevent it from doing so.[30] This argument was maintained in the 1970s by MPs such as Michael Foot and Enoch Powell, but it has tended to recede in prominence in recent years. More significant has been the argument of those who have continued to press for reform internal to the House.

Internal reformers contend that the failure of the reforms of the 1960s and early 1970s did not demonstrate the failure of structural and procedural reforms as such. Since 1979 they have been able to point to the experience of the departmental select committees. They argue the case for further strengthening of the select committees, for a reform of standing committees (favoring the development of special standing committees), for improved research facilities for members individually and the House collectively, for automatic timetabling of lengthy bills, and for greater public dissemination of the work of the House. They favor broadcasting proceedings of the House, and they achieved success in this regard in 1988 after several previous attempts. Pressure for such reform comes from a number of MPs, grouped in a Commons' Reform Group, and from the Commons' Select Committee on Procedure, which has issued several reports since its 1978 report recommending the departmental select committees proposing further reforms.

Finally, there is the approach associated with this writer, an approach subsumed elsewhere under the appellation of the "Norton view."[31] This approach allows for the maintenance of government effectiveness, with the political process remaining executive-centered, while on the other side making possible an effective House of Commons, the House fulfilling and being seen to fulfill the function of subjecting governmental actions and measures to scrutiny and influence. The balance between executive and Commons would be maintained, and this balance could be jeopardized by the implementation of a new electoral system (see Chapter 5). The approach posited by this author makes possible such a balance. It draws on recent experience as the basis for arguing not only what should be but also what can be.

This approach stipulates the need for an attitudinal change on the part of MPs as a prerequisite for effective procedural reform. Relying on the government to introduce effective procedural change—designed to act as possible critics of that very same government—is an inherently flawed stance, as witnessed by the failure of the modest reforms of the 1960s. No amount of structural or procedural changes will make any significant difference unless accompanied by the political will to make such changes effective. Hence, if the House of Commons is to become a more effective scrutineer and influencer of government, it is up to MPs themselves to make it so. Such an argument before 1970 would have been considered idealistic, indeed naive. Since the 1970s however, it has been given credence by the behavioral changes that have taken place. As we have seen, they provided the basis for the most important structural reform of the twentieth century: the introduction of the departmental select committees. By flexing their political muscle, MPs have started to craft the tools necessary for consistent and effective scrutiny of executive actions; by using that same muscle, they can reform the procedures for legislative scrutiny. The behavioral changes may not prove permanent (though the select committees spawned by them are now accepted as an established part of the political landscape); they nonetheless demonstrate what can be achieved. They point the way. Members can ensure effective scrutiny and influence of government if they have the political will to do so. A House in which the government of the day can normally be assured a majority, but a majority it cannot take for granted, is the most practical way of ensuring the existence of a government that can govern but that is responsive to the House of Commons. If the House is seen publicly to be fulfilling its limited but not unimportant role, it will be achieving as much as one would hope.

The House of Lords

The debate on parliamentary reform has not been confined to the House of Commons. The House of Lords continues in its accustomed role as the subject of disparate proposals for change. The hiatus following the failure of the 1969 Parliament (No. 2) Bill has given way to pressure for radical change, including total abolition, from a number of Labour politicans and for less radical surgery from Conservatives and others. The views now expressed on Lords' reform may be summarized for convenience under four heads, the "four Rs": retain, reform, replace, and remove altogether.

Many who find the hereditary basis of the House of Lords unacceptable often express amazement that there are people other than hereditary peers who are prepared to defend the House as it currently exists. Yet a number of observers are prepared to make a case for the retention of the House in its current form, doing so on grounds of principle and practicality. They contend that the hereditary principle provides peers who are able to render an opinion free of external pressures, since they are beholden to no party or patron, and that it provides peers with not only a wide range of experience but also a wide range of views. The House boasts not only a large number of independent peers (known as "cross-bench" peers because of the benches they occupy in the House, no such benches existing in the Commons), it also has two Communist members. Members give freely of their services in order to ensure that the House fulfills its functions, and defenders contend that those functions are well fulfilled. In the absence of an acceptable alternative, the defenders contend, why not leave well enough alone? The House does its job and there is little public pressure for change.

Reformers take a different view. Many Conservatives and some Labour supporters (notably a number of Labour peers) are of the opinion that if the Upper House—indeed, any second chamber—is to survive, the existing House must be reformed or replaced; otherwise, it may fall victim to the onslaught of Labour abolitionists. Change is sought in order to conserve. Moderate reformers seek change based on the existing House. They favor a measure on lines similar to those of the 1969 bill. Such a measure was proposed by a working group of Labour peers in 1980. Other reformers seek to replace the existing House either with a completely new elected or appointed chamber or one that forms something of a hybrid between the existing chamber and an elected House. Two Conservative committees have recommended a House chosen mainly or wholly by election.[32] They argue that such election would enhance the legitimacy of the second chamber and, in so doing, create a chamber that had an acceptable basis to act as a safeguard against an over-mighty House of Commons.

Other radical proposals for replacement have included a House based on regional representation and one based on functional representation. A House comprising representatives of the regions of the United Kingdom, a proposal popular with those who support devolution, is seen as a means of providing a countervailing force against the centralizing tendencies of government. The Labour party in 1989 came out in favor of an elected chamber, designed to "reflect the interests and aspirations of the regions and nations of Britain." A House formed of representatives of groups such as the trades unions and industry would allow for the cooption of sectional groups into the formal political process, enhancing the consent of such groups.

The most radical step—to abolish the House of Lords and not replace it at all, creating a unicameral legislature—has been advocated by some politicians for many years. One leading Labour politican, Tony Benn, has made it clear that he believes abolition should be the first task of any future Labour government. A second chamber, however composed, is seen as a potential obstacle to the passage of Socialist legislation. The case for doing away with it has been most succinctly put by Labour Peer Lord Wedderburn: "Either the second chamber is less democratic than the Commons in which case it should not be able to delay legislation," he said, "or it is just as democratic, then there is no point in having two chambers."[33] The functions of the Upper House, so abolitionists argue, could be transferred to a reformed House of Commons.

Although at the national level defenders of the existing House of

Lords are in a minority, those who favor reform have difficulty finding a measure on which they can agree. Each reform proposal has its detractors: an appointed House would be little better than the existing House; an elected chamber would either duplicate the Commons or (if elected by a procedure different from that for the Lower House) be a potential obstruction to measures emanating from it; a House based on functional representation would further enhance the position of already over-powerful groups; and the absence of a second chamber would generate too many pressures for the remaining chamber, as well as doing away altogether with a necessary constitutional safeguard. It has been such disagreement among those who favor change that has resulted in no significant change taking place. The only measures affecting the Upper House that have been passed in the past 30 years have been those providing for the creation of life peers—a development that has breathed new life into the chamber—and for hereditary peers to disclaim their titles should they so choose. Although such changes are more radical than any made affecting the Commons, the House has undergone no fundamental change. Defenders of the House see this as no bad thing. Others believe that the longer it remains unreformed, the greater the pressure for it to be swept away altogether. The great democratic wave identified by Shaftesbury may yet swell and sweep it away.

CONCLUSION

Parliament continues to enjoy popular support as a legitimate political institution. Its output, by virtue of the doctrine of parliamentary sovereignty, is binding upon all and cannot be struck down by the courts. It is the institution from which the political apex of government is drawn and from which government derives its popular legitimacy. It has the characteristics of an arena assembly, seeking through debate to subject government to scrutiny and some measures of influence, and providing the broad limits within which government may govern.

Recent decades have witnessed a growing realization that neither popular support for it as a legitimating political body nor its modest powers has been as great as was previously believed. The mode of election and the adversary relationship between two parties have been identified as undermining the claim of the House of Commons to be a representative assembly. The hereditary basis of the Lords continues to be used as sufficient reason for denying the House any claim to be considered an appropriate political institution. Party hegemony has been identified as constricting Parliament's ability to exercise even the modest powers ascribed to it. A consequence of these factors has been modestly successful pressure for change within the House in order to restore to Parliament both popular support and the political will to exercise modest powers in the making of public policy. Pressure for more radical reform grew in the 1970s and 1980s. What has been lacking among proponents of more radical reform has been agreement as to what form change should take. Although many may agree on ends, agreement as to means is notably absent. Electoral reformers seek to generate a parliamentary system that reflects and seeks to generate consensus. In their preference for their own scheme of reform, consensus is the one thing they lack.

NOTES

1. However, under Article I, section 7(1), of the Constitution all revenue-raising bills must originate in the House of Representatives.
2. M. Mezey, *Comparative Legislatures* (Duke University Press, 1979), Ch. 2.
3. See H. W. Stanley and R. G. Niemi, *Vital Statistics on American Politics*, 2nd ed. (Congressional Quarterly, 1990), pp. 192–94.
4. Mezey, p. 37.
5. R. H. S. Crossman, "Introduction" to W. Bagehot, *The English Constitution* (Fontana, 1963 ed.), p. 39.
6. N. Polsby, "Legislatures" in F. I. Greenstein and N. Polsby (eds.), *Handbook of Political Science*, Vol. 5 (Addison-Wesley, 1975). See also P. Norton (ed.), *Legislatures* (Oxford University Press, 1990).
7. J. A. G. Griffith, *Parliamentary Scrutiny of Government Bills* (George Allen & Unwin, 1974), p. 93.
8. Ibid., p. 159.
9. G. Drewry, "Legislation," in M. Ryle and P. G. Richards (eds.), *The Commons Under Scrutiny* (Routledge, 1988), p. 135. See also D. Marsh and M. Read, *Private Members' Bills* (Cambridge University Press, 1987).
10. P. G. Richards, *Parliament and Conscience* (George Allen & Unwin, 1970).
11. R. L. Borthwick, "The Floor of the House," in Ryle and Richards, p. 57.
12. See P. Norton, *The Commons in Perspective* (Blackwell, 1981), pp. 111–14; and H. Irwin, "Opportunities for Backbenchers," in Ryle and Richards, pp. 77–82.
13. S. J. Downs, "The House of Commons: Structural Changes," in P. Norton (ed.), *Parliament in the 1980s* (Blackwell, 1985), pp. 53–54.
14. D. Shell, "Specialist Select Committees," *Parliamentary Affairs*, 23 (4), Autumn 1970, p. 380.
15. Figure calculated from series of written parliamentary answers on ministers' correspondence with members, July 1989. See generally P. Norton, "The Importance of MP-to-Minister Correspondence," *Parliamentary Affairs*, 35 (1), Winter 1982, pp. 59–72.
16. R. Jowell, S. Witherspoon, and L. Brook. "British Social Attitudes: The 1987 Report" (Gower, 1987).
17. B. Cain, J. Ferejohn, and P. Fiorina, "The Roots of Legislator Popularity in

Great Britain and the United States," *California Institute of Technology: Social Science Working Paper 288*, October 1979, p. 6.

18. See Norton, *Commons in Perspective*, pp. 115–17; H. B. Berrington, *Backbench Opinion in the House of Commons 1945–1955* (Pergamon Press, 1973); and S. E. Finer *et al.*, *Backbench Opinion in the House of Commons 1955–1959* (Pergamon, 1961).

19. S. H. Beer, *Modern British Politics* (Faber, 1969 ed.), p. 350.

20. P. Norton, *Conservative Dissidents* (Temple Smith, 1978), Ch. 9.

21. S. H. Beer, *Britain Against Itself* (Faber & Faber, 1982), p. 190.

22. P. Norton and D. Wood, "Constituency Service by Members of Parliament: Does It Contribute to a Personal Vote?" *Parliamentary Affairs*, 1990. See also B. Cain, J. Ferejohn, and M. Fiorina, *The Personal Vote* (Harvard University Press, 1987).

23. *Parliamentary Debates (Hansard)*, Vol. 188, cols. 1925–26 (1867).

24. See C. Grantham and C. M. Hodgson, "The House of Lords: Structural Changes," in Norton, *Parliament in the 1980s*, pp. 114–35.

25. The House appointed a select committee to discuss the issue and in two succeeding sessions passed a Bill of Rights. See P. Norton, *The Constitution In Flux* (Blackwell, 1982), p. 246.

26. N. Baldwin, "The House of Lords: Behavioural Changes," in Norton, *Parliament in the 1980s*, pp. 96–113.

27. J. Morgan, "The House of Lords in the 1980s," *The Parliamentarian*, 62 (1), January 1981, p. 18.

28. B. Crick, *The Reform of Parliament* (Weidenfeld & Nicolson, 1964).

29. S. E. Finer (ed.), *Adversary Politics and Electoral Reform* (Wigram, 1975); S. A. Walkland, "Whither the Commons?" in S. A. Walkland and M. Ryle (eds.), *The Commons Today* (Fontana, 1981), Ch. 12.

30. R. Butt, *The Power of Parliament* (Constable, 1967).

31. P. Norton, "The Norton View," in D. Judge (ed.), *The Politics of Parliamentary Reform* (Heinemann, 1983); Norton, *The Commons in Perspective*, Ch. 9.

32. Report of the Conservative Review Committee, *The House of Lords* (Conservative Central Office, 1978); and Report of the Constitutional Reform Committee of the Society of Conservative Lawyers, *House of Lords Reform?* (Macmillan, 1978).

33. Quoted in H. Hebert, "The Lords under the Microscope" *The Guardian*, March 1, 1979.

CHAPTER 12

The Monarchy
Strength through Weakness

In the United States, the head of state is the president. In the United Kingdom, the head of state is the monarch. Both fulfill certain formal duties associated with the position. Beyond that there is little similarity between the two. In terms of history, determination of incumbency, powers, and current responsibilities, the United States presidency and the British monarchy have virtually nothing in common. The president is both head of state and political head of the administration. He operates directly and personally at the heart of the political decision-making process. The monarch, as head of state, stands above political decision making. In political terms, he or she serves not to decide but primarily to perform a symbolic role. The president serves by virtue of election; the monarch reigns by virtue of birth.

The monarchy is the oldest secular institution in Britain. It predates Parliament by some four centuries and the law courts by three centuries. The present monarch is able to trace her descent from King Egbert, who united England under his rule in 829 A.D. The continuity of the institution has been broken only once, during the period of military rule by Oliver Cromwell. There have been various interruptions in the direct line of succession, but the hereditary principle has been preserved since at least the eleventh century. The succession itself is governed by certain principles of common law and by statute. The throne descends to the eldest son, or in the absence of a son, the eldest daughter. By the Act of Settlement of 1700, affirmed by the Treaty of Union in 1707, the Crown was to descend to the heirs of the granddaughter of James I, Princess Sophia; this line has been confirmed by later acts.[1]

For several centuries, there was no separation of powers: executive, legislative, and judicial power was exercised by the king. With the growth of Parliament (and its power of the purse) as well as the courts, the direct exercise of these functions progressively declined. As we have seen (Chapter 3), the conflict between King and Parliament in the seventeenth century resulted in the Settlement of 1688 and the establishment of what was essentially a limited constitutional monarchy. The monarch nonetheless remained at the head of government, in practice as well as formally. Those responsible for the Bill of Rights of 1689 wanted "a real, working, governing king, a king with a policy,"[2] albeit a king governing with the consent of Parliament. The centrality of the monarch to governing was to decline in the eighteenth century with the king's increasing dependence on his ministers. During this century, one can see the divorce of the positions of head of state and political head of government, formerly united in the person of the king. The former remained with the king, the latter in practice became vested in his chief minister. The withdrawal of the monarch largely but by no means exclusively from active participation in political life was to be a marked feature of the succeeding century. Queen Victoria's reign (1837–1901) marked the transition from a monarch still active in political life to one fulfilling primarily a formal role, part of what Bagehot had identified as the "dignified" part of the Constitution.[3] The twentieth century has realized the move toward a politically neutral monarchy, standing now well removed from the partisan fray of party government.

The years since 1688 have witnessed various landmarks on this path toward a neutral monarchy divorced from active partisan decision making. The last occasion a monarch vetoed a piece of legislation was when Queen Anne did in 1707, the last time a monarch dismissed a ministry was in 1834, and the last occasion on which the monarch clearly exercised a personal choice in the selection of a prime minister was Queen Victoria's summoning Lord Rosebery in 1894. (Monarchs have on occasion subsequently had to exercise a choice in the selection of prime ministers but, as we shall see, have acted under advice.) The last monarch to attempt to veto cabinet appointments, with some measure of success, was Queen Victoria. She was also the last monarch to be instrumental in pushing successfully for the enactment of particular legislation: on at least two occasions she virtually initiated legislation, the 1874 Public Worship Regulation Act and the 1876 Royal Titles Act.[4] She may also be described as the last monarch to indulge, albeit within a limited circle, in partisan expression. Initially a Whig, she became for all intents and purposes a vehement Conservative; she clearly adored her Conservative prime minister, Disraeli, and made little secret of her utter disdain for the Liberal leader, William Gladstone. Partisan expression declined significantly under her successors. Indeed, according to Frank Hardie, this was a notable feature of the first half of the twentieth century: "Since 1901 the trend towards a real political neutrality, not merely a matter of appearances, has been steady, reign by reign."[5]

The result of these developments has been that twentieth-century monarchs have come to occupy a position in which they are called on to fulfill two primary tasks. One is to represent the unity of the nation. The other is to carry out certain political functions on the advice of ministers. The weakness of the monarch in being able to exercise independent decisions in the latter task has ensured the strength of the monarchy in fulfilling the first.

The Crown in Britain is the symbol of supreme executive authority. It serves essentially as a substitute for the concept of the State, a concept not well developed in Britain and one that has not made an impact on the national consciousness. The monarch is the person on whom the Crown is constitutionally conferred. Various public duties are carried out in the name of the Crown (for example, public prosecutions) and, as the person in whom the Crown vests, the monarch's name attaches to both government and the armed forces. The armed services are Her Majesty's Services. Her Majesty is Commander-in-Chief. People go to war to fight for "Queen and Country." The government is Her Majesty's government, ministers are Her Majesty's ministers. Even the Opposition in Parliament is titled Her Majesty's Loyal Opposition. Postage stamps and coins bear the Queen's image. (British postage stamps are unique: the monarch's head substitutes for the name of the nation.) The Queen personifies what for Americans is represented by the Stars and Stripes. The pageantry associated with the monarchy serves as a living expression of national unity. It provides the opportunity for citizens to indulge in that expression of unity and to escape from the drudgery of everyday life: it gives expression to pride in being British.

In order that the Queen may embody the unity of the nation, it is imperative that she not only abstain from partisan activity but be seen to abstain, indeed be seen to transcend political activity. The political functions she performs, such as the appointment of the prime minister, the appointment of ministers, the dispensing of honors, and the assent of legislation, are governed by convention. She acts on the advice of her ministers and is recognized as so acting. When the Queen's Speech is read from the throne on the opening of Parliament, the speech is handed to the Queen by the Lord Chancellor and subsequently handed back to him, signifying that it is the government's responsibility. Government is carried on in the name of the Queen and not by the Queen.

The formal exercise of political functions by the monarch serves a useful purpose. It provides a sense of duty for government (fulfilling duties as Her Majesty's ministers is a reminder that they are in office to perform a service to the nation) and it provides a significant sense of continuity. Governments may come and governments may go, but the Queen continues to reign. When Queen Elizabeth II ascended to the throne in 1952, Winston Churchill was prime minister. She has been served by eight separate prime ministers. By being the person to whom prime ministers submit their resignations and who summons the new premier, the monarch gives a sense of continuity, one that arguably could not be provided by any other form of head of state in a free society.

The continuity provided by the monarch has another and, from the perspective of government, very useful aspect. Each prime minister has a regular audience with the Queen, usually at least once a week when the sovereign is in London; under a practice initiated by Harold Macmillan, the PM sends in advance a list of points he or she would like to raise. The Queen receives the minutes of cabinet meetings and cabinet committee meetings. She also receives copies of all important Foreign and Commonwealth Office telegrams. According to her various prime ministers, she is an assiduous reader of all such papers. Apart from almost 40 years' experience of meeting with her prime ministers, the Queen is also head of the Commonwealth and has traveled extensively, building personal links with other heads of state. This experience she can and does bring to bear in her meetings with the prime minister, doing so in a nonpartisan context (raising issues in the form of questions) and in an environment where the prime minister does not have to deal with an opponent or political rival. The audience provides the premier with a unique opportunity, as Sir Ian Gilmour expressed it, "to explain decisions and policies to a disinterested observer in the fullest privacy."[6] Successive prime ministers have attested to the value of such meetings. According to Harold Macmillan, "the Queen was a great support, because she is the one person you can talk to."[7] Labour prime ministers Harold Wilson and James Callaghan expressed similar views. The only two prime ministers with whom relationships have reputedly been a little cool have been, ironically—given Conservative support for the monarchy—Conservatives Edward Heath and Margaret Thatcher; the Queen, according to some reports, was distressed at the strains Mrs. Thatcher's refusal to endorse sanctions against South Africa was placing on the Commonwealth. The Queen attaches much importance to her role as head of the Commonwealth; according to a 1988 Gallup poll, so do most of her subjects.[8]

Prime ministers have reason also be to grateful to the monarch for the fulfillment of various formal duties. In the United States, the president as head of state has to fulfill a number of time-consuming tasks, including receiving new ambassadors, presenting medals, and attending a number of formal nonpolitical functions. The president is not trained to carry out these tasks and the time given over to them is at the expense of time that could be used for running the administration. In Britain, the formal tasks are carried out by the monarch or, in some cases, by other members of the royal family. The physical distinction between head of state and head of government allows for ceremonial duties to be carried out by someone schooled for the task and eliminates the conflicting time demands faced by any political leader cum head of state.

By being scrupulously neutral in performing her duties, the Queen is able to fulfill her task of representing the unity of the nation. The hereditary principle in this context is a benefit rather than a hindrance. It helps provide a monarch prepared for the task, one free of the partisan implications that can inhere in the election of a head of state. A hereditary monarchy, as a number of observers have pointed out, serves also to prevent the growth of competing dynastic families. By fulfilling her duties in the way that she does, the Queen serves also to overcome any perceptions of incompatibility between a hereditary monarchy and a presumed democratic society. Indeed, there are those who see the monarch as fulfilling an essential role to protect democratic institutions. In the unlikely

TABLE 12.1. IMPORTANCE OF FUNCTIONS FULFILLED BY THE ROYAL FAMILY, 1988

Here are some possible functions of the Royal Family. Please tell me for each of them whether you think they are very important functions for the Royal Family, quite important, not very important or not at all important.

Response	Very	Quite	Not Very	Not at All	Don't Know
To represent the United Kingdom at home and abroad	67	25	4	2	1
To set a standard of good citizenship and family life	59	26	8	4	3
To maintain the continuity of British traditions whichever party is in government	51	34	9	3	2
To distract people from the real problems affecting the country	9	16	25	42	5
To preserve the class system in Britain	13	16	23	43	5
To unite the people despite their political, economic and class differences	52	30	8	6	4
To preserve a Christian morality in Britain	43	26	17	10	4
To ensure that the armed forces owe their allegiance to the Crown rather than to the government of the day	52	24	10	7	7

The poll was conducted in December 1988. *(Source:* Gallup Political Index, *Report No. 341, January 1989, p. 10.)*

event of an attempt to impose military or otherwise nondemocratic government, the monarch would be the most effective barrier to its realization. A monarch, as Gilmour observed, can engage the affections and loyalty of the armed forces more readily than can a president.[9] Almost paradoxically, the monarchy serves as a backstop, an ultimate safeguard, to protect those political institutions that have superseded it as the governing force in the United Kingdom.

The importance of these various functions has been variously recognized by the public. A 1988 Gallup Poll found that more than 80% of respondents judged the uniting, or figurehead, functions of the Queen to be very or quite important (Table 12.1). More than 70% attached importance to maintaining the political neutrality of the armed forces. Less than 30% considered important what have been described by some critics as essentially divisive functions: preserving the British class system and distracting people from the real problems of the country. There would appear to be, then, broad agreement on the monarch's functions. Debate on the monarchy is focused on other aspects.

THE CURRENT DEBATE

The main areas of debate concerning the monarchy have been those essentially of (1) its existence, (2) its cost, and (3) the monarch's exercise of certain political powers not clearly governed by convention. The first two are the products of criticism, the third of speculation.

Existence of the Monarchy

The continued existence of the monarchy has been challenged by various politicians and writers. The institution has been attacked as anachronistic, undemocratic, costly, and a bastion of privilege and conservatism, indefensible in a democratic age. Various Labour MPs have put the case for abolition as, more recently, have writers Tom Nairn, in *The Enchanted Glass—Britain and Its Monarchy* (1988), and Edgar Wilson, in *The Myth of British Monarchy* (1989). To Wilson, the various arguments put forward to support the monarchy are essentially myths, generated in order to justify the existing order. Far from being neutral, he contends that the institution is arbitrary "and exercises a pernicious influence."[10] Such critics believe that the necessary functions fulfilled by the Queen as head of state could be equally well fulfilled by an elected president. A number of Labour MPs have expressed support for a presidential system, albeit one based on the lines of the West German rather than the American model—that is, they favor separate election of the head of state and the head of government.

Most countries in the world have a nonhereditary head of state. So, they ask, why not Britain?

Supporters of the monarchy have defended it on the grounds that it enjoys popular support, is efficient, and performs functions that could not be carried out as well (or at all) by an elected or nominated head of state. The survey data make clear that the monarchy enjoys popular support. The 1988 Gallup poll found that 82% of respondents were in favor of the monarchy as it currently existed (Table 12.2). When the question was put another way—"Would you prefer an elected Head of State, such as a President, to an hereditary king or queen?"—80% said they preferred a hereditary king or queen. A Gallup Poll in 1973 had elicited the same response. A MORI poll in January 1989 suggested a slightly different picture. Though a majority of respondents felt that Britain would be worse off if the monarchy was abolished, the proportion was down from 1984 (from 77% to 58%); those feeling it would make no difference rose from 16% to 34%. However, believing it will make no difference is not the same as supporting change. Only 7% of respondents—up from 5% in 1984—felt that the country would be better off with an elected head of state.[11]

An elected head of state, according to defenders of the existing system, could not perform the uniting task as well as the Queen—in part because election would be potentially divisive and in part because he or she would not have been prepared for the office in the way that members of the royal family are. The Queen stands above political activity in a way that others are unlikely to be able to emulate, and her experience would be difficult to match, especially by presidents serving for fixed terms of office. For defenders, the pageantry—and in the eyes of some, the romance—of the monarchy is a positive rather than a negative aspect of its existence, contributing to a sense of pride in the nation. According to Harold Macmillan, who took a romanticized view of the monarchy, replacing the

TABLE 12.2. ATTITUDES TOWARD THE MONARCHY, 1988

Q: Would you describe yourself as in favour of or against the Monarchy as it exists at present, with the Queen as Head of State, acting on the advice of the Government?

Response	%
Favour	82
Against	14
Don't Know	5

The survey was conducted in December 1988. *(Source:* Gallup Political Index, *Report No. 341, January 1989, p. 10.)*

Queen with a president would be disastrous. He expressed himself in characteristic style:

> Imagine if at this moment, instead of the Queen, we had a gentleman in evening clothes, ill-made, probably from Moss Bros., with a white tie, going about everywhere, who had been elected by some deal made between the extreme Right and the extreme Left . . . ! Then we would all wait for the next one, another little man, who is it going to be? . . . "Give it to 'X,' you know he's been such a bad Chancellor of the Exchequer, instead of getting rid of him, let's make him the next President. . . ." Can you imagine it? I mean, it doesn't make sense, that would be the final destruction of colour and life and the sense of the past in this country, wouldn't it . . .?[12]

Critics would respond that Macmillan's analysis has not necessarily been borne out by experience elsewhere. The response of supporters of the monarchy would doubtless be that Britain is not "elsewhere."

The Cost of Monarchy

More substantial criticisms have been leveled at the cost of the monarchy. Expenditure for the exercise of the Queen's public duties is met from the Civil List.[13] This covers such items as staff costs, the upkeep of royal residences, the cost of state dinners and other functions, and transportation to official functions. Provision is also made for the expenses incurred in fulfilling public duties by other members of the royal family to be met from public funds. (The exception is Prince Charles, the Prince of Wales, whose income derives from the Duchy of Cornwall.)[14] When other costs are included that are not covered by the Civil List but paid instead by government departments, such as maintenance costs of royal castles and of aircraft of the Queen's Flight, the annual public expenditure on the monarchy exceeds £20 million ($33 million). This expenditure has been criticized on a number of grounds. One is that, in absolute terms, it is too high, certainly by comparison with what it would cost to maintain an elected president. The 1988 Gallup Poll found the public divided on the cost (Table 12.3). Though half of the respondents felt the expenditure was "about right," 40% thought it was too much. A second criticism is that the country does not get particular value for money from certain members of the royal family, especially junior members. The 1989 MORI poll found that senior members such as the Queen, Prince Charles, and Princess Anne were judged to be hard-working and cost effective. However, when asked which two or three members of the royal family represented the worst value for money to the British taxpayer, 37% of respondents identified

TABLE 12.3. ATTITUDES TOWARD COST OF THE MONARCHY, 1988

Q: Last year £5.25 million was spent on supporting the Royal Family in their public functions. Do you think that this is too much, too little or about right?

Response	%
Too much	40
Too little	4
About right	51
Don't know	5

The survey was conducted in December 1988. The £5.25 million referred to was the amount provided under the Civil List. (*Source:* Gallup Political Index, *Report No. 341, January 1989, p. 10.*)

Sarah, Duchess of York, and 23% identified her husband, Prince Andrew. The Queen's sister, Princess Margaret, came third (identified by 14%), closely followed by the Queen's youngest son, Prince Edward (13%).[15] Various critics have argued for such royals, variously described as "hangers on," to be removed from the Civil List and to be dependent on earned income. A third criticism is that the expenditure is not necessary given the Queen's personal wealth. The Queen is one of the richest women in the world. (*Fortune* magazine in 1987 estimated her wealth to be in the region of £4.5 billion—more than $7 billion.) Her wealth and income are not subject to taxation. Labour critics in particular have argued that the Queen should pay taxes and/or use her personal wealth to help maintain the monarchy. In support of this view, 91 Labour MPs in 1975 voted against an increase in the Civil List.

Defenders of the monarchy point out that much of the Queen's wealth is in the form of national assets, not realizable in cash terms and held in trust for the nation. Furthermore, they argue, if one takes into account income from Crown Lands (surrendered to the state by the monarchy in return for regular provision under the Civil List) as well as the intangible benefits that accrue from having a monarch rather than a president (for example, increased tourism and international goodwill), then the country makes a net profit from the institution. Furthermore, increases in the Civil List, often referred to as the "Queen's pay rises," are usually to meet increased staff costs. Whether serving a monarch or a president, employees have to be paid. In 1975 the then Chancellor of the Exchequer, Denis Healey, pointed out that the total annual expenditure by the Exchequer or the taxpayer on the monarchy was about equal to the cost of holding one general election.[16] The prevailing opinion would (just) appear to be that, on balance, the expenditure is justified.

The Exercise of Political Powers

The debate surrounding those powers of the Queen not clearly governed by convention is of a different nature. As we have seen, the exercise of most of the political powers vested in the monarch is governed largely by convention. In most cases, this entails the Queen's acting on the advice of her ministers. However, certain important powers remain vested in the monarch that on occasion may require a choice among alternative options, a choice not clearly dictated by convention. The most obvious and important power involved here is that of choosing a prime minister.

It is a convention of the constitution that the Queen will select as prime minister that person whom she considers capable of ensuring a majority in the House of Commons. In practice, this usually creates no problems. If a party obtains an overall majority in a general election, the Queen summons the leader of that party. But what happens if there is no party leader to be summoned or if no party is returned with an overall majority at a general election? The first possibility no longer faces the Queen, though until recently it did. Until 1965, the Conservative party had no formal mechanism for choosing a leader. The leader was expected to "emerge" following soundings of one sort or another within the party. In the event of a Conservative prime minister's retiring with no successor immediately apparent, or with different contenders for the succession, the choice was left to the monarch. In 1957 the Queen was faced with summoning someone to succeed Sir Anthony Eden as prime minister. After consulting with senior statesmen, she sent for Harold Macmillan instead of, as many assumed she would, R. A. Butler. In 1963 she was confronted with the difficult task of appointing a prime minister in succession to Macmillan. After taking the advice of her outgoing prime minister, she summoned Lord Home (or Sir Alec Douglas-Home, as he quickly became after renouncing his title in order to seek a seat in the House of Commons). The choice was a controversial one[17] and, though the decision was essentially that of Macmillan, it embroiled the Crown in political controversy. The prospect of any repetition was avoided when the Conservative party in 1964 introduced a procedure for the election of the party leader. The party was thus in a position to elect a leader and avoid the Queen's having to make a selection on its behalf.

The second possibility, a party having no overall majority, is one over which many commentators have mused in recent years. What should the Queen do in the event of no party having a parliamentary majority? If the Conservatives were returned at a future election with a plurality of seats but not an absolute majority, and the third party holding the balance of power refused to support the Conservatives under their existing leader, what should the Queen do? Should she summon a Conservative who would be acceptable to that third party, or should she automatically summon the leader of the second largest party in the House? There is no clear convention to guide the Queen. She would be saddled, as David Watt observed, "with a highly controversial and thankless responsibility."[18] It is one she would almost certainly prefer to do without.

One other power that has produced a similar debate is the power to dissolve Parliament. The usual practice is for the prime minister to recommend a dissolution to the Queen and for Her Majesty to accede to the request. There is some doubt, though, as to whether it is considered a convention for the Queen automatically to concede a dissolution. Various hypothetical circumstances have been postulated to demonstrate a case for not considering it such a convention. In the event of a cabinet's breaking up (possibly after two general elections in close succession) and the prime minister's preference for a dissolution rather than a coalition with another party being opposed by most ministers, would the Queen be justified in withholding her consent to her prime minister's request? Lord Blake has argued that in such or similar circumstances the Queen would not be obliged to grant a dissolution.[19] When the Tribune Group, a group of Labour MPs, argued in 1974 that the prime minister had an absolute right to determine the date of an election, a senior minister responded, "Constitutional lawyers of the highest authority are of the clear opinion that the Sovereign is not in all circumstances bound to grant a Prime Minister's request for a dissolution."[20] The problem is one of determining the circumstances that would justify the Queen's denying a dissolution, and whether, whatever the circumstances, such an action could be taken without seriously damaging the Queen's reputation for being above the partisan fray. "For the monarch," wrote Kingsley Martin, "the only safe rule is always to follow the Premier's advice."[21] If that rule were to be accepted as a convention, it would strengthen rather than weaken the position of the Queen. As we have seen, any involvement, however unwilling, in the political fray could jeopardize the ability of the monarchy to fulfill its central role of embodying the unity of the nation.

One alternative, recommended by Labour MP Tony Benn, is for the power of dissolution (indeed, all prerogative powers) to be transferred to the Speaker of the House of Commons.[22] This, Benn noted, would avoid the Queen's being drawn into the heart of political debate, transferring instead the power to someone who "knows the Commons intimately and is therefore specially qualified to reach a judgment about the appropriate moment for granting a dissolution and who is most likely to command a majority."[23] The recommendation has been variously rejected, some critics of Mr. Benn viewing it as a disguised attempt to take a step on the road of abolishing the monarchy altogether.[24] Others have argued that it would unnecessarily reduce the Queen to a limited figurehead role, since there was no instance of a modern monarch actually abusing the prerogative powers. It is assumed that the hypothetical situation of one political crisis is insufficient to justify such a constitutionally radical move.

CONCLUSION

The Queen fulfills the task of representing the unity of the nation as well as carrying out certain political functions largely but not exclusively governed by convention. Her role as a political actor is circumscribed, necessarily so in order for her to fulfill her unifying role, and any real choice she is called on to exercise in political decision making is the product of circumstances and unclear conventions and not of any personal desire on her part. The monarchy occupies a central position in the British polity, a valuable one in embodying the unity of the nation, and a formal but nonetheless necessary one in fulfilling certain political duties. In the eyes of some, it is the most efficient element of the constitution. It is also the most popular.

NOTES

1. This paragraph is based on *The Monarchy in Britain*, Central Office of Information Reference Pamphlet 118 (Her Majesty's Stationery Office, 1975), p. 1.
2. F. W. Maitland, *Constitutional History of England*, quoted in H. V. Wiseman (ed.), *Parliament and the Executive* (Routledge and Kegan Paul, 1966), p. 5.
3. W. Bagehot, *The English Constitution* (Fontana, 1963 ed.), p. 61.
4. F. Hardie, *The Political Influence of the British Monarchy 1868–1952* (Batsford, 1970), p. 67.
5. Ibid., p. 188.
6. I. Gilmour, *The Body Politic*, rev. ed. (Hutchinson, 1970), p. 317.
7. A. Horne, *Macmillan*, Vol. II: 1957–1986 (Macmillan, 1989), p. 168.
8. A Gallup poll in December 1988 found that 82% of respondents judged the Queen's role as head of the Commonwealth to be very or fairly valuable. *Gallup Political Index*, Report No. 341, January 1989, p. 9.
9. Gilmour, p. 313.
10. E. Wilson, *The Myth of British Monarchy* (Journeyman/Republic, 1989), p. 178.
11. *British Public Opinion*, February 1989, p. 5.
12. Quoted in Horne, pp. 170–71.
13. Private expenditure as sovereign, such as gifts to visiting dignitaries, is met from the Privy Purse (the income from the Duchy of Lancaster), and personal expenditure as an individual, such as wedding or Christmas gifts, is met from the Queen's personal wealth.

14. Prince Charles, among other titles, is Duke of Cornwall, and the Duchy encompasses a number of revenue-generating estates.
15. *British Public Opinion*, February 1989, p. 5.
16. *House of Commons Debates* (*Hansard*), Vol. 887, col. 628.
17. See R. Churchill, *The Fight for the Tory Leadership* (Heinemann, 1964); I. Macleod, "The Tory Leadership," *Spectator*, January 17, 1964; and P. Norton and A. Aughey, *Conservatives and Conservatism* (Temple Smith, 1981), pp. 243–45.
18. D. Watt, "If the Queen Has to Choose, Who Will It Be?" *The Times*, December 11, 1981.
19. Lord Blake, *The Office of Prime Minister* (Oxford University Press, 1975), pp. 60–61.
20. E. Short, quoted in Blake, p. 60.
21. K. Martin, *The Crown and the Establishment* (Penguin, 1963).
22. *New Socialist*, August 1982. Reported in *The Daily Telegraph*, August 27, 1982.
23. Ibid.
24. Editorial, *The Sunday Express*, August 28, 1982.

PART V

Enforcement and Feedback

CHAPTER 13

Enforcement
The Courts and the Police

The United States Supreme Court, as one American expert observed, is neither a court nor a political agency: "it is inseparably both."[1] This special status derives from the court's power of constitutional interpretation, a power effectively read into the constitution by Chief Justice John Marshall in his opinion in *Marbury* v. *Madison* in 1803. "It is emphatically the province and duty of the judicial department," declared Marshall, "to say what the law is." The Constitution amounts to a paramount law and, in the event of the ordinary law conflicting with it, the Court must resolve the conflict: "This is of the very essence of judicial duty."[2]

The chief justice's reasoning did not go unquestioned.[3] Nonetheless, acceptance of the Court as the arbiter of constitutional disputes was underpinned by the Lockean philosophy inherent in American society[4] and has been reinforced by reasons of practicality (somebody has to perform the task) and of history (the judiciary has, in effect, always performed it). When Richard Nixon's attorney, James St. Clair, sought to argue in the case of *United States* v. *Nixon* (1974) that the president should interpret his own powers under the Constitution, he was more than one and a half centuries too late in putting forth such an argument. Acceptance of the Court's power of constitutional interpretation was too well established to be overthrown. The Court remains the judicial arbiter of a document that in inherently political and one that by its own declaration constitutes the supreme law of the land—hence the Court's dual and inseparable roles.

The position of the British judiciary in the political process is significantly different from that of its American counterpart. There are two principal reasons for this. For one thing, there are inherent difficulties in seeking to interpret a constitution whose boundaries are not clearly delineated. For another, the judiciary labors under the self-imposed doctrine of parliamentary sovereignty. The courts have no power to declare unconstitutional an act of Parliament. If the judicial interpretation of an act conflicts with the intentions of Parliament, a new act may be passed making explicit Parliament's wishes: the courts are duty-bound to enforce the new act. The last word, in short, rests with Parliament.

These difficulties are crucial to an understanding of the American and British courts. They serve to explain why the United States Supreme Court (indeed, the United States judiciary, given that any court can declare an act unconstitutional) may be deemed to form part of the political decision-making process in the United States, whereas the judiciary would not form part of that process in Britain. Nonetheless, such differences should not be overstated. A number of caveats need to be entered to the distinctions that have just been drawn.

On the American side, it is important to record that the Supreme Court will decide a case on the basis of constitutional interpretation only where it cannot be resolved by statutory interpretation. A random sample of cases in a 60-year period (1912–1972) reveals that only a minority of cases are resolved by resorting to constitutional interpretation.[5] The Court itself will seek to avoid, especially on grounds of nonjusticiability, those cases it considers to be political. Nor is it free of the constraints imposed by other political bodies. Congress can limit, and on occasion has limited (as in the instance of *Ex Parte McCardle*), the Court's appellate jurisdiction. The Court itself is dependent on the executive for the enforcement of its decisions. While it may seek either to give a lead to or to restrain the actions of Congress or the president, it will rarely beat a path too far ahead or too far behind what is politically acceptable. And in practice it has rarely struck down federal legislation. Up to 1985, only 134 or 135 provisions of federal law were struck down as unconstitutional, and this was out of a total of some 91,000 public and private laws passed.[6] (The Court was somewhat more active in striking down state law.) Although the power to strike down a measure serves as "an omnipresent and potentially omnipotent check upon the legislative branches of government," it is a power that, as Henry Abraham observed, "courts are understandably loathe to invoke."[7]

On the British side, the courts retain the power of statutory—and common law—interpretation and can determine, in any case brought before them, whether the purported exercise of a power is authorized by law. As a result, the executive actions of ministers and administrative authorities can, when challenged, come within their purview. The determination of the courts in such cases can always be overridden by a new act of Parliament authorizing that which the courts have struck down, but by having to determine such cases, the courts are brought into the political limelight. This relative prominence has been especially evident in recent years, when the higher judiciary has been active in reviewing a number of important executive actions. Furthermore, British entry into the European Community has added a new judicial dimension to the Constitution. The 1972 European Communities Act provided that, in the event of a conflict between the provisions of EC law and domestic law, the former was to prevail. Section 3(1) of the act provided that any disputes as to the interpretation, effect, and validity of the EC Treaties, or of any legislation made under them, was to be treated by British judges as a matter of law. Cases that reached the House of Lords (the highest domestic court of appeal) had, under the provisions of the Rome Treaty, to be referred to the Court of Justice of the European Communities for a definitive ruling, and lower courts could request that the European Court make a ruling on the meaning and interpretation of the treaties. The act created a new role for the British judiciary.

The British judiciary clearly cannot be described as standing divorced totally from the political fray. Nonetheless, despite the foregoing qualifications, the basic difference between the United States and British courts remains. Courts in the United States have the power, however rarely exercised it might be, to strike down legislative measures and executive actions as unconstitutional. British courts have no such power, however much they might like to have it. It is this fundamental difference that explains why United States courts are accorded a more prominent place in analyses of American politics than is the case with British politics. In studies of British politics, the judiciary constitutes but a marginal consideration.

THE JUDICIAL SYSTEM

The administration of justice is one of the prerogatives of the Crown, but it is a prerogative that has long been exercisable only through duly appointed courts and judges. Apart from a number of specialized courts and various tribunals, the basic organizational division within the court system is that between criminal and civil. There is no such distinction in the United States court system. A simplified outline of the court system in England and Wales is provided in Figure 13.1. (Scotland and Northern Ireland have different systems.) The Court of Appeal, the Crown Court, and the High Court together constitute what is known (confusingly, from the perspective

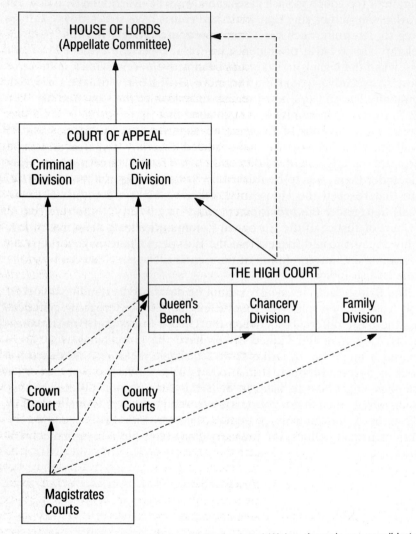

Figure 13.1. The Court System in England and Wales. Appeals are possible to higher courts as shown by arrows, usually through the immediate superior court or, in certain cases (shown by dotted lines), through another route. Tribunals and specialist courts are omitted.

of the American student) as the Supreme Court. At the apex of the structure sits the House of Lords.

Criminal Cases

Minor criminal cases are tried summarily in magistrates' courts. The courts, presided over by unpaid lay magistrates (except in the case of one or two of the largest cities, which have legally qualified, full-time, paid magistrates known as stipendiary magistrates), have the power to levy fines and, depending on the offense, impose a prison sentence not exceeding six months. Stipendiary magistrates sit alone. Lay magistrates sit in a bench of between two and seven and are normally advised on legal points by the legally qualified clerk of the court. Cases dealt with by magistrates cover such matters as motoring offenses, assault charges, and offenses against public order (for example, breach of the peace). The courts also have a limited civil jurisdiction, primarily in matrimonial proceedings, and have semiadministrative functions in the licensing of public houses, betting shops, and clubs.

For many years magistrates' courts were linked closely with the police. Until 1952, magistrates' courts in London were known as police courts and were often attached to police stations. Until 1986, the decision whether to prosecute—and the prosecution itself—was undertaken by the police. Since October 1986, responsibility for the independent review and prosecution of all criminal cases instituted by police forces in England and Wales has, with certain exceptions, rested with the Crown Prosecution Service (CPS), headed by the Director of Public Prosecutions (the DPP). (In Scotland, responsibility for prosecution rests with the Crown Office and Procurator Fiscal Service.) Members of the CPS are lawyers, but since the inception of the service, difficulties have been experienced in recruiting a sufficient number of well-qualified staff; private practice is more lucrative.

In 1987–1988 the CPS dealt with some 1.5 million defendants in magistrates' courts. More than nine out of every ten cases are heard and determined by magistrates, a total of about 2 million cases a year. Appeals from magistrates' courts are possible to the Crown Court or, in certain cases, to the High Court (to the Queen's Bench Division on points of law and to the Family Division in matrimonial cases). Serious criminal cases—indictable offenses—are tried before a jury in the Crown Court. In 1987–1988 the CPS proceeded against some 135,000 defendants in the Crown Court. The Crown Court has nearly 100 centers, divided into six court circuits. Cases are heard either by a High Court judge (who will normally preside over the most serious cases), a Circuit judge, or a Recorder. Circuit judges are full-time, salaried judges; recorders are part-time and salaried, and when not presiding at court, they pursue their normal legal practice. Judges and recorders are legally qualified and to be eligible for appointment must have practiced for at least ten years as either solicitors or barristers.

Appeals from the Crown Court may be taken on a point of law to the Queen's Bench Division of the High Court but usually are taken to the Criminal Division of the Court of Appeal. Appeals against conviction are possible on points of law (as of right) and on a question of fact (with the leave of the trial judge or Court of Appeal). The Appeal Court may quash a conviction or uphold it: it can also vary the sentence imposed by the lower court. Appeals against sentence, if not a sentence fixed by law, are also possible with the leave of the Appeal Court. Since February 1989 the power has existed (and been used) for the Attorney–General to refer to the court those sentences that appear to the prosecuting authorities to be unduly lenient. The Criminal Division of the Appeal Court comprises a presiding judge, known as the Lord Chief Justice; 27 Lords Justices of Appeal; and a number of *ex officio* members. Three members of the court normally sit to hear a case.

From the Court of Appeal, an appeal to the House of Lords is possible if the court certifies that a point of law of general public importance is involved and it appears to the court or the House that the point ought to be considered by the highest court of appeal. For judicial purposes, the House of Lords does not comprise all members of the House. Instead, the task is undertaken by an appellate committee that will comprise usually five but sometimes as many as seven peers drawn from the Lord Chancellor, Lords of Appeal in Ordinary (life peers appointed for the purpose of undertaking such tasks), and such peers as hold or have previously held high judicial office. The committee meets in a Committee Room of the House of Lords, though its judgment will still be delivered in the full chamber. In 1966 the Lords of Appeal in Ordinary announced that they would no longer consider themselves bound by their previous decisions, and the House is now prepared to depart from a previous decision when it appears right to do so.

Civil Cases

In civil proceedings, minor cases involving small sums of money are heard by county courts, of which there are 274; more important cases go to the High Court. The High Court comprises the Queen's Bench Division, covering mainly matters of common law; the Chancery Division, dealing mainly with equity cases; and the Family Division, for cases of divorce and custody. County courts are presided over by Circuit judges. The High Court comprises the Lord Chief Justice, who presides over the Queen's Bench Division; the Lord Chancellor, who is nominally president of the

Chancery Court but who' never sits (a vice-chancellor, in practice, presides); the President of the Family Division; and up to a total of 75 judges known as Puisne (pronounced *puny*) judges. In civil cases the judges normally sit alone, though a Divisional Court of two or more judges may be formed, especially in the Queen's Bench Division, which has important responsibilities in the issuing of writs of habeas corpus and orders of mandamus, certiorari, and prohibition. Like other senior judicial posts, Puisne judges are appointed from among eminent lawyers of long standing.

Appeals in certain instances may go to the High Court. Appeals from county courts in bankruptcy cases are heard by a Divisional Court of the Chancery Division. Appeals against the decisions of magistrates' courts in matrimonial proceedings are heard by a Divisional Court of the Family Division. And appeals on points of law may be taken from a magistrate's court to a Divisional Court of the Queen's Bench Division.

Appeals from county courts (those not going to the High Court) and from the High Court go to the Civil Division of the Court of Appeal—presided over by the Master of the Rolls—and from there may go to the House of Lords. In exceptional cases—on a point of law of exceptional difficulty calling for a reconsideration of a binding precedent—an appeal may go directly (with the leave of the House) from the High Court to the House of Lords. In the instance of European Community law, any case that reaches the House of Lords must, under the provisions of the 1972 European Communities Act, be referred to the Court of the European Communities for a definitive ruling.

The Judiciary

Concerning the judiciary itself—its recruitment, appointment, and relationship to and with the executive—a number of important points are deserving of mention. Magistrates' courts, with the exception of those presided over by stipendiary magistrates, are staffed by lay magistrates, known as Justices of the Peace, of which there are currently almost 28,000. These magistrates are not legally qualified, though they do now receive some basic training; they are usually prominent local citizens and are appointed by the Lord Chancellor. Any citizen can recommend the name of an individual for appointment as a magistrate, though in practice, recommendations tend to come from local political parties and civic bodies.

Above the level of magistrates are the legally qualified judges, who are drawn from the ranks of the legal profession. Lawyers in Britain are divided into solicitors and barristers; there is no equivalent distinction in the United States. (There are also far fewer lawyers per head of population in Britain than in the United States.)[8] A solicitor is a lawyer who undertakes ordinary legal business for clients. A barrister gives expert legal advice to solicitors and their clients and conducts cases in court. Barristers have enjoyed an exclusive right to appear before certain courts; under proposals announced by the Lord Chancellor in 1989, solicitors are also to enjoy certain rights of audience. There is statutory provision as to how long one must have served as a solicitor or barrister before being eligible for appointment as a judge. Usually, judges are drawn from the ranks of barristers (occasionally a solicitor is appointed as a recorder, but none has been appointed to higher judicial office) and have generally been in legal practice for longer than the minimum period required. Those appointed are regarded as the outstanding members of their profession. The status of a judge is superior to that of a judge in the United States. Elevation to judicial office is regarded as a step up the professional ladder, something to be sought after, rather than a position one settles for if unable to establish oneself as a leading corporate lawyer.

Although judges are recruited from the ranks of well-qualified lawyers and are usually appointed or promoted on the basis of legal merit, their appointment is made by members of the executive branch. Formally, all judges are appointed by the Crown. By convention, senior judicial appointments, those above the level of Puisne judges, are made by the Crown on the advice of the prime minister. Other judicial appointments are made by the Crown on the advice of the Lord Chancellor. In making recommendations, the prime minister will usually consult the Lord Chancellor. It is rare for judicial appointments to be the subject of political controversy, although that has been known to happen.[9] Such appointments are not subject to any form of parliamentary approval.

The method of appointment of judges, coupled with the unusual position of the Lord Chancellor and of certain senior judges, may raise doubts as to the independence of the judiciary. The Lord Chancellor is living proof that the separation of personnel exercised in the United States between branches of government is not rigidly adhered to in the United Kingdom. The Lord Chancellor is a member of the cabinet, he presides over the House of Lords (though his position as presiding officer is not dissimilar to that of the vice president with relation to the Senate in the United States),[10] and he is the head of the judiciary. He not only advises the Crown on the appointment of judges and magistrates, he also is himself a judge, as Lord Chancellor. He is a member of the appellate committee of the House of Lords and, if he takes part in hearing an appeal, which sometimes he does, then he presides. Furthermore, he is not the only person in government who occupies a position in the judicial hierarchy. The positions of Attorney-General and Solicitor-General, as well as those of Law Officers for Scotland (Lord Advocate and Solicitor-General for

Scotland), are political appointments and form part of the government. Also, the Lords of Appeal in Ordinary are life peers. As members of the House of Lords, they are free to take part in parliamentary proceedings.

Despite this overlap, and despite the ability of Parliament to overrule the courts through new legislation, the judiciary in Britain is independent. This independence is achieved in a number of ways, by statute, common law, parliamentary rules, and an acceptance by government that the rule of law requires abstention from interference with the conduct of litigation. Judges of superior courts (the High Court and above, with the exception of the Lord Chancellor) cannot be removed except for misbehavior in office, and their salaries are fixed by statute in order to avoid annual debate. They serve in office until they reach a statutory retiring age of 75 years. They enjoy immunity from civil proceedings for anything said or done while acting in a judicial capacity. Judges of lower courts are also immune if acting within their jurisdiction. By custom, questions are not asked in either House of Parliament about the conduct of courts in particular cases, reference may not be made in debate to matters awaiting or under adjudication before the courts (*sub judice* rules also prevent media comment on pending cases), and reflections may not be cast in debate upon the character or motives of a judge. Judges are not eligible for election to the House of Commons, and those who are members of the House of Lords, with the obvious exception of the Lord Chancellor, abstain from party political activities.

Two authors have suggested that another fact that promotes judicial independence is that judges "are all drawn from the bar after successful careers as barristers, a profession which tends to foster self-confidence and independence of mind."[11] Also, service as a judge is not seen as a stepping-stone to other things. One makes a career in the law, a career in which one's standing with colleagues and superiors is important and is essentially independent of partisan implications.

The degree to which judicial independence has been maintained is reflected in the fact that since judges of superior courts were accorded security of tenure under the Act of Settlement of 1700, only one judge has been removed from office—an Irish judge in 1830. He was found to have misappropriated money belonging to litigants and to have ceased to perform his judicial duties many years previously![12] In 1973, 180 Labour MPs signed a motion calling for the dismissal of the judge who presided over the new (and, in the event, short-lived) National Industrial Relations Court, a Court regarded by the MPs as a political court set up to restrain the trade unions. The motion wase never debated and it was very much the exception that proved the rule.

Although, as we shall see, the judiciary has not been free of criticism, the principle of judicial independence is a feature of the British Constitution and, in interpreting and applying the law, judges are generally more skilled and better regarded than their American counterparts (especially those that serve in the state courts) and maintain probably a greater degree of judicial decorum in the proceedings before them. The rules and ethics of the legal profession also prevent much of the degrading touting for business by lawyers that is a feature of many American courts.[13]

Nonetheless, some of the problems experienced by the American judicial system find reflection, albeit not quite on such a grand or obvious scale, in Britain. The use of plea bargaining generates similar problems.[14] There are delays in bringing defendants to trial. In London the average wait between committal and trial is 20 weeks. Although there are now various schemes, including legal advice centers, to provide advice to less well-off individuals, the cost of legal advice and various legal services (not least some straightforward legal services on which solicitors enjoy a monopoly) is a problem for many citizens.[15] For those citizens involved in lawsuits, it can be an expensive business.

THE CURRENT DEBATE

During the course of the past decade or so, the judiciary has on occasion entered the political limelight. This activity has been occasioned, on one hand, by the exercise of power already vested in the courts and, on the other, by various calls for the judges to be vested with new powers. The powers exercised and the powers proposed have implications for the maintenance of political authority.

The courts have the power to review executive actions to determine whether they are carried out within the limits of the relevant authorizing act. If the action is deemed by the courts to be *ultra vires* (beyond the powers), it is void. A court may also declare void an action if it deems that the principles of natural justice have not been observed or if the action has entailed the abuse or unreasonable exercise of power. The power to declare an action *ultra vires* is a corollary of the principle of parliamentary sovereignty. The power to void an action for failing to observe the principles of natural justice is derived from common law. Until the 1960s, neither power was much used. In part, this may have been due to the realization that the executive dominated the legislature and could thus obtain legitimation of past or proposed actions; it may concomitantly have been due to a lack of will on the part of judges. They were, and more recently have been, accused of not being too sympathetic to the claims of the individual when those claims were pitted against the demands of government. Denied the power to question acts of Parliament and unwilling to exercise their powers over acts of the executive, few judicial decisions entered the realms of controversy. This was to change beginning in the mid-1960s.

Professor John Griffith has referred to "the emergence of a period of judicial activism or intervention which began in the early 1960s and has been growing in strength every since."[16] A number of judges, apparently concerned about the encroachment of executive power in the field of individual liberties, became more assertive in the exercise of their common-law power to review the executive actions of ministers and administrative authorities. In four cases during the 1960s, the courts adopted an activist line in reviewing the exercise of powers by administrative bodies and, in two instances, by ministers.[17] The courts have maintained their activist stance since that time, in a number of controversial cases holding that ministers have exceeded their powers. Thus, for example, a 1981 decision by the environment secretary to reduce the central government grant to certain London boroughs was quashed by the High Court on the grounds that he had failed to listen to representations made late on behalf of the authorities and in so doing had not validly exercised his discretion under the provisions of the relevant act of Parliament. In 1985 a decision by the transport secretary to require the Greater London Council to pay £50 million to support the London Transport Authority set up in 1984 was quashed by the High Court. The government introduced legislation to reverse the court's decision. Cases involving ministerial actions have not been the only ones in which the courts have rendered politically contentious decisions. In 1981, in the *Greater London Council* (GLC) case, the Court of Appeal quashed an extra rate levied by the Labour-controlled GLC to pay for its policy of reducing fares on London Transport's bus and underground services: the court held the GLC's action to be an abuse of its powers and *ultra vires*. The court's judgment was upheld by the House of Lords.

The foregoing cases proved politically contentious not only for the holding of the courts in each case but also, in a number of instances, because of the *obiter dicta* (incidental remarks) of the judges. In particular, the comments of the Master of the Rolls, Lord Denning, in two cases provoked fears that the courts were seeking to usurp the functions of government and Parliament. In once case, Lord Denning declared that the Attorney-General's discretion to refuse consent to a particular action (a relator action) was not unfettered. If the Attorney-General takes into account things he should not take into account, or fails to take into account things he should, "then his decision can be overridden by the courts. Not directly, but indirectly."[18] In the *GLC* case, his Lordship declared that a manifesto issued by a political party (the Labour party had fought the GLC elections on a manifesto that included its cheap fares proposal) "was not to be regarded as a gospel. It was not a covenant."[19] His Lordship, declared

The Economist, was "demonstrating his popular thesis that judges are a higher form of animal than politicians."[20] Labour politicians were somewhat more disparaging.

In such cases, the exercise by the courts of their powers has brought them into the realms of political controversy. They have also entered the sphere of political debate as a consequence of proposals to extend their powers. As we have already mentioned, the European Communities Act of 1972 ensured a new judicial dimension to the British Constitution. Some politicians and jurists sought to extend that judicial dimension further through the enactment of a bill of rights.

Pressures for the enactment of a bill of rights, if possible with some degree of entrenchment (that is, with extraordinary provisions to limit the possibility of amendment), have built up since the latter half of the 1970s. Such a bill was initially advocated by some jurists and various Liberal and Conservative politicians, especially in the House of Lords. The case for it gained a boost in the late 1980s, when "Charter '88," a constitutional reform movement supported by well-known figures on the left, made a bill of rights a central feature of its manifesto. Advocates consider that Parliament is no longer capable of resisting the encroachment of government on rights previously considered inviolate. Britain, according to Lord Hailsham, labors under an "elective dictatorship."[21] If the rights of the individual are to be protected, some new means of protection is necessary to supplement or replace that provided inadequately by Parliament. The answer is deemed to lay in a bill of rights, that stipulates the rights of the individual, possibly a bill akin to that of the United States. Such a measure would then be subject to interpretation by the courts, which, if the bill enjoyed a degree of entrenchment, would be able to strike down conflicting measures as being contrary to its provisions. It is not axiomatic that the courts would enjoy such a power. Nonetheless, that is the clear intention of those who advocate the measure. They seek to put certain rights beyond the reach of government and place them into the care of the courts. Lord Scarman has imputed to society a wish for judges to defend the liberties of the individual from arbitrary acts of government.[22] "Let us keep in mind," he wrote in 1989, "that in a pluralist society many minorities have no real opportunity of acquiring political power and rely on the law's protection against oppression by the majority."[23]

Both the exercise of the power to review ministerial and administrative actions and the proposal for a judicially protected bill of rights have met with criticism from a number of sources. The actions of the courts in certain cases, and the *obiter dicta* of Lord Denning, have been taken to confirm the impression that judges are conservative in outlook and adhere to a restricted view of society. According to Griffith, the most senior judges "by their training and education and pursuit of their professions as barristers, acquired a strikingly homogeneous collection of attitudes, beliefs and principles, which to them represent the public interest."[24] The public interest is construed to favor law and order and the interests of the state (in time of perceived threat) over the rights of the individual, property rights over personal human rights, and, in Griffith's view, "the promotion of certain political views normally associated with the Conservative Party."[25] The latter, asserted Griffith, was reflected in cases involving trade unions, race relations, and the striking down of ministerial decisions during a period of Labour government. It is a view that has been reinforced by the *GLC* case of 1981 and by the *Ponting* case of 1985, in which the judge, Mr. Justice McCowan, interpreted the interests of the state to be whatever the government declared to be the interests of the state.

Such perceptions of the attitudes and actions of judges has fueled opposition to the introduction of a bill of rights. To an American weaned on an entrenched bill of rights interpreted by independent magistrates, opposition to an entrenched bill of rights is difficult to comprehend. Britain, however, lacks those characteristics that have underpinned the American's acceptance of constitutional interpretation by the United States Supreme Court. "Federalism apart," one analyst writes, "judicial review as it has worked in America would be inconceivable without the national acceptance of the Lockian creed."[26] Such a creed has not found universal assent in Britain.

Weaned on the doctrine of parliamentary sovereignty, Britons have come to regard constitutional disputes as matters for resolution by political debate and not litigation. Whereas constitutional interpretation by the courts in the United States may serve as a support of the political system, in Britain it could serve to undermine it. "I should hate to rely upon the appointed judiciary rather than upon the elected members of a legislature for the rights of the people," declared an MP, perhaps not altogether disinterestedly.[27] If the courts are seen as not being impartial arbiters and become what Lord Joseph has termed "a party political football"—a possibility even more likely in the event of their being empowered to interpret a bill of rights whose provisions would be politically contentious—then respect for judges and the judicial process is undermined.

Whereas Americans may be largely if not wholly agreed on the provisions of the Bill of Rights, there is no such agreement in Britain as to what should be included in a British bill. It would be a politically contentious document, and anybody vested with the responsibility of its interpretation would be drawn inexorably into the political fray. Some jurists would not be averse to being drawn into that fray. Many politicians and some judges would prefer to defend the judiciary from the perils of such a course. Despite growing pressure in favor of a bill of rights, the chances of its realization in the near future are slim.

THE POLICE FORCE

Respected at home and admired abroad, the British police force has been regarded for many years as a paragon among police forces. In the past ten to twenty years it has undergone major changes. It has also become a topic of public debate because of the problem of police accountability, accusations of corruption in certain forces, and strained relations between the police and particular elements of the community. Like police forces elsewhere, it has also been at the sharp end in tackling a rise in the recorded incidence of crime.

In the United Kingdom there are 52 police forces (43 in England and Wales, 8 in Scotland, and 1 in Northern Ireland), each responsible for law enforcement in its area. Outside the London metropolis each force is under the direction of a chief constable. The Metropolitan Police Force, with its headquarters in New Scotland Yard, is under the control of a commissioner. (There is a separate City of London force.) The number of police officers has grown throughout the century and at the end of 1987 stood at 145,800. There is approximately one police officer for every 400 people in England and Wales, roughly the same ratio as in the United States. The police force relies for its effectiveness on the consent and the cooperation of the community. As far as possible, the police have sought to operate as a part of the local community. Police officers live in the community they serve (that is, they live in local houses rather than in barracks), they have limited but original powers, and for many years they patrolled their allotted beats on foot. Remarkable in American terms is the fact that, with certain exceptions (the Diplomatic Protection Group, for example, and police in Northern Ireland), they are not armed: police constables on beat patrol carry only a truncheon (a wooden baton). Although in some parts of the community the police have always been treated with suspicion, popular trust in the police has been a feature of recent British history, a view fostered by the police: children have often been taught to look up with respect to the local policeman on the beat, often portrayed as a kindly figure, ready to pass the time of day with residents and obligingly telling children the time or seeing them safely across the road.

It has also been a nonpolitical force in that it has been kept largely at one remove from direct governmental control. (Only the Special Branch, which carries out arrests on behalf of the intelligence services, could be described as fulfilling a political role.) The fear of a national police force under government control has prevented the creation of such a force. Each force is accountable to the Police Authority, a public body. Each authority comprises local councillors, who constitute two-thirds of the members, and magistrates. The exception is in London, where the Police Authority is the Home Secretary. A chief constable, the head of each force, has to submit an annual report to his authority, and the authority can require him to supply a report on any topic, other than on the operational deployment of his force (or anything that could be against the public interest, as confirmed by the Home Secretary). The authority also appoints senior officers above the rank of Chief Superintendent. Funding of the police is provided by local authorities, supplemented by grants from central government. This funding provides, or could provide, both the police authorities and the Home Secretary with leverage in seeking to ensure police accountability. In practice, chief constables have tended to achieve autonomy in their activities, local authorities being more concerned with the provision of funds than the policies for which those funds are intended.

Pitted against the fear of centralized government control has been the desire for greater operational efficiency. Problems arising from the existence of too many autonomous police forces (such as the 40,000 police forces that exist in the United States) has encouraged the amalgamation of forces, reducing the number in England and Wales from a little under 200 in the 1920s to the present 43. Perceptions of the police force as a local, well-trained force (all officers undergo a standard training) that is free of political direction, combined with a crime rate considered low by international standards (not least when compared with the United States) helped produce the positive view of the police force held at home and abroad, particularly in the 1950s and, to a lesser extent, the 1960s.

Since the latter half of the 1960s, the public attitude toward the police has undergone some change. In part, this is attributable to certain changes in the police force itself. From being the local constable on the beat with nothing more than a whistle to summon assistance, the policeman was transferred to driving a car (known as panda cars because of their appearance) and was equipped with a personal radio. By being in a car, able to respond more quickly to calls for assistance (the rationale for the move), the police officer had less direct contact with the local citizenry. By having a personal radio he or she was able to summon the assistance of colleagues: there was less need to appeal to local citizens or pursue a diplomatic approach in handling quarrelsome characters. There also emerged a new breed of more professional chief constable, more self-assertive and imposing his own views on policing onto his own forces.

The police force also came under pressure as a result of an increase in the crime rate, or at least an increase in the number of offenses known to the police. Indictable offenses in England and Wales known to the police in

1960 totaled 797,500. This figure rose to 1.6 million in 1971, to 2.9 million in 1981, and by 1987 had reached 3.9 million (see Table 13.1). Of these latter cases, only 33% were classified as having been cleared up. Public concern at the rise in crime, or perceived rise, generated what has been termed a "moral panic."[28] The police were increasingly hard-pressed to deal with the situation, and their operational methods came in for criticism. Many observers felt that policemen were more effective on beat patrol, acting as visible deterrents, than they were in cars responding to an event after it had happened. Also, a number of television series (some American imports, some home-produced) portrayed police behavior as more aggressive than the image previously conveyed.

On top of this moral panic, in the late 1970s and early 1980s there arose what a number of observers described as a crisis of confidence in the police.[29] Though the crisis peaked in the 1980s, the developments that came together to generate it have remained. Among the most significant were—and remain—accountability and corruption. The high-profile activity of certain chief constables, such as John Anderton in Greater Manchester, produced conflicts with some police authorities and a vigorous debate as to the accountability of chief constables and their forces. The debate acquired partisan overtones. The 1981 Labour party conference approved a proposal that police policies must be approved by police authorities. Sensing a left-wing attack on the forces of law and order, the Conservatives responded by defending the police force. The debate continued throughout the decade, chief constables retaining and defending their autonomy in operational matters.

Corruption had been a problem in the case of the Metropolitan Police;

TABLE 13.1. NOTIFIABLE OFFENSES RECORDED BY THE POLICE, 1987

Notifiable offense recorded	England and Wales (thousands)
Violence against the person	141.0
Sexual offenses of which, rape and attempted rape 2.5	25.2
Burglary	900.1
Robbery	32.6
Drugs offenses	7.1
Theft and handling stolen goods of which, theft of vehicles 389.6	2,052.0
Fraud and forgery	133.0
Criminal damage	589.0
Other notifiable offenses	12.2
Total notifiable offenses	3,892.2

Source: Social Trends 19 (Her Majesty's Stationery Office, 1989), p. 186.

between 1972 and 1977 the commissioner, Sir Robert Mark, had removed more than 450 officers. In 1976 there was the biggest trial involving detectives seen in London since 1877. Allegations continued to be made and a new investigation, "Operation Countryman" was instigated. It produced few prosecutions, a result attributed not to lack of corruption but to lack of tangible evidence.[30] Continuing allegations affected both police morale and public confidence. In 1965 a Gallup Poll found that 23% of respondents believed that there were cases of violence and corruption in the police force, albeit very scattered; 8% believed cases of corruption and violence "occur too often." In 1981, 45% of respondents believed there were scattered cases of violence and corruption, 16% believing such cases occurred too often. In 1985 the figures were similar: 43% believed there were scattered cases, and 17% believed they occurred too often.[31] Cases of corruption and malpractice have continued to make the headlines. In 1989 the chief constable of the West Midlands, Geoffrey Dear, removed from operational duty every member of his 53-member criminal investigation department, having earlier wound up its serious crime squad following allegations of fabricated evidence.

There have also been accusations of the police taking an aggressive or biased stance toward particular communities. Britain witnessed a number of riots in urban areas in the 1980s, especially in Bristol, Liverpool, Handsworth in Birmingham, and the Brixton and Tottenham areas of London. One of the reasons given for the riots in certain areas was the attitude taken by the police toward the local black community. There were allegations of racism on the part of some police officers and of a heavy-handed approach by the police generally in dealing with black suspects. Police officers were accused of picking on black youths and detaining them under the so-called "sus" law, a law (since replaced) that permitted arrest on suspicion of someone about to commit a crime. One unit of the Metropolitan Police, the Special Patrol Group, came in for particular criticism because of the aggressive tactics it was alleged to employ in responding to public disturbances. Further tension was generated by the death of a black woman of a heart attack during a police search and by the accidental shooting of another during a police raid. The death of Cynthia Jarrett, in Tottenham, precipitated a riot in which a policeman was killed.

Various attempts have been made to deal with these problems. In 1985 an Independent Police Complaints Authority came into being with powers to supervise the investigation of serious complaints against police officers. Under the provisions of the 1984 Police and Criminal Evidence Act, the police are required to make arrangements for obtaining the views of people about the policing in their area; most areas now have police/community consultative groups. Greater efforts have been made to improve relations with the ethnic communities, and racially discriminatory behavior is now an offense under the Police Discipline Code. Police conduct, however, remains a topic of concern. Relations with blacks in some cities remain poor. The police have had little success in recruiting blacks into their ranks. The acquisition of riot control gear, and the training of officers for riot control, have further undermined the image of the lone "bobby on the beat." There have also been disputes between some chief constables and their police authorities over the acquisition of such equipment. The mass use of police during the miners' strike of 1984–1985 also gave rise to fears of a more politicized, and a more national, police force. The omnibus Police and Criminal Evidence Act has also been criticized for extending police powers of search and arrest (though it also extends in some areas the rights of suspects), and the 1986 Public Order Act has been criticized for giving the police greater power over the holding of public demonstrations.

Compared with the position of the 1950s and 1960s, the police force in Britain has changed markedly and become far more a topic of critical concern. Against this situation, though, must be set a number of qualifications. For one thing, the picture presented of the police in the 1950s is an idealized one. Various cases of corruption occurred then, and there were some conflicts between chief constables and their watch committees (police authorities). Concern was such that a Royal Commission on the Police was appointed in 1960. Hence, the change over time is not as great as may appear. Furthermore, public confidence in the police remains relatively high. In a 1985 Gallup poll, 83% of respondents said they had a "great deal" or "quite a lot of confidence" in the police. Only 5% said they had no confidence at all in them. Respondents also ranked the honesty and ethical standards of police officers as second only to that of doctors, and 76% expressed themselves satisfied in general with the way the police did their job.[32] A more recent poll, in 1988, found that 69% of respondents considered that the police offered good value for money, a better rating than was achieved by any other range of public services, including the National Health Service, schools, and universities.[33] In short, though there has been a decline in police morale and public confidence, it has been relative. In absolute terms, public confidence remains high, and so too, in most areas of the country, does police morale. Police recruitment picked up in the 1980s and pay and conditions improved.

Relative to conditions presumed previously to have existed, the police force in Britain is facing a more difficult time than before: difficulties with some police authorities, problems in keeping order among and building links with particular sections of the community, and incidents of corruption and bias within its own ranks. It has also changed in character, taking on more the character of an organized mass force than that of a collection of beat-walking individuals. Yet it remains, by international standards, a professional and well-respected body, still largely unarmed and still enjoying the confidence of the public.

NOTES

1. J. J. Magee, "Constitutional Vagaries and American Judicial Review," *Hull Papers in Politics No. 10* (Hull University Politics Department, 1979).
2. Marshall, C. J., *Marbury* v. *Madison*, 1803, 5 U.S. (1Cranch), 137 2 L. Ed.60. H. W. Chase and C. R. Ducat, *Constitutional Interpretation* (West Publishing, 1974), p. 26.
3. See the cogent argument advanced by J. Gibson in his dissenting opinion in *Eakin* v. *Raub*, 1825, Supreme Court of Pennsylvania, 12 S. & R. 330. Chase and Ducat, pp. 27–33.
4. See L. Hartz, *The Liberal Tradition in America* (Harcourt, Brace & World, 1955), especially p. 9.
5. Taking cases in which the Court rendered a full opinion, all cases in every twentieth volume of the *U.S. Reports* were analyzed, starting with Volume 230 (the Court's October term 1912). Of the 10 terms covered, in only 3 did the number of cases determined by constitutional interpretation outnumber those determined by statutory interpretation. Of the total of 471 cases studied, 264 were decided by statutory interpretation and 207 by constitutional interpretation. (Drawn from research undertaken by the author while a Thouron Scholar at the University of Pennsylvania.)
6. H. J. Abraham, *The Judicial Process*, 5th ed. (Oxford University Press, 1986), p. 293.
7. Ibid.
8. There is approximately one lawyer for every 600 people in the United States, compared with one for every 1,600 people in Britain. (*The Economist*, November 5, 1977, p. 45.) Another difference is that barristers and solicitors (they take different examinations) have to meet one set of national standards in Britain. In the United States there is some variety in the standards set by the 50 State Bar Associations.
9. The appointment of Lord Donaldson as Master of the Rolls in 1982 aroused controversy. The judge had presided over the short-lived National Industrial Relations Court set up under the provisions of the 1971 Industrial Relations Act and was regarded as a political enemy by the Labour party and the trade unions.
10. Like the vice president, the Lord Chancellor exercises few powers as presiding officer: the Lords have minimal rules of procedure and all Lords who wish to participate do so. The task of presiding is often handed over to one of a panel of peers appointed for the purpose.
11. T. C. Hartley and J. A. G. Griffith, *Government and Law*, 2nd ed. (Weidenfeld & Nicolson, 1981), p. 181.
12. E. C. S. Wade and G. Godfrey Phillips, *Constitutional and Administrative Law*, 9th ed. by A. W. Bradley (Longman, 1977), p. 371. Judges of inferior

courts may be removed by the Lord Chancellor on grounds of incapacity or misbehavior, and magistrates may be dismissed by the Lord Chancellor as he thinks fit. Occasionally, magistrates have been dismissed for failing to fulfill their duties, and in 1977 a Scottish sheriff (a judicial rather than a police position) was dismissed for engaging in political activities.

13. See especially the excellent but now dated L. Downie Jr., *Justice Denied* (Penguin, 1971).
14. P. Knightley and E. Potter, "How Lawyers Bend Justice," *Sunday Times*, July 11, 1982, p. 25.
15. P. Knightley and E. Potter, "How Solicitors Get Rich," *Sunday Times*, July 18, 1982, p. 25.
16. J. A. G. Griffith, *The Politics of the Judiciary*, 2nd ed. (Fontana, 1981), p. 210.
17. *Ridge* v. *Baldwin* (1964), *Anisminic* v. *Foreign Compensation Commission* (1968), *Conway* v. *Rimmer* (1968), and *Padfield* v. *Minister of Agriculture, Fisheries and Food* (1968). See P. Norton, *The Constitution in Flux* (Blackwell, 1982), pp. 136–38.
18. Quoted in Griffith, pp. 130–31.
19. *The Times*, Law Report, November 11, 1981.
20. *The Economist*, November 14, 1981, p. 19.
21. Lord Hailsham, *Elective Dictatorship* (BBC, 1976).
22. Sir L. Scarman, *English Law—The New Dimension* (Stevens, 1974), p. 86.
23. Lord Scarman, "A Bill of Rights Could Become the Conscience of the Nation," *The Independent*, June 9, 1989.
24. Griffith, p. 193.
25. Griffith, p. 195.
26. Hartz, p. 9.
27. *House of Commons Debates* (*Hansard*), Sixth Series, Vol. 2, col. 1256.
28. A. K. Bottomley and C. Coleman, "Law and Order: Crime Problem, Moral Panic, or Penal Crisis?" in P. Norton (ed.), *Law and Order in British Politics* (Gower, 1984), pp. 38–59.
29. Said by a solicitor at a seminar attended by the author. See also K. Warren, MP, and D. Tredinnick, *Protecting the Police* (Conservative Political Centre, 1982), p. 7.
30. "World in Action," August 2, 1982; *The Guardian*, August 4, 1982.
31. G. Heald and R. J. Wybrow, *The Gallup Survey of Britain* (Gallup, 1986), p. 266; N. Webb and R. Wybrow, *The Gallup Report: Your Opinions in 1981* (Sphere Books, 1982), p. 123.
32. Heald and Wybrow, p. 74.
33. *Gallup Political Index*, Report No. 333, May 1988, p. 12.

CHAPTER 14

Communication
and Feedback
The Mass Media

Communication is an essential and integral part of any society. It is a necessary if not always well-used tool of the politician's trade. To influence others, one must communicate. With the advent of a mass electorate, politicians have had to communicate with a large audience. In the eighteenth century, when affairs of state were the concern of an aristocratic elite, communication by word of mouth or by letter was often sufficient in order to reach those with political influence. In the nineteenth century, the newspaper became more important as a medium of communication, especially toward the end of the century. (The only other medium of mass communication, or at least one capable of reaching a large audience, was political pamphleteering.) In the twentieth century, newspapers have remained important but have been supplemented by radio and more recently have been overshadowed though not quite supplanted by television.

Other forms of communicating by a single medium to a large number of people have also been developed. These now include records, videocassettes (a recent phenomenon in Britain), films, and books. Although some of these have served as vehicles for political communication and, more especially, influence, their impact is limited. They are rarely used to fulfill such functions and their audiences are relatively small. Book reading and cinema going are minority interests. In Britain, as in the United States, the primary *mass* media for communicating political information remain television, radio, and newspapers. It is with these three media that this chapter is concerned.

PRESS AND BROADCASTING IN BRITAIN

Despite an increase in the sophistication of mass communication, the sheer size and diversity of the United States has militated against the development of "national" newspapers. The number of daily newspapers with anything other than a geographically limited readership can be counted probably on the fingers of one hand. Even the titles of most of the exceptions—*The Washington Post*, the *New York Times*, *The Wall Street Journal*—imply specific parochial interests; *USA Today* stands alone in its explicitly national orientation. In Britain, by contrast, factors of geography and demography have tended to encourage the development of a national daily press. The country is geographically small, with most of the population living in England, the greatest concentration living in the nation's capital. Despite some exceptions, the press in Britain is London-based and national (which often means London) in its orientation. The newspaper emerged as a medium of political information and influence at the turn of the century and has remained an important medium since. By international comparison, Britons remain great newspaper readers.

The advent of "popular" newspapers, those designed to appeal (in both content and price) to artisans and the lower middle class, took place in the 1890s, a development made possible by advances in adult literacy and in printing technology. The first such newspaper was the *Daily Mail*, founded in 1896 by Alfred Harmsworth (later Lord Northcliffe). It was followed by the *Daily Express* in 1900, the *Daily Mirror* in 1903, and the *Daily Sketch* in 1908. They built up mass readerships not enjoyed by the more sedate and serious newspapers such as *The Times*, the doyen of influential newspapers founded in 1788; the *Morning Post* (merged with the *Daily Telegraph* in 1937); or the *Manchester Guardian*, one of the few significant newspapers with a regional orientation. The mass circulation of the new popular "dailies" attracted advertisers, and income from advertising came to constitute a (and in some cases, the) main form of revenue, thus allowing the publishers to keep down the cost of their papers. Harmsworth boasted that he was able to sell a one-penny paper for half-a-penny.[1] The newspapers themselves were largely in the hands of a few wealthy individuals, known in the early decades of the century as the "press barons." The Harmsworth family was especially influential (owning the *Mail*, the *Mirror* and, from 1908 to 1922, *The Times*), as was the Canadian Max Aitken (Lord Beaverbrook), who acquired control of the *Daily Express* in 1916. Although the papers were run as essentially commercial enterprises, proprietors were not averse to using their newspapers in attempts to influence political developments. In the early 1930s the conservative leader, Stanley Baldwin, bitterly assailed the press barons for seeking to engineer his removal from the party leadership, uttering the memorable observation that they exercised "power without responsibility—the prerogative of the harlot through the ages." The attempt to oust Baldwin was one that many critics of the press would regard as the tip of a very sizable iceberg. Overt political partisanship remains a feature of British newspapers.

Newspaper circulation continued to grow in the first decades of the century. By 1945 the circulation of the main daily newspapers had reached nearly 13 million. Throughout the 1950s it exceeded 16 million, dropping to below 16 million in the 1960s and to just below 15 million in the 1970s and 1980s. (In 1988, national newspapers had a circulation of 14.8 million on weekdays.) However, given that each copy of a newspaper is usually read by more than one person (and most households order only one daily paper), the figures reveal that a majority of adults in Britain continue to read a daily newspaper. On an average day, two out of three people over the age of 15 read a national newspaper.[2] Relative to the size of population, newspaper circulation is greater in Britain than in the United States and most other developed countries.

Of the national newspapers currently available, there is in terms of numbers a relatively wide choice. There are in addition a variety of national Sunday newspapers, weekly magazines of news and current affairs (preeminent among them being *The Economist*), regional daily newspapers, and a host of local daily and weekly papers: hardly any community is without its "local" publication. In total, there are about 130 daily newspapers, 1,700 weekly newspapers, and some 7,500 periodical publications. Table 14.1 lists the principal national newspapers, along with the names of their owners and their sales figures.

Until the 1980s, most national newspapers were edited and printed on Fleet Street, and the name of the street became synonymous with the national press. In the 1980s newspapers, taking advantage of new computer technology, began to move out, thereby weakening the influence of the traditionally powerful print unions. Led by the publications of News International, most relocated in the docklands of London. The last national newspaper left Fleet Street in 1989.

Although journalists may differ in their political beliefs, individual newspapers tend to adopt a particular though not always committed editorial position in support of a political party or general political persuasion. The party that benefits most from editorial preferences is the Conservative party (see Table 14.2). The *Daily Telegraph* is generally regarded as *the* Conservative newspaper and is widely read by Conservatives, as

TABLE 14.1. NATIONAL NEWSPAPERS: OWNERS AND SALES

Newspaper	Owner	Average sale July–Dec. 1988	% change 1987 to 1988
Daily Newspapers			
The Sun	News International	4,219,052	+4.3
Daily Mirror	Mirror Group	3,156,516	+0.9
The Star	United Newspapers	966,533	−15.0
Daily Mail	Associated Newspapers	1,758,689	−2.8
Daily Express	United Newspapers	1,637,066	−3.2
Today	News International	548,362	+61.4
Daily Telegraph	Daily Telegraph	1,127,674	−3.6
Guardian	Guardian	438,054	−4.8
The Times	News International	436,298	−2.5
Independent	Newspaper Publishing	387,103	+7.3
Financial Times	Pearson	278,577	−9.2
Morning Star	Morning Star Co-operative	29,000[a]	
Sunday Newspapers			
News of the World	News International	5,360,479	+5.2
Sunday Mirror	Mirror Group	2,953,079	+2.0
Sunday People	Mirror Group	2,743,451	−3.9
Sunday Express	United Newspapers	2,032,798	−8.8
Mail on Sunday	Associated Newspapers	1,919,295	+3.5
Sunday Times	News International	1,314,504	+5.2
Observer	Lonrho International	722,008	−5.6
Sunday Telegraph	Daily Telegraph	693,431	−6.1

[a] Estimate. Figure not audited by Audit Bureau of Circulations. *(Sources:* Britain 1989 *(Her Majesty's Stationery Office, 1989), p. 426; Audit Bureau of Circulations.)*

Table 14.2 reveals. The *Daily Mail, Daily Star,* Daily Express, and *The Sun* (formerly a Labour supporter) also tend to fall within the Conservative camp, though not always giving editorial support to specific Conservative policies (the *Express,* for example, was a long-standing opponent of British membership in the European Community). *The Times* is often considered to be a Conservative-leaning newspaper, though for part of the 1980s it appeared particularly sympathetic to the Social Democratic party. *The Daily Mirror* is the only mass circulation daily newspaper that remains a consistent supporter of the Labour party. *The Guardian* (now national in its orientation) is a radical newspaper, its center-left position putting it somewhere between the Labour party and the center parties. *The Morning Star*, with its small but committed readership, is the paper of the Communist party. The two newest newspapers—*Today* (a tabloid) and *The Independent* (part of the quality press), both beginning publication in 1986— have added some variety, *The Independent* attempting deliberately to live up to its name, *Today* leaning more to the center parties.

TABLE 14.2. NATIONAL NEWSPAPERS: POLITICAL PROFILE, GENERAL ELECTION 1987

	Con. %	Lab. %	All %	Bias[a] %	Political content[b] %
Dailies					
Times	56*	12	27	61(C)	42.7
Guardian	22	54*	19	40(All)	41.1
Telegraph	80*	5	10	85(C)	31.6
Financial Times	48*	17	29		16.4
Independent	34	34	27	17(All)	39.7
Today	43	17	40*	14(All)	45.3
Express	70*	9	18	86(C)	59.1
Mail	60*	13	19	75(C)	63.1
Mirror	20	55*	21	82(C)	26.8
Sun	41*	31	19	53(C)	29.7
Star	28*	46	18	5(C)	22.2
Sundays					
Times	58*	15	23	68(C)	50.6
Observer	28	49	18	23(L)	53.6
Telegraph	78*	9	9	76(C)	46.2
Express	64*	6	25	79(C)	32.8
News of the World	37*	33	23	31(C)	26.1
Mail	61*	14	20	62(C)	36.5
Mirror	25	49*	19	65(L)	14.6
People	36	38*	20	31(L)	49.9

*How the papers "voted." [a] Readers' perception of papers' political views.
[b] Percentage of front page devoted to election or polls. *(Source:* UK Press Gazette, *June 22, 1987, p. 25.)*

Critics on the left ascribe the Conservative bias of the press to the nature of ownership, newspapers being part and parcel of a capitalist system, with more and more newspapers coming within the control of fewer hands. Table 14.2 reveals the extent of owner concentration. Foremost among the present-day "press barons" is Rupert Murdoch, owner of News International, whose media empire includes both tabloids (*Sun, News of the World*) and the quality *Times*. A similar concentration is to be found in other media, with a considerable overlap of ownership.

Whereas newspapers, being owned by private concerns, are free to express their partisan preferences (and do so), the broadcasting media are more constrained. Initially, the British Broadcasting Corporation (the BBC) enjoyed a monopoly on radio and television broadcasting. The BBC is a quasi-autonomous state corporation that came into being on January 1, 1927. (It succeeded an independent company, the British Broadcasting Company Ltd.) It was granted a license to broadcast under Royal Charter and it was and remains financed by a license fee levied originally on radio receivers (abolished in 1971) and subsequently, from 1946 onward, on television sets. The first scheduled public television service was started in 1936, though it was suspended during the Second World War. The 1950s witnessed the growth of television: more sets were purchased and more services became available.

In 1954 the BBC's monopoly was ended with the creation of the Independent Television Authority. This body was authorized to license program-contracting companies to transmit in certain areas of the country and to finance their operations by carrying paid advertisements. The first commercial independent television (ITV) channel was broadcast in 1955. Television was well established in Britain by the 1960s (more than 10 million television licenses were issued in 1960) and witnessed further expansion both in that and succeeding decades. In 1964 a second BBC channel, BBC2, began transmission, catering more to minority tastes, especially in the spheres of culture and education. In 1967 the BBC began experimenting with local radio stations to supplement their (by then) four national services; 20 new stations were established within six years. In the 1970s the establishment of independent local radio stations was authorized for the first time, and 19 such stations were established in 1976. In November 1982 a fourth television channel (Channel 4), in independent hands, began transmission and early in 1983 both the BBC and, on independent television, a new franchise (TV-AM) began early morning transmissions—"breakfast television." Cable television also became available (though it attacted relatively few subscribers), and in 1989 the first satellite television channel—Sky Television—began broadcasting. By the end of the 1980s the viewer or listener was offered what was, by British standards, a considerable variety of programs emanating from different television channels and radio stations, though the two main television channels—BBC1 and ITV (divided up into regional networks)—retained the mass audiences. Significant inroads into their viewing figures were apparent, but these were more the product of an increase in the use of videorecorders (and of fewer people watching television) than of a large shift of viewers to Channel 4 television or an increase in radio listening. By 1989, more than 50% of households owned two or more television sets and owned or rented a videorecorder.[3]

In their coverage of politics, both the BBC and the independent stations—television and radio—are required to be impartial. The concept of equal time has been applied to the two main parties, though the advent of significant third parties (and of more fringe candidates in parliamentary by-elections) has created problems in determining the allocation of time to other parties. During general election campaigns, no paid political advertisements are permitted on radio or television, though both media carry an agreed-upon number of party election broadcasts (the number agreed upon by the parties and the broadcasting authorities), which are scripted and presented by the parties themselves, the broadcasting media transmitting them without comment.

The BBC and the independent companies come under the control of separate semi-autonomous bodies—the BBC Board of Governors and the Independent Broadcasting Authority—which position themselves as a cushion between the broadcasting companies and the government of the day. Although some critics see the media (and the BBC in particular) as unduly subservient to government, the broadcasting authorities appear to pride themselves on their independence of government, an independence that sometimes may generate tension between the two, as in 1982 over the Falklands War and in 1988 over a program on the shooting of three members of the IRA in Gibraltar.

POLITICAL INFLUENCE

The mass media, by the content and method of their communicating or failing to communicate information, can exert tremendous political influence. Political evaluations and actions of politician and citizen are based on receipt of information. How that information is portrayed and transmitted can significantly affect both the evaluation and the action taken on the basis of that evaluation.

The political information transmitted by the mass media is, of necessity, limited. Newspapers do not have the space nor broadcasting media the air time to transmit comprehensive coverage of daily events (nationally or worldwide) of political significance. Nor do they have the inclination to do so. Although newspapers and the broadcasting media constitute the primary means of transmitting political information to a mass audience, they do not exist exclusively or indeed even primarily to fulfill such a function. Television and radio are essentially media of entertainment. Newspapers may make some claim, by virtue of the written word, to be more a medium of information, but the information transmitted is not usually on the subject of political behavior. Although the so-called quality newspapers (*The Times*, *Daily Telegraph*, and *Guardian*) devote a significant proportion of space to reporting and commenting on political events, the mass readership papers do not.

Indeed, the trend has been away from covering political items to what publishers consider human-interest stories.[4] This is in line with what newspapers see as consumer demands at a time of intense competition for readers. A survey in the 1960s found that newspaper readers were most likely to read thoroughly (that is, from beginning to end) articles covering tragedies and celebrities as well as cartoons and letter columns. More readers (41%) thoroughly read the horoscopes than they did stories on home politics (37%) or international politics (29%).[5] In the 1970s and 1980s, as the circulation war among newspapers became more intense, *The Sun* and the *Daily Star* competed against one another to publish pictures of half-naked females, and most of the popular dailies sought to attract new readers through running competitions offering large cash prizes.

Nonetheless, the role of the mass media in transmitting political information remains of vital significance. Indeed, the significance of newspapers and television as media of communication has increased in the twentieth century not only because of the increase in the size of the audiences but also because of the increase in sophistication of communication technology. Television, in particular, is important not only for the content of what it conveys but also for the method and speed by which it conveys that content. Not only can various happenings—a bomb blast in Northern Ireland, candidates addressing meetings, politicians arguing with one another—be portrayed visually and in sound (and, nowadays, in color), but they can also be transmitted shortly after or even at the time of happening. Receiving information with such immediacy, and in such a form, can affect viewers' evaluations in a way not possible when this medium of communication did not exist. As Hedley Donovan queried once in *Time* magazine: "Could the Civil War have survived the 7 P.M. news? Could George Washington have held his command after a TV special on Valley Forge?"[6] Media coverage of the Vietnam War clearly affected the American public's perception of the wisdom, or lack of it, in such an action. In Britain, recognition of the implications of media coverage influenced the government in its actions and its control of information during the Falklands War in 1982. The government controlled the means of transmitting news from the Task Force to Britain, and facilities for the quick transmission of television pictures were not made available. To have shown on television during the conflict "pictures of the sort of realism that the Americans had during the Vietnamese war," to be seen by servicemen's families, would, in the words of one commanding officer, "have had a very serious effect" on troop morale.[7] Media coverage of particular events such as riots may extend beyond constituting an impartial recording of those events to being an alleged instigator of them. The activities of the media themselves may constitute political issues.

The way in which information is channeled, then, is not neutral in its effect. The mass media, in short, exert political influence. This influence may be primary, affecting the recipient of the communication, or it may be secondary, affecting a party independent of the communication process (e.g., a politician whose capacity to achieve a particular action is limited by public reaction to news of a certain event as, for instance, President Johnson in the Vietnam War).[8] The influence of the media may be seen as especially important in terms of the legitimacy of the political system, the partisan support of electors, and the behavior of politicians. The influence exerted in each case may be described as that of enhancing, of reinforcing, and of constraining, respectively.

The media fulfill a function of latent legitimation of the political system. By operating within that system and accepting its norms, newspapers and television help to maintain its popular legitimacy. When a political crisis arises, journalists and TV reporters descend upon ministers and MPs for comment, hence accepting and reinforcing the legitimacy of those questioned to comment on the matter at hand. There is regular coverage of parliamentary proceedings. What political leaders and members of the royal family do in a public and often in a private capacity is considered newsworthy. By according this degree of status to such figures and to the institutions they occupy and represent, the media serve to reinforce the legitimacy of such bodies. Where a body does not enjoy popular legitimacy, the media probably could not create it. Where it does exist, however, they can and do reinforce it by the very nature of their activities.

At times, certain media may also fulfill the more conscious role of overt legitimation. Coverage of the activities of the royal family, for example, may go beyond reporting to a clear statement of editorial approval. At times of national crisis, some newspapers consider it not only their duty but that of their readers to support the national effort, and vigorously exhort their readers to provide such support. The most recent and obvious example was that of a number of national newspapers, most notably *The Sun*, during the Falklands War in 1982. Reporting of the war was merged with vigorous, not to say crude, editorializing in support of the British effort, any critics being roundly condemned as unpatriotic. The broadcasting media, by virtue of their charters, sought to take a more detached position.

On party political preferences, the media may be seen as having primarily a reinforcing effect. This is in line with the findings of various studies of the effect of mass communication. Persuasive mass communication, according to Klapper's classic study, tends to serve far more heavily in the interests of reinforcement and of minor change than of converting opinions.[9] There is a marked tendency for the recipients of communications to indulge in a process of selective exposure, perception, and retention. This phenomenon was borne out by Butler and Stokes' study in Britain on the effects of newspaper reading.[10] Most readers chose a newspaper whose partisan stance was in line with their own stance or, for young people, with that of their parents; when the children absorbed and accepted the preferences of their parents, they continued to read the same newspaper.

The effect of reading any given partisan newspaper was characterized by Butler and Stokes as "magnetic": "Readers who are already close to their paper's party will tend to be held close; those at some distance will tend to be pulled towards it."[11] A similar finding emerged from the more recent study of Dunleavy and Husbands. In their study of media influence on voting in 1983, they found that the greater the exposure to Conservative newspapers, the greater the likelihood to vote Conservative. The relationship remained strong even when social class was controlled for. "Within all the class categories used the Conservative vote is some 30 percentage points lower among people primarily exposed to non-Tory messages than it is amongst readers of the Tory press, a high level of association that has few parallels amongst either social background or issue influences. . . . The difference is even more marked when we compare the two extreme groups, those exposed to a predominantly Tory message and those receiving a predominantly non-Tory one; the differences in Conservative support range from 36 to 58 points."[12] The relationships they established were, they concluded, too close to be attributable solely or even mainly to partisan self-selection. Hence, according to their analysis, newspaper reading can have a significant political influence. The beneficiary of such influence is the Conservative party. In the 1983 general election, 75% of national daily newspaper readers were advised to vote Conservative (an all-time high, compared with an average of 54% in the eight postwar elections to 1970), and in the 1987 election the proportion was 67%.[13]

Media coverage also serves to have a constraining effect on politicians' behavior. In order to achieve their aims, politicians must be able to communicate with others, at what may be described as the horizontal level (i.e., with fellow politicians, civil servants, and other policy makers) as well as the vertical (i.e., politician to the public), and they must also at times ensure the noncommunication of material. Most politicians crave the attention of the media. Such attention enhances their legitimacy and provides them with the means to influence others. Political behavior may often be geared, in consequence, to the needs of television and newspapers. Press conferences are now *de rigueur* during election campaigns. (They are not so necessary at other times, because Parliament provides ministers with an authoritative and structured forum for communicating their views, an important facility not available to the president and cabinet secretaries in the United States.)[14] Texts of speeches are given in advance of delivery to journalists and TV reporters. Meetings are organized so as to present a good televisual effect and also timed to meet newspaper deadlines or to get onto the early television evening news. The effect or presumed effect of the televising of particular politicians may even influence the careers of political leaders. A politician whose words in print may be persuasive may come across as hesitant and bumbling on television; he or she may physically not be photogenic. The Conservative leader in the 1964 general election, Sir Alec Douglas-Home, suffered badly from coming across as a poor performer on television; his Labour opposite number, Harold Wilson, came across as a confident, dynamic young leader. (There are certain parallels with the American public's perception of the television performances of Richard Nixon and John Kennedy in the 1960 presidential election campaign.) The Labour leader, Michael Foot, suffered a similar fate in the 1983 general election campaign. When the television cameras entered the Commons in 1989, Margaret Thatcher was judged to come across well on the screen whereas her Labour rival, Neil Kinnock, came across as negative and hectoring. Politicians are thus constrained not only in how they behave in seeking to put across a particular message but also in how they look and how they present themselves before the television cameras.

The media may constrain a politician also in terms of what substantive actions or policies he or she may wish to pursue. Knowledge that one's activities may be observed and reported may deter a minister, for example, from engaging in a policy or particular action that is thought to be unpopular or likely to incur the wrath of one's colleagues or supporters. In the Falklands War in 1982, the British policy makers were keen to achieve a quick military victory with as few casualties as possible. They were conscious that reports of heavy losses or a long-drawn-out and indecisive campaign could have an effect on public morale similar to that of media coverage of the Vietnam War on morale in the United States. Civil servants and other public officials may decide not to pursue a particular line, albeit a secret one, for fear that details may be leaked to the press and television. The effect of media reporting may thus limit the options that policy makers believe are open to them.

Thus despite their not seeking to act primarily as channels of political information and influence, the mass media in Britain constitute an integral part of the political process. Through reading newspapers and watching television (or listening to radio), citizens receive information that helps shape and reinforce their political attitudes and that, by its presentation, reinforces the legitimacy of the political system and may at times help modify their attitudes. By similarly reading newspapers and watching news and current affairs programs, politicians are aware of the material that is being communicated to the public. Their perceptions of the likely impact of this material may influence their behavior, even if the communication does not have the impact expected.

The media also serve to communicate information to political leaders on how particular policies and programs are being received. Investigative work by journalists or television researchers may present new public evidence on a particular issue—a feature of television programs such as "World in Action" (ITV) and "Panorama" (BBC). The reporting of evidence researched by others, the coverage of demonstrations, or the publication of opinion polls commissioned by the newspaper or program serve to inform both the public and political leaders of attitudes and responses to policies and the actions of policy makers.

That the media are instrinsically significant and influential in the political process is a statement of fact. Whether the effect and influence of the media are desirable is another question and a point of current contention.

CURRENT DEBATE

The media serve to convey information. They also form part of contemporary political debate. This stems in part, especially in the case of national newspapers, from their own practices.

The activities of the popular press in particular in obtaining stories has proved a cause of controversy in recent years. The harassment of individuals by journalists and television crews—camping outside their homes, constantly telephoning, pursuing them down the street whenever they venture out—has been a cause of serious complaint, ranging from pursuit of aged and innocent relatives of figures in the public eye to the engulfing of the then-Lady Diana Spencer whenever she appeared publicly following speculation as to her likely engagement to the Prince of Wales. Following her marriage, press pursuit of the Princess reached such a level—especially during the period of her first pregnancy—that the tabloid press incurred the public displeasure of the Queen, who summoned editors to Buckingham Palace to request that the privacy of the Princess be respected. The use of money to elicit exclusive stories has similarly incurred public criticism, particularly in instances when it has been employed to obtain evidence from witnesses involved in pending court cases.

Extensive criticism has also been generated by many of the stories that have resulted, the press having considerable license to criticize and abuse. The position has been exacerbated by the limited means available to those attacked by the press to achieve a redress of grievance. The only means available are to sue for libel or to report the matter to the Press Council. Neither is considered a particularly effective course of action. Newspapers have the resources to defend themselves against any libel actions. For individuals, the cost of pursuing a case through the courts is, in most cases, financially prohibitive. (Legal aid is not available in such cases.) Only those with personal wealth are in a position to sustain a libel action. Among those who have done so in recent years are Jeffrey Archer, the novelist and former deputy chairman of the Conservative party, who successfully sued *The Star*, and Elton John, the singer, successful in a major action against

The Sun, settled out of court for a seven-figure sum. Reporting cases to the Press Council is a course of action open to all. The problem here is the lack of powers available to the Council. A nonstatutory body established by the newspaper industry in 1953, it can investigate complaints against newspapers and, if it finds the camplaint justified, can censure the newspaper. Papers are under a moral obligation to publish the Council's findings. However, such reports are often buried in the inner pages and on occasion treated almost with contempt. Despite that, complaints continue to be made to the Council in increasing numbers. The number of cases received in 1976 was 534; in 1986 it had doubled to 1,136.[15]

Public lack of confidence in the press—a Gallup poll in 1985 found that it vied with trade unions as the least trusted institution in Britain[16]—has led to various proposals to provide more effective means of redress. These have included providing legal aid in libel cases, strengthening the Press Council, strengthening the law of defamation, and allowing a statutory right of reply. In 1989, attempts were made to achieve the latter two proposals through private members' bills introduced in the House of Commons. At the same time, the government made it clear that it was up to the press to put its own house in order if it was to avoid legislation. To forestall such action, national newspapers began appointing in-house "ombudsmen" for the purpose of adjudication on readers' complaints. In effect, they began to acquire their own individual "press councils."

In their political influence, the media have attracted disparate criticism. Their effect as legitimizers and as supporters or alleged supporters of the Conservative party has come in for particular complaint.

Fulfilling the function of latent legitimation has attracted criticism from left-wing bodies opposed to the existing political system. They see the media as buttressing opposition to change. Radical critics such as the Glasgow University Media Group have argued that rather than devoting space to the activities of the royal family or to interviewing MPs, television and newspapers should give greater coverage to the activities and the opinions of factory workers and the unemployed. Such criticism from the left of the political spectrum is an enduring feature of debate, but on occasion criticism is leveled by government and other elements of the existing political system. Such criticism often stems from media coverage of bodies and activities that are opposed to the existing political order. In particular, reporting on the Irish Republican Army (IRA) in Northern Ireland, and especially the interviewing of IRA leaders and sympathizers, generates a strong reaction from political leaders in Britain. By communicating details of IRA activity, by using to some extent IRA terminology (including its name), and by showing IRA leaders and activities (the firing of guns over the coffin of a dead IRA member, for example), the media are seen as giving legitimation to an illegal organization. The response of the media, especially the broadcasting media (which are most sensitive to criticisms from government sources), is that coverage does not imply approval and that to fail to report what is going on in the province would constitute a form of censorship. Despite such criticism probably resulting in a more cautious approach to the coverage of IRA activity in the province, the government in 1988 introduced restrictions (similar to those already in existence in the Irish Republic) on the broadcast of speeches by members of the IRA and supporting organizations.

Criticism of the media function of legitimation has extended, more obviously, to its overt attempts to reinforce the legitimacy of particular institutions or of specific actions. Opponents of the monarchy decry the extent not only of coverage given the royal family by the media but also the editorializing and some degree of sycophancy in its support. Those who opposed sending the British Task Force to retake the invaded Falkland Islands in 1982 found themselves at the receiving end of intense press criticism, being characterized as unpatriotic or (if foreign) villainous. The conflict was portrayed, especially by the *Sun* newspaper, in terms of a clear contest between right and wrong, between the British and the anti-British.

And just as the media may be accused of indulging in overt attempts at legitimation, they are accused also of seeking to deny the legitimacy of certain bodies and types of activity. Among bodies or activities portrayed as being in some respect not legitimate, and hence deserving of public disapproval, are strikes (and, some critics suggest, trade unions generally), communists, homosexuals, large demonstrations by certain groups, and individuals who manage to obtain more social security payments than they are entitled to (dubbed "social security scroungers").[17] A number of Labour politicians on the left, such as Tony Benn, also consider themselves as falling within this broad category.

On occasion, the media have also come under pressure from the government of the day for failing to indulge in more overt approval of particular actions. This has been notable at times of national crisis, especially when British troops have been in action abroad: for example, during the Suez crisis in 1956 and the Falklands War in 1982. In the latter instance, though some newspapers were enthusiastic in their support of the British action, some media—notably television—were accused of treating Argentinian news releases as being on a par with those of the British and of seeking to present in a neutral fashion both sides of the dispute. The BBC came in for special condemnation from Conservative MPs when a "Panorama" program devoted itself to a study of the Conservative critics of the action. Such programs were taken by some Conservatives as reinforcing their belief that the BBC was manned by left-wing sympathizers.

The media have also come under much criticism from Labour politicians, especially on the left wing of the party, for consciously favoring the

Conservative party and, in 1981 and 1982, the Social Democrats. The partisan preference of the national daily newspapers I have recorded already. Many Labour politicians consider the broadcasting media to share a similar bias, albeit one less consciously expressed. The result is seen as a consensus among the media in support often of Conservative and certainly of conservative policies, whether introduced by a Conservative or Labour government.[18] In 1981—and here, there is some measure of agreement between Conservative and Labour politicians—the media were accused of treating the new Social Democratic party sympathetically and certainly uncritically. "The Social Democrats," declared Tony Benn, "have been the beneficiaries of the greatest display of media support ever given to any group of MPs in recent history. . . . [They] were launched upon their venture with a fanfare of publicity that rivalled the coverage accorded to the American space programme or a royal tour."[19] To many established Labour and Conservative politicians, the publicity-conscious SDP was essentially a media creation.

That newspapers do indulge in political bias has not generally been a point of contention. No one, least of all the more vociferous newspapers, has sought to deny it. Rather, the newspapers have been attacked by opponents for the views they have expressed and not for making claims to be objective. The position is somewhat different with the broadcasting media, which do make a claim to be neutral and objective. Their defense to charges of bias has tended to take the form of pointing out that they have been criticized by politicians both on the political left and on the right (Mrs. Thatcher has been a well-known critic of the BBC) and that this fact, in some way, implies that they have pursued a neutral course. Such a defense has had little effect on their critics. Labour activists, as Mr. Benn put it, "feel that the BBC is an instrument being used by the centre against the left—and it is no answer to be told that Mrs. Thatcher does not like the BBC either."[20]

The argument that the SDP was purely a media creation cannot be proven. Although extensive media coverage facilitated the new party in getting its message conveyed to a mass audience (and the claim that much of the coverage was at first fairly uncritical may be justified), the SDP was unable to maintain a high level of support despite continuing media coverage. It is also pertinent to note the unexpected performance of the Green party in the 1989 European Parliament elections: it achieved 15% of the poll without extensive media coverage.

The failure of extensive allegedly sympathetic coverage of the SDP to maintain public support for the party is important also in responses to claims that the media, when combining on a particular issue, can determine popular attitudes on that issue. It is the case, as a number of Labour critics have noted, that the media may express the same opinion on a particular issue—for example, supporting continued British membership of the European Community in the 1975 referendum and supporting Denis Healey against Michael Foot in the contest for the Labour party leadership in 1980. However, while such support may clearly or presumably be useful to the causes in question, it does not follow that the support has been either necessary or sufficient to influence public opinion (or the opinion of the audience in question) toward supporting the line advocated. In 1980, despite media support, Denis Healey failed in his bid to become leader of the Labour party. Earlier, in the February 1974 general election, all major national newspapers but one supported the return to office of Edward Heath's Conservative government. In the event, the leader of the Labour party, Harold Wilson, was summoned to form a minority government.

Other criticisms of media influence have centered on their ability to set the agenda of political debate and on the extent to which events may be manufactured for the benefit of media coverage. The former is an important but possibly overstated point. By selecting certain material and events to cover, newspapers and news programs can influence the agenda of political debate. However, in order for that debate to be sustained, the media have to find some apparently solid base on which to pursue it and it has to be considered a salient issue by those who participate in the debate. If an issue fails to elicit a response or, worse still, produces a counterproductive response (readers or viewers objecting to the line taken), then media coverage may be affected accordingly—that is, the issue may not be pursued or the editorial policy may be changed. In the case of newspapers, it is important to recall that their primary concern is to sell copies. Taking an unpopular political line that could jeopardize sales of the newspaper would be unlikely to find favor with the proprietors. Although the significance of the media in helping set the agenda of political debate is great, the preceding qualification is important. They can rarely help influence that debate by operating in a political vacuum.

Finally, the accusation that events are created for the benefit of media coverage is an important and contemporary one. Clearly, politicians and others, as we have seen, modify their actions in order to try to ensure media coverage. Where controversy arises is in the cases of violent demonstrations or specific acts of violence being carried out, allegedly, in order to attract media attention. By being present on the streets of Belfast or, during riots in the 1980s, in the streets of Liverpool or Brixton, television crews were regarded as encouraging—not actively, but passively, by virtue of their presence waiting for something to happen—the stoning of troops or police by rioters. Again, it is important to stress that rioting is unlikely to take place merely for its own sake (so-called "copycat" riots in other parts of Britain following some of the riots of the 1980s quickly subsided), but had camera crews not been present, the incidents that occurred might not have been as extensive or as violent as they were. The problem for the media, primarily the broadcasting media, is deciding what to do in such circumstances. Once rioting has begun, they can hardly ignore it. Yet, once present at the scene, they are open to claims that their presence served to instigate continued or renewed rioting. For producers and reporters, it remains a delicate problem.

CONCLUSION

The mass media in Britain play a significant, indeed vital, role in the political process. They serve to communicate information to a mass audience. By virtue of the way in which they present that information, they can and do exert influence on attitudes toward the political system, on partisan support, on attitudes toward particular issues, and on politicians' behavior. They help set the agenda of political debate. Not only do they help communicate contemporary political debate, they are themselves in part the subject of that debate. They remain the subject of criticism, especially on grounds of political bias, from politicians on the political left and sometimes on the right of the political spectrum. Nonetheless, their role and influence, though great, should not be exaggerated: as we have seen, various qualifications need to be entered. Not least, it is important to record that, though constituting the primary means for communicating political information to a mass audience, the national newspapers and the broadcasting media remain first and foremost commercial concerns intent on maintaining readership and viewing figures. In order to achieve a large audience, they must remain media of entertainment. The most thoroughly read stories in newspapers are those dealing with tragedies and with celebrities (the celebrities attracting most consistent interest almost certainly being members of the royal family). The most watched television programs in 1988 and 1989 were "Neighbours," an Australian soap opera; "Coronation Street," in ITV soap opera popular for more than two decades; and "Eastenders," the BBC's answer to "Coronation Street." Current affairs programs (as opposed to news programs, which do appear) rarely make an appearance in the TV ratings.

NOTES

1. J. Whale, *The Politics of the Media* (Fontana, 1977), p. 86.
2. *Britain 1989* (Her Majesty's Stationery Office, 1989), p. 425.
3. Ibid., p. 435.
4. J. Curran and J. Seaton, *Power Without Responsibility* (Fontana, 1981), p. 123.
5. See ibid., p. 124.

6. "Fluctuations on the Presidential Exchange," *Time*, November 9, 1981, p. 60.
7. *The Handling of Press and Public Information during the Falklands Conflict, First Report from the Select Committee on Defence*, Session 1982–1983, Vol. I: Report and Minutes of Proceedings, HC 17-1 (Her Majesty's Stationery Office, 1982), p. xiv.
8. See C. Seymour-Ure, *The Political Impact of the Mass Media* (Constable, 1974), p. 22.
9. J. Klapper, *The Effects of Mass Communication* (Free Press, 1960), pp. 15–18.
10. D. Butler and D. Stokes, *Political Change in Britain* (Penguin, 1971), pp. 281–300.
11. Ibid., p. 291.
12. P. Dunleavy and C. T. Husbands, "Media Influences on Voting in 1983," in J. Anderson and A. Cochrane (eds.), *A State of Crisis* (Hodder & Stoughton, 1989), pp. 291–92.
13. "Political Allegiances in Step with the Readers' Intentions," *UK Press Gazette*, June 22, 1987, p. 25.
14. See the conclusion of C. Seymour-Ure, *The American President: Power and Communication* (Macmillan, 1982).
15. *33rd Annual Report of the Press Council* (Press Council, 1986), p. 11.
16. G. Heald and R. J. Wybrow, *The Gallup Survey of Britain* (Gallup, 1986), p. 153
17. See, e.g., S. Cohen and J. Young (eds.), *The Manufacture of News*, rev. ed. (Constable, 1981), passim.
18. This point is developed in T. Benn, *Arguments for Democracy* (Penguin, 1982), Ch. 6, especially p. 115.
19. Ibid., p. 111.
20. Ibid., p. 110.

PART VI
Conclusion

CHAPTER 15

Flux and Strength
A Book with Two Themes

Most political science texts develop particular themes or arguments. This book is no exception. Indeed, it has two themes. What is unusual is that only one of these themes derives explicitly from what I have written in the body of the text. The other theme is drawn from what is absent in my earlier pages. "Listen, Watson." "I hear nothing, Holmes." "Precisely." The first theme, clear from the chapters, is that of a constitution in flux. The second, the hidden or covert, theme is that of the continuing strength of the political culture.

CONSTITUTIONAL FLUX

The period of the past 25 years has been notable for actual and demanded change in the institutions and practices of British government. There have been reforms, and, more especially, advocacy of radical reforms in existing institutions such as the civil service, the judiciary, the House of Commons, the House of Lords, and the structures of regional and local government. There have been changes in relationships and significant calls for further changes: between prime minister and cabinet, between government and groups, between the judiciary and the executive, between government and the citizen. There have been often vigorous demands for the introduction of what would constitute new dimensions to the Constitution: a bill of rights, membership in the European Community federal or regional government, and the regular use of referendums. The ultimate demand is for a new, written constitution. Some of these demands have been met; others, as we have seen, have been stoutly resisted by government.

The result of these developments is that the constitutional landscape in Britain is clearly not what it was at the beginning of the 1970s. Britain is now a member of a supranational body with legislative powers, the European Community. The relationship between the institutions of the Community and the institutions of United Kingdom government changed significantly toward the end of the 1980s. Northern Ireland is governed directly by the United Kingdom government. Various constitutional innovations have been tried in the province. A formal body has been created through which a foreign government may make representations on behalf of a particular community in part of the United Kingdom. National referendums are no longer alien to constitutional practice. The structure of local government has been changed, as has the relationship between central and local government and the basis for funding local government. Direct elections have been held for members to serve in a supranational Parliament. For the election of members of the European Parliament from Northern Ireland, a system of proportional representation has been employed. Civil rights have been variously modified, restricted, and extended. The powers of central government have been strengthened. At the same time, the extent of public ownership has been significantly reduced. In the 1970s, trade union rights were extended; in the 1980s, they were restricted.

During the period, various conventions of the constitution also underwent modification or erosion. The principle of collective responsibility was twice suspended in order to allow ministers to speak and vote against particular government policies. The principle was also eroded by the growing practice of leaks and semipublic disputes; in the Labour government of the 1970s Tony Benn was a minister in clear disagreement with government policy, and in the Conservative government of the 1980s Peter Walker occupied a similar position. The application of the convention of collective responsibility to confidence votes in the House of Commons was shown to have a more restrictive application than was previously assumed.[1] The principle of individual ministerial responsibility was also whittled away at the edges by the increasing public visibility of civil servants, especially before select committees of the House of Commons, and by the establishment, beginning in 1989, of executive agencies within departments.

The period also witnessed major attempts at reform, beginning in 1969 with the Parliament (No. 2) Bill (see Chapter 11) and followed in 1976 by the Scotland and Wales Bill (see Chapter 9). Both failed, the first because of parliamentary indifference, the second as a consequence of hurdles erected by Parliament. Various attempts to establish power-sharing executives in Northern Ireland also fell foul of opposition from the Unionist parties in Northern Ireland (Chapter 9). Measures to implement the Fulton Report on the Civil Service were, at best, only partially successful. These were all attempts at reform initiated by government. Various efforts to achieve reform were made also by nongovernment parties or by individual parliamentarians, most notably the introduction of a bill of rights, a measure regularly receiving a majority in the House of Lords. In the latter half of the 1980s, Alliance and then SLD MPs regularly introduced private members' bills designed to introduce proportional representation for local elections. Other private members' bills of constitutional import ranged from a measure to introduce fixed-term elections to one to terminate British jurisdiction in Northern Ireland.

Given the uneven and disparate reformulations of the constitutional landscape, traditional textbooks on the British constitution very soon became out of date. Not only did the books change, but so did those who were writing them. Books by constitutional lawyers began to give way to works produced by political scientists or by a combination of political scientists and a new breed of (often reform-minded) law lecturers.[2] The works reflected the change in the nature of constitutional debate. The constitution was far more at the heart of political debate, constitutional change often being offered as a solution or partial solution to some of the nation's political, economic, and social ills. As it became drawn into the maelstrom of political debate, so there began to emerge a number of different approaches to constitutional change. These approaches succeeded the often unarticulated consensus that had prevailed in the 1950s and part of the 1960s.

By the beginning of the 1980s, six separate approaches were discernible. The High Tory approach favored the existing constitutional framework, arguing for things to be left as they were. The Socialist approach argued for a constitutional reformulation that would permit a strong party-dominated central government to fulfill a party program free of external constraints. The Marxist approach largely rejected institutional change, regarding it as an attempt by the ruling state elite to maintain the interests of finance capital; it waited instead for the crisis of capitalism to result in a collapse of the existing political system. The group approach sought the more extensive incorporation of groups into the governmental process. The liberal approach (not confined to the Liberal party) sought constitutional reform that would defend the individual in society and allow for the generation of consensus-building constitutional rules. The sixth and final approach, the traditional approach, sought limited change in order to maintain a balance between strong government and an effective Parliament, the emphasis being on the maintenance of parliamentary sovereignty and parliamentary (and party) government.[3] These approaches were not all well developed nor were they coterminous with existing political parties. Their more obvious emergence and articulation served to generate a vigorous but confused debate about the structure and the future of the British Constitution.

By the early 1980s the description of the Constitution as being in a state of flux would thus appear both apt and accurate. That it should be in such a state is not surprising. As economic policies failed to have the desired effect in restoring the nation's economic health, attention began to turn to institutional change as a possible solution. At times of economic malaise, when government has had difficulty in maintaining effectiveness and/or consent, there has been a tendency to look to constitutional change as a palliative or a means of dealing with the problem, of producing a system capable of being effective and maintaining consent. At the time of the depression in the 1930s, for example, the implications for the Constitution were noted by Conservative leader Stanley Baldwin. "There is bound to be unrest," he reflected, "when more questions are being put than statesmen can answer. Within the House of Commons itself there is a growing sense of the need for overhauling the ship of State."[4] Disappointment with the working of representative government, he said, was no new thing. "It recurs periodically and we are in one of the fermenting periods now. It may be uncomfortable but it is not surprising."[5]

The economic and political problems of the 1970s encouraged growing demands for constitutional change. Advocates of the liberal approach, who pressed in particular for electoral reform and a bill of rights, tended to make much of the running in debate. Support for a bill of rights was pronounced among Conservative and Liberal jurists in the House of Lords. In the first half of the 1980s constitutional debate receded in prominence, in part because of improvements in some economic indicators and in part because some prominent Conservative advocates of reform (notably Lord Hailsham) were brought into government; there was also a recognition that there was unlikely to be any liberal reforms by a government wedded essentially to the traditional approach. However, as we have seen (Chapter 3), pressure for a new constitutional settlement grew in prominence in the wake of the 1987 general election. Perceptions of a more powerful, centralized government—with consequent implications for civil liberties— and the recognition by some on the left that the Labour party might be more likely to achieve power under a different constitutional system generated a new configuration in the debate. Advocates of the liberal approach in the 1970s and early 1980s were drawn largely from the center and center-right of the political spectrum. In the latter half of the 1980s the centrists were joined by a number on the left—those who previously would have been associated with the socialist approach. The signatories of "Charter '88," a manifesto issued in 1988 by supporters of a new constitution, comprised leading members of center parties and noted left-wing writers, including Marxists Ralph Miliband and Martin Jacques (editor of *Marxism Today*). This pressure for change was accompanied by a range of publications, including a continuous stream of literature from the Constitutional Reform Centre, a body formed in 1984 to press for a new constitution "in line with the needs of contemporary society."[6] Constitutional change was back on the agenda.

In short, the demands for constitutional change in recent years have been significant. However, in historical perspective, they are not unusual. From the perspective of the languid 1950s they may appear surprising, but historically the 1950s constitute a decade more atypical than subsequent decades. Pressure for political and constitutional change has littered the historical landscape, an observation borne out by a study of the development of parliamentary government in Britain (Chapter 3). Demands for constitutional change may be more virulent in some decades than in others, but rarely have such demands been totally absent from the agenda of political debate. Even in the 1950s and early 1960s, the period from which many generalizations have been drawn about British political behavior, modest constitutional changes were carried out by government (the introduction of life peerages, for example). Less modest proposals, not least concerning the House of Lords, were being put forward by more radical reformers.[7] Given the apparent failure of the political system at various times since then to meet demands and expectations that it had appeared capable of meeting in earlier decades, it is hardly surprising that the pressure on the institutions of government became much greater, with the Constitution being dragged back into the fray of political debate as it had been in the 1930s and earlier.

Thus, that the Constitution should be a matter of political controversy is not something that should be a cause of wonder. Apprised of the contemporary debate, the appropriate response should be, "Oh yes, only to be expected" and not "Good heavens, how surprising." And yet there does remain something that *is* remarkable about the constitutional ferment of recent years. Given the problems variously faced by the nation, problems worse than those faced by many other Western industrialized nations, it is amazing that the force for change has not been greater. The basic constitutional structure remains intact. Pressure for change has not overwhelmed or gone beyond the Constitution—that is, the people have not taken to the streets to demand action. (For those who might query this assertion, read on.) Indeed, looked at from this perspective, what emerges as being far more deserving of attention than what has happened over the past two decades is what has *not* happened. Why has the political system proved relatively resilient at a time of acute stress? Why have demands for reform not been more strident? Why have such demands been channeled through largely conventional avenues rather than through more radical action? The explanation, I suggest, lies in the continuing strength of the political culture.

THE STRENGTH OF THE POLITICAL CULTURE

Since the 1960s, Britain has faced various serious economic problems. A number of explanations have been offered as to the cause of these problems (Chapter 3). Economic problems have generated political and social problems. Government has, for most of the period, lacked the resources it previously had for meeting rising demands and expectations. Its failure to meet those demands has led to demands for political and institutional change as well as to social tension. As we have seen, the 1970s and 1980s witnessed a relative desertion by voters of the two main parties; in the 1983 and 1987 general elections, one in four voters who went to the polls cast their ballots for center parties. Scottish nationalism became an important force north of the border. In the 1980s, public order broke down in a number of cities, starting in the St. Paul's district of Bristol in 1980, followed by Liverpool, London, and a number of other cities in 1981, and by the Handsworth district of Birmingham and the Brixton and Tottenham districts of London in 1985. Government has variously had difficulty in mobilizing support among affected groups in order to ensure the implementation of its policies, those groups standing out for results that will favor their own interests; the groups have been varied, ranging from traditional manual unions to the medical profession. Hence the problems of recent years. All of this is true.

According to some analyses, these problems both reflect and are in part the product of a decline in the "civic culture" in Britain. In particular, Samuel Beer has contended that the growth of technocratic and populist attitudes, the latter engendered by a "romantic revolt in politics," has served to undermine the hierarchic and organic values that formed the civic culture in Britain. The consequence has been a decline, indeed a collapse, in the civic culture, producing distrust in government and demands for more radical participatory democracy. Thus, coupled with pluralist stagnation, provides an explanation for political fragmentation and immobilism in Britain.[8] All of this, I would suggest, is not true.

Let me first of all express the thrust of my own argument before explaining why Professor Beer's well-expressed points are wrong. In Chapter 2, I argued that the strength of the political culture lay in the convergence of the orientations toward problem solving, the political system, cooperation and individuality, and other people. Those orientations, I suggested, were congruent with one another and had been molded and reinforced by the experience of history. Recognition of the apparent strength of the political culture, certainly of the corollary of having a culture and a political system that worked and were different from those of other countries, reinforced pride in the political system and encouraged a rather romanticized teaching of its attributes. Indeed, I would suggest that these developments imparted to the political culture a momentum that has resulted in a strengthening of that culture over past decades, not a weakening. The events of more recent years point to its continuing strength. Viewed from a deeper historical and cultural perspective than that of the 1950s and 1960s, the political and social tensions of the past twenty years are unusual only in that they were not more severe. Certainly, they can be understood and should be understood within the context of the well-established civic culture.

Consider the following quotation. It is a lengthy one but, important for the purposes of my argument, it could have been much longer:

In 1919, following demobilisation, serious rioting occurred throughout the country. In May and June there were race riots in South Wales, the East End [of London,] and Liverpool when whites attacked blacks. In Cardiff three people were shot dead. In July the Peace Day celebrations were attended by riots in Wolverhampton, Salisbury, Epsom, Luton, Essex, Coventry and Swindon. In Luton the town hall was destroyed by arson. Police and firemen were attacked by bricks, stones and bottles and there was widespread looting. On the first of August the police in Liverpool went on strike, and severe rioting and widespread looting began, continuing for four days and nights. Steel helmeted troops and tanks were sent in. There were bayonet charges and shooting. In July and August there were also riots and battles between police and youths in London: in Greenwich, Hammersmith, Tottenham, Edmonton, Wood Green, Barking and Brixton.[9]

This was not an isolated period in British history. There were clashes before the First World War between the police and the suffragettes (demanding votes for women) and between police and strikers. On a number of occasion troops were called out to assist the police. During a railway and dock strike in 1911, the Home Secretary, Winston Churchill, actually sent a gunboat up the River Mersey. He despatched troops to guard Manchester railway stations. According to one newspaper, he sent troops "hither and thither as though Armageddon was upon us."[10] There was rioting on various occasions in the 1920s and 1930s. There were clashes between police and demonstrators during the General Strike of 1926. In 1931 thousands of unemployed demonstrators fought with the police in Glasgow; there was entensive damage. Violent clashes took place for two days between demonstrators and police in Birkenhead, resulting in many injuries.[11] Public disorder, in short, is not unknown in Britain in the twentieth century.

Various caveats must now be entered. The violence and disorder in the early part of the century were significant but (1) they were less common than in the eighteenth and nineteenth centuries,[12] (2) they were less extensive than in many other Western countries, and (3) they remained exceptional. For an illustration of the second point, one need look no further than the United States. In the three-year period 1902 to 1904, about 200 people were killed and 2,000 injured in the United States in the violence that accompanied various strikes and lockouts.[13] In 1914 in the so-called Ludlow Massacre, National Guardsmen killed a number of striking coal miners and set fire to their tents. There were 16 deaths in the Little Steel Strike of 1937.[14] Lynch-mob violence remained a feature of the American South and race riots occurred in the North. Between 1915 and 1919 there were 22 racial disturbances in United States cities, the most violent being in Chicago in 1919, when 15 whites and 23 blacks were killed.[15] Violent clashes have been far more a feature of the American than the British historical landscape.

That the clashes in Britain were exceptional is significant and central to my argument. The early part of the century was marked by the orientations identified in Chapter 2. A desire to reach agreement, "to work things out," and to accept established authority remained predominant features of the political culture. Despite clashes between police and demonstrators, most strikes and demonstrations were peaceful. Every year there were several hundred industrial stoppages involving several hundred-thousand workers.[16] Despite clashes during the General Strike of 1926, the most noteworthy feature of the dispute was its peacefulness and the desire to reach some form of agreement. "Paradoxically," wrote A. H. Halsey, "the General Strike of 1926, which may reasonably be described as a moment of tense confrontation between the two main classes, . . . provides unmistakable evidence of a consensual political culture."[17] He discerned this consensus as much in the actions of the political elite as in the activities of police and strikers. The union leaders were keen not to be seen as threatening the Constitution. Prime Minister Stanley Baldwin, for his part, was keen to heal any social wounds caused by the dispute. He discouraged his supporters from seeking further to restrict the unions once the strike was over, invoking in the House of Commons the prayer "Give Peace in our time, O Lord."[18] What disputes there were tended to be conducted more often than not in a very British fashion, according to accepted norms. Similarly, when sailors (hit by a pay cut) refused to set sail on exercises, in the "Invergordon Mutiny" of 1931, there were no serious outbreaks of violence and force was not necessary to bring the incident to an end; a compromise was found and the ships were sent back to their home ports. The long-term effect of the action was an improvement in sailors' welfare.[19] Winston Churchill provided an idiosyncratic but nonetheless British response when berated by a fellow cabinet minister for having sent troops to northern cities. "Now, Charlie," he said, "don't be cross. It was such fun."[20]

My contention, then, is that the orientations of the political culture, as identified in Chapter 2, were well developed by the beginning of the twentieth century and became more marked as the century progressed. This development was reflected in the decline in violent clashes and public disorder. The strength of the political culture helps explain both the nature and the extent of the political conflicts and the public disorder in the 1970s and 1980s. The orientation toward the political system ensured that the controversies surrounding the institutions of government were essentially disparate and were conducted according to the accepted "rules of the game." Those parties seeking radical constitutional change, whether liberal or socialist, were prepared to seek that change through the existing electoral and parliamentary framework. Despite the Conservative and Labour parties becoming more polarized in the policies they advocated, both parties have remained wedded to the essentials of British parliamentary government. Left-wing politician Tony Benn is as ardent a parliamentarian as is Mrs. Margaret Thatcher. Parliament remains the accepted legitimate forum in which political battles must be fought. Left-wing Labour MPs are among the most assiduous attenders of parliamentary debates. Advocacy of extra-parliamentary action—in essence, of taking to the streets to press for change—remains remarkable for its rarity and for the fate of those who pursue it. Few advocate it, and even fewer appear to try it (see below). Public demonstrations are popular but in this, as in clashes between competing groups, there is nothing new. What remains unusual is the reluctance to consider action that goes beyond the norms of the political culture, such as the use of violence or of political strikes. Trade union leaders retain the fear that characterized their predecessors of the 1920s—that of taking "political" as opposed to "industrial" action. Industrial action in Britain continues to take the form of wage militancy rather than political militancy.[21]

Despite the riots of 1981 and 1985 violence and public disorder remain uncommon to contemporary Britain. Even during the riots, serious violence was rare. Fatalities have been rare: one youth died after being hit by a police vehicle in Liverpool, two Asian shopkeepers died in a fire during the Handsworth riots, and one policeman was killed by a mob in Tottenham. (Compare this with the experience of race riots in Miami.) Military force equivalent to calling out the National Guard has not been used or, as far as is known, contemplated. There is also no monocausal explanation of the riots. Some appear the product of mounting tension between police and black youths, others of spontaneous violence between white gangs and blacks.[22] The riots themselves, at least in Liverpool, appeared to follow well-ordered patterns, with a clear "us" and "them" division between the police and the rioters, members of the public being allowed to stand on the side and spectate. One anecdote by a Liverpool resident reflects the British nature of the rioting. As a gang of predominantly black youths was marching up one street, setting fire to a number of buildings, a local white resident rushed out to try to persuade them not to set fire to the local squash club building on the grounds that it was of architectural importance. Apparently, the gang and the resident were engaged in discussion for several minutes before the decision was taken that the building should be burned.[23] Such an exchange is hardly conceivable in the context of riots in, say, Miami, Los Angeles, or Chicago.

It is possible that at this stage some readers, looking at the problem from a United Kingdom rather than a British perspective, are getting irritated with my line of argument. What, they may well ask, is the position in Northern Ireland? Is that not an example of a society in which violence is rife and political strikes have been held, most notably that of the Ulster Workers Council in 1974 (the strike that effectively brought down the new Northern Ireland Executive)? Indeed yes, but this reinforces rather than undermines my argument. The *British* political culture is precisely that: British. The culture and history of Northern Ireland, as I sought to show in Chapter 9, is totally distinct. It is precisely because of this gulf between the British and Northern Ireland cultures that the problems of Northern Ireland are so incomprehensible to the British mind. It also helps explain why, as I suggested in Chapter 9, the British government has had difficulty in knowing how to handle the problem, since policy is often premised on the British assumption that problems can be solved by discussion, by reasonable people gathering round a table to resolve their differences.[24] The British political culture also helps provide a partial explanation for the continued presence of troops in Northern Ireland. Opinion polls, as we have seen, reveal that most people in Britain would prefer to withdraw troops from the province. They remain, in part because of the sense of responsibility shared by political leaders, who believe that to pursue a policy of withdrawal would result in a bloodbath.

So much, then, for a basic statement of my argument. Let me now pursue it further, from a negative perspective, by dissecting the threads of Beer's argument. A confluence of technocratic and populist attitudes, he argues, have undermined the values of the traditional civic culture, thus explaining a decline in deference, class decomposition, and lack of trust in government. The changes, he claims, are sufficient to argue that the decline in the civic culture can be described as a "collapse."[25] In fact, the changes he claims to discern are relative and have so far effected no fundamental change in the political culture.

Let us consider briefly the different elements that Professor Beer identifies, both the new attitudes and their presumed effects. The assertion of *technocratic values*, he concedes, had a limited impact on the populace and is presented in his work primarily in order to help isolate and characterize the more powerful influence of populist values.[26] Nonetheless, he contends that "the technocratic attack," "an exaggerated assertion of the scientific ethos," helped shape in critical ways the behavior of the political elite: it found reflection in the reform of the civil service following the Fulton Committee report in 1968 and in Edward Heath's managerial approach as prime minister, with the introduction of Program Analysis and Review (PAR) and the Central Policy Review Staff (CPRS). Yet even this is to state too much. As previous chapters have shown, primarily Chapter 8, those reforms failed to overcome the self-interest and incremental-policy style of government, a style facilitated by the existing political culture. Far from the reforms having a significant impact on the traditional processes of government, those processes in effect smothered the new managerialism. The CPRS and PAR exist no longer, and the managerialism of Edward Heath was short-lived, Mr. Heath being replaced by a leader who adheres to a philosophy that, taken to its logical conclusion, has an antimanagerial bias.

What, then, of the *romantic revolt?* Professor Beer concedes that the reasons for the occurrence of this "revolt" and for the method of its occurrence are not clear. Possible explanations that he discusses, but does not fully align himself with, are post-material reaction to affluence, a reaction to the failure of government to meet expectations, and a reaction to a centralized bureaucratic state.[27] Whatever the causes, the new romanticism took the form of emphasizing cultural values as well as demanding wider and more intense participation. It was also radically decentralizing.

It was a revolt that found reflection in the cultural and political upheavals of the 1960s. It had to be seen within the context of a wider far-reaching assault on the values of society. "The ethos was the same in all spheres," Beer writes. "No explanation of political developments can satisfy that does not recognise this connection."[28] On the left of the political spectrum, Marcuse and the New Left writers had a major impact on young students. Beer continues, "No one who was a university teacher in those days [the 1960s] can doubt the power of a book, such as Brown's *Life Against Death* or Marcuse's *Eros and Civilisation*, to work a 'conversion.' "[29] But the new populism reached wider. Pop music served as one transmission belt for new messages that broke with established values. The songs of the Beatles are accorded special attention. "I doubt," writes Beer, that they ever used the word 'democratic' or 'participation' in a song, but it would be hard to find a stronger case against exclusion than *Eleanor Rigby* or in favor of inclusion than *Sergeant Pepper*. And if you are looking for a secular hymn to agape, *All You Need Is Love* should do. The localism of their songs is fundamental."[30]

The romantic revolt, the new populism, extended into the 1970s, constituting a new orthodoxy of dissent. It found reflection in workers' attitudes, emphasizing principles rather than material benefits when striking, and has had an impact on the political parties. There has been a populist thrust within the Labour party, stressing participation and being less willing to accept established authority within the party. Within the Conservative party, it has found reflection in the rise of neoliberalism and a decline in the traditions of deference, authority, and acceptance of an organic society. There has been, declared Beer, "a waning of Toryism."[31] The parties most in tune with and benefiting most from this new romanticism—with its emphasis on values, participation, and decentralization—were the Liberal party and, after 1981, the Social Democratic party.

Possibly the kindest comment that can be made about this thesis is that it is vague. The more you try to come to grips with it, the more the sand seeps through your fingers. The threads of the argument are thin and tenuous, resting on little empirical verification. In asserting that no university teacher in the 1960s could doubt the power of writings such as those by Marcuse and Brown to work a "conversion," Beer is clearly drawing on his own recollections as a university teacher. This, with all due respect, tells us little about changes in the political culture. I, as an undergraduate in the very late 1960s, can put forward the conflicting assertion that few British students were "converted" by any such works and that few students had read Marcuse and even fewer had heard of Brown. Such anecdotal assertions take the argument not very far forward. Far more relevant, and observable, is the comparative behavior of students in different countries during the 1960s. While students were facing National Guardsmen on campuses in the United States and rioting students in France came close to toppling the French government, British students were mostly getting on with their studies and a number at a minority of campuses were engaging in occasional bouts of public disorder. What needs to be explained is not why there were sit-ins and demonstrations by students in some British universities but why those students did not emulate their foreign counterparts. The answer, I would suggest, is to be found in the continuing strength of the political culture.

As for the relevance of the pop music of the 1960s, one reviewer of *Britain Against Itself* wrote, "I cannot take seriously a discussion of the lyrics of the Beatles, although I'm willing to admit that the rock, pop and teenage culture generally are symptomatic of a change."[32] Some of the music of the period may indeed have served to convey messages that broke with established values. However, the interpretation of their meaning by Beer is not necessarily the interpretation given by those responsible for the music, nor is it necessarily the same as that rendered by those who listened to the music. Music means different things to different people. *Eleanor Rigby* had quite an impact on this writer, but how I interpret it bears no resemblance to Beer's interpretation. The fact that music that conveys a message of change or a challenge to existing values is popular does not mean necessarily that the message has won approval.[33] If the pop culture of the 1960s is symptomatic of change, there is little empirical evidence to demonstrate what that change is, other than a change in musical tastes and behavior. Certainly, there is little to demonstrate a connection between the lyrics of Beatle songs and Beer's "new populism."

Moving to more relevant ground, the assertion of the new populism in workers' behavior and in the political parties is not sufficient to bear the weight that Beer gives it. There may indeed have been a greater fragmentation in the union movement in the 1960s and 1970s, local groups starting to regulate their own behavior, but the cause of this was not some new populism that was sweeping across the land but rather the failure of government to meet the demands of the unions. When union leaders became unable to produce the goods for their members, local groups began to get what they could for themselves, and in that there is nothing surprising. Such changes may have engendered some change in attitudes, but not to an extent that has threatened the existing political culture. Union attitudes and behavior, looked at in broad historical perspective, have not departed dramatically from those of earlier periods. In taking strike action, workers may indeed, as Beer suggests, emphasize the importance of the principles at stake ("Money doesn't count when you're fighting for principle," he quotes one striker as saying), but he presents no evidence that such expressions are new. One might be forgiven for suggesting that it would be surprising if such assertions were not made. If a worker is out on strike for any length of time and ends up losing more money through lost wages than would be gained by the claimed pay rise, how can he justify his action? Furthermore, looked at from the perspective of member participation, the greater demands for participation that form part of the romantic revolt can hardly be said to have swept through the trade union movement. The prevailing ethos remains one of nonparticipation.

As for the political parties, the attempts within the Labour party to introduce populist themes are hardly new to the traditions of the party. An emphasis on the individual, on electing regional authorities (responsible for planning), on opening up civil-service decision making to "much greater scrutiny and political control," on liberalizing the Officials Secret Act, and on moving toward employees' control and self-management—the items singled out by Beer—have well-established lineages. They may have become more pronounced but they are best understood within the context of the strands that form the Labour party and the divisions between those strands that have existed since the party's formation (see Chapter 6). Furthermore, one of the most significant features of Neil Kinnock's leadership has been the assertion of authority by the leader; an unwillingness to accept such authority by the party has, if anything, been reversed.

Beer's argument concerning the Conservative party is similarly overdrawn. As we have seen (Chapter 6), neoliberalism is one well-established strand of Conservatism. It has become more prominent in recent years, especially since the election of Mrs. Thatcher as party leader, but its significance should not be exaggerated. The party, as I said in Chapter 6, now has a leader more identified with the neoliberal wing than was the case before, but the government she heads has not pursued a vigorous neoliberal policy nor has the Conservative party as a whole become neoliberal. Outside of its economic policy, the government has pursued many traditional Tory policies, and on economic policy most of the parliamentary party remains agnostic (that is, in the event of neoliberal policies failing, it will turn to support other policies). Beer's claim to substantiate the "waning of Toryism" rests largely on the writings of two Conservatives (one of the works a somewhat idiosyncratic one and, as its author conceded to this writer, somewhat self-indulgent) and their failing to address themselves to the issues of deference and authority. Within the Conservative party, deference and attitudes toward authority may be less marked than in the 1950s, but any change is relative. Deference and the relationship between leaders and led within the party remain fundamentally unchanged.[34] And, as we have seen, the parties identified as the main beneficiaries of this new romanticism—the center parties—have fallen on hard times since 1987.

So much, then, for the supposed "romantic revolt." This is not to say that some of the changes mentioned by Beer have not taken place (neoliberalism clearly is more prominent in the Conservative party than it was previously), but the changes will not bear the weight of the analysis given them. What, then, of the developments that Beer hypothesized were the result of his supposed romantic revolt?

Class decomposition is discussed primarily in terms of the decline in the class–party nexus.[35] This decline I have charted in Chapters 5 and 6. The decline is significant but, as is argued in Chapter 5, class remains the most important predictor of voting behavior. Although class may have declined in significance, class-related factors, notably home ownership, have grown in importance. If one goes beyond the class–party nexus, class remains central to British society (see Chapter 1). There is a greater social mobility than before, as Goldthorpe has shown, and a "service class" may be emerging, but to contend as Beer does that there has been class decomposition and a reintegration of the working class into competitive society by a new plurality of groups is again to take the argument further than the empirical evidence will allow. It is also to emphasize the economic over the social. Class provides a social orientation for which groups have provided no substitute.

As for a *decline of leadership and weakening of party government*, these are not particular features of recent British history and can hardly be described as notable features of the Thatcher era. As I interpret Beer's thesis, leadership decline results from the failure of government to mobilize consent and to impose policies on disparate groups. This argument, as we have seen, remains current, forming part of the thesis of adversarial politics (Chapter 3). In response, let me make a number of points. First, it can be contended that there was a notable absence of leadership during the collectivist era of the 1950s, the product of an unwillingness to break from the collectivist consensus and give a lead. (If this is the case, what has leadership "declined" from?) Second, insofar as there is a problem of getting groups to support, or at least acquiesce in, the implementation of new departures in public policy, this is not exclusive to recent decades. It has been apparent at different times in British history—for example, in the first two decades of the century—and is explicable in terms of the political culture. Third, it can hardly be argued that the premiership of Margaret Thatcher has been notable for an absence of leadership. That leadership has proved notably more effective than recent leaderships in ensuring group compliance with public policy. In the latter half of the 1980s union resistance largely crumbled; whereas the Heath government had faltered and ultimately failed in the face of a threatened national miners' strike, the Thatcher government proved willing, and ultimately successful, in resisting such a strike. Trade unions were effectively constrained by legal sanction. Groups willing and able to defend the self-interest of members declined in number throughout the 1980s; those that did resist with some effect, such as doctors in 1989, were exceptional. If not actually "mobilizing" support, the reduction of group resistance by government proved a notable feature of the 1980s. Insofar as there may have been a relative failure of government to mobilize support, it is relative only to an ideal state postulated by advocates of the adversary politics thesis; it is not relative to the reality of British peacetime experience.

As for a weakening of strong party government, this again tells little about a change in the political culture of Britain. It has been apparent at various times in modern British history. The period of "strong" two-party government, from 1945 to 1970, is much more an atypical one than the period since 1970. It is also relevant to remind ourselves of Nevil Johnson's observation (cited in Chapter 6) that a decline in voting support for one or both main parties is not in itself proof of a decline in support for a two-party system. Indeed, as we have been, there is survey evidence that citizens wish to retain the benefits of a two-party system—principally a government with an overall majority—even if this is at the expense of a "fairer" electoral system.

Finally, what of *trust in government?* Beer cites a decline in such trust as empirical verification of a waning of deference that underpins the positive orientation toward government. He calls in aid the analyses of Alan Marsh and Vivien Hart (the latter using the findings of the Royal Commission on the Constitution: see Chapter 9), who interpret a decline in such trust as reflecting a change in values.[36] The biggest change, according to Beer, is a decline or a collapse in deference.

Let us look at the evidence. Both Marsh and the Royal Commission detected a significant fraction of the population expressing distrust in government. The responses to the Royal Commission question on the existing system of running the country are given in Table 15.1. As it shows, only 5% of respondents thought the existing system worked extremely well and could not be improved. Marsh found that when asked, "How much do you trust the government in Westminster [sic] to do what is right?" 47% responded with "Only some of the time" and 10% responded "Almost never."

Much has also been made by some writers of the findings of Barnes, Kaase, et al. as to the preparedness of the British public to engage in direct action. These findings, reproduced in Table 15.2, are interpreted to suggest that significant micro-level political changes had taken place between the mid-1960s and the 1970s.[37] More Britons than before appeared willing to engage in direct action than to defer to government. Is this not sufficient evidence for providing a *prima facie* case for Beer's thesis? The simple answer is: no. I would offer three principal points in refutation.

First, even the survey evidence presented is not, on the face of it, sufficient to demonstrate a high or, especially, a *rising* level of mistrust in

TABLE 15.1. TRUST IN GOVERNMENT (1), 1970

Question: **Which of these statements best expresses your opinion on the present system of running Britain?**

"Works extremely well and could not be improved"	5%
"Could be improved in small ways but mainly works well"	43%
"Could be improved quite a lot"	35%
"Needs a great deal of improvement"	14%
"Don't know"	4%

Source: Royal Commission on the Constitution, Research Papers 7, reproduced in V. Hart, Distrust and Democracy (Cambridge University Press, 1978), p. 60. Copyright 1978 HMSO. Reprinted by permission.

TABLE 15.2. WILLINGNESS TO ENGAGE IN DIRECT ACTION

The preparedness of the British public to engage in direct action

Action	Percentage Answering				
	"Have Done"	"Would Do"	"Might Do"	"Would Never do"	Missing Data
Petitions	22	31	22	21	4
Lawful demonstration	6	25	24	42	4
Boycotts	5	17	23	47	7
Rent strikes	2	10	20	65	4
Unofficial strikes	5	7	15	69	3
Occupying buildings	1	6	13	77	3
Blocking traffic	1	7	15	74	2
Damaging property	1	1	2	95	2
Personal violence	0	1	4	93	2

Source: Barnes, Kaase, et al., Political Action (1979), reproduced in D. Sanders and E. Tanenbaum, "Direct Action and Political Culture: The Changing Political Consciousness of the British Public," European Journal of Political Research, 11, 1983, p. 47.

government. It is not clear that the survey responses can bear the weight of interpretation given them. The fact that 35% of respondents in the Royal Commission survey believed that the system of government "could be improved quite a lot" does not demonstrate a lack of *trust* in that system. Similarly, the fact that almost half the respondents in the Marsh survey trusted government to do what is right "only some of the time" tells us nothing about trust in the *system* of government. Governments (which is what the question was really about) are not infallible and it would have been remarkable had most Britons expected government to do what was right all the time. More significantly for our purposes, there is little if anything to demonstrate changes in the level of trust over a period of time. There are no comparable data for, say, the 1920s and 1930s. That there may have been some decline in trust from the 1950s to the 1970s and early 1980s may not be surprising, but has it declined compared with earlier decades of the century? From my earlier observations on public disorder during the early years of this century, I suspect not. There are no survey data to dispel that suspicion. Sanders and Tanenbaum, in using the data of Barnes et al., concede that the database is fragile and are able only to suggest "micro-level" changes.[38] This is hardly sufficient for demonstrating a collapse of the civic culture in Britain. Indeed, what is remarkable about the findings given in Table 15.2 is not, as Sanders and Tanenbaum claim, "the proportion of the mass population willing to undertake direct political activities such as boycotts, demonstrations and strikes in situations where these activities had hitherto been deemed 'illegitimate' or 'unacceptable,'"[39] but precisely the opposite. Table 15.2 is remarkable for the proportion of people who "would never" engage even in activities that are lawful and have not been considered illegitimate or unacceptable, never mind the overwhelming proportion who would never engage in more dubious activities. Bearing in mind the extent of public disorder in the early part of this century, Table 15.2 would appear rather to support my argument as to the continuing strength of the political culture. It suggests an essentially law-abiding population, one not avidly disposed to taking direct political action.

The fact that there was *some* distrust of the system of government in the 1970s is not sufficient to bear out Beer's thesis, nor is it surprising. It is surprising to Beer and others because of the assumptions that they make about the political culture. However, if one accepts that the deference accorded government is contingent, not certain (Chapter 2), then the failure of government to meet expectations could be expected to produce a greater expression of distrust in government than was the case in the heady days of Almond and Verba's research for *The Civic Culture* (1963). What should be considered surprising, given Beer's assumptions about the political culture, is the proportion of respondents who did not express any distrust in government and, much more importantly, the fact that distrust did not appear to increase during the 1970s. This provides the second point of refutation. A survey by Louis Moss of adults in England and Wales in 1978 revealed responses very similar to those obtained in 1970 by the Royal Commission on the Constitution (Table 15.3). Questions similar to those asked by Marsh also elicited no increase in the proportions giving nontrusting responses.[40]

Other surveys in the 1970s of attitudes toward specific elements of the constitutional structure, such as the House of Commons, also failed to elicit the negative response expected by some critics. A National Opinion Poll (NOP) undertaken for Granada Television in 1973 on the attitudes toward Parliament "failed to demonstrate the extent of disaffection they expected. So in the end they discarded the poll and used the dissatisfaction of many MPs and civil servants as their framework."[41] (Of those ques-

TABLE 15.3. TRUST IN GOVERNMENT (2), 1978

Respondents were asked their opinion "on the present system of running the government of this country."

"On the whole it works well and probably could not be improved"	4%
"It could be improved in small ways but mainly works well"	53%
"It could be improved a lot"	30%
"It needs a great deal of improvement"	11%

Source: L. Moss, "Attitudes Towards Government," SSRC Research Report HR 5427 (1980), Appendix, p. 28. Reprinted by permission.

tioned, 55% had said that "Parliament works very well or fairly well"; only 8% thought that their MPs were doing "a poor job.") A MORI poll carried out for *The Sunday Times* in 1977 on how well institutions performed found that "Parliament emerges with surprisingly little egg on its face," only 8% of respondents considering that Parliament did "a bad job."[42] Nor did polls in this period suggest that dissatisfaction with government had swelled to the level of demanding significant institutional change. Indeed, an Opinion Research Centre (ORC) poll in 1977 found that respondents gave constitutional change "a very low priority" in relation to other issues.[43] People were more concerned that government should deal with problems such as rising prices and unemployment.

The third point of refutation derives from putting the data in comparative perspective. When compared with the position in, particularly, the United States, levels of trust in government in Britain appear remarkably high and stable. Given the trauma of Vietnam and then Watergate, one might hypothesize that there would be a significant decline in trust in government among Americans in the late 1960s and 1970s. That is precisely what happened (Table 15.4). In the case of the United Kingdom, one might hypothesize that, with the political and economic problems of the 1970s (minority government, rising unemployment, an inflation rate that at one point exceeded 25%, and industrial conflict), trust in the system of government would decline markedly, albeit not as much as in the United States. Yet this hypothesis was not borne out by the data. The decline that took place was markedly modest compared with what might be expected. What was remarkable about the 1970s was the extent to which trust in the system of government was maintained.

In short, then, the arguments advanced by Beer and others are not sufficient to justify the claim that there has been a collapse of the civil culture. The data offered are not sufficient individually and collectively to bear the weight of the argument. Beer's narrow, time-bound focus has obscured the wider reality, and that wider reality is the continuing strength

TABLE 15.4. TRUST IN GOVERNMENT, USA: 1958–1978

Attitude	Year							
	1958 (%)	1964 (%)	1968 (%)	1970 (%)	1972 (%)	1974 (%)	1976 (%)	1978 (%)
Cynical	11	19	26	36	36	50	53	52
In-Between	25	18	24	25	24	24	23	26
Trusting	58	61	48	38	38	24	22	19

Source: W. E. Miller, "Misreading the Public Purse," Public Opinion, Oct.–Nov. 1979, p. 11, reproduced in A. Ranney, Channels of Power (Basic Books, 1983), p. 78.

of the political culture. This is borne out by survey data of more recent years. The basic characteristics of the political culture remain intact. Britons retain their positive attitude to one another and their 'allegiant attitude toward the institutions of government. As we have seen (Chapter 2, Table 2.2), eight out of ten Britons are quite or very proud to be British. Compared with other West European nations, the strength of national pride is remarkable (Table 15.5). Again, as we have seen (Chapter 2, Table 2.1), nine out of ten Britons consider Parliament to be important or very important (a majority saying very important) in the life of the country; again, in international perspective, the figures are remarkable. More generally, satisfaction with the way democracy works remains at a healthy level and showed an increase in the period from 1973 to 1986 (Table 15.6). Most respondents in 1986 were found to be fairly or very satisfied with the way democracy works; of the other big West European countries, only West Germany produced a higher proportion.

And when a law is introduced that citizens strongly opppose, what do they do? Do they take to the streets in protest? Do they form groups or utilize existing groups, as the Beer argument would suggest? No. As the Barnes data suggest, few Britons do, or are inclined to, participate in direct action. This fact is reinforced by the British Social Attitude Surveys of the 1980s. The 1986 survey revealed that a majority of respondents would sign a petition and/or, at the individual level, contact their MPs (Table 15.7). Contacting an MP is considered more effective than signing a petition, and contacting the media, though rarely done, is the only form of action deemed more effective in influencing government than contacting the member of Parliament. These findings bear out the findings of an earlier survey.[44] More people try to influence government now than twenty or thirty years ago, but such attempts at influence are channeled through traditional avenues; MPs are increasingly active as conduits for constituents' demands (Chapter 11.)[45] There is little evidence of a dysfunctional political system or, more accurately, little evidence of widespread percep-

TABLE 15.5. PUBLIC FEELINGS OF NATIONAL PRIDE, 1983

	France %	West Germany %	UK %	Italy %
Very proud	36	17	57	40
Quite proud	39	39	35	44
Not very proud	14	24	5	10
Not at all proud	5	9	2	4
Don't know	6	11	1	2
Index[a]	3.14	2.73	3.49	3.23

[a] Range from "very proud" = 4, to "not at all proud" = 1. (Source: Euro-Barometre, June 1983, p. 54.)

TABLE 15.6. PUBLIC SATISFACTION WITH THE WAY DEMOCRACY WORKS, 1973–1986

	France		West Germany		UK		Italy	
	Sept. 1973 %	*Oct. 1986* %	*Sept. 1973* %	*Oct. 1986* %	*Sept. 1973* %	*Oct. 1986* %	*Sept. 1973* %	*Oct. 1986* %
Very satisfied	4	6	5	12	7	11	2	2
Fairly satisfied	37	44	39	59	37	42	25	23
Not very satisfied	16	10	11	4	20	14	30	25
Don't know	13	12	1	3	2	7	1	5
Index[a]	2.33	2.51	2.38	2.83	2.32	2.52	1.99	2.04

[a] Range from "very satisfied" = 4, to "not satisfied" = 0. (*Source:* Euro-Barometre, *December 1986, pp. 26–27.*)

tions of one. Pressure for constitutional change, as we have seen, has increased in recent years. However, there is little evidence that such pressure comes from anything other than an elite body comprising, essentially, the politically dispossessed of the political center and, after 1987, parts of the left. A Harris Poll taken in 1973 found that 82% of those interviewed agreed with the statement that, "On the whole, the British system of government works pretty well."[46] There is no evidence, *pace* Professor Beer, to suggest any significant shift of opinion since then among the populace. The political culture remains notably intact. Debate as to constitutional change takes place at a rarified level.[47]

TABLE 15.7. MEANS OF INFLUENCING GOVERNMENT, 1986

	Would Do %	Had Ever Done %	Believed "Very" or "Quite" Effective %
Sign petition	65	34	45
Contact your MP	52	11	50
Contact radio, TV, or newspaper	15	3	58
Speak to influential person	15	3	38
Contact government department	12	3	26
Go on protest or demonstration	11	6	21
Raise issue in organization you already belong to	10	5	32
Form group of like-minded people	8	2	26

Source: R. Jowell, S. Witherspoon, and L. Brook, British Social Attitudes: The 1987 Report *(Aldershot: Gower, 1987), p. 56.*

CONCLUSION

The political culture of Britain may have helped facilitate some structural problems but, nonetheless, it helps provide a breathing space for government in attempting to deal with the nation's problems, problems which I would suggest are essentially economic. The orientations toward problem solving and cooperation have encouraged piecemeal change in the political system. Indeed, the nature of that change has been such that, rather than there being a danger of centralized, prime ministerial power in Britain, there is instead a danger of constitutional fragmentation, of power being wielded by disparate actors (prime minister, cabinet, civil service, ministers, the institutions of the European Community, policy communities); the nature of this fragmentations has been sketched throughout this volume. Such fragmentation does not generate a need for constitutional change but rather emphasizes the need for strong, coherent government, basically, in common parlance, "a government that can govern."[48] The political culture favors a strong executive and has done so for several centuries.[49] If the executive authority has gone beyond what is acceptable to the political community, it has been checked—exceptionally by, or through the threat of, force (*Magna Carta*, the English Civil War, the Glorious Revolution), more commonly by Parliament. Parliament provides the bounds of executive action. Within those bounds, the task of government is to pursue a coherent strategy. Britons continue to defer to government that appears to know what it is doing. When governments are punished by the electorate, the punishment is for being weak, not strong. The Thatcher government won reelection in 1983 and 1987 because it was able to convey that it was a strong government that knew what it was doing. There was no great shift in values, no rallying to the philosophy of the Prime Minister ("Thatcherism"); indeed, Mrs. Thatcher continued as prime minister despite Thatcherism, not because of it.[50] For governments prepared to take strong action, the political culture provides a far more supportive environment than has often been assumed to be the case; even some cabinet ministers in the 1980s were amazed by the willingness of the population to accept without greater social unrest an unemployment level in excess of 3 million. In short, the culture and the political structures combine to facilitate a strong government that is prepared to be strong.

Thus, one has the paradox of the British political culture. The increasing fragmentation militates against decisive leadership, but if such a leadership is attempted, it provides the potential for the popular support for its realization. However, government itself does not exist independently of the political culture and is constrained by the reciprocal relationship between governors and governed (Chapter 2). It can go only so far, and at the end of the day its policies need to bear fruit. But the political culture is stronger and permits of more determined government than many have been prepared to admit.

NOTES

1. See P. Norton, "Government Defeats in the House of Commons: Myth and Reality," *Public Law*, Winter 1978, pp. 360–78.
2. Thus, for example, J. Jowell and D. Oliver (eds.), *The Changing Constitution* (Clarendon Press, 1985); P. McAuslan and J. F. McEldowney (eds.), *Law, Legitimacy and the Constitution* (Sweet and Maxwell, 1985); and I. Harden and N. Lewis, *The Noble Lie* (Hutchinson, 1987).
3. P. Norton, *The Constitution in Flux* (Basil Blackwell, 1982), conclusions.
4. S. Baldwin, *The Torch of Freedom*, 4th ed. (Hodder & Stoughton, 1937), p. 50.
5. Ibid.
6. It produces a regular newsletter, briefing documents, and various publications. See, e.g., R. Holme and M. Elliott (eds.), *1688–1988: Time for a New Constitution* (Macmillan, 1988).
7. See A. W. Benn, *The Privy Council as a Second Chamber*, Fabian Tract 305 (Frabian Society, 1957); and Lord Chorley, B. Crick, and D. Chapman, *Reform of the Lords*, Fabian Research Series 169 (Fabian Society, 1954).
8. S. H. Beer, *Britain Against Itself* (Faber and Faber, 1982).
9. S. Field and P. Southgate, *Public Disorder*, Home Office Research Study No. 72 (Her Majesty's Stationery Office, 1982), pp. 4–5.
10. A. G. Gardiner in the *Daily News*, quoted by S. Reynolds, book review, *Punch*, July 13, 1983, p. 60.
11. Field and Southgate, p. 5.
12. Ibid.
13. *To Establish Justice, To Insure Domestic Tranquility*, the Final Report of the National Commission on the Causes and Prevention of Violence (Bantam Books, 1970), p. 52.
14. Ibid.
15. Ibid.
16. D. Butler and A. Sloman, *British Political Facts 1900–1979*, 5th ed. (Macmillan, 1980), pp. 340–41.
17. A. H. Halsey, *Change in British Society*, 2nd ed. (Oxford University Press, 1981), p. 70.
18. Quoted in ibid., p. 71.
19. A. Ereira, *The Invergordon Mutiny* (Routledge & Kegan Paul, 1981).
20. Reynolds, p. 60.
21. A. W. Cox, "Strikes, Free Collective Bargaining and Public Order," in P. Norton (ed.), *Law and Order and British Politics* (Gower, 1984).
22. See, e.g., J. Rex, "Law and Order in Multi-Racial Areas: The Problems After Scarman," in Norton, *Law and Order and British Politics*, pp. 100–114.
23. Recounted to the author on a visit to Liverpool in 1982.

24. See above, Chapter 9, and Norton, *The Constitution in Flux*, Ch. 10.
25. Beer, p. 119.
26. Ibid., p. 120. This paragraph is based on pp. 120–26.
27. Ibid., pp. 143–48.
28. Ibid., p. 134.
29. Ibid., p. 137.
30. Ibid., p. 142.
31. Ibid., pp. 169–80.
32. B. M. Jones, book review, *Teaching Politics*, 12 (2), May 1983, p. 262.
33. Thus, for example, in the 1980s Tom Robinson's song "Glad to Be Gay" proved to be quite popular, but apparently many of those who sang along with the words at concerts had little understanding of the message even though it was quite obvious.
34. See P. Norton and A. Aughey, *Conservatives and Conservatism* (Temple Smith, 1981), Chs. 5 and 6; and P. Norton, "Mrs. Thatcher and the Conservative Party: Another Institution 'Handbagged'?" in K. Minogue and M. Biddiss (eds.), *Thatcherism: Personality and Politics* (Macmillan, 1987), pp. 21–37.
35. Beer, pp. 79–83.
36. Beer, pp. 114–18; A. Marsh, *Protest and Political Consciousness* (Sage, 1977); V. Hart, *Distrust and Democracy* (Cambridge University Press, 1978).
37. D. Sanders and E. Tanenbaum, "Direct Action and Political Culture: The Changing Political Consciousness and the British Public," *European Journal of Political Research*, 11, 1983, p. 46.
38. Ibid.
39. Ibid.
40. Of respondents, 24.8% thought that they could trust government to do what was right "all or most of the time," 68.4% thought they could trust it to do what was right "some of the time," and fewer than 7% responded with "none of the time." L. Moss, "Attitudes Towards Government," *SSRC Research Report HR 5427* (1980), p. 296.
41. Granada TV, *The State of the Nation* (Granada TV, 1973), p. 201.
42. P. Kellner, "Who Runs Britain?" *Sunday Times*, September 18, 1977.
43. Cited in S. E. Finer, *The Changing British Party System 1945–1979* (American Enterprise Institute, 1980), p. 176.
44. R. Jowell and S. Witherspoon, *British Social Attitudes: The 1985 Report* (Gower, 1985), p. 12.
45. P. Norton and D. Wood, "Constituency Service by Members of Parliament: Does It Contribute to a Personal Vote?" *Parliamentary Affairs*, 43 (2), 1990.
46. Hart, p. 217, n. 42.
47. At one seminar in London, convened in 1986 to discuss constitutional reform—comprising essentially academics, former civil servants, and politicians—one leading participant declared: "Let's face it, there are only 25 people in this country really committed to constitutional reform, and they are all sat in this room." Though exaggerated for the sake of emphasis, no one sought to challenge the assertion.

48. See P. Norton, "The Changing Constitution: Parts 1 and 2," *Contemporary Record*, 3 (1) and 3 (2), 1989.

49. See P. Norton, *Parliament in Perspective* (Hull University Press, 1987), pp. 12–13.

50. See I. Crewe and D. D. Searing, "Ideological Change in the British Conservative Party," *American Political Science Review*, 82 (2), June 1988.

Select Reading List

This is neither a bibliography of works used nor a comprehensive survey of available literature. Rather, it is a brief *guide* to the main and, in particular, the most recent texts available for student use. Chapter footnotes provide a pointer to further reading for students whose intellectual appetite is not satiated by what follows.

PART 1: INTRODUCTION

There are various reference works that provide useful facts and figures on contemporary Britain. The most regular and helpful of these are *Britain: An Official Handbook*, published annually by Her Majesty's Stationery Office, London; and *Social Trends*, compiled annually by the Central Statistical Office and also published by HMSO.

For a succinct introduction to political culture, see D. Kavanagh, *Political Culture* (London: Macmillan, 1972). The classic work on the subject is G. Almond and S. Verba, *The Civil Culture* (Princeton, N.J.: Princeton University Press, 1963). See also their more recent compilation, which they edited, *The Civic Culture Revisited* (Boston: Little, Brown, 1980); and S. H. Beer, *Britain Against Itself* (London: Faber and Faber, 1982). *British Social Attitudes*, published annually (Aldershot: Gower), provides analysis and the findings of the surveys conducted by Social and Community Planning Research. The volumes provide valuable material on contemporary attitudes on a range of issues and treat a number of the concerns covered in *The Civic Culture*.

The history of Britain is treated in numerous works, including the 15-volume *Oxford University of England*, published by Oxford University Press. A recent and highly acclaimed political history of Britain has been produced, in three volumes, by W. H. Greenleaf: *The British Political Tradition, Vol. 1: The Rise of Collectivism* (London: Longman, 1983); *Vol. 2: The Ideological Heritage* (London: Longman, 1983); *Vol. 3: A Much Governed Nation* (London: Longman, 1987). Unfortunately, the price of the three volumes, individually as well as collectively, dictates that they will be available primarily for library consultation.

There are a number of other works by political scientists that also offer a historical perspective in analyzing political developments and the nation's problems. Among the more influential—written from different perspectives—are S. Brittan, *The Economic Consequences of Democracy* (London: Temple Smith, 1977; rev. ed. 1989); K. Middlemas, *Politics in Industrial Society* (London: Andre Deutsch, 1979); S. H. Beer, *Britain Against Itself* (London: Faber and Faber, 1982); A. Gamble, *Britain in Decline* (London: Macmillan, 1985 ed.); and D. Marquand, *The Unprincipled Society: New Demands and Old Politics* (London: Fontana, 1988).

PART II: THE POLITICAL ENVIRONMENT

Recent years have witnessed a significant growth in the number of texts putting the Constitution in a political context. R. Brazier, *Constitutional Practice* (Oxford: Oxford University Press, 1988) provides a useful introduction to the subject. Recent contributions to the debate on the Constitution include Lord Hailsham, *Elective Dictatorship* (London: British Broadcasting Corporation, 1976); N. Johnson, *In Search of the Constitution* (London: Methuen, 1980 ed.); P. Norton, *The Constitution in Flux* (Oxford: Basil Blackwell, 1982); J. Jowell and D. Oliver (eds.), *The Changing Constitution* (Oxford: Oxford University Press, 1985); C. Graham and T. Prosser (eds.), *Waiving the Rules* (Milton Keynes: Open University Press, 1988); and R. Holme and M. Elliott (eds.), *1688–1988: Time for a New Constitution* (London: Macmillan, 1988). All bar the Norton text are essentially tracts favoring reform.

The standard works on British general elections are those published in the Nuffield election series, authored or coauthored by D. Butler and published after each election under the title of *The British General Election of . . . .* The most recent edition is D. Butler and D. Kavanagh, *The British*

General Election of 1987 (London: Macmillan, 1988). There is also now a short brief guide: D. Butler, *British General Elections since 1945* (Oxford: Basil Blackwell, 1989). The legal aspect of elections is well treated in H. F. Rawlings, *Law and the Electoral Process* (London: Sweet & Maxwell, 1988).

   D. Denver, *Elections and Voting Behaviour in Britain* (London: Philip Allan, 1989) provides a brief introduction to the subject. The principal works offering explanations of voting behavior are D. Butler and D. Stokes, *Political Change in Britain*, 2nd ed. (London: Macmillan, 1974); B. Sarlvik and I. Crewe, *Decade of Dealignment* (Cambridge: Cambridge University Press, 1983); M. Franklin, *The Decline of Class Voting in Britain* (Oxford: Oxford University Press, 1985); P. Dunleavy and C. T. Husbands, *British Democracy at the Crossroads* (London: George Allen & Unwin, 1985); A. Heath, R. Jowell, and J. Curtice, *How Britain Votes* (London: Pergamon, 1985); R. Rose and I. McAllister, *Voters Begin to Choose* (London: Sage, 1986); and R. J. Johnston, C. J. Pattie, and J. G. Allsop, *A Nation Dividing? The Electoral Map of Great Britain 1979–87* (London: Longman, 1988). The principal—and critical—works analyzing the political effects of the electoral system are S. E. Finer (ed.), *Adversary Politics and Electoral Reform* (London: Wigram, 1975); and A. Gamble and S. A. Walkland, *The British Party System and Economic Policy 1945–1983* (Oxford: Oxford University Press, 1984).

   The classic but now dated work on political parties is R. McKenzie, *British Political Parties*, 2nd rev. ed. (London: Heinemann, 1964). A recent introductory text is S. J. Ingle, *The British Party System*, 2nd ed. (Oxford: Basil Blackwell, 1989). The best history of the Conservative party is R. Blake, *The Conservative Party from Peel to Thatcher* (London: Fontana, 1985). For a comprehensive treatment of the party's philosophy, history, organization, electoral support, and leadership, see P. Norton and A. Aughey, *Conservatives and Conservatism* (London: Temple Smith, 1981); a new introductory text on the party by Norton will be appearing in the near future. There are many books on different aspects of the Labour party, especially polemical tracts, but few that provide a good overview of the party. The best but now dated overview is provided by D. Kavanagh (ed.), *The Politics of the Labour Party* (London: George Allen & Unwin, 1982). On recent developments, see especially E. Shaw, *Discipline and Discord in the Labour Party* (Manchester: Manchester University Press, 1988); and E. Deakins, *What Future for Labour?* (London: Hilary Shipman, 1988). On the former Liberal party, see V. Bogdanor (ed.), *Liberal Party Politics* (Oxford: Oxford University Press, 1983); and on the Social Democratic party see P. Lee Sykes, *Losing from the Inside* (Reading: Transaction Publishers, 1988). There is, as yet, no substantial work on the newly formed Social and Liberal Democratic party. On the financing of political parties, see especially M. Pinto-Duschinsky, *British Political Finance 1830–1980* (Washington, D.C.: American Enterprise Institute, 1981); and K. Ewing, *The Funding of Political Parties in Britain* (Cambridge: Cambridge University Press, 1987).

An invaluable study of the effect of political parties in office is provided in R. Rose, *Do Parties Make a Difference?* 2nd ed. (London: Macmillan, 1983), providing an effective rejoinder to the thesis advanced in S. E. Finer, *Adversary Politics and Electoral Reform.*

On the development of group influence in British politics, see especially the seminal S. H. Beer, *Modern British Politics*, 3rd ed. (London: Faber and Faber, 1982). See also R. Kimber and J. Richardson (eds.), *Pressure Groups In Britain* (London: Dent, 1974); and J. Richardson and G. Jordan, *Governing Under Pressure* (Oxford: Martin Robertson, 1979). On Parliament and pressure groups, see especially M. Rush (ed.), *Parliament and Pressure Politics* (Oxford: Oxford University Press, 1990). Several books on lobbying have now appeared, the most substantial being C. Miller, *Lobbying Government*, 2nd ed. (Oxford: Basil Blackwell, 1989). G. Alderman, *Pressure Groups and Government in Great Britain* (London: Longman, 1984) provides a useful overview.

PART III: GOVERNMENTAL DECISION MAKING

There is, as yet, no good, up-to-date single-author work on the premiership in Britain. The main work is A. King (ed.), *The British Prime Minister*, 2nd ed. (London: Macmillan, 1985). For a short history of the office, there is Lord Blake, *The Office of Prime Minister* (Oxford: Oxford University Press, 1975).

Though there is little material on the prime minister qua prime minister, there is a voluminous literature on the Thatcher premiership, encompassing the individual (that is, Mrs. Thatcher), her philosophy ("Thatcherism"), and her period of government. Of the works on Mrs. Thatcher, see especially H. Young, *One of Us* (London: Macmillan, 1989). On Thatcherism, see K. Minogue and M. Biddiss (eds.), *Thatcherism: Personality and Politics* (London: Macmillan, 1987); D. Kavanagh, *Thatcherism and British Politics* (Oxford: Oxford University Press, 1987); and A. Gamble, *The Free Economy and the Strong State* (London: Macmillan, 1988). On the Thatcher government, see in particular P. Riddell, *The Thatcher Decade* (Oxford: Basil Blackwell, 1989).

For a good historical work on the cabinet, see J. P. Mackintosh, *The British Cabinet*, 3rd ed. (London: Stevens, 1977). For the present position of the cabinet, see P. Hennessy, *Cabinet* (Oxford: Basil Blackwell, 1986). For a radical analysis, see B. Sedgemore, *The Secret Constitution* (London:

Hodder and Stoughton, 1980). K. Theakston, *Junior Ministers* (Oxford: Basil Blackwell, 1987) explores a much neglected aspect of government.

The civil service is well treated in two recent works: G. Drewry and T. Burton, *The Civil Service Today* (Oxford: Basil Blackwell, 1988), a good introduction to the subject; and P. Hennessy, *Whitehall* (London: Secker and Warburg, 1989), a massive and exhaustive study which also covers the structure of government departments. It is also relevant to consult Sedgemore, *The Secret Constitution* (as above); *The Civil Service: Eleventh Report from the Expenditure Committee of the House of Commons*, HC 535 (London: HMSO, 1977); and *Civil Servants and Ministers: Duties and Responsibilities, Seventh Report from the Treasury and Civil Service Committee of the House of Commons 1985–86*, HC 91 (London: HMSO, 1986).

On subnational government, see, for local government, J. Gyford, S. Leach, and C. Game, *The Changing Politics of Local Government* (London: Unwin Hyman, 1989). S. J. Bailey and R. Paddison, *The Reform of Local Government Finance in Britain* (London: Routledge, 1988) provides a background to the introduction of the community charge. On regional government, see especially R. A. W. Rhodes, *Beyond Westminster and Whitehall: The Sub-Central Governments of Britain* (London: Unwin Hyman, 1988). On Scotland, see especially J. G. Kellas, *The Scottish Political System*, 4th ed. (Cambridge: Cambridge University Press, 1989). The literature on Northern Ireland is extensive. On the debate surrounding the province, see especially R. Rose, *Governing without Consensus* (London: Faber and Faber, 1971); A. J. Ward, *Northern Ireland: Living with the Stress* (London: Aldwych Press, 1987); F. Wright, *Northern Ireland: A Comparative Analysis* (Dublin: Gill and Macmillan, 1987); and, for a recent introductory overview, P. Arthur and K. Jeffrey, *Northern Ireland since 1968* (Oxford: Basil Blackwell, 1988).

On the history of Britain's applications to join the European Community, see R. J. Lieber, *British Politics and European Unity* (Berkeley: University of California Press, 1970); U. Kitzinger, *The Second Try* (Oxford: Pergamon Press, 1968); and U. Kitzinger, *Diplomacy and Persuasion* (London: Thames and Hudson, 1973). On the position since British entry, see F. Gregory, *Dilemmas of Government* (Oxford: Martin Robertson, 1983); A. Daltrop, *Politics and the European Community*, 2nd ed. (London: Longman, 1986), and S. George, *An Awkward Partner* (Oxford: University Press, 1990).

PART IV: SCRUTINY AND LEGITIMATION

The most recent works on the House of Commons are P. Norton (ed.), *Parliament in the 1980s* (Oxford: Basil Blackwell, 1985); P. Norton, *Parliament in Perspective* (Hull: Hull University Press, 1987), a short monograph; M. Ryle and P. G. Richards (eds.), *The Commons Under Scrutiny* (London: Routledge, 1988); and P. Silk, *How Parliament Works*, rev. ed. (London: 1989). The major work on select committees is G. Drewry (ed.), *The New Select Committees*, 2nd ed. (Oxford: Oxford University Press, 1989). The constituency activity of MPs is covered in B. Cain, J. Ferejohn, and M. Fiorina, *The Personal Vote* (Cambridge, Mass.: Harvard University Press, 1987). There is now an up-to-date work on the Upper House: D. Shell, *The House of Lords* (Oxford: Philip Allan, 1988). A good review of literature on Parliament published since the early 1970s is provided by S. C. Patterson, "Understanding the British Parliament," *Political Studies*, 37 (3), September 1989, pp. 449–62.

On the debate on parliamentary reform, see the classic work by B. Crick: *The Reform of Parliament*, rev. 2nd ed. (London: Weidenfeld & Nicolson, 1970); as well as P. Norton, *The Commons in Perspective* (Oxford: Martin Robertson, 1981), Ch. 9; D. Judge (ed.), *The Politics of Parliamentary Reform* (London: Heinemann, 1983); and P. Norton, *Parliament in Perspective*.

There are numerous biographies and sketches of members of the royal family but few recent works dealing with the role of the monarch in a political context. F. Hardie, *The Political Influence of the British Monarchy 1868–1952* (London: Batsford, 1970) provides a good introduction; and C. Hibbert, *The Court of St. James* (London: Weidenfeld & Nicolson, 1979; New York: Gill, 1983) provides a good overview. E. Wilson, *The Myth of British Monarchy* (London: Journeyman/Republic, 1989) provides a radical critique.

PART V: ENFORCEMENT AND FEEDBACK

There are several works, usually entitled *Constitutional and Administrative Law*, which provide introductions to the English (and sometimes the Scottish) legal system. At the heart of the debate surrounding the judiciary is the critique of J. A. G. Griffith: *The Politics of the Judiciary*, 2nd ed. (London: Fontana, 1981). A. Paterson, *The Law Lords* (London: Macmillan, 1982) provides a useful insight into the operation of the higher judiciary. On the police force, see R. Reiner, *The Politics of the Police* (Brighton: Wheatsheaf Books, 1985); and J. Benyon and C. Bourn (eds.), *The Police: Powers, Procedures and Proprieties* (London: Pergamon Books, 1986). For works on the more general question of law of order, see P. Norton (ed.), *Law and Order and British Politics* (Aldershot: Gower, 1984); and J. Benyon (ed.), *Scarman and After* (London: Pergamon, 1984).

On the mass media, recent works include J. Tunstall, *The Media in Britain* (London: Constable, 1983); J. Seaton and B. Pimlott, *The Media in*

British Politics (Aldershot: Avebury, 1987); J. Curran and P. Seaton, *Power without Responsibility*, 3rd ed. (London: Methuen, 1988); and—a good basic introduction—R. Negrine, *Politics and the Mass Media in Britain* (London: Routledge, 1989). For the use made of the press by Downing Street, see especially M. Cockerall, M. Walker, and P. Hennessy, *Sources Close to the Prime Minister* (London: Macmillan, 1984). The role of the media in general election campaigns is covered in each volume of the Nuffield *British General Election* series.

Glossary

Back-bencher. A member of either House of Parliament who is neither a government minister nor a spokesperson for the opposition. The name derives from where the members sit: on the back benches.

Barrister. A specialist lawyer who appears on behalf of clients in superior courts and is retained through a solicitor.

Bobby. Colloquial name for a policeman (not used much now) that was derived from the first name of the Home Secretary, Sir Robert Peel, responsible for the creation of the (Metropolitan) police force in 1829.

Buckingham Palace. The official London residence of the Queen. When the prime minister "goes to the Palace" for an audience (i.e., meeting) with the Queen, the reference is to Buckingham Palace.

By-election. The election to return a member of Parliament (MP) in a constituency in which a vacancy has occurred (usually because of the death or resignation of the incumbent). A vacancy can be filled only by means of an election. By agreement between the parties, the precise date of a by-election is usually determined by the party that previously held the seat. Like general elections, by-elections are traditionally held on a Thursday.

Chequers. The official country residence of the prime minister, located close to London, near Princes Risborough in Buckinghamshire. It was given to the nation by Lord Lee of Fareham in 1917.

Chief Constable. The professional head of each police force, except in London, where the Metropolitan and City of London forces are each headed by a commissioner.

The City. The City of London, occupying one square mile in the heart of London; it is the traditional home of the Bank of England, the Stock Exchange, and the nation's other financial institutions.

Collective ministerial responsibility. The answerability of all members of the government for decisions taken by the cabinet.

Commonwealth. A voluntary association of independent states and territories. The Commonwealth evolved from the British Empire and exists now to provide cultural, sporting, and some political links among member states. The Queen is Head of the Commonwealth.

Constituency. An electoral area equivalent in nature to a congressional district. Each is known by a geographical name rather than by number. Each constituency elects one member of Parliament.

Contest an election. To stand for election.

Conventions of the constitution. Informal constitutional rules treated as binding by those to whom they are directed.

Devolution. The devolving of powers by national government to subordinate assemblies.

Dissolution. The dissolving of Parliament to prepare for a general election, that is, the election of a new Parliament.

Division lobbies. The voting lobbies in the two Houses of Parliament. When members vote (divide), they enter lobbies on the two sides of the chamber; the "aye" lobby is to the right of the presiding officer, the "no" lobby to the left.

Downing Street. A small cul-de-sac off Whitehall housing three principal houses—numbers 10, 11 and 12. No. 10 is the official London residence of the Prime Minister, No. 11 the official London residence of the Chancellor of the Exchequer, and No. 12 houses the office of the Government Chief Whip in the House of Commons.

Empire. The British Empire comprised countries under British sovereignty (though some were self-governing) and in 1918 it encompassed well over a quarter of the human race and more than a quarter of the world's land surface. It began to wither as various dominions gained independence. From the 1920s onward, it came to be called the British Commonwealth of Nations, now known simply as the Commonwealth.

Erskine May. The manual of parliamentary procedure—"the parliamentary bible"—the full title of which is *Erskine May's Treatise on the Law, Privileges, Proceedings and Usage of Parliament*. Sir Thomas Erskine May was a nineteenth-century clerk of the House of Commons. The book is now in its twenty-first edition; new editions are compiled by clerks under the direction of the Clerk of the House.

Field a candidate. To put up a candidate for election.

Fleet Street. A street in central London, a continuation of the Strand (off Trafalgar Square), which traditionally has housed the main national newspapers. The name is still used to refer to the British press, even though no national newspapers are still based there; the last newspaper left in 1989. Most have relocated in the docklands area of east London.

Free votes. Parliamentary votes in which parties have not formally requested their members to vote in a particular way.

Front benchers. The front bench on the Government side of the House of Commons (known as the Treasury bench, and extending halfway down the chamber) is by custom reserved for ministers, and the equivalent bench on the Opposition side of the House is reserved for spokesmen of the official Opposition party. Hence, those who occupy them are known as front benchers. Front benches also exist in the House of Lords.

General election. The election of a new House of Commons.

Going to the country. The calling of a general election; hence "the Prime Minister has decided to go to the country" means that the premier has requested a dissolution and the election of a new House of Commons.

Individual ministerial responsibility. The answerability of ministers to the Crown (formally) and to Parliament (politically) for their official actions and those of civil servants within their particular departments.

Lord Chancellor. A political appointee (a member of the cabinet) who is head of the judiciary. He is also formally the presiding officer of the House of Lords, though this entails no significant powers.

Lord Chief Justice. A senior, professional judge who heads both the Queen's Bench division of the High Court and the Criminal division of the Court of Appeal.

Master of the Rolls. A senior, professional judge who presides over the Civil division of the Court of Appeal.

Member of Parliament (MP). A member of the House of Commons. No such designation applies to members of the House of Lords, who are known by their titles.

"New" Commonwealth countries. A term employed to refer to Asian and African countries that were granted independence by Britain in the 1940s, thus distinguishing them from the "old" Commonwealth countries of Canada, Australia, and New Zealand.

Officials. A reference usually, though not exclusively, to civil servants.

Peer. A member of the peerage (i.e., a lord).

PM. Prime minister.

Premier. Alternative term used to refer to the prime minister.

Private Members. All members of Parliament who are not ministers. The term is not synonymous with back-benchers, since opposition front benchers are private members.

Quango. Quasi-autonomous nongovernment organization.

Rt. Hon. Right Honorable. This title—as, for example, the Rt. Hon. Margaret Thatcher MP—denotes a member of the Privy Council. The Council, historically, was an important advisory body to the Crown but is now largely ceremonial in nature. However, membership in the Council is still important because members can receive state secrets. All members of the cabinet and other senior ministers are sworn in as members of the Privy Council. Once sworn, they remain members for life.

Scotland Yard. The headquarters of the Metropolitan police force. The name derives from the location of the original headquarters—Scotland Yard, Westminster (just off Whitehall). It now occupies a modern building in Broadway, Westminster, close to the Home Office.

Second reading. Parliamentary debate on the principle of a bill.

Speaker. The presiding officer of the House of Commons, selected by the House from among its members. The Speaker has the power the select members in debate (through "catching the Speaker's eye"), to select amendments in debate, and to discipline members, though all within fairly well-defined limits and procedures. After election to the post, the Speaker ceases to be a member of a political party (seeking reelection at a general election simply as "Mr. Speaker"), operates as a nonpartisan figure, and leads an isolated parliamentary existence.

Tabling a motion. The act of submitting a motion for debate. This is a positive move and should not be confused with the American equivalent, which means to shelve a motion.

Tory. A colloquial name for a member of the Conservative party, deriving from the name of the party, the Tory party, from which the Conservative party evolved in the 1830s. The term also refers to a specific strand of thought within British Conservatism.

Ulster. The northern nine counties of Ireland form the historic region of Ulster. However, the name (Ulster) is often used, especially by Unionists, to refer to the northern six counties that now constitute Northern Ireland. Since Northern Ireland was formed, it has been common to refer to it as a province of the United Kingdom.

Upper House. The House of Lords. (The House of Commons is the Lower House, though it is rarely referred to as such.)

Vote of confidence. A formal motion expressing confidence (or no confidence) in the government, *or* a vote on a motion on which the government has declared that, if defeated, it will resign or request a dissolution. Such motions are discussed only in the House of Commons.

Wapping. An area in the docklands of London to which a number of national newspapers have relocated from Fleet Street.

Westminster. A district of London. The name is usually employed to refer to the Palace of Westminster, which houses the two Houses of Parliament.

Whipped votes. Votes in Parliament in which the parties have requested their members to vote in a particular manner. Such requests are issued through a weekly written document known as the written whip. The request in the whip is given emphasis by underlining. The most important votes during which all party members are expected to be present and vote in unison are underlined three times. The term "three-line whip" derives from this practice. If there is a free vote (see above), there is no underlining.

Whips. Apart from the weekly written whip, there are members of each parliamentary party designated as whips. They act as channels of communication between party leaders and back-benchers, and largely as business managers. They are responsible for ensuring that party members know what business is being transacted and that they are present to vote when necessary and, on occasion, to speak when insufficient members have volunteered to take part in a debate. Contact between the whip's offices, especially the government and Opposition chief whips, is known as contact "through the usual channels."

Whitehall. London street, between the Palace of Westminster and Trafalgar Square, traditionally housing most government departments. The name is still employed to denote the environment occupied by ministers, and especially civil servants, even though most departments are now located elsewhere.

Whitehall Mandarins. The name employed on occasion to refer to the senior civil servants in government departments.

Index